From Kathy Z.   2007, Christmas.

D1551977

MINNESOTA HOOPS

Minnesota Hoops

BASKETBALL IN THE NORTH STAR STATE

Marc Hugunin

Stew Thornley

MINNESOTA HISTORICAL SOCIETY PRESS

All photo credits are on p. 281.

www.mhspress.org

The Minnesota Historical Society Press is a member of the Association of American University Presses.

Book design: Wesley B. Tanner/Passim Editions
Manufactured in the United States of America

10   9   8   7   6   5   4   3   2   1

♾ The paper used in this publication meets the minimum requirements of the American National Standard for Information Sciences—Permanence for Printed Library Materials, ANSI Z39.48–1984.

Library of Congress Cataloging-in-Publication Data

Hugunin, Marc, 1949–
  Minnesota hoops : basketball in the North Star State / Marc Hugunin, Stew Thornley.
      p. cm.
  Includes bibliographical references and index.
  ISBN-13: 978-0-87351-574-0 (cloth : alk. paper)
  ISBN-10: 0-87351-574-9 (cloth : alk. paper)
  1. Basketball—Minnesota—History. 2. College sports—Minnesota—History. I. Thornley, Stew. II. Title.
  GV885.72.M6H84 2006
  796.32309776—dc22   2006014473

Frontispiece: *George Mikan led the Minneapolis Lakers to six league championships in seven years and was voted the greatest basketball player of the first half of the twentieth century.*

Junior college transfer Vince Grier led the Gopher men to a surprising 21–11 record and an NCAA tournament bid in 2005.

MARC HUGUNIN DEDICATES THIS BOOK TO
THE MEMORY OF HIS FATHER
Dr. Leonard S. Hugunin
(1910–1967)

STEW THORNLEY DEDICATES THIS BOOK TO
HIS DAD
Howard Thornley
(1924–1987)
WHO TOOK HIM TO WILLIAMS ARENA
ON MANY OCCASIONS

Contents

Acknowledgments

THE AUTHORS WISH TO THANK Greg Britton, Michael Hanson, Pam McClanahan, Will Powers, and Alison Vandenberg of the Minnesota Historical Society Press for their support and editing of the project and Alan Holst, George Rekela, and Paul Rittenhouse for reviewing the manuscript and making valuable suggestions. Thank you also to Dana Johnson, the director of development for Hamline University Athletics, who reviewed the Hamline chapter and provided valuable information.

Joel Rippel of the *Star Tribune* was extremely helpful in sharing his research on the University of Minnesota women's basketball program, as well as information concerning the Gophers' attempt to hire John Wooden as coach in 1948. Sara Berhow, Becky Bohm, and Kyle Coughlin of the University of Minnesota media relations department were also of great assistance.

We would also like to thank Mike Cristaldi, Matt Slieter, and Paul Thompson of the Minnesota Timberwolves for their help with information and images. Previous members of the Timberwolves staff who also aided our research include Tim Bryant, Tim Leiweke, Bill Robertson, Kent Wipf, and Marv Wolfenson. Thanks also to Russ Granik, who was deputy commissioner of the National Basketball Association when interviewed in 1989.

Paul Harris, Eric Jacobson, Jerry Janzen, Pat Lewis, Howard Luloff, Gregg Nelson, and Steve Smith, who, in addition to Alan Holst and Paul Rittenhouse, are members of an electronic discussion group on Minnesota basketball, helped with their many comments and suggestions, as did Robert Bradley, John Grasso, Rob Heflin, Clay Kallam, and Ray LeBov of the Association of Professional Basketball Research and basketball historian Bill Himmelman.

Thanks also goes to Tony Geer, who provided some invaluable information on the history of women's basketball in Minnesota.

We would also like to thank the players, coaches, and others who consented to being interviewed: Marie "Scooter" Barnette (DeLorme), Don "Swede" Carlson, Mike DeWane, Doris Draving, Harold Gifford, Bud Grant, Ellen Mosher Hanson, Mark Hanson, Sid Hartman, Lusia Harris-Stewart, Dick Higgins, Dee Hopfenspirger (formerly DeMaras "Dee" Mercie), Tony Jaros, Dan Klinkhammer, Marie Kocurek, John Kundla, Terry Kunze, Mary Manderfeld, Paul McDonald, George Mikan, Vern Mikkelsen, Gordy Nevers, Mark Olberding, Eva Olofson, Jim Pollard, Paul Presthus, Dick Schnittker, Diane Scovill, Lynnette Sjoquist, and Julia Yeater.

Finally, we offer our thanks to the following coaches, athletic directors, sports information directors, and archivists who provided information and photographs: Jim Cella, Concordia College; Mike Durbin, College of St. Benedict; Ellen Gilloy, Minnesota State High School League; Candy Hart, Hamline University; Michael Herzberg, Winona State University; Eric Hilleman, Carleton College; Dieter Humbert, Rainy River Community College; Karen Kraft, Anoka-Ramsey Community College; Ryan Klinkner, St. John's University; Eugene McGivern, St. Thomas University; Sharon Schroeder, Goodhue County Historical Society; Lisa Sjoberg, Concordia College; Lori K. Ulferts, St. Cloud State University.

Hamline dominated Gustavus Adolphus and the MIAC for almost a quarter century under legendary coach Joe Hutton.

Introduction

Although not as famous, Minnesota's basketball tradition rivals those of basketball hotbeds like Indiana, Kansas, Kentucky, New York City, and Philadelphia. Consider the following: The first basketball game ever played between two college teams occurred in St. Paul in 1895, and a team from Red Wing played one of the first basketball games ever seen in Asia. The Minnesota Gopher and Hamline University men have each won three national collegiate championships, and Hamline was once rated fifth in the nation among *all* colleges and universities. In the forties and fifties, Minnesota was home to the six-time world champion Minneapolis Lakers. And today, Minnesota has more kids playing basketball per capita than does almost any other state, and those kids have won dozens of national titles over the past fifteen years. The history of basketball in Minnesota, in other words, is vastly richer than most basketball fans know.

But research and publications concerning that history have been rare, and what passes for common knowledge of that history contains many misconceptions. *Minnesota Hoops* aims to bust many of the myths that have infiltrated the history of Minnesota basketball and illuminate many of the stories that have been forgotten. It has been written many times and in many places, for example, that old-time Carleton College athletic director Claude J. Hunt founded the state high school basketball tournament. The Minnesota State High School League (MSHSL) even honored Hunt in 1957 with a plaque that says so. We now know, however, that Hunt had yet to set foot on the Carleton campus by the time of the first tournament. Then there is the MSHSL record book, which shows that the first two-class high school tournament was held in 1971, leaving out the fact that a small school tournament was held throughout most of the 1920s.

Former stars and their stories have also been lost through time and neglect. When in 2000 the Minnesota Gophers announced their all-century team—a team with one player picked from each decade—three of the all-time greats were nowhere to be seen. In 1950, Frank J. Lawler, class of 1912, was selected as the greatest Gopher of the half century, but by 2000, he was no longer regarded as the best Minnesota player of even the 1910s. John Kundla, better remembered today because of a distinguished career as the Lakers' and the Gophers' coach, was selected as the player of the 1930s, ahead of teammate Marty Rolek, who had earned All-America honors in 1938. Perhaps, the greatest oversight was the omission of Jim McIntyre, arguably one of the two greatest Minnesota schoolboy hoopsters ever. He went on to become one of only three consensus All-Americans the Gophers have ever had.

Not all of the misconceptions are ours today, however. You will learn, for example, that until about 1940 the game was played at a walk because many physical educators believed erroneously, as we now know, that strenuous physical exercise—like playing basketball on the run—was "too hard on young growing bodies." Moreover, they believed that young women who played basketball jeopardized their ability to become pregnant.

Myths and misconceptions aside, the ultimate truth is that for over a hundred years Minnesota basketball fans have ridden a roller coaster up to the thrill of victory and down to the agony of defeat, caring passionately about the success of their favorite teams. Today, Minnesota basketball fans are enjoying one of the two longest ascents in the history of Minnesota basketball. At least, the authors hope that Minnesotans are enjoying the game today, because this is the second golden age of the game in the North Star State. These are the good old days of Minnesota basketball. And considering the number of Minnesota kids playing ball today and the truly amazing skills that they are now demonstrating, maybe someday—maybe soon—those Hoosiers and Jayhawks will start calling Minnesota "America's basketball hotbed."

MINNESOTA HOOPS

Basketball Comes to Minnesota, 1892–1924

Basketball came to Minnesota the same way it spread throughout the rest of the United States during the 1890s—directly from the YMCA International Training School in Springfield, Massachusetts. It was there that Dr. James A. Naismith invented basketball in 1891, and it was there that he staged the first game ever played, on December 21, with nine men on a side and peach baskets for goals. More games were staged in January 1892, and they were witnessed by dozens of students and instructors at the school. Naismith and his disciples were America's first generation of trained physical educators, and over the next decade they carried the game wherever they went. Three of them—Max J. Exner, Raymond P. Kaighn, and Dr. Louis J. Cooke—brought the game to Minnesota.

When Exner, in 1892, and Kaighn, the following year, arrived, there were no basketball teams in the state. When Cooke came in 1895, there were still few halls in which a proper game could be played, nor any fans clamoring to see the game. There was no Big Ten, no NCAA, no high school league, and no high school tournament, and published schedules and eligibility rules did not exist. There was no accepted body of strategies, tactics, and techniques for playing the game, and the rules themselves were primitive. By the time of Cooke's retirement as the University of Minnesota's basketball coach in 1924, however, the game had become deeply entrenched in both high schools and colleges. Facilities, administrative bodies, and procedures had been created, and coaching had become established. The work of the game's pioneers had been completed. Only the rules remained primitive. Perfecting them was left to the following generations of basketball leadership.

In twenty-seven years as head basketball coach at the University of Minnesota, Dr. Louis J. Cooke won four Big Ten and three national championships.

1 *The Four Pioneers*

Within a month of Dr. James A. Naismith's invention of basketball, his original thirteen rules were published and widely disseminated through a variety of YMCA publications. Surely that is how Dr. James C. Elsom, physical education director at the Minneapolis Y, heard about the game. Soon, its gymnasium was set aside for basketball every Tuesday and Saturday evening. These pick-up games were the first games of basketball played in Minnesota.

First to teach basketball in Minnesota at the college level was Max J. Exner, Naismith's roommate at the YMCA Training School in Springfield, Massachusetts. In the fall of 1892, he both enrolled as an undergraduate at Carleton College in Northfield, Minnesota, and began serving as its first director of physical education and as coach of its men's intercollegiate athletic teams. In return, the college provided for his tuition and room and board. Sometime in 1893, Max taught basketball to his women's physical education classes. The women played among themselves—never against an intercollegiate opponent—and there is no evidence that he showed the game to the men. When Exner left Carleton to pursue a medical degree, the game was forgotten for a decade. Later, the YMCA sent Exner to China to open a school for physical educators. Naismith credits him with introducing basketball to the Chinese. Still later, he became a leading expert in the field of sexual health and venereal disease.

Next, in the fall of 1893, Raymond P. Kaighn, who had played in Naismith's December 12, 1891, "demonstration game" of basketball, came to St. Paul's Hamline University. Like Exner, he pursued a bachelor's degree and also earned his tuition and room and board

In 1892 at Carleton College, Max J. Exner became Minnesota's first collegiate director of physical education. Twenty years later, according to Dr. James A. Naismith, Exner introduced the game to the Chinese.

by serving as a director of physical education and athletics. Thanks to Kaighn, what is generally regarded as the first intercollegiate game anywhere was played in St. Paul. In the fall of 1894, he organized Hamline's first basketball team and then lined up a winter game against the Minnesota Aggies of the Minnesota School of Agriculture and Mining, now the St. Paul campus of the University of Minnesota. The Aggies defeated Hamline, 9–3, on February 9, 1895, and later won a rematch, 9–6. Like Naismith's 1891 game, these games resembled modern basketball very little. They were played on a handball court with nine-foot ceilings in the basement of Science Hall, with nine men on a side, goalies, and peach baskets for hoops.

Dr. Louis J. Cooke, the fourth of the four pioneers, came to Minnesota in the summer of 1895 to replace Elsom as physical education director at the Minneapolis Y. Elsom had left in 1894 to go to the University of Wisconsin at Madison, where he remained as a professor of physical education for more than four decades.

The early physical educators were of two kinds: those whose passion was physical education and public health for the masses and those who loved elite, competitive athletics. Like Exner and Naismith himself—who to this day is the only Kansas University basketball coach with a losing record—Elsom was of the first kind. He became the Wisconsin Badgers' first basketball coach in 1898, winning twenty-five games while losing just fourteen over six years. He also coached gymnastics from 1902 to 1909. But he returned to physical education, which by 1910 had become differentiated from the field of elite athletics. He taught and authored three books—a handbook for student exercise, a guide to community education, and a collection of social games and dances "suitable for community and social use."

Cooke was among the second kind of physical educators, and he brought to the Minneapolis Y a résumé that was exactly typical of the time. Cooke spent two summers at the YMCA Training School and then went to the University of Vermont, where he starred as a baseball pitcher. Like many of the early physical educators—including Naismith and Cooke's colleague Dr. Henry L. Williams, the Gophers' football coach—he also received a medical degree. But he earned his living as a physical educator in his hometown of Toledo, Ohio, then moving on to Duluth; Burlington, Vermont; and finally Minneapolis. He quickly organized the Twin City Basket Ball League, which over the next several years included the Twin Cities militia, Company A; Hamline University and Macalester College; U of M teams from the Minneapolis and St. Paul campuses; several teams from the Minneapolis Y; and, eventually, a team from the St. Paul Y. Cooke's own first string from the Minneapolis Y, along with the Minnesota Aggies, dominated the league in the early going. Unbeknownst to Cooke, the YMCA was in a state of fiscal crisis at the time of his arrival, owing to the difficulty in paying off the cost of the very facility that had made the first games of basketball possible. Thus, in February 1897, the YMCA was happy to give the U of M half of Cooke's time. The U paid half of his compensation.

Cooke's move was in perfect alignment with the shift in basketball's center of gravity—from the YMCAs to the colleges—that was then taking place throughout the United States. At the U, his initial duties were limited to managing the natatorium. By the following fall, however, Cooke was working full-time at the U as director of the university's gymnasium, director of physical education, and coach of the intercollegiate basketball team.

Coming to the U four years after Kaighn arrived at Hamline, Cooke was nevertheless among the earliest professional (full-time, paid) coaches in American intercollegiate athletics. And the Gophers had another significant asset in their quest for basketball respectability: the University Armory, which had opened in the fall of 1896. One of the largest armories in the country, it was not designed for basketball yet proved to be ideally suited to the new game. In fact, it was probably the finest basketball facility in the state.

Still, it would be two more years before the U—the

Minneapolis campus under Doc Cooke, that is—fielded competitive teams. The Aggies beat the Minneapolis campus ten straight times before Cooke's team beat the Aggies for the first time, 20–9, during the 1898–1899 season. The Gophers never played the Aggies again after 1901, though the Aggies fielded a separate team as late as the 1940s.

The Gophers also continued to fare poorly against the Minneapolis Y, winning just six of twenty games through 1900. Yet, as the colleges and universities increased their commitment to the game, the Y quickly readjusted its goals from fielding elite teams to providing wholesome exercise for the masses. As a result, the Gophers would not play the Minneapolis Y after 1899 or the St. Paul Y after 1900–1901. Their final games against any Y were two games, a win and a loss, against the Chicago West Side Y in 1903–1904.

Thus, by 1899 the Gophers were looking for new opponents. They found them mainly, though not exclusively, among neighboring land grant universities—their future Big Ten opponents. The Gophers' first-ever winning record, 10–3 in 1900, was probably due to the fact that Iowa and Wisconsin were not as good as the Aggies and the Y, whom they replaced in the Gophers' schedule.

At least, that is the conclusion of St. Bonaventure accounting professor Patrick Premo, developer in the 1990s of the Premo Power Poll rankings of early college basketball. Premo ranked the 5–5 Gophers of 1899 as the number five college team in the nation, while the 10–3 Gophers of 1900 are not ranked among the top ten. The fact is that Iowa, whom the Gophers defeated 30–4, was a terrible team. The Hawkeyes' first winning Big Ten season would not come until 1920–1921, and Cooke went 28–8 against them over a twenty-five-year period. Meanwhile the Gophers of 1899–1900 split four games against the Superior Normal school and edged Minneapolis Central High just 14–8 and 8–7.

The 1900–1901 schedule does not appear to have been any more demanding, but the Gophers clearly were improved. They easily dispatched Central High and its star center George Tuck by a score of 27–4, and Wisconsin, who had been beaten just 18–15 the year before, was clobbered 42–15. Premo ranked the 11–3 Gophers the number seven college team in the nation.

Yet the fact is that the colleges still were not the best teams in the land, as was demonstrated at a historic national tournament at the University of Chicago. The Gophers played and lost two games to the Ravenswood YMCA, 20–12, and to the Silent Five, a team of deaf players from New York City, 24–20. The college teams were not the best ones, but they quickly became the most visible as the twentieth century dawned. This was just as true in Minnesota, and especially in the Twin Cities, as it was almost everywhere in the United States.

In 1891 in Springfield, Massachusetts, Raymond P. Kaighn played in the world's first basketball game. In 1895, he staged the first intercollegiate game anywhere, pitting his Hamline squad against a team from the Minnesota Ag School.

2 The Birth of Golden Gophers Basketball

IN THE 1901–1902 SEASON the Minnesota Gophers established themselves as the state's premier, though not necessarily best, basketball team. What the U had going for it primarily was a large following—a cadre of fans with the youthful enthusiasm and leisure time to attend games. This meant revenue, which in turn enabled the U to promote their games and to travel as needed to play other big-name teams. The games brought newspaper coverage, which produced still more fans. No other teams at any level were able to create this kind of synergy. Thus, "big-time" basketball came to be synonymous in most places with major college ball—and, in Minnesota, with the University of Minnesota Gophers.

Minneapolis Central phenom George Tuck became a Gopher in 1901. The schedule was strengthened considerably, and still Coach Louis J. Cooke's five won all fifteen games by an average score of 36–9. The highlight was a meeting with the barnstorming team from Yale at the University Armory in December 1901. Yale was considered to be the best team in the East every season from 1896 to 1901, and it was recognized retroactively by the Helms Foundation as national champions in 1901 and 1903. Nevertheless, the Gophers prevailed, 32–23, and later they were honored as 1902 national champs by both the Helms Foundation and the Premo Poll. In order to appreciate Cooke's pioneering role as one of the earliest professional coaches, consider that Yale's 1901 national champs did not have a coach. Nor did the champions of 1904 and 1905 (Columbia) and 1906 (Dartmouth).

The 1902–1903 Gophers were even more dominant, winning all eleven of their games by an average score of 41–9. Lacking a win over a big time, interregional opponent, however, the Gophers modestly declined to claim another national championship. Premo awarded the team another mythical title anyway, though Helms preferred once-beaten Yale.

The Gophers' star and leading scorer for those two unbeaten seasons was forward William Deering, who had learned the game at the Y in Fargo, North Dakota, and also played at Fargo College, now North Dakota State University. In addition, the Gophers benefited from the heady guard play of veteran Michael Kiefer, whose late steals helped to seal the victory over Yale. Kiefer was then in his sixth year as a Gopher, and he would continue to play for three more years until he completed medical school in 1905. His nine years in a Gophers uniform is one record that will never be broken. Finally, Tuck dominated around the basket and went on to become the Gophers' first All-American in 1905.

The Gophers would not repeat their unbeaten seasons or national championships until 1919 (and after that, never again), but four more successful seasons followed through 1907. The first two of these years (1903–1904 and 1904–1905) saw grueling eastern barnstorming trips that resulted in ten wins, seven losses, and a tie. Three of the losses came at the hands of semiprofessional teams Washington Continental and Schenectady Company E. But the 1903–1904 team beat Williams College, rated eleventh that year, 10–6. Another highlight was a road sweep of Purdue, 32–22, and Ohio State, 31–18, sandwiched around a 28–23 win over Indiana high school powerhouse Crawfordsville. The Gophers finished 10–2 and were rated number two by Premo.

The following year, despite Tuck's All-America season, the Gophers slumped to 7–7–1 against the toughest schedule Coach Cooke would ever face. Two of the

Around the turn of the century, George Tuck played basketball at Minneapolis Central High School, who gave the Minnesota Gophers tougher games than did most college rivals. In 1905, he became the Gophers' first All-American.

Cooke at work in his office (left). Note the Little Brown Jug hanging above his head. This photo could have been taken any time between 1903, when the Gophers football team won the jug, and 1909, when the Michigan Wolverines won it back.

losses were to the top two teams in the country according to the Premo Poll—Columbia 27–15 and Williams 32–11. The relative quality of play in the East and the Midwest may be illustrated by the Gophers' record of 3–2–1 against eastern colleges and 5–1 against future Big Ten opponents. Differences in the style of play were described by Yale star W. C. Hyatt, who said, "The Minnesota and Wisconsin men played in the style prevalent among most of the girl colleges in the East, that is, the 'no contact' game." Such, at least, was one man's opinion.

The Wisconsin Badgers of 1903–1905 would be remembered later as a powerhouse, largely because of the exploits of Christian Steinmetz, the first college player to score 1,000 career points and one of only two college players to score 50 points in a game before George Mikan did it in 1945. But the Gophers took six of their

first seven games against Wisconsin through late 1906, and the Badgers never rated ahead of Minnesota in the Premo Poll until 1908.

The Helms and Premo national championships were purely mythical and were handed out thirty-five and ninety years, respectively, after the fact. But it is true that by 1905 or so, various teams at all levels were quite routinely claiming the championship of this or that piece of geography. Every such claim was immediately and hotly disputed by some other claimant.

The desire for clear and undisputed championship opportunities, then, was one of the reasons for the formation of the college conferences. The New England Intercollegiate Basketball League was the first in 1901, followed a year later by the Eastern Intercollegiate League, the forerunner to the Ivy League. The Western Conference, later the Big Ten, began basketball competition in 1905 with Chicago, Illinois, Iowa, Indiana, Minnesota, Purdue, and Wisconsin. (Football play had begun a decade earlier.) Northwestern joined for the league's second campaign; Ohio State joined in 1913. Michigan had been a charter member, but it was booted from the conference about the time basketball play began because of a lack of administrative oversight of the players' academic eligibility. The Wolverines rejoined the conference in both sports in 1918.

Minnesota won or tied for the first two conference basketball titles. In 1905–1906, the Gophers went 6–1 in the conference despite a narrow average scoring margin of 22–20. Their final four victories included 2-point games at Illinois and Chicago, a 3-point win against the Chicago Maroons, and a 6-point win over second-place Wisconsin at home. Guard Garfield Brown, who averaged 6 points per game, was named as the Gophers' second All-American. The following year, the Gophers had to defeat Chicago 21–10 in their final game to tie the Maroons and Wisconsin for the title at 6–2. These two championship teams later were rated by Premo as the number three (1906) and eight (1907) teams in the nation.

Chicago then put together a string of four straight Big Ten titles behind six-foot-three center John Schom-

There were no basketball arenas in the early days, but armories were as well suited to the game as any existing facilities. Until 1925, the Minnesota Gophers played at the University Armory, which still stands on the East Bank of the Minneapolis campus. That year they moved to the Kenwood Armory, increasing seating capacity from 2,000 to 6,000.

mer and another of the early professional coaches, Joseph Raycroft. Schommer led the conference in scoring three times, was named national Player of the Year in 1909, and later invented the modern backboard. The 1908 team also participated in the first postseason match games between the best teams in the East and West. Pennsylvania was the eastern champ and was favored to beat the Maroons. Instead, Chicago won two games in Philadelphia to claim the national title. This title was just as mythical as the others of that day, however: the Premo poll later projected unbeaten Wabash College, Indiana (26–0) as its champion. Premo recognized Chicago as national champs in 1907 and 1909, while Helms picked the Maroons all three times.

Wabash was a bona fide powerhouse. The Gophers did not meet the 1908 championship Wabash team, but they did play their 1906 Premo national championship team. Although the Gophers won the Big Ten title and ranked number three nationally and the game came during a road trip in which they beat Purdue and Illinois, both by a 27–25 score, and Chicago, 31–29, the Minnesota team lost to Wabash, 26–16. Cooke's boys then slumped to a 5–12 conference record combined over the next two seasons (1907–1909) before rebounding in the early 1910s.

3 *Minnesota's First Hoops Hotbed*

I N 1896, BASKETBALL ARRIVED in the Queen City of Red Wing, which quickly became Minnesota's leading hotbed of basketball action, the one place where the game was embraced with Hoosier-like enthusiasm. By 1898, senior men's teams had played as far away as San Francisco and Manila. In 1906, they barnstormed their way throughout the western United States, winning twenty-six of thirty-two games in a period of just thirty-six days. To earlier claims of the championships of Minnesota and the old Northwest was added a new claim to the championship of half a continent. Red Wing High School then won state high school championships in 1915, 1920, 1922, and 1933, all in just twenty-one years of tournament play. No Minnesota high school would exceed Red Wing's record of four titles through the remaining sixty-seven years of the twentieth century despite the advent of multiple classes and championships beginning in 1971.

All of this excitement was initiated by none other than Dr. Louis J. Cooke, still eighteen months removed from becoming the Gophers' coach. Cooke came to Red Wing to inquire into local interest in starting a YMCA, but he also talked up the game of basketball among officers of the local militia. Company G Lieutenant Oscar Seebach had no interest in a Y, but he saw the potential for this new game to help keep the men in fighting trim. Basketball teams were quickly organized, and the first three games of basketball in Red Wing history were staged at the local armory in November 1896.

There were (and are) three ingredients necessary for a good game of basketball. One is vigorous young folks in numbers sufficient to make up two teams. Another is a hall large enough to accommodate a game. And the third is a philosophical bent toward physical fitness. The militias were among the few institutions at the time that had all three.

A mere two months later, the company got its first real test, against Cooke's first string at the Minneapolis Y, and flunked. In addition to its obvious disadvantage in experience, the militia was also playing for the first time in an unfamiliar hall. So Company G was routed 19–1. Another month later, the Y traveled to Red Wing for a rematch. Company G fared better on its home court but still lost 13–7. From this time forward, the company was obsessed with the idea of beating Cooke's team. The notion that basketball might serve to enhance the fitness of the entire company was quickly forgotten, and an elite five was formed. With the new focus, success came quickly, and by March 1898, the company defeated the Y, 22–18. A 14–4 win over the Minnesota Aggies followed, and on the first of many occasions, Company G claimed the championship of the state of Minnesota. It was perhaps the strongest such claim they would ever make.

Athletic activity in the Queen City came to a halt when Company G was mustered into the Thirteenth Minnesota Volunteers for service in the Spanish-American War. During a layover in San Francisco, they played and lost a game of basketball to the Central YMCA, 12–10. Then, in the Philippines, they played a series of games among themselves and perhaps—the historical evidence is ambiguous—against a squad from Stillwater's Company K. These may have been the first basketball games played in Asia.

Upon its return, and over the next seven seasons, the team would change identities from Company G to the Red Wing Athletic Club to the Foresters and, finally, to the Red Men. Yet they consisted of and were known as the "Steady Seven"—the seven being Charles Ahlers, H. M. Bird, Goodwin Esterly, brothers Charles and John Fisher, and brothers Ed and Mike Kappel. According to one report, the seven averaged five feet and eleven and a half inches in height and 191.5 pounds.

The Steady Seven suffered but one home court loss

The first Company G team from Red Wing c. 1897. Front row, left to right: George Haustein, Carl Heglund, and Ralph Melendy; middle row: Ed Neill, Ed Kappel, Charles Fisher, and George Erickson; back row: E. S. Mellinger, John Fisher, Carl Reckner, Charles Ahlers, George Buel, Theo. Eke, and Charles Burnsen. Ahlers and Burnsen were shot two years later in the Philippines in the Spanish-American War. Burnsen died, while Ahlers survived and, with the Fishers and Kappel, went on to become a member of the Steady Seven.

among about fifty games between 1897 and 1908, that to the Minneapolis Victors and center George Tuck, 14–12, in 1901. The 1902 team barnstormed through the state of Wisconsin and finished with a record of 15–2–1. One of the losses was to Fond du Lac Company E, widely regarded as the best team between Chicago and the Rocky Mountains, 27–26. On this record they based another claim as champions of the Midwest (exclusive, apparently, of Wisconsin), though the Gophers defeated Company E to finish unbeaten at 15–0.

It was in the fall of 1905 that the Steady Seven accepted the sponsorship of the Red Wing Tribe No. 31 of the Improved Order of Red Men and traveled all the way to the Pacific Ocean in search of tougher competition. The Red Men won eight victories before losing its first game, 24–16, in Spokane, Washington. Finally, on February 23, 1906, came the game the Red Men had waited for the most anxiously. They rose to the occasion, defeating Stockton's "champions of California," 20–14, before a crowd of 1,400, the largest crowd up to that time to see a basketball game in that state. The return trip consisted of twelve more wins and two losses. The Red Men played and won seven games before and after the tour for a season total of thirty-three wins and

six defeats. The championship of the western United States, including, of course, Minnesota and the Northwest, was claimed.

Over the next two years, the Red Men probably looked as good as ever to the casual observer. But by 1909, only Ahlers and Esterly remained of the seven, and their trip to Wisconsin began with six straight losses, after which the local paper simply quit reporting their scores. In the end, when the Steady Seven began to retire, one by one, their steadiness turned out to be a liability. They had not recruited a new player in almost a decade. They had no feeder system, no lifeline to the community. A year or two earlier, some of the younger basketball stars might have been honored to play alongside the remaining members of the Steady Seven. Now, the idea of simply filling their empty shoes had no appeal for young men like Ben Hawkins and Al Rehder.

And so, the Red Men never played again.

Meanwhile, Company G had fielded a team again in 1902, after a lapse of just two seasons. But it was not an elite team and made no pretense of competing with the seven. The company defeated the high school, 56–6, in 1908, however, and it would be three years after this

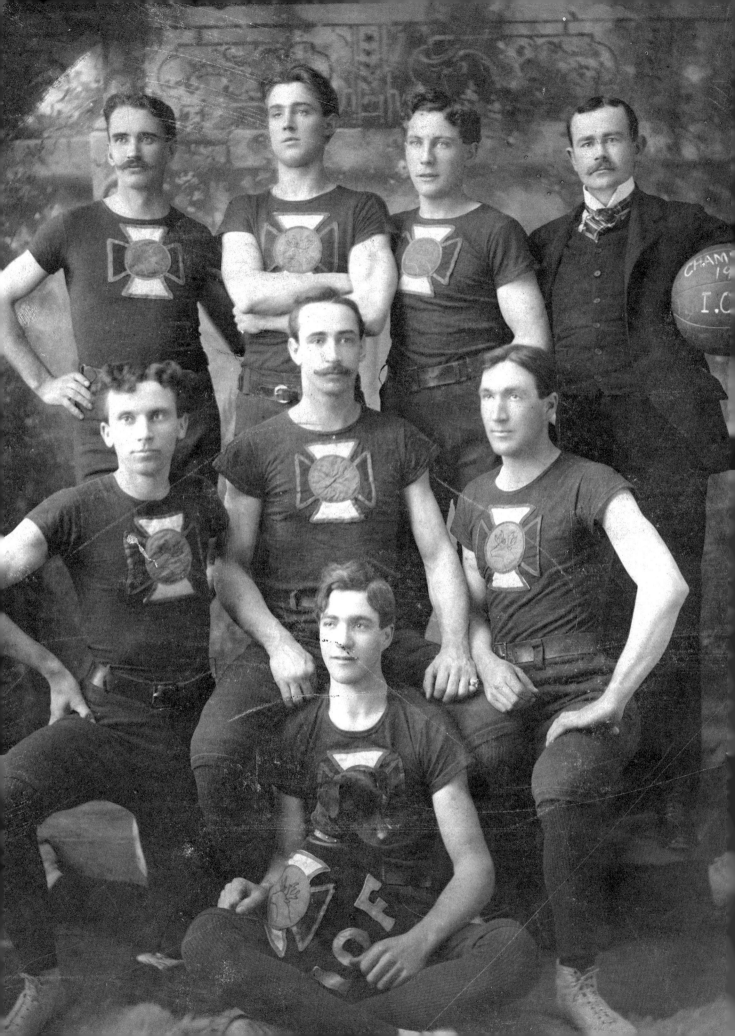

embarrassment before the latter would field a team again.

In 1909, Company G once more became, if only by default, the best team in Red Wing, and they quickly renewed efforts to gain recognition as the best team in Minnesota. They split two games with what was generally regarded as the state's second best senior men's team, St. Joseph's Church of Minneapolis. They won at home, 48–25, with Rehder scoring 28 points, and lost in Minneapolis, 52–12. In 1910, they were embarrassed in two games with the best team, the Ascensions from Ascension Church, also of Minneapolis. On February 4 in Red Wing, the Ascensions quit the game in a disagreement over the officiating. Red Wing partisans charged that the Ascensions had walked off the court because of their fear of losing to the G men. This was very unlikely, however, as the Ascensions led the disputed game 6–2 at the time they left the floor and also had won the earlier game, 50–18.

Rehder, a guard, and center Hawkins were Red Wing's new stars. But early in the 1912–1913 season, Hawkins left to join Fond du Lac's perennially powerful Company E. Nevertheless, no less an authority than Ahlers, star center of the Steady Seven, said that "Company G is as good as the old Red Men," largely in recognition of Rehder's play. At the time of his death in 1955, Judge Al Rehder was remembered "as the best shortstop to ever appear on a local diamond. He made a similar reputation in basketball."

In 1913, the company was designated by a new letter, L, and Hawkins appeared in Red Wing with Company E for the first time. E defeated L, 32–13. The 1913–1914 season passed uneventfully, though the losses to Hawkins and Fond du Lac continued to mount up, 34–14 and 58–24. The company managed to split a pair of games with St. Joe's, however, winning 43–35 in 1913 but losing 20–18 in 1914. The Ascensions had as of yet refused to meet the Red Wingers again after the debacle of 1910.

The 1914–1915 season saw a major breakthrough for the men from Red Wing. They split a pair of games with Fond du Lac and defeated St. Joe's, 30–26. They completed their season with a pair of wins, one over the Ascensions, 29–13, and one over Fond du Lac, 20–16, as Rehder scored 21 points in the two games and manager Bill Conlin scored 8 against Fond du Lac. The company won only twelve of twenty-three games, but eight of the losses were to barnstorming teams from New York—the Nationals, Oswego, and "national champion" Troy. (Contrary to the usual hyperbole, the Troy Trojans were the genuine article, featuring perhaps America's greatest basketball player in six-foot-five center Ed Wachter.) In any event, the western title was claimed, despite a pair of problematic losses to Chaska, 24–10 and 39–22.

Then in 1916, the company left nothing to chance, again claiming the midwestern title after a 20–0 season in which the team enjoyed a 53–16 average scoring advantage. But the heyday of elite, senior men's basketball in Red Wing had passed. In his unpublished history of Red Wing, long-time city clerk S. T. Irvine notes the city's basketball champions of 1901, 1902, 1906, and 1915. In the first three cases, he is of course referring to the Steady Seven, but in the latter case he referred not to the company or the Red Men but to the high school team.

And why not? Company L in 1915 defeated the Ascensions and Fond du Lac, each for the first time. But when they played the high school on January 1, 1915, they lost 21–19 in what the local paper called a "New Year's surprise."

The Steady Seven represented the city of Red Wing against all comers from 1900 through 1908. On their home court they won perhaps fifty games while losing only one. They are shown here in 1901, when they played as the Foresters. Front row, seated: Goodwin Esterly; middle row, left to right: Charles Fisher, Charles Ahlers, and Ed Kappel; back row: H. M. Bird, John Fisher, Mike Kappel, and Edmund P. Neill (manager).

4 *The High Schools Take the Court*

THE FIRST MINNESOTA high school team of any note was that from Minneapolis Central, which produced center George Tuck, later the first Gophers All-American in 1905. Even after Tuck became a Gopher, Central gave the U tougher games than many of their college opponents.

Stillwater also fielded competitive teams in the early years, claiming the state high school championship in 1903 after defeating Central, 26–21. Stillwater won twelve games that year while losing only one to the St. Cloud Normal School, 24–13; that same season, the rapid decline of the Minnesota Aggies was dramatized in a 48–8 rout by Stillwater. In 1906, Central won the championship of the first high school conference, the short-lived Tri-City, with a record of 4–0, while Stillwater finished second with five wins and three losses.

Initially, Minnesota's high schools were ill-suited to support the game of basketball. Schools at that time had no gymnasiums or auditoriums, and they lacked the faculty capacity and expertise to supervise athletic activities. Most important, the high schools had not yet developed a philosophy consistent with extracurricular and social activities. The game thus took root in the YMCAs, colleges, and militias. But not every community had a Y or a college or an armory, and in such communities the game languished for a decade or more. It would be about 1910 before basketball was played much beyond the state's largest cities. In most such communities it was the high schools that eventually took the lead. For every boy or young man who played basketball at a Y, college, or militia, dozens would one day play at their local high school.

For most Minnesota communities, then, the true "arrival" of the game of basketball was signaled by the first boys state high school basketball tournament, held at Carleton College in April 1913. More than just the game of basketball, the tournament also signaled

the arrival of physical education and its attendant philosophy of muscular Christianity in Minnesota's secondary schools. Dr. James A. Naismith was not only a physical educator and a doctor but also an ordained minister. And like basketball, muscular Christianity was invented at Springfield, where Naismith's boss, Dr. Luther J. Gulick, taught that the body is the temple in which the spirit resides and that a healthy body is a necessary condition for healthy morals. This philosophy swept across the United States, no doubt because it validated the sporting interests that American boys and young men and, to a lesser extent, girls and young women had already adopted.

This, then, is the early history of basketball in a nutshell: Boys and girls, and young men and women, played the game because it was fun. Their parents, educators, and community leaders embraced the game and brought it into the schools because it promised mental, moral, and spiritual as well as purely physical improvement.

Although the first official tournament was played in 1913, there was almost universal recognition of Madison High School as Minnesota's first, albeit mythical, statewide high school champion in 1911. Madison featured brothers "Butch" and "Slip" Little and cousins Grant and Len Jacobson. (Grant was the son of Jake Jacobson, Speaker of the Minnesota House of Representatives and 1912 Republican gubernatorial candidate.) Slip and Grant went on to play on Hamline's powerhouse teams of the early 1910s, though it was Butch who was the captain and Len the high scorer in most of the games for which box scores were published. Then again, the fifth starter, Dahl, was said to be the star of a 36–19 win over highly regarded New Ulm. Madison then arranged match games with Zumbrota, who claimed the championship of southeastern Minnesota, and Ada, claimants to the championship of northern

Minnesota. Madison beat Zumbrota easily, 43–15, at Madison, then beat Ada, 29–20, on a neutral court at Willmar.

Following Madison's lead, the so-called Northfield tournament had a definite southern Minnesota flavor during its nine-year run from 1913 to 1922. Southern Minnesota schools claimed fourteen of twenty spots in the championship finals, and nearby Red Wing won three of the ten early tournaments (then added a fourth in 1933). Rochester, Waseca, and Albert Lea ran off three straight titles from 1917 through 1919. Winona (1914), Mountain Lake (1913, 1915, 1917), New Ulm (1919, 1921), Mankato (1920), and Madison (1922) all finished as runners-up.

Maybe the shorter train rides helped the southeastern teams cope with the brutal two-a-day scheduling. The number of teams varied from nine in 1914 to sixteen in 1920, so prior to 1920 some teams usually received a first-round bye. But fifteen of the twenty championship finalists from 1914 to 1922 were playing their

Madison High School claimed the mythical championship of Minnesota in 1911 after winning match games against Zumbrota, 43–15, and Ada, 29–20. Stars Grant Jacobson and "Slip" Little went on to play for Hamline's powerful team.

fourth game in just two or three days, with a banquet in between. In 1920, the *Red Wing Republican* reported that, despite the banquet, Winger Carl "Cully" Lidberg had lost twelve pounds at the tournament; center Wal-

---

The Big Game

Fosston High School 29, Mountain Lake High School 27
April 5, 1913

Fosston High School won the first Minnesota high school basketball tournament, held at Carleton College in Northfield, in what was described as "a complete surprise." Fosston, after all, was the smallest team in the tournament by height and weight, and it represented one of the smallest schools from one of the smallest towns in the field.

Mankato and Stillwater were the favorites to win the title. But Mankato's star Earl Kimble (or Kimball) injured his knee in a first-round win over Faribault, and he was unable play through the rest of the tournament. So Mankato was surprised by Luverne, 26–22, in the second round. Stillwater held Madison without a field goal in a 32–5 first-round victory, then drew a bye in the second round. Now heavily favored to win the title, the Ponies instead joined Mankato on the sideline as a result of a shocking semifinal loss to Mountain Lake, 31–24. Meanwhile, Fosston's "Jack Pine Savages," as they fancied themselves, cruised to the finals without having to face any of the big boys. They easily defeated Willmar, 29–20; Plainview, 38–27; and Luverne, 38–28.

In the finals, Fosston defeated Mountain Lake by virtue of "some very clever teamwork." Mountain Lake jumped off to

an early 6–1 lead, though whether they did this primarily with "long shots" or "clever passing," the latter usually Fosston's forte, depends on which game description you prefer. Fosston, then, "by some clever short passes got the sphere under the basket three times and each time a ringer resulted." The half ended in a 16–16 tie. The two teams played evenly again through much of the second half, but finally Fosston, "by a series of clever and sure short passes" and "by some very clever teamwork and good shots," opened up a 5-point lead. The closest Mountain Lake could come thereafter was at the final score of 29–27.

Ralph "Curly" Movold, who later would coach at North Dakota State University, scored 11 points for Fosston, all of them from the free throw line, while Peter Guenther led the Lakers with 9 points. Over the course of the four games, Guenther scored 71 points. Thirty years later, this would still be the third highest total ever.

"Fosston's performance is all the more wonderful when we consider the fact that they did not even have a coach," the *Northfield Independent* reported. Fosston bewildered their opponents with a unique style of play that featured short, sharp passes thrown while the Fosston players ran in a series of tight circles—they literally ran rings around their opponents. This unique style, it turned out, came out of the expedient of holding practices in a classroom.

Red Wing High School won the first of four state titles in 1915. Front row, center, Raymond "Rucca" Hanson was their captain, coach, and star but was banned from the state tournament because he attended a beer bust a week earlier. Red Wing won anyway.

ter Seig, ten; and guard Robert Brown, eight. In finals that matched a team that had received a first-round bye against a team that had not, the better rested team won two of three. Only Rochester, led by future Gopher and All–Big Ten guard Fred Enke, overcame the effects of the extra game, beating Mountain Lake 19–8 in 1917.

It's more likely, of course, that these southern towns had more success simply because they were Minnesota's more mature and populous cities.

How They Played the Game

If you could return to Northfield for these first ten tournaments, you would find that it was an era of competing styles and strategies of play. It featured a faster pace and higher scoring than during the years immediately following.

When Naismith went to work at the University of Kansas, he was met by an eager young disciple named Forrest "Phog" Allen, who said he wanted to be a basketball coach. "You don't coach the game, Forrest," Naismith told him, "You just play it." This was a time, then, when the adults let the kids "just play it."

The physical education establishment simply could not meet the demand for qualified coaches until after World War I. Only thirty-one of sixty-six colleges listed in Spalding's guide to the 1908–1909 season had full-time coaches. And if this was true at the college level, no wonder that Fosston's 1913 champions did not have a coach. As late as 1915, the champions from Red Wing went through the regular season without a coach. Only at state tournament time did Bill Conlin, manager of the local Company L team, take on the role.

Left to their own devices, the boys did what boys do. They ran; they jumped; they played with more enthusiasm than discipline; they flung the spheroid at the goal (as they used to say). And they did the latter with enough frequency and skill to routinely score up to 20 or 30, sometimes even 40, and on two occasions 50 points in a game, even against state tournament–caliber opposition. Mountain Lake clobbered Red Wing, 49–28, in the very first tournament, and in 1914, Stillwater routed Aitkin, 57–11. No team scored more than those 57 points in a tournament game for almost a quarter century.

Teams ran up these relatively high scores the same

way they do today—because of mismatches in the skills of the opposing teams and with high-scoring offensive strategies. Blowouts were also exaggerated by the center jump rule. The ball was put into play after each basket by virtue of a jump ball at midcourt. A team with a tall player, such as Stillwater's Harold Gillen in 1914 and Albert Lea's Leonard Thune in 1919, could maintain control of the ball through virtually an entire game. This is how scores like those of the 1914 and 1919 championship games—Stillwater 30, Winona 4, in 1914; Albert Lea 37, New Ulm 8, in 1919—could occur. With Gillen and Thune dominating possession of the ball, "designated shooters" Ronald Parkhurst of Stillwater and Gordy Malmer of Albert Lea scored 18 and 23 points, respectively, totals that would be unheard of during the "dead ball" era of the 1920s and early 1930s.

Forwards were usually the designated scorers, as in ice hockey, and so they were usually the best, though not the biggest, athletes on the squad. Guards primarily played defense, as their name implies, chasing the opposing forwards all the way down to the baseline—again as in ice hockey. Guards were often the tallest players on the team. The importance of a designated shooter was enhanced by the rule that allowed one player to shoot all of a team's free throws, regardless of who had actually been the victim of the foul. In addition, free throws were awarded to the opposing team when a violation, like traveling, was committed. Sometimes, off and on during the game's early days, rules awarded two free throws if a player was fouled in the act of shooting, even if the shot went in the hoop.

In 1921, Minneapolis Central's Martin Norton set a tournament record that still stands today by making 37 free throws. Will Sheehan of Luverne shot at least 51 free throws in 1913; the Minnesota State High School League (MSHSL) erroneously lists Jim Hill's 40 free throw attempts in 1967 as the record. "Cheap free throws" mercifully were abandoned in 1923 in an effort to put more action back into the game.

Brothers in Arms

Along with Fosston's historic champions, the most colorful teams to appear in the Northfield tournaments

Four Members of The Tribune All City Floor Quint

Martin Norton (second from left) won All-America honors at the national high school tournament in Chicago in 1920 and then led Minneapolis Central to the state title in 1921. He set free throw records that still stand, and forty years later, sportswriter Halsey Hall selected Norton to his all-time tournament five.

Minnesota Mysteries and Myths
Who Founded the State High School Tournament?

For fifty years or more, old-timers gathered at the state tournament and reminisced about the first tournament held at Carleton College in Northfield in 1913. From time to time a newspaper reporter would overhear and publish their reminiscences, until they became accepted as the official tournament history. The old-timers remembered long-time Carleton athletic director Claude J. Hunt as the tourney's founder, for example. So the Minnesota State High School League (MSHSL) gave him a plaque honoring him as such in 1957. Some also remembered Fosston native and Gophers All-American Francis H. "Dobie" Stadsvold coaching Fosston to the first state title. (Others remembered that "Dr. Stadsvold" treated the blisters on the Fosston boys' feet.) So he was a "special honoree" on the occasion of the tournament's fiftieth anniversary in 1963.

The only problem with these reminiscences is that neither Hunt nor Stadsvold was actually in attendance at the first tournament.

The tournament was held on April 1–4, 1913. Hunt first set foot on the Carleton College campus when he became athletic director and coach in the fall of that year. As anyone can ascertain by reading the campus newspaper, *The Carletonia*, for 1913, the tournament was founded by the Faculty Committee on Athletics with assistance from Philosophy Professor Leal A. Headley, the head of the school's student recruiting program.

First among equals on the committee was Rev. Fred B. Hill, a professor of biblical literature. Hill had attended Carleton and was remembered as a star pitcher on the baseball team. He then went East, where he earned a doctorate in theology, was ordained as a minister, and married the heiress Deborah Sayles. Upon his return to Carleton, he and Mrs. Hill contributed $60,000 to the college for the construction of the Sayles-Hill Gymnasium, named in honor of the Hills' parents. When Donald J. Cowling became president of the college in 1908, Hill gave him a home to live in and a lifetime membership in the Minneapolis Club. Thus, when Hill suggested that Carleton should host a basketball tournament, all were enthusiastic in their support, especially since he offered to defray the participants' travel costs. When the tournament participants met after the Friday night banquet, they created a committee, charged it with assuring that another tournament would be held in 1914, and appointed Hill as its chair-

Contrary to published reports, it was the Rev. Fred B. Hill who was primarily responsible for the founding of the Minnesota state high school basketball tournament in 1913. A baseball star in Carleton's class of 1900, he returned to the college in 1907 as a professor of biblical literature and promptly spent $60,000 of his own money to build the Sayles-Hill Gymnasium.

man. He was the first leader of what would in 1916 become the MSHSL.

It would be twenty years before basketball fans began to inquire as to the tournament's origins and history. By then, Hill was already dead and forgotten, a victim of the influenza epidemic of 1919. In fairness, Hunt was never quoted as claiming to have founded the tournament, though he also was never quoted as protesting the same. Stadsvold, on the other hand, is quoted in Fosston's *Centennial History* as "recall[ing] that famous day when [Fosston] won the state trophy." Stadsvold was a son of Fosston's wealthiest and most prominent family. Add to that his status as a Gophers basketball star, and he was a local celebrity whose comings and goings were slavishly chronicled in the local newspaper, *The Thirteen Towns*. He was home for the Easter break on the day the team left for Carleton, and he returned to school at the U of M the next day. If *The Thirteen Towns* failed to report that he was in Northfield with the team, it can only be because he was not there.

The following year the paper reported quite unequivocally that Stadsvold was with the team in Northfield, though only as a chaperone, not as a coach. The boys' blisters surely occurred in 1914, when they were forced to play five games in five days. Whether they were treated by Stadsvold or by Fosston's real doctor, Dr. Porter, who also chaperoned the team, *The Thirteen Towns* did not say.

were the first of many state champions from Minnesota's Mesabi Iron Range—Virginia in 1916—and the three Red Wing teams to win at Carleton College in 1915, 1920, and 1922.

Virginia was declared co-favorite with Little Falls in 1916 as a result of the sound thrashings they handed out in the regional playoffs. Rush City upset Little Falls in the first round, however, and after two victories, "Virginia was being conceded the state high school basketball championship," according to the local *Virginia Daily Enterprise*. This was despite a close call, a 33–30 overtime win over Austin in the semifinal. But for once, obvious hometown boosterism turned out to be correct, as Virginia clobbered St. Paul Mechanic Arts, 20–9, in the final. Center William and brother J. Rooney made all-state, and a year later William was the first player ever selected to the all-tournament team in two different years.

Just before the tournament began, it was reported that "Virginia players realize that the tournament offi-cials will not be as lenient as Range referees in the matter of calling fouls. They have been cautioned against playing rough." Whether because of or in spite of their rough and spirited play, Iron Range high schools continued to leave their mark on the state tournament for almost fifty years. Not only did Iron Range teams dominate their region—that is to say, they routinely defeated teams in the Duluth area in the playoffs—but in every decade and every era before the 1960s, at least one Iron Range squad would follow Virginia's lead in claiming a state title.

Meanwhile, it's common to find brothers, cousins, fathers and sons, uncles and nephews on team rosters from a particular community over the years. But Red Wing perfected the art. The Browns helped the Wingers win three titles—Donald in 1915, Robert in 1920, and Kenneth in 1920 and 1922. The Maetzold cousins, Russell or "Butsie" and Jim, played in five tournaments, made all-tournament three times, and won two titles. Butsie went on to greater fame as a Hopkins

Minnesota State High School Champions through 1924

Year	Documented Mythical Championships	W–L	Authors' Choice: Postseason MVPs
1903	Stillwater 26 Mpls. Central 21	12–1	
1906	Mpls. Central	4–0	
1911	Madison 29 Ada 20	N/A	Slip Little, Madison, G

Year	Tournament Championship Game	W–L	Authors' Choice: Postseason MVPs
1913	Fosston 29 Mountain Lake 27	14–1	Peter Guenther, Mountain Lake, F
1914	Stillwater 30 Winona 4	14–2	Ronald Parkhurst, Stillwater, F
1915	Red Wing 30 Mountain Lake 18	15–1	Gerhard Hiebert, Mountain Lake, F
1916	Virginia 20 St. Paul Mechanic Arts 9	13–2	William Rooney, Virginia, C
1917	Rochester 19 Mountain Lake 8	11–2	Fred Enke, Rochester, G
1918	Waseca 29 Duluth Central 10	13–0	Lester Juhnke, Waseca, F
1919	Albert Lea 37 New Ulm 8	17–0	Gordy Malmer, Albert Lea, F
1920	Red Wing 21 Mankato 10	15–2	Carl Lidberg, Red Wing, F
1921	Mpls. Central 19 New Ulm 15	13–1	Martin Norton, Mpls. Central, F
1922	Red Wing 34 Madison 27	19–0	Butsie Maetzold, Red Wing, G
1923	Aurora 24 Austin 14	17–2	Paul Danculovic, Aurora, C
	East Chain 35 Raymond 26[a]		
	Duluth Cathedral 30 St. John's 16[b]		
1924	Two Harbors 21 Mpls. South 12	21–2	Mally Nydahl, Mpls. South, G
	Stewart 12 Brewster 7[a]		
	Duluth Cathedral 30 St. Thomas 22[b]		

[a] Tournament for the high school departments in graded schools.
[b] Catholic tournament.

High School coach, where his football teams went 88–6–5 over eighteen years, won ten conference titles, were unbeaten and untied nine times, and were unscored upon in 1933 and 1937. His basketball teams went 508–62 over twenty-nine years, winning nineteen conference, five region, and two state titles, one in 1952 and the other in 1953. Second cousin Leslie Maetzold also played in the 1941 tourney for tiny Lester Prairie. Dick Seebach was the star of the 1933 champions and went on to become a starting guard for the 1937 Minnesota Gophers, who won their only Big Ten conference title between 1919 and 1972. It was Dick's second cousin, Oscar, who first brought the game of basketball to Red Wing in 1896 through his acquaintance with Louis Cooke.

But it was the Nordlys who made up the greatest family dynasty of the tournament's single-class era. Olaf Martin "Marty" Nordly was Red Wing's greatest athlete of the nineteenth century. He led the city's greatest town baseball team to the championship of southern Minnesota in 1892. He once owned and operated a gymnasium, and he was a recognized expert in the gymnastic event of Indian club swinging. His oldest son, Louis (pronounced "Louie"), was the designated shooter and top scorer on the 1915 team, despite the presence of teammate Neal Arntson, who went on to win All–Big Ten honors for the Minnesota Gophers in 1921. Carl was the greatest athlete of the four brothers, yet his 1919 Wingers lost their only state tournament game. He went on to win eleven varsity letters at Carleton, plus all-conference honors in basketball three times, and then coached at Carleton and at Roch-

ester High School. He joined the U of M as a professor of physical education, in which capacity he remained from 1935 through 1955. In 1942, he was also named the Gophers' basketball coach, but after two years of disappointing results, he stepped down.

H. Oliver Nordly, known as "Hon" from his initials, was a sophomore forward on the 1920 championship team. In 1921, Nordly and Maetzold returned but lost in the first round; starters and 1922 all-staters Chuck Hartupee and K. Brown stayed at home because of illness. In 1922, Nordly took over the designated scorer's role, though it was Brown who led the way with 18 points in the championship win over Madison. Nordly and Maetzold made the first all-tournament team; Brown and Hartupee, the second. Nordly went on to coach Rochester to the 1931, 1933, and 1937 tournaments, and he later coached at Northern Iowa Teachers College (now Northern Iowa) for fifteen years. Harold "Tubby" Nordly and the 1929 Red Wing team lost in the final to Moorhead's defending champions in a 20–16 overtime thriller, and Tubby was named to the all-tournament five. He went on to play a reserve role for Carleton's greatest team, the Victory Five.

By 1923, the tournament had grown too big for the Carleton campus and was moved to the Kenwood Armory in Minneapolis, where it was housed for five years until the U of M Field House was opened in 1928. Aurora, under coach Harold Taylor, defeated Austin in 1923 to become the first state champ crowned in the Twin Cities—and the second from Minnesota's Mesabi Iron Range.

5 Victorian Attitudes Trump Women's Basketball

SEVERAL OBSERVERS NOTED the absence of the big-city boys from Minneapolis, St. Paul, and Duluth from the first Northfield tournament. But no one noted, nor much less lamented, the absence of Minnesota's girls, who would not have a tournament of their own until sixty-one years later. Nevertheless, from the beginning girls and young women across the country had embraced the game of basketball with as much enthusiasm—and in almost as large numbers—as their brothers did. The women's physical education classes at Carleton College, for example, were the second venue in the state (after the Minneapolis YMCA) in which basketball was played. Meanwhile, on October 20, 1905, the first game of basketball ever witnessed in the village of Fosston matched two women's teams. A week later, the first high school game matched two girls teams. It would be another year before a boys team would be formed in Fosston. But change—in this case, the overthrow of Victorian ideas of womanhood—came slowly. The 1913 season that saw the boys win the state championship also marked the end of girls interscholastic basketball in Fosston for more than sixty years.

Change was hard in Red Wing, too. The women of the town followed the men by about three years in organizing a team, and they worked more or less continually from 1899 to 1901 to do so. In the end the effort was abandoned because there were no opponents to be found. The high school girls played in 1904 and 1905, but they only participated in two interscholastic games, both against Rochester.

Marian Bemis Johnson, coauthor with Dorothy McIntyre of *Daughters of the Game*, has estimated that as many as three hundred Minnesota high schools fielded girls basketball teams from the turn of the twentieth century through 1942. Girls basketball was primarily a small-town phenomenon, according to Johnson. "The whole attitude had to do with classism," Johnson told

the *Star Tribune* in 1999. "It was the upper class who was concerned about the role of a lady. In rural communities, there was no one out there that belonged to this class."

In Minneapolis, however, no girl enrolled in the public high schools appears to have played interscholastic basketball after about 1908. From 1900 to 1908, the bulk of the games played by the Minnesota Lady Gophers were against the girls from Minneapolis Central, East, North, and South high schools. Several boarding schools or "settlement houses," such as Drummond and Stanley Hall, had teams right through the time of World War II, however, and the very first game ever played by the Lady Gophers was a 12–6 win over Stanley Hall in 1900.

Over the next eight years, the Lady Gophers won an estimated forty-six games while losing just five against the local high schools and boarding schools, plus the University of Nebraska; the Superior, Wisconsin, and Valley City, North Dakota, Normal Schools; the occasional YWCA; and the Minnesota Aggies. After the 1908 season, however, members of the faculty decided the activity was inappropriate, and the Board of Regents voted to abolish basketball and all intercollegiate athletics for women.

Opposition to the girls game was not confined to the big cities, however. Marie Keeler from Belle Plaine told Bemis Johnson that her own mother was appalled when she learned that her daughter was playing ball, "embarrassing your family and making a spectacle out of yourself." Victorian attitudes saw athletics, simply enough, as a threat to femininity. Because a woman "should always preserve her inborn sense of modesty and innocence, she must never be seen by the opposite sex when she is likely to forget herself"—for example, when she might get caught up in the emotional excitement of a competitive game. "The emotional strain attendant

Lee Bro

upon competition would be injurious," according to a report by women physical educators.

Physical educator and future First Lady Lou Henry Hoover (wife of Herbert Hoover) is often characterized as a leading conspirator against girls and women's athletics. In 1923, she helped form the Women's Division of the National Amateur Athletic Federation (WD-NAAF), which took the general position that competitive athletics were bad for girls and women. Women physical educators had advocated for physical education for women, and they tried to make it clear that they simply wanted to avoid the "mistakes" of physical education for men. What mistakes are those? "The earmarks of bad athletics," they said, "will always centre around intensive coaching of a few [and] neglect of the many." The men had found the siren song of elite athletics to be irresistible and, without fully recognizing the choice they were making, had almost invariably chosen to divert scarce educational resources from physical education for the many to elite athletics for the few. The women instead wanted to return to the ideals that the YMCAs had formulated in the 1890s: since physical education promised mental, moral, and spiritual as well as purely physical improvement, every boy and girl should benefit from such an education.

Recent scholarship has found Hoover to have been a "crusader for causes benefiting children and women" and "a champion for girls' and women's recreational sport." In fact, she believed that, given the Victorian

From the very beginning, Minnesota girls and women embraced the game of basketball with the same enthusiasm as their brothers. Here is some action from 1934, probably from a Minneapolis Park and Rec League game.

antipathy to physical activity, "those who do not want to play must be persuaded to play." Her preference for physical education for all rather than elite athletics for the few seems to have been misinterpreted. As noted physical educator Mabel Lee wrote, "We were fighting to correct abuses and to abolish only the wrong kind of sports." Unfortunately, their crusade may have resulted in fewer opportunities not simply for those girls and women interested in elite competition but also for the many who would have benefited from general physical activity.

In any event, Bemis Johnson and McIntyre uncovered in their research a letter from Harold Jack, the state supervisor of health and physical education, which was sent to Minnesota school districts in 1938. It reads, in part, "It is recommended that the interscholastic program be dropped and that the Girls' Athletic Association program be installed in its place." The following year his department reported that the number of high schools offering interscholastic competition for girls dropped from ninety-two in 1938–1939 to thirty-eight in 1939–1940. Jack described this as "a change for the better."

The role of Lou Hoover and the WD-NAAF as villains in the decline of girls and women's athletics, in summary, has been overstated. To the degree that the future First Lady's beliefs about elite, competitive athletics for girls and women carried the day, it was because they reflected those of a majority of Americans and even of women who were physical educators.

Between 1900 and 1909, the University of Minnesota Lady Gophers won an estimated forty-six games while losing just five. The first string from 1907 included Florence Schuyler, Rose Marie Schaller Joyce, Julia Bearnes, Florence Hofflin, and Madge Bogart.

6 *The Best of the Rest*

THE BEST TEAMS IN MINNESOTA in the early going included the Minneapolis Y in 1896 and 1897, Red Wing Company G in 1898, and perhaps Macalester College in 1899. The University of Minnesota emerged as a power in 1900, and from that point forward, the Gophers often fielded the state's best amateur team. Still, a variety of senior men's teams—from the 1906 Red Men and 1913 Ascensions to Carleton College in 1933 and the 1943 Rock Spring Sparklers—could from time to time make legitimate claims to being the best basketball team in the state.

For many years, the Ascensions, "Father Harrigan's boys," representing Ascension Catholic Church on the near north side of Minneapolis, were among the best of the senior teams. As late as 1941 (by that time, without Father Harrington), the Ascensions won the state Amateur Athletic Union (AAU) title and played in the national AAU tourney with a roster of former Gophers: Gordie Addington, Johnny Dick, John Kundla, Butch Nash, and Marty Rolek. The Ascensions were so good that in 1910 they sent their junior team (with players of high school age), the Ascension Cadets, into action against the St. Cloud Athletic Association. This was in spite of the fact that the St. Cloud AA was a senior men's team that was winning games by scores like 74–25 over Anoka and 62–14 over Melrose. The Cadets won easily, 58–17. When the Ascensions sent their first or senior team into battle, scores like 72–32 and 92–31 were the norm. And when New Ulm High School beat the Ascensions, 40–28, on March 10, 1911, it was front page news in the *Brown County Journal*.

The Duluth Boat Club finished its 1913 season with a record of 9–1 and wanted the opportunity to play for a state championship, so it invited the four best teams in the Twin Cities—the Ascensions, Company F, the "Ineligibles," and St. Joseph's Church—to Duluth for a tournament. All declined, unfortunately, and both the

Ascensions and the Ineligibles gave as their reason the fact that former Gophers Frank Lawler and R. M. Rosenwald were busy with their medical school studies. The fact is that these teams, with their heavily overlapping rosters, could hardly have all competed in the same tournament. Lawler primarily played with the Ineligibles, a group of Gopher alumni, but he was also the star of the Company F team and occasionally played with the Ascensions. Ascensions manager Fred Chicken also played for Company F, as did center Fred Nord of St. Joe's. Rosenwald played for the Ineligibles, Company F, and occasionally the Ascensions.

As if that were not enough, Lawler played for the Stillwater Hibernians, champions of the Stillwater city league. Most likely, he played for the Hibernians only in the playoffs, but he helped them defeat the Woodsmen, 23–17, with three baskets and then Company K, 12–10, as he scored 11 of his team's 12 points.

Nor was it clear that any of these was the best senior team in the state. The Ascensions split with Fond du Lac Company E, losing 33–22 and then winning easily 46–27. They also lost to the Hopkins Athletic Club, 43–28, and barely squeaked past the barnstorming New York Nationals, 33–32. St. Joe's lost to Company E, 35–34; the Nationals, 53–32; Fond du Lac, 27–16; plus a shocker to Willmar High School, 22–18; nevertheless, they defeated the Ineligibles, 16–15. Company F, even with Lawler, Chicken, Nord, and Rosenwald in their lineup, lost to the Nationals, 35–34. Although Fond du Lac defeated them twice, 43–23 and 28–25, the Nationals were the best barnstorming team to visit the Twin Cities and were a more or less constant presence in Minnesota and western Wisconsin from mid-February through the end of March. They won just three of seven against Minnesota's better teams, however.

Meanwhile, Company G lost to the Ascensions, St.

Famous Ascension Team of 1913

The Ascensions, representing Ascension Church on Minneapolis's near north side, were the leading senior men's team in the state from 1907 through the onset of World War II. The 1913 team (shown here) went 40–0 and concluded their first eight years of play with a record of 190–10. Front row, left to right: Frank Collins, Bill Donahue, Art Barry, and Jack Riley; back row: Al Beck, Al Von, and Jack Barry.

Joe's, and the Nationals but beat an outstanding Chaska team. Chaska lost to Red Wing and the Ascensions but defeated Company E, 23–20; they also easily beat the Nationals. Scores of 32–20 or 52–30 were reported, and perhaps these were in fact two separate games. A Chaska-Hopkins game was announced, but no score was published.

There is no reason to believe that the Duluth Boat Club could have stayed with any of them. Duluth's one loss was to the Shamrock club of Superior, Wisconsin. On a late January visit to the Twin Cities area, the Shamrocks were demolished by the Ascensions, 58–17,

and also lost to St. Joe's, 19–11. Chaska or Hopkins was perhaps better than the perennially dominant Ascensions. All three, and perhaps all of the above, were better than the woeful Minnesota Gophers in this particular year.

But the Gophers quickly bounced back, and the small colleges, especially Hamline and Carleton, also improved rapidly after 1910. Basketball at Hamline, as elsewhere, had languished in the decade of the 1900s. But Carleton and Hamline built new gymnasiums in 1908 and 1909, respectively, and in 1910 the Minnesota-Dakota Intercollegiate Athletic

Conference was formed. Hamline enjoyed immediate success, and by 1920 the basketball team had won six conference championships, the baseball team three, and the football team two.

The Minnesota Collegiate Athletic Conference (MCAC), the forerunner to the Minnesota Intercollegiate Athletic Conference (MIAC), was formed in 1913, and several teams competed simultaneously in the Minnesota-Dakota and Minnesota conferences. Hamline won the first three MCAC basketball titles behind the exploits of "Slip" Little and Grant Jacobson from Madison's 1911 state high school champs. But how good were they, really? It is hard to say, because by now the colleges were for the most part playing just among themselves. But on January 26, the Winona YMCA clobbered the St. Paul Y, featuring Grant Jacobson, 51–30. Parr, Winona's star center, scored 32 points and completely dominated his older rival. A year later, he would score a near-record 25 points in a state tournament game while leading Winona to second place, even though he would be completely outclassed by Stillwater's Harold Gillen in the final.

Precious few boys were attending college yet, and perhaps, the small colleges were not very good at all. Carleton set out to change all of that in 1913. They launched a recruiting campaign designed to bring "strong men" to the school. Most college students at this time were women, and Carleton wanted "that substantial equilibrium of the sexes which characterizes a normal, well ordered community." Of course, Carleton also founded the state high school tournament, and no less an authority than the tournament's founder, Rev. Fred B. Hill, said, "The tournament advertises Carleton and we admit it is held in part to advertise the college. . . . Advertising is the thing nowadays." As a result, several high school basketball stars who had the good fortune to play in the tournament followed up by coming to Carleton to play college ball in the Sayles Hill gym. The most notable among them was Carl Nordly of Red Wing. Others included Mervyn Welshons and "Red" Hollands of Stillwater, Frank Balzer of Mountain Lake, Eddie Kruse and Lester Kitzman of Rochester's 1917 state champions, and Chauncey Fleckenstein of Faribault.

By 1916, Hamline had been defeated for the first time, and Carleton claimed its first MCAC championship. Seven more titles followed in succession un-

til 1923, when Carleton left MIAC in search of tougher competition. Memorable victories included a 20–19 defeat of the University of Iowa at Iowa City in 1915. In 1924, they clobbered the Michigan Aggies, now Michigan State, at East Lansing shortly after the University of Michigan Wolverines had beaten them in a much closer game. The *Minneapolis Tribune* speculated that the unbeaten Carls could have contended for the Big Ten title.

Perhaps even more memorable than these victories was a 1921 defeat at the hands of the Indiana Hoosiers. George "Windy" Levis, who had coached Carleton from 1917 through 1919, was now the Hoosiers' coach, and he had been replaced at Carleton by Indiana grad Everett Dean. So the Hoosiers stopped off in Northfield on their way home from a 25–23 win over the Gophers in Minneapolis. The visiting Hoosiers edged the Carls, 24–23, after which Levis said, "Carleton has a wonderful team. It is my opinion that it could beat half the Big Ten teams and give any of them a close battle."

Success continued throughout the decade, and at one time Carleton had won forty-six straight conference games, sixty-four consecutive home games, and seven consecutive Midwest Conference titles. Their greatest team was the Victory Five in 1932. The Carls won their fifth straight Midwest Conference title at 7–0 and finished 17–1 overall. Their only loss was to the Minnesota Gophers, 19–14, but their nonconference schedule also included victories over Chicago, DePaul, Iowa, Iowa State, Nebraska, and Oklahoma A&M. Forward Dick Arney, from Marshalltown, Iowa, led the team in scoring at 10.4 points per game and earned Little All-America honors. The Gophers were defeated the following year, 31–21, and again in 1934–1935 by a score of 29–26. Wisconsin grad Marshall Diebold was now coach, and in 1933, Carleton also won at his alma mater, 34–29.

Perhaps the most remarkable of Carleton's achievements, however, was the development of so many coaches of note. The earliest were themselves participants in the Northfield tournament. George Peterson coached Austin's 1916 team, for example; Art Rolfe brought his Red Wing teams to Northfield in 1919 and 1920; and Reginald Kramer led Madison to the 1922 championship game. The next were future Gophers basketball coaches Ozzie Cowles, a Browns Valley native, and Carl Nordly of Red Wing, each of whom earned eleven varsity letters and all-conference hoops honors in 1922. Cowles then coached Rochester into the 1923 state tournament before succeeding Everett Dean at Carleton. From there Cowles went to Dartmouth, where he won six straight Ivy League titles and was NCAA tournament runner-up to Dean and Stanford in 1942, before becoming Gophers coach in 1949. Nordly succeeded Cowles at Rochester and later served as Gophers coach from 1942 through 1944. In 1924 Nordly won all-conference honors for a third time, now joined by Joe Hutton and Herman Woock. Hutton went on to become a national Hall of Fame coach at Hamline University, while Woock became a Minnesota Hall of Fame coach at Crosby-Ironton High School. Carl Nordly's brother Oliver or "Hon" also won all-conference honors at Carleton, then coached at Rochester and Northern Iowa Teachers College in Cedar Rapids.

A decade later, the Victory Five produced another clutch of great coaches, including Dick Arney, Verl "Gus" Young, and Chet Raasch. Like Red Wing and Rochester, Austin High School felt the pull of Carleton's gravity. In addition to Coach Peterson, Arney (1935) and Young (1939), from Wadena, Minnesota, coached Austin to the state tournament. Raasch, who had been Red Wing's center in the 1929 and 1930 state tournaments, coached Tracy to the big show in 1940. Young went on to a particularly colorful career, coaching high school ball at Warroad, Buffalo, and Hutchinson in addition to Austin, then as an assistant at Carleton and head coach at Gustavus Adolphus College from 1949 to 1957. Finally, he was hired to conduct community relations for the professional Minnesota Pipers of the American Basketball Association and eventually became head coach for the final part of the 1968–1969 season.

Small College Conference Champions, 1913–1942

Year	Minnesota Collegiate Conference Champion(s)		Year	MIAC Champion
1913	Hamline		1921	Carleton
1914	Hamline		1922	Carleton
1915	Hamline		1923	Carleton
1916	Carleton		1924	St. Thomas
1917	Carleton		1925	Gustavus
1918	Carleton, St. Thomas		1926	Gustavus
1919	Carleton		1927	Augsburg
1920	Carleton		1928	Gustavus
			1929	St. Olaf
			1930	St. Olaf
			1931	Concordia
			1932	Hamline

Year	MIAC Champion(s)	Northern Teachers Conference Champion
1933	Hamline	Mankato Teachers
1934	Hamline	Duluth Teachers
1935	Hamline	Duluth Teachers
1936	Hamline	Duluth Teachers
1937	Macalester	Duluth Teachers
1938	Gustavus, Hamline	Winona Teachers[a]
1939	Hamline, St. Mary's	Winona Teachers[a]
1940	St. Mary's (Hamline)[a]	Bemidji Teachers[a]
1941	Hamline (St. Mary's)[a]	Bemidji Teachers[a]
1942	Hamline[a]	Bemidji Teachers[a]

[a] Participated in National Association of Intercollegiate Basketball (NAIB) tournament.

7 The Ups and Downs of Doc Cooke's Gophers

AFTER A ROCKY START, the Gophers under Doc Cooke had known almost nothing but success after 1900. Now they began to experience a cycle of ups and downs that would characterize Golden Gophers basketball for the next one hundred years. They simply were not very good from 1907 through 1909, but they bounced back to 10–3 in 1909–1910 and 9–4 in 1910–1911. Frank Lawler, one of four prominent basketball-playing brothers from Minneapolis, scored 8 points per game to lead the Big Ten and earned All-America honors in 1911. In 1950, he was voted the greatest Gophers player ever.

The U claims to this day a share of the Big Ten title in 1911 at 8–4, though the Big Ten long had listed the Gophers in second place at 7–4. Now, for unknown reasons, the conference has acknowledged the Gophers' claim. Yet the Gophers' own records show two victories each over Wisconsin, Iowa, and Purdue and one against Chicago. Where that eighth phantom win came from even the Gophers cannot say, so it appears Minnesota really did finish 7–4 (9–4 including two nonconference victories over Nebraska) and in second place in the conference.

Despite Lawler's continuing efforts, the Gophers slumped to 7–6 and fourth place in the conference in 1912. Then came 1913 and near disaster. The team was bereft of veteran talent, and newcomers Lawrence "Bee" Lawler, Frank's younger brother, and Francis "Dobie" Stadsvold were counted on to lead the team. The first game against Hamline was a preview of what was to come, however, and that was a terrible embarrassment, a 30–15 defeat. In their final nonconference game, the Gophers managed to defeat Nebraska, 20–11, as Bee Lawler starred, and Bee also starred in a 26–10 victory at Iowa. But these two wins represented his, and the team's, high point. Stadsvold showed more promise as the year went on, but his services were lost to the team before the end of February because of academic problems. These coincided with what was reported as a severe ankle injury that would have ended his season anyway. With the loss of Stadsvold, the team's play deteriorated. Their only two conference victories were early and on the road, at Iowa City and at Purdue. Later in the year, they managed to lose to both on their own home court at the University Armory.

The big news surrounding the Gophers basketball team in 1913, however, was the banning on February 21 of the traditional postgame dance because of "the prevalence of 'lagging' and the 'tango.'" The Gophers athletic department was already having difficulty paying its bills. A $5 student fee to support the department had been proposed, though it does not appear to have been adopted. The elimination of the postgame dance caused an immediate and disastrous drop in attendance and further reduced the department's receipts.

The department quickly reversed itself. "The great stretches of empty chairs were so vast . . . [that] the return of dancing is necessary or basketball will show the greatest deficit since its establishment as a college sport," the *Minneapolis Tribune* reported. "The board will not even dictate what dances may be danced." Even after the postgame dances were reinstated, however, the crowds were very small, and "enthusiasm was at a very low ebb."

But the Gophers' roller-coaster ride took them back up to the top of the Big Ten by 1917. The road back to respectability was substantially served by the rapid development of Minnesota high school ball, and the two stars of the 1917 team are representative of the state of basketball before and after that development.

Stadsvold was "before." By the time of his graduation from Fosston High School in 1910, he had played a mere twenty-two interscholastic games, and there had never been any other teams on which to play. Further, he had never played for a trained coach, so he came to the U as a rough and unpolished athlete. He did not play

The crowning achievement of Cooke's career was his 1919 national championship squad. Front row, left to right: *Norman Kingsley, Arnold Oss, Erling Platou (captain), Miles Lawler, and Joel Hultkrans;* second row: *Kearney, Sidney Hammer, Fred Enke, and James McMillan;* back row: *Coach Cooke.*

varsity ball until his third year in school, and it would be seven years after his high school graduation—in 1917, at the age of twenty-six—before he would be ready to achieve his All-America potential.

Harold Gillen was five years younger than Stadsvold and represented "after." He played sixteen interscholastic games in his senior season alone and had played for senior men's teams throughout his high school career, for a total of perhaps one hundred competitive games of basketball. He was ready to contribute to the Gophers from the moment he stepped on to the U of M campus in the fall of 1914. And so he, too, earned All-America honors for Cooke's squad in 1917 at the age of twenty-one.

Together Gillen and Stadsvold led the Gophers to a 10–2 conference record and to seventeen victories overall, the most a Cooke team would ever earn in a single season. In fact, no Gophers team would win seventeen games again for thirty years. The Premo Poll retroactively ranked them fourth in the nation, their first time back among the top twenty in ten years.

The Gophers placed second in the Big Ten in 1918 at 7–3 (9–3 overall) and even defeated conference champion Wisconsin, 19–11, in Madison. Then came the crowning achievement of Cooke's career, another undefeated (13–0) national championship team. This was the second-highest-scoring team in Big Ten history at 35.5 points per game, including a school record of 68

Gophers Annual Record, 1895–1924

Year	Overall Record	Big Ten Record
1895–1896	4–7[a]	

Coach Dr. Louis J. Cooke

Year	Overall Record	Big Ten Record
1896–1897	3–6–1	
1897–1898	5–8–1[a]	
1898–1899	5–5[a]	
1899–1900	10–3[a]	
1900–1901	11–1	
1901–1902	15–0[b]	
1902–1903	13–0[c]	
1903–1904	10–2	
1904–1905	7–7–1	
1905–1906	13–2	6–1 (1st)
1906–1907	10–2[a]	6–2 (1st tie)
1907–1908	12–7[a]	4–6 (4th)
1908–1909	8–6	3–6 (5th)
1909–1910	10–3	7–3 (2nd)
1910–1911	9–4[a, d]	7–4 (2nd)
1911–1912	7–6	6–6 (4th)
1912–1913	4–9[a]	2–8 (7th)
1913–1914	4–11[a]	4–8 (6th)
1914–1915	11–6[a]	6–6 (4th)
1915–1916	11–6[a]	6–6 (4th)
1916–1917	17–2[a]	10–2 (1st tie)
1917–1918	13–3[a]	7–3 (2nd)
1918–1919	13–0[b]	10–0 (1st)
1919–1920	7–9[a,d]	3–9 (7th tie)
1920–1921	10–5	7–5 (4th)
1921–1922	5–8[a]	5–7 (8th)
1922–1923	2–13	1–11 (9th)
1923–1924	9–8	5–7 (8th)

	Overall Record	Big Ten Record
Cooke Totals	254–142–3	105–100
	.640	.512

	Overall Record	Big Ten Record
Gopher Totals		
1895–1924	258–149–3	105–100
	.633	.512

[a] Five different sources were consulted for the Gophers' early win-loss records, and there are discrepancies in these seasons. All of the records shown here are based on lists of actual opponents and game scores. Cooke's career totals as shown here, then, disagree with those in other published sources.
[b] Helms and Premo national champions.
[c] Premo national champion.
[d] The Gophers' claim of a tie for the 1911 Big Ten title appears invalid, while 1920 records disagree whether the Gophers defeated Michigan, 30–16, or lost to the Wolverines by that score.

Authors' Choice: Minnesota All-Stars, 1892–1924

Center George Tuck, Minneapolis Central High School and University of Minnesota. The Gophers won their first twenty-nine games after Tuck joined the team for the 1901–1902 season, and they finished 45–9–1 for Tuck's four-year career. He became the Gophers' first All-American in 1905.

Forward Frank Lawler, University of Minnesota. In 1950, Lawler was voted the Gophers' best player of the previous half century. He led the Big Ten in scoring and won All-America honors in 1911.

Forward Martin Norton, Minneapolis Central High School. Norton won All-America honors at a national high school tournament in Chicago in 1920. The following year, he led Central to the Minnesota state title while setting a free throw shooting record that still stands. More than forty years later, long-time newspaperman and broadcaster Halsey Hall picked Norton for his all-time high school tournament five.

Guard Erling Platou, University of Minnesota. Platou led the 1919 Gophers to an unbeaten season, a Big Ten Title, and, later, a retroactive Helms Foundation national championship. Helms also honored him as national Player of the Year for his then remarkable average of 11.6 points per game. Both Lawler and Platou went on to become doctors, Lawler at the Veteran's Administration, Platou at the University Medical School.

Guard Al Rehder, Red Wing Company G and L. Better known is Russell "Butsie" Maetzold, who led Red Wing High School to two state titles in 1920 and 1922 and then won all-state college honors four times at Hamline. But Rehder played just a decade earlier, and though he played neither high school nor college ball, he was more highly regarded by Red Wing basketball fans at the time.

SECOND TEAM *Center* Ben Hawkins, Red Wing Company G; *forwards* Carl Nordly, Red Wing High School and Carleton College, and Arnold Oss, University of Minnesota; *guards* Fred Enke, Rochester High School and University of Minnesota, and Butsie Maetzold, Red Wing High School and Hamline University.

points in a single game (against Wisconsin-Stout) that stood until 1946. Only two of the wins were by less than a double-digit margin, those coming on a late-season road trip to Indiana (20–14) and Purdue (26–21). Guard Erling Platou led the way at 11.8 points per game, forward Arnold Oss added 9.4, and center Norman Kingsley, 7.4, this at a time when many teams did not score much more than 20 points per game.

The Gophers had nowhere else to go after 1919, and so their fortunes declined. The next five years saw them finish seventh, fourth, sixth, ninth, and eighth in the Big Ten, winning just twenty-one of sixty conference games. A highlight was the one-two punch in 1921 of Oss, the Big Ten's official scoring leader with 3.67 field goals per game, and Neal Arntsen, the team's designated free throw shooter, who outscored Oss 8.8 to 7.5 points per game. Oss, from Lidgerwood, North Dakota, won All–Big Ten

and All-America honors in football as well as hoops.

Great things were expected in 1923–1924, but the season ended in a disappointing 5–7 conference record. The following fall, before the opening of the 1924–1925 season, Cooke announced his retirement. His remarkable twenty-seven-year tenure ended, like that of so many coaches, on a low note. Yet he had won four (not five, as Gopher records claim) Big Ten titles and fielded three (counting the 1903 Premo Poll) national championship teams. His overall record was 254–142–3 (.640), though just 105–100 (.512) in the Big Ten. (Almost one-third of his losses occurred in his first two and final three seasons. Setting those aside, his winning percentage during his "prime" was .705.)

More important, Cooke had made the University of Minnesota Gophers the premier basketball program in the state. It had not been obvious to anyone when Cooke first arrived in the state in 1895 that it should be so.

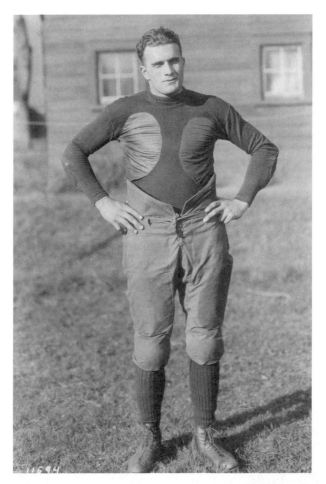

Arnold Oss, from Lidgerwood, North Dakota, won All-America honors in both football and basketball. He scored 9.4 points per game for the 1919 national champs and then led the Big Ten in scoring in 1921 with 3.67 field goals per game.

The Coaches Take Charge, 1924–1942

From its founding in 1891 to World War I, the game of basketball spread so rapidly that the nascent physical education establishment could not produce enough trained coaches to meet demand. Before the turn of the century, the YMCA International Training School at Springfield, Massachusetts, was the only school in the United States that was training physical educators and coaches. By the 1910s, physical education departments were springing up at places like Carleton and Hamline and all over the country. By 1920, the opportunity to learn how to coach was widely available, and trained coaches, in turn, were teaching more and more boys at a younger and younger age.

It was no surprise that the coaches brought more discipline and strategy to the game than the kids themselves did. That's what they were paid to do. In Minnesota, that usually meant the adoption of strategies developed by coach Walter "Doc" Meanwell at the University of Wisconsin—ideas that were taught at Carleton and widely disseminated by its graduates.

Unfortunately, Meanwell's complex strategies, in the hands of lesser coaches and players, often had the effect of slowing the game almost to a crawl. So the coaches constantly tinkered with the rules for twenty years in an effort to add more action back into their game.

Minnesota basketball also began to show signs of weakness. Carleton, under coaches Everett Dean, Ozzie Cowles, and Marshall Diebold, thrived, as did Hamline later under coach Joe Hutton. But Minnesota high schools won only half of their games at the national tournament in Chicago from 1923 to 1929, though Minneapolis DeLaSalle won a national Catholic title in 1931. Meanwhile, the U of M struggled more often than not, except for one brief, shining season in 1937. But after winning 65 percent of its games under Dr. Louis J. Cooke, the Gophers won barely 52 percent of their games from 1924 through the first retirement of coach Dave MacMillan in 1942.

Yet, despite the slow-paced games, attendance at Minnesota high school championship games increased from little more than 2,000 in 1920 to more than 8,000 in 1939. And despite the Gophers' struggles, their attendance record skyrocketed from around 2,500 to 15,800 over the same twenty years. The fans, at least, seemed to be happy with Minnesota basketball just the way it was.

In his prime, coach Joe Hutton and his Hamline Pipers won seventeen MIAC titles in twenty tries, and over twenty-four years only once finished lower than second in the league.

8 The Midwestern Style

BY THE TIME OF WORLD WAR I, the first generation of professional (full-time, paid) college coaches—including Dr. Louis J. Cooke at Minnesota; Forrest "Phog" Allen at Kansas (1906–1956); George Keogan, a Detroit Lakes, Minnesota, native, U of M graduate, and Notre Dame coach (1916–1943); Ward "Piggy" Lambert at Purdue (1917, 1919–1946); and Walter "Doc" Meanwell of Wisconsin (1912–1917, 1921–1934)—had begun to impose order on the strategic chaos that was early basketball.

Easily the most influential of them in the Upper Midwest, including Minnesota, was Meanwell. Though he had never played the game himself, he had definite ideas about how it *should* be played. "The game got completely out of hand," he said. "It was so rough that many schools dropped basketball between the years 1905 and 1915. I decided to buck the trend and stress finesse." Meanwell held doggedly to the belief that the passing game represented finesse and precision, while dribbling was a rough and primitive tactic. So his Wisconsin System, which as it spread became known as the "Midwestern Style," was a five-man motion offense featuring a weave pattern and short passes. Rarely did the Badgers ever dribble the ball. And the motion enabled Meanwell to pioneer the screen for the shooter.

In his first three seasons at Wisconsin, Meanwell's teams went 44–1. His 1912, 1914, and 1916 teams later were declared national champions by the Helms Foundation, and he won nine conference titles—including his stints at Wisconsin and Missouri—in his first twelve years in college coaching. So his style became all the rage. Compared to their eastern rivals, midwest-

Verl "Gus" Young was one of several Carleton grads who went on to a notable coaching career. After coaching at Warroad, Buffalo, Hutchinson, and Austin high schools, Young won three MIAC titles at Gustavus Adolphus and coached the ABA's Minnesota Pipers for a portion of the 1968–1969 season.

In 1922, Carl Nordly (pictured here), Ozzie Cowles, and Joe Hutton were teammates at Carleton College. Nordly and Cowles went on to coach the University of Minnesota Gophers, while Hutton gained fame as coach of the Hamline Pipers.

ern colleges featured less holding on defense, less dribbling, more passing, and more one-handed and pivot shooting.

In Minnesota, Meanwell's influence flowed largely through Minnesota's "cradle of coaches," Carleton College. George "Windy" Levis had been an All-America center at Wisconsin. He became Carleton coach in 1917 and immediately installed the Wisconsin System. Levis then moved to Indiana, where he coached the Hoosiers' first All-American, Everett Dean. Dean then became Carleton coach and taught Meanwell's system to future Gophers coaches Ozzie Cowles and Carl Nordly and future Hamline coach Joe Hutton, among many others. Later, Marshall Diebold came to Northfield from Wis-

Carleton and Hamline, seen here in action in 1926, both promoted the control style of play and turned out dozens of coaches who carried that legacy right up to the present day.

consin, where he, too, had played for Meanwell. All of them passed Meanwell's gospel along to another generation of Minnesota coaches.

As late as 1972, three of the four Class AA high school tournament semifinalists were coached by Hutton disciples. They were Joe Hutton Jr. at Bloomington Lincoln, Oscar Haddorff at Austin, and Ziggy Kauls at Class AA champion Mounds View. All of them played the same deliberate, ball control style of play that had been taught decades earlier at Wisconsin, Carleton, and Hamline. And wherever the so-called control game went, controversy was sure to follow. In the 1930s, Northwestern coach Arthur "Dutch" Lonborg protested the lack of action, saying it was "more than the spectator can be expected to bear." In 1949, *Minneapolis Tribune* columnist Dick Cullum noted "the asser-

tion, in some quarters, that the so-called control style of basketball, as played in Minnesota, is uninteresting." In 1975, *Minneapolis Tribune* columnist Bruce Brothers wrote of the high school tournament, "Teams have been slowing it down, stressing defense and playing conservative basketball. . . . [and] the argument was raging as to whether this year's . . . basketball tournaments were a good show or not. . . . Is there a relationship between that style and the poor attendance?"

In 1927, at Meanwell's urging, the rules committee voted 9–8 to outlaw dribbling. They then adjourned to watch the greatest professional team in the United States, the Original Celtics, who like Meanwell disdained the dribble. After the game, Meanwell again praised the passing game. But Nat Holman, a member of the Celtics who also coached at the City College of New York, argued passionately that college players, much less younger men and boys, should not be expected to play like professionals and needed the dribble as well as the pass to maneuver. The committee voted again, this time to keep the dribble. So as the 1930s dawned, basketball retained both the pass and the dribble to keep the ball moving.

Unfortunately, as Holman suggested, Meanwell's was a complex and difficult style for less skillful athletes (and coaches) to employ. Methods for stopping it were being developed—in particular, the zone defense, which came to dominate the late 1920s. The stall was then invented by another Doc—coach "Doc" Carlson of Pittsburgh—to counteract the zone defense, and as a result games seemed to grind to a halt. One guard, called the "back" or "stationary" or "standing" guard, rarely advanced much beyond midcourt.

How much had the game really changed from, say, 1913 to 1935? In the very first Northfield tournament of 1913, the average game score had been 34–21, a level that would not be reached again until 1935. As late as 1922, the average was about 29–20. In 1922, "the cheap free throw" was eliminated—that is, free throws would no longer be shot for technical violations like traveling. Beginning in 1923, there would also be no more "designated shooter" of all of a team's free throws. These rule changes may have quickened the pace of the game, though it's hard to tell, but the loss of the "cheap free throw" had the immediate impact of further depressing scoring. By 1925, the average state high school tournament score was at an all-time low of 21–11. Fortunately, by 1933, it had crept back up at least to 27–19.

The memories of players from that period, reported decades later, provide insights into the development of the game. In 1953, a run-and-gun Red Wing team went into the state tournament unbeaten with a stunning 92–73 regional triumph over Braham, stimulating much reminiscing about earlier editions of the Winger dynasty. Louis Nordly, high scorer for the 1915 team, told a *Minneapolis Tribune* reporter, "We used to run a lot in our day, too. We didn't play any standing guard." Meanwhile, Art Lillyblad, all-state guard for the 1933 champs, said, "It's a different game today: the kids . . . run more." Pat Rogers, high scorer for Glencoe in their 1931 title game win over Buffalo, described the game of his era for the *St. Paul Pioneer Press/Dispatch* during the 1984 tournament. "These kids today are so much

Minnesota Mysteries and Myths
"Too Hard on Young, Growing Bodies"

The slow-down, ball control style of play popular in the 1920s and 1930s was often described as "winning basketball." It also had the benefit of teaching "discipline" to boys and young men. Another rationale for the slow-down game was not discussed so much and only really came to light in the late '30s. With the elimination in 1937 of the center jump after each basket, sportswriters—and coaches, apparently—formed the impression that the game was being played at a vastly faster pace. Fans loved it, but coaches were not so sure. A 1941 coaches' poll conducted by the *Minneapolis Tribune* came up with the following suggestions for improving the game:

- Bring back the center jump;
- Slow down the game, give the kids a breather;
- Slow up the game—it's too hard on young, growing bodies.

The demise of girls and women's ball reflected a similar concern for potentially negative effects of strenuous exercise. In this case, the concern was focused on the women's child-bearing function. One study showed that strenuous physical activity in the school caused the number, extent, and flow of menstruations to be diminished, and this in turn was taken as evidence of a reduction in fertility. Therefore, "what is needed is a restriction in quantity of competition in any form."

Ruth Dahlke recalled being told in about 1928 that her Sherburn High School team was being disbanded because "it was detrimental to our health." At least Dahlke was able to continue to play basketball at what is now Minnesota State University–Mankato. Marie Keeler remembered that her Belle Plaine High School team was disbanded in 1926. Her teacher told her that "they wouldn't be able to have kids with all that bouncing around." Having abused herself with three years of high school ball, Keeler went on to have eleven healthy children. She was ninety-one years old when interviewed by the *Star Tribune* in 1999.

Of course, the notion that a game that was played on the run, rather than at a walk, would be too hard on growing bodies seems just as ludicrous today as the idea that girls who competed in athletics would be unable to have babies. But such was the evolution in thinking that had to precede the evolution of the game itself.

Carleton's greatest team, the Victory Five of 1932, was also referred to as the eleventh member of the Big Ten. Left to right: Ron "Boots" Taylor, Chet Raasch, Dick Arney, Marshall Diebold (coach), Matt Thoeny, and Eric J. "Joey" Strom.

Authors' Choice:
Minnesota All-Stars, 1924–1942

Center Clint Wager, Winona High School and St. Mary's College. One of the state's first big, scoring centers, the six-foot-five-and-a-half Wager led St. Mary's to the only two MIAC titles in its history and led the conference in scoring twice. He then played seven seasons of professional ball in the National Basketball League (NBL) and National Basketball Association (NBA) as well as pro football in the National Football League (NFL).

Forward John Kundla, Minneapolis Central High School and University of Minnesota. In 1937, Kundla led the Gophers to their only Big Ten championship between 1919 and 1972, scoring 9 points per game in his sophomore year. He then led the Gophers to thirty wins and just ten losses over the next two seasons.

Forward Dick Arney, Carleton College. Carleton was unbeaten in Midwest Conference play from 1928 to 1934 and beat the Minnesota Gophers in 1932–1933 and 1935–1936. The best team of this golden era was the so-called Victory Five of 1932, and Arney was its star. He earned Little All-

America honors, then went on to coach Austin to the state title in 1935.

Guard Marty Rolek, Minneapolis Edison High School and University of Minnesota. Rolek was the primary ball handler for the 1937 Big Ten champion Gophers, then earned All-America honors in 1938.

Guard Willie Warhol, Minneapolis Edison High School and University of Minnesota. Warhol was the star of the best Minnesota high school team of the era, then played at the U—even helping out at the center spot for a while—at a time when the Gophers' program was struggling.

SECOND TEAM *Center* Hans Rortvedt, Henning Schools and Augsburg College; *forwards* Arnie Johnson, Gonvick High School and Bemidji Teachers College, and Johnny Norlander, Virginia High School and Hamline University; *guards* Johnny Dick, Buhl High School and University of Minnesota, and Ray Moran, Moorhead High School and Concordia College (Moorhead).

faster," he said. "*We just walked through the plays.* . . . In . . . four games, we took one shot beyond the free throw line. Just about everything then was a 'pot shot,'" a shot from under the basket, a layup. "*There was discipline in those days*" (emphasis added).

Despite more rule changes, scoring increased only slowly. In 1931, Glencoe beat Chisholm, 15–14, in a semifinal, and as late as 1933, Red Wing beat Minneapolis North, 16–13, in the state title game. The elimination of what had seemed like an endless parade to the free throw line way back in 1923 had not changed that perception of a slow-moving game, but fortunately the next innovation did the trick. Since Naismith's time, every basket was followed by a jump ball at midcourt, like a hockey face-off. Then, on March 17, 1937, came the long-awaited and much-discussed elimination of the center jump after each basket. Now the defensive team would simply bring the ball back into play from their opponents' baseline based on the concept of alternating possessions. Sportswriters reported that the game was now being played at a breakneck pace. They called the new style "the firewagon fast break." But it's hard to know what really happened because, compared to 1937, scoring increased only slightly and even fell back in 1939.

Field goal attempts and shooting percentages were only very rarely reported before the World War II years, but in 1922, Carleton swept a pair of games, 54–8 against Coe and 48–8 against Concordia (Moorhead), while shooting 35 percent. "A strong team," it was reported, "is usually playing very well when its shooting percentage is over .200." In 1936, Buhl upset Minneapolis Edison in the high school tournament by making 16 of 32 shots, or 50 percent. Edison, meanwhile, shot 23 percent, connecting on 14 of 63 attempts. "Experts figure that from 18 to 20 percent is a good average," the report continued, and this was at a time when "just about everything . . . was a 'pot shot.'" Then, in the 1940 high school tournament, the four semifinalists took 185 shots, each converting 19 to 23 percent of them. Teams, in short, were taking—and making—about the same number of shots in 1940 that they were in 1920. Perhaps the players simply were moving around more rapidly in the interim of twenty to thirty seconds or so between shots.

The evolution of basketball in the 1920s and 1930s, then, can be summarized as follows: Having taken the air out of the ball in the early 1920s, the coaches struggled for twenty years to add some excitement back into their game. Still, many of the coaches were not sure they had gotten it right. Those who wanted faster and higher scoring and those who liked to hang on to the ball would, in fact, battle in the decade after World War II for basketball's soul.

9 *March Madness Captures the High Schools*

JUST AS THE GAME ON THE COURT was evolving, the Minnesota high school basketball tournament saw a variety of changes and experiments, too. From the Kenwood Armory (1923–1927), the state tournament moved to the University of Minnesota Field House from 1927 to 1932, the Minneapolis Auditorium from 1933 to 1938, the St. Paul Auditorium for two years, and then back to the Minneapolis Auditorium. Championship game attendance at the Kenwood Armory was about the same (3,500) as in the final year at Northfield, but attendance grew to around 7,000 to 8,000 after the tournament moved to the Field House. It hovered there for a decade, finally hitting the 10,000 mark in 1938. The highest pre–World War II total for the three-day tournament was 35,900 in 1941, while the single game record increased to 12,500 in 1942.

The tournament's increasing popularity was primarily due to two factors. One was the availability of the tournament via a statewide radio network beginning in 1938. The other was the occasional success of the small-town Cinderellas. From 1938 through 1942 a series of small-town teams won five championships in a row. The very first Cinderella, however, was Gaylord in 1926, and it is surely the best remembered champion of the 1920s.

Gaylord did not even have a basketball team until five years before, and for several seasons they went without a coach. Then, in the fall of 1925, the players themselves recruited the local barber, B. F. Borchert, as their coach. Why they did so—what skills or experience or qualifications he had—is not known. Maybe he cut their hair well. Apparently, he could coach; Gaylord won seven consecutive upsets in the postseason. They were expected to lose to New Ulm as early as a District 20 semifinal. They won easily, 33–17. They were expected to lose to Sleepy Eye in the district final, but they won in a 35–11 rout. They were expected to lose

each of their regional games but won easily, 27–8 over heavily favored St. Peter and 25–12 over Tracy, to earn their way to the state tournament in Minneapolis. And, of course, they followed that up by winning three more upsets there.

Gaylord immediately captured the fancy of the fans (and the press) in a way that no team had ever done. They somehow impressed themselves on spectators as an underdog, a Cinderella, and thus created the type. They did it first by knocking off future powerhouse Moorhead, 18–14, as Bennie Lichttenegger scored 13 points. Next they defeated Austin, also a future power, 22–12 in the semis, as Lichttenegger again led the way with 16 points. They then met a Gilbert team that was as much of a Cinderella as Gaylord, having beaten Minneapolis Edison and Buffalo, tournament runner-up the previous year, in their first two games.

Maybe there was something about Gaylord's style of play, the way they carried themselves, or the color of their uniforms, or perhaps it was simply the fact that they were again expected to lose. Whatever it was, it made Gaylord the sentimental favorite, and when they won, it was as if every small town in Minnesota had won—with the exception, of course, of Gilbert. They were the most popular champion ever, and the state tournament was now more firmly imprinted on the map of Minnesota sports than ever before.

Oddly, if the game of basketball during this era was sometimes lacking in action, then that championship, with a final score of 13–9, was such a game. Yet nobody seemed to mind. After the final game, a hat literally was passed through the crowd at the Kenwood Armory to raise money to finance Gaylord's trip to the national high school tournament in Chicago, and $500 was raised in this way. Then, as quickly as they had emerged, Gaylord returned to the anonymity of the western Minnesota prairie, not qualifying for another tournament until 1969 and never again in the twentieth century winning a single tournament game.

From Gopher Prairie to the Windy City

Gaylord was one of seven Minnesota state champions authorized to participate in the national high school basketball tournament in Chicago from 1923 through 1929, though six other Minnesota teams also made the trip to the Windy City. Overall, the thirteen Minnesota teams won fourteen games and lost fourteen in Chicago. Only four of the thirteen earned more than one victory.

Duluth Central was the first in 1913, defeating Crawfordsville, Indiana, 34–16, to take third place against nationwide competition that was vastly stronger competition than Fosston faced in Northfield. Based on its stellar play in Chicago, Duluth probably

was the state's best team and its star, "Bunk" Harris, one of the best players that year. In 1920, Minneapolis Central also took third place as the only team ever to opt out of the Minnesota tourney in favor of the national. Among three victories was one over Ishpeming, Michigan, coached by future Chisholm, Minnesota, coach Harvey Roels. Their only loss was to Crawfordsville, 21–16. Martin Norton, state tournament MVP in 1921, earned All-America honors for his efforts in 1920. Duluth Cathedral lost to the eventual national champions from Lexington, Kentucky, 37–26 in the third round in 1922. Clarence Smith and Johnny Benda, who later

On March 29, 1941, at the Minneapolis Auditorium, an estimated 10,000 fans watched Buhl defeat Minneapolis Washburn and Red Wing knock off Bemidji in semifinal action at the Minnesota state high school basketball tournament. Attendance at the annual event skyrocketed in the decade spanning the late 1930s to the aftermath of World War II. By the 1950s, it had become almost impossible to get a ticket to what Minnesotans called the "big show."

coached St. John's College for
many years, were named All-
Americans.

It didn't hurt Gaylord's historical standing that they, too,
won two national tournament
games in 1926, a total that no
other Minnesota state champ
matched. In the first game,
Gaylord raced to a 14–7 halftime lead over Memphis, Tennessee, then held on to win,
25–24. Gaylord then clobbered
Atlanta Technical High, 23–7,
before losing to Fargo, North
Dakota, 25–20. Fargo's perennially powerful team went on to
the national final before losing
to Fitchburg, Massachusetts,
25–14.

In 1919, a national Catholic
tournament was launched, also

St. Paul Mechanic Arts won two state championships in a period of just six years. The 1925 squad (shown here) hammered Buffalo, 20–8, in the final. Then the 1930 team beat Moorhead, 23–13, preventing the Spuds from becoming the tournament's first three-peater.

in Chicago, though Minnesota teams participated beginning only in 1924. The highlight of Minnesota's participation was Minneapolis DeLaSalle's 1931 national
Catholic championship. DeLaSalle defeated Jasper
Academy from Indiana, 23–21, in the final to avenge a
2-point first-round loss to Jasper in the previous year.
Their star was American Indian center Ray Buffalo,
who later became a softball legend on the Minneapolis sandlots. Overall the record of Minnesota's Catholic
teams in Chicago was not good, however, with six wins
and eleven losses prior to DeLaSalle's championship
season and just four wins and twenty-one more losses
through 1940.

Spuds Turn Tables, Mash Opposition

The Moorhead Spuds put together the first back-to-
back state titles in 1928 and 1929, behind the leadership
of legendary coach Glen Hanna and guard Earl Moran.
Moran became the first player and one of only two to
earn all-state honors three times before the end of the
single class era in 1971. Moran and teammate Carroll
"Shorty" Malvey were the only boys through 1971 ever
to start in three finals.

The Spuds' tournament finalists in 1928, 1929, and

1930 were among a record eight consecutive Moorhead
teams to appear in the tournament between 1924 and
1931. Prior to 1928, however, the highlight had been
a Sportsmanship Trophy in 1924. Then in 1928, the
Spuds survived Virginia by 1, clobbered New Prague by
20, and came back from an 8–1 deficit to beat Minneapolis Edison, 29–16. Cliff Halmrast's 20 points were the
most in any championship round game between 1922
and 1944.

In 1929, Moorhead was said to be better than the
previous year because of more balanced scoring from
Pat Hilde, Malvey, and Moran. They edged Ely by 3
and Red Wing by 4 in overtime in the final. In between,
they dominated St. Cloud, 31–18, as Hilde scored 17. In
1930, the press again said that this was the Spuds' best
team ever, and why not? Three starters, two of them—
Moran and Malvey—all-staters, returned from the
1929 champion team. But all-state forward Hilde's season ended in January when he turned twenty, exceed-
ing the age limit. So the Trainers of St. Paul Mechanic
Arts were able to dominate Moorhead, 23–13, in the
final. In 1931, Concordia College won its first Minnesota Intercollegiate Athletic Conference (MIAC) title
as former Spuds Halmrast, Hilde, and Moran all made
the all-state college team. Malvey was also a member

of that team, and all four are now honored in the Concordia Athletic Hall of Fame.

The Iron Range Picks Up the Pace

Scoring gradually increased in the 1930s, and as it did, one of the fortunate legacies of the Midwestern Style became more and more apparent—that is, balanced scoring. Where older offenses had relied on a designated shooter, Doc Meanwell's offense got everybody involved. Before 1934, it had been rare when two players from the same team scored in double figures in the same game. Now there might be three. The high school tournament, for example, saw Edward Turk (16), Pete Burich (12), and Gordon Burich (10) of Chisholm do it in a semifinal win over Moorhead in 1934. In 1936, Johnny Dick, Mike Peinovich, and Velko Rajacich each scored 12 for Buhl in a thrilling first-round win over Minneapolis Edison. Then, in 1937, it was Edison's turn, with Joe Mernik (18), Donald "Swede" Carlson

(11), and Willie Warhol (11) doing the honors in a 62–23 semifinal rout of New Ulm.

It is no coincidence that teams from Minnesota's Mesabi Iron Range accounted for two of these three cases. Scoring was about the same in 1934 as it was in 1913. Then, between 1934 and 1956, team scoring records, on the average, doubled. More often than not, the new team scoring records were the handiwork of teams from the Range. Why?

As always, the most successful coaches tended to dictate the style of play for everybody. On the Range during the 1930s, that meant Harvey Roels and his Chisholm Bluestreaks, who played a fast-paced style that produced "a point a minute," including a state tournament record of more than 37 points per game in their championship season of 1934. Roels was followed by Herman Woock of Crosby-Ironton and Archie Skalbeck and then Art Stock at Virginia from the 1930s through about the time of World War II. In the

---

Minnesota Mysteries and Myths

Minnesota's First Two-Class State High School Tournament

In 1965, Art Tverra, star of Minneapolis South's 1927 state champions, was surprised to read in the *Minneapolis Tribune* that 1927 state Class B champion, Henning, had issued a challenge to South. What's more, reporter Merrill Swanson wrote, the Mill City team had declined it. Tverra responded by calling the *Tribune* to say, Oh yeah? Says who? "If they still want to play us," he added, "let's go."

Other readers were likely as surprised as Tverra (sometimes Tveraa or Tvera), because most fans were unaware that there had ever been a Class B state tournament. It was an invitational, Swanson reported, that was not sanctioned but also not banned by the Minnesota State High School League (MSHSL).

Like most latter-day recollections, this one was not quite accurate, though it is true that the tourney was neither sanctioned nor operated by the MSHSL. It was hosted and operated by Hamline University in an obvious attempt to replicate archrival Carleton's fabulously successful tournament. But at the time it was not referred to as Class B, nor was it ever an invitational. Technically, it was the "graded" or the "department" tournament—that is, participants represented "high school departments" in "graded schools,"

which technically were not considered to be high schools at all. In 1923, and 1924, any "high school department" that wanted could compete, and so twenty-six and then forty-four teams did. From 1925 through 1927, district and regional playoffs were initiated.

The highlight of these five tournaments was the 1927 performance of Hans Rortvedt, who was described as a "giant center." Rortvedt scored 22 points in one game and 37 overall, leading Henning to the title by an average margin of 32–18. In 1928, Rortvedt led Augsburg to the MIAC title game, where the Auggies lost to Gustavus Adolphus, and won first-team all-state honors as a freshman. Still later, he won recognition playing with the amateur Rock Spring Sparklers from Shakopee.

The other four tournaments were won by East Chain, Stewart, Chisago City, and Brewster.

Then, in 1928 and 1929, the MSHSL launched what it did call a Class B postseason competition at the district level. Each district had the option of crowning a Class B champion, which was then seeded into the Class A district playoffs. Only one Class B champion ever made it to a Class A district final—Columbia Heights, who lost to defending state runner-up Excelsior, 32–13, in 1928. Thereafter, for more than forty years, the smaller schools would agitate for the reinstatement of a tournament of their own.

Johnny Dick of Buhl played in the 1935 and 1936 state tournaments and then went on to play for the Minnesota Gophers. He was called "pound for pound, the best all-around player the tournament has ever seen." Of course, he weighed only 130 pounds.

1940s and 1950s, Mario Retica at Buhl and later Hibbing led the way, followed finally by Bob McDonald of Chisholm throughout the last quarter of the twentieth century.

All of them, to some extent, favored an up-tempo game. The pace of the game is often dictated by the defense, and the Range was always known for an aggressive, pressing defensive style that forced their opponents to run, too. Buhl's 1942 state champs, under Retica, combined a pressing defense with Meanwell's ball control offense.

The city fathers of Chisholm set out in 1923 to obtain the services of the best coach that money could buy. That coach turned out to be Harvey Roels, who had already won two state championships—at Appleton, Wisconsin, in 1919 and Ishpeming, Michigan, in 1920—and who would one day become one of the first ten basketball coaches enshrined in the Minnesota Basketball Coaches Association Hall of Fame. Success at the level Iron Rangers aspired to was some time in coming, though by the end of 1929 the Roelsmen, as the *Mesaba Miner* called them, had an excellent record of 81–29. They had had a 17–1 season in 1925–1926 and 15–3 records in 1924–1925 and 1928–1929 but no state tournament entry. Then, beginning in 1930, came a string of five consecutive entries, five straight twenty-win seasons, a total record of 103 wins and just nine losses, and finally, in 1934, a coveted state title.

Coming into the state tournament with excellent win-loss records and a strong Iron Range tradition, Chisholm was among the favorites in 1930 and 1932 and was rated as a clear favorite in 1931 and 1934. If a semifinal loss to two-time defending champion Moorhead in 1930 was disappointing, then the 15–14 upset defeat at the hands of Glencoe the following year was devastating. Chisholm's 1931 squad was its first "point-a-minute" team, and six-foot-two guard Joe Malkovich was regarded as the best player in the tournament. But the Bluestreaks squandered a 9–5 halftime lead and clung desperately to a 14–13 lead, and to the ball, with one minute remaining. Then disaster struck: Glencoe stole the ball, and guard LeRoy Karstens sank the game-winning field goal.

The 1932 team, led by colorful guard Onerato "Joe" Belluzzo, took runner-up honors, and the *Mesabi Miner* seemed well enough pleased with that accomplishment. In 1934, it would not be pleased with anything less than a title, despite the Bluestreaks' poorest record coming into the tournament in five years at 18–2. What's more, the 'Streaks were very fortunate to survive the region final with a 15–12 win over Gilbert, when Gilbert went 0 for 7 from the free throw line. Yet the Bluestreaks again scored at a point-a-minute clip—twice that, in fact, in a 69–4 rout of hapless Hill City in a district game. They had four starters back from the 1933 tournament, including excellent size in Gordon Burich and Edward Turk, both six foot three. Fans were pleased when the Roelsmen outclassed Cass Lake,

Minneapolis Edison's 1937 state champs were regarded as the greatest high school team before World War II. Left to right, front row: Stan Fudro, Joe Mernik, Teddy Pilacinski, and George Rapacz; back row: Bob Johnson, Willie Warhol, Don Carlson, and Wally Andrewski.

33–12, in the first round. They were delirious when they avenged their 1930 defeat to Moorhead by the outlandish score of 50–17. And they were beside themselves with joy when a St. Paul Mechanic Arts rally fell just short, 29–27, in the title game. Gophers coach Dave MacMillan reported in the *Minneapolis Tribune* that Gordon Burich's ability to control the tip-off was the deciding factor in the game.

Success had come in the nick of time. Four starters graduated from the championship team, and the Roelsmen would not return to the tournament until 1940, with another colorful, high-scoring guard named Orlando Bonicelli. After that, it would be 1960, with Belluzzo as coach, before the 'Streaks came back again. But it was the years from 1930 to 1934 that made Roels's reputation as a coach and launched Chisholm as the greatest dynasty on the Range and one of the greatest in tournament history.

Buhl or Edison?

Buhl, meanwhile, claimed consecutive state titles in 1941 and 1942, and most observers agreed that either

Minneapolis Edison's 1937 champs or Buhl's two-time winners was the best team of the era. When old-timers spoke of Buhl, however, they often referred to 1935 and 1936. The 1936 team was at the time regarded as the greatest Iron Range team ever, though their failure to win a state title suggests otherwise. In addition, scrappy forward Johnny Dick was regarded as one of the greatest players in tournament history. Otis Dypwick, later U of M sports information director, wrote, "Pound for pound, he is the best all-around player the tournament has ever seen."

Dypwick did not mean this as faint praise, but the fact is that Dick only weighed in at 120 pounds and was a mere five foot three in 1935. He was described as a long shot artist, and why not? How many open shots would he get closer to the hoop? He did sprout six inches between 1935 and 1936 but came back still weighing only 130 pounds.

As highly regarded as Buhl was, they were the victims of two huge upsets. In 1935, they were beaten by Glencoe, 22–14, in the first round, but that was nothing compared to 1936, when the field was regarded as the strongest ever, with Bemidji, Minneapolis Edison, and

The starting five for Buhl's 1941 state champions. Left to right: Bob Delich, Russell Willberg, John Klarich, Ed Nylund, and George "Pecky" Smilanich. The Bulldogs were coached by "Muxie" Anderson (not pictured). All but Lubotina and Coach Anderson returned to win a second title in 1942.

Buhl returning from the 1935 tournament. Bemidji and Edison brought all-state players back, but Buhl matched that with Dick and two other returning starters. All three teams were regarded as title threats. Bemidji was perhaps slightly favored, but observers noted that Buhl had defeated Coleraine three times while Coleraine had beaten Bemidji. After a first-round win over Edison, 41–32, in what was described as one of the greatest tourney games ever, Buhl became a heavy favorite to go all the way.

Instead, unsung Wadena knocked them off, 28–27, as Wadena center Schiller outscored Buhl center and star Peinovich, 9–0. And yet it was Peinovich, not Schiller, who made the all-state team, along with Dick. Buhl's loss was attributed in the media to exhaustion from playing in the toughest conference and the toughest region in the state. Buhl players are also said to have stayed up most of the night celebrating their win over Edison and to have completely underestimated Wadena. Buhl then swamped Red Wing, 35–16, for third place. As Dick left the floor late in the game, he received what was described as the longest and loudest ovation in tournament history.

Along with Dick, Edison stars Willie Warhol and Don "Swede" Carlson went on to play Golden Gophers basketball. Edison's other guard, Joe Mernik, also went on to an athletic career at the U of M and kicked the extra point that won the 1940 national championship for

the Gophers football team in a thrilling 7–6 win over Michigan. Center Norm Galloway of Bemidji's champions also started his college career at the U but transferred to Bemidji Teachers College.

Buhl returned to the tournament in 1941 and 1942, and they won the state's second back-to-back championships. In fact, after Minneapolis Edison's championship in 1937, Buhl's titles were the fourth and fifth consecutive titles for small towns—their best run ever during the single-class era.

Edison had finished up with fifteen wins and one loss, won three tournament games by an average score of 46–25, and placed three players—guards Mernik and Warhol and center Walt Andrewski—on the five-man all-tournament squad. In 1938, Thief River Falls won its second title of the decade and finished with the best record, 27–0, in state history at that time. Center Loren Stadum became the only player in the twentieth century to win all-tournament honors without starting in a single game.

In both 1939 and 1940, Minneapolis Marshall, with center Donald "Red" Mattson, was the pretournament favorite. But in 1939 Mountain Lake, three times a runner-up, finally won a state title, 37–31 over Marshall, behind the play of brothers Hank and Ruben Epp. Marshall played Breckenridge in the semifinals both years, winning easily in 1939 before losing a shocker, 32–30, in 1940. Breckenridge went on to defeat perennial power Red Wing in the final, 43–40. Red Wing returned to its seventh title game in 1941, losing to Buhl, 31–29.

In 1942, Buhl, master of the close call, beat Chisholm, 43–41, in overtime in the opening round of the District 28 playoffs on their way to the state tournament. They then held on to edge Marshall High School (the one from the city of Marshall, not the Minneapolis version), 30–29, for their second straight title and a new state record at 28–0. Walter Chapman, Minneapolis Marshall coach, christened Buhl as Minnesota's best high school team ever, better even than Edison's 1937 powerhouse. Chapman made his comment before the title game, however, and he based his choice on the superior pivot play of Buhl center Ed Nylund. But the next evening, Marshall held Nylund to just 1 point.

Minnesota State High School Champions, 1925–1942

Year	Championship Game Score	W–L	Authors' Choice: Postseason MVPs
1925	St. Paul Mechanic Arts 20 Buffalo 8	17–1–1	John Matyas, New Prague, F
	Chisago City 17 Ceylon 11[a]		
	St. Thomas 27 St. Cloud Cathedral 10[b]		
1926	Gaylord 13 Gilbert 9	20–3–1	Ben Lichttenegger, Gaylord, F
	Brewster 24 Hitterdal 22[a]		
	St. Thomas 29 Bird Island St. Mary's 12[b]		
1927	Mpls. South 32 Excelsior 13	12–5	Hans Rortvedt, Henning, C
	Henning 28 Chisago City 18[a]		
	DeLaSalle 28 Superior Cathedral 12[b]		
1928	Moorhead 29 Mpls. Edison 16	19–3	Cliff Halmrast, Moorhead, F
	St. Cloud Cathedral 32 DeLaSalle 25[b]		
1929	Moorhead 20 Red Wing 16 (OT)	24–3	Earl Moran, Moorhead, G
	St. C. Cathedral 37 Austin St. Augustine 16[b]		
1930	St. Paul Mechanic Arts 23 Moorhead 13	22–2	James Delmont, St. Paul Mechanic Arts, F
	St. John's 23 Cretin 18[b]		
1931	Glencoe 22 Buffalo 14	16–3	Ray Buffalo, DeLaSalle, C
	DeLaSalle 23 Jasper Academy (Indiana) 21[c]	24–3	
1932	Thief River Falls 21 Chisholm 15	23–0	John Chommie, Thief River Falls, G
1933	Red Wing 16 Mpls. North 13	22–3	Dick Seebach, Red Wing, G
1934	Chisholm 29 St. Paul Mechanic Arts 27	21–2	Gordon Burich, Chisholm, F
1935	Austin 26 Glencoe 24 (OT)	16–6	Art Hanson, Austin, F
1936	Bemidji 26 Wadena 20	21–4	Norman Galloway, Bemidji, C
1937	Mpls. Edison 37 Virginia 24	15–1	Willie Warhol, Mpls. Edison, G
1938	Thief River Falls 31 Mpls. North 29	27–0	Roy Lee, Thief River Falls, G
1939	Mountain Lake 37 Mpls. Marshall 31	23–1	Don "Red" Mattson, Mpls. Marshall, F
1940	Breckenridge 43 Red Wing 40	28–3	Melvin Ruud, Breckenridge, F
1941	Buhl 31 Red Wing 29	26–3	Ed Nylund, Buhl, C
	Duluth Cathedral 26 Cretin 21[b]		
1942	Buhl 30 Marshall 29	28–0	John Klarich, Buhl, F
	Cretin 38 Duluth Cathedral 34[b]		

Note: From 1923 to 1930, the Catholic tournament was a northwestern tournament that included teams from western Wisconsin and the eastern Dakotas, though Minnesota schools won every championship.
[a] Tournament for the high school departments in graded schools.
[b] Catholic tournament.
[c] Catholic national tournament.

10   *Get the Ball, Pass the Ball, and Put It in the Basket*

HAROLD TAYLOR HAD COACHED his Aurora High School team to the Minnesota state title in 1923, and on the strength of that performance he had become assistant to Minnesota Gophers coach Louis J. Cooke for the 1923–1924 season. In the fall of 1924, with Cooke's sudden retirement, Taylor became the second head coach in Gopher history. The Taylor years were eventful ones, as the team moved from the University Armory to the Kenwood Armory in downtown Minneapolis in midseason in 1925. Kenwood's capacity of 6,500, compared to the old Armory's 2,000, enabled game attendance to soar. On the court, the Gophers featured the efforts of forward Ray "Black" Rasey, called by one observer the best player the Gophers had ever had. In 1925, Rasey set a conference record by scoring 20 points in a 36–16 trouncing of the Purdue Boilermakers.

But the Gophers struggled under Taylor, winning fewer than 40 percent of their games overall and just one of every three Big Ten conference games. In 1927, Taylor was dismissed, and a proper search for a new coach was conducted. On March 9, the *Minneapolis Tribune* advanced an all-star cast of candidates, including Everett Dean of Indiana (formerly of Carleton); Minnesota native and Notre Dame coach George Keogan; Purdue's Piggy Lambert, inventor of the fast break; Doc Meanwell of Wisconsin, the Midwest's most successful and influential coach; former Gophers All-American Francis "Dobie" Stadsvold, then coaching at West Virginia; and several others. All were reported, somewhat implausibly, to be anxious to leave their current employer to come to Minneapolis. But the Gopher job went instead to dark horse Dave MacMillan. Over a period of seven seasons, MacMillan had led the University of Idaho to a 93–25 record, including a 19–1 record in 1921–1922. His .727 winning percentage remains the highest ever for an Idaho coach with more than two years on the job.

The Canny Scot

Raised in New York City, MacMillan was of Scotch-Irish descent and quickly became known as the "Canny Scot." He is often said to have been a member of the New York Celtics, forerunner to the Original Celtics, who as a team were inducted as charter members of the Basketball Hall of Fame in 1959. Celtics' historian Murry Nelson reports, however, that MacMillan's name does not appear on the rosters of any of the Celtics teams, though he acknowledged, "That doesn't mean that he might not have played a game or two."

In any event, MacMillan based his style of play on that of the Celtics. Otis Dypwick, long-time Gophers sports information director, later wrote that MacMillan "introduced the deft, snappy passing, and sound blocking plays featured by the Celts. This was an innovation at Minnesota, and caused side-line observers to raise their eyes dubiously. 'Mac' was unperturbed by the initial reaction and the difficulty experienced in imparting this intricate offense to unseasoned material." MacMillan emphasized short, hard passes from all angles, with players moving rapidly under the basket for set shots. "Get the ball, pass the ball, and put it in the basket" was his dictum. "It is effective basketball and when the plays are worked to precision, it is winning basketball," he wrote.

Midway through MacMillan's first season on the job, the Gophers were on the move again, abandoning the Kenwood Armory for an on-campus home, the new University of Minnesota Field House. With a capacity of 9,500, it was more than large enough to accommodate the still-growing number of Minnesota fans. The Gophers held their first practice in the Field House on January 31, 1928. The *Minneapolis Tribune* reported, "The players experienced a little difficulty in adjusting themselves to the new playing court, because of the

The Gophers' new U of M Field House, shown here—inside and out—during the late stages of construction in 1927, had an official capacity of 9,500. The facility, later renamed Williams Arena, has stood at the corner of University Avenue and Oak Street since the 1920s.

'give' on the floor, which is made up of 126 sections and elevated 16 inches above ground level on a cinder base. Viewed from a vantage point in the lofty second balcony, the playing court presents the appearance of a rectangular centerpiece perched on the black dirt below. It occupies less than one-third of the ground space within this vast enclosure."

Two days later, the Gophers held a practice game against the team from nearby Augsburg College, and on February 4, 1928, the first official game was played in the new Field House. Three years earlier, the Kenwood had been christened with a 32–20 loss to Ohio State. Now, Ohio State would again provide the opposition, and a crowd of more than 11,000—25 percent above the official capacity—turned out for the historic occasion. Once more, the Gophers lost, this time in overtime by a score of 42–40. Dr. James A. Naismith was on hand for the game and took part in a dedication ceremony.

The Field House was eventually named Williams Arena in honor of Dr. Henry L. Williams, who served simultaneously as a football coach and a physician at the University of Minnesota and was one of the country's leading football strategists in the early part of the twentieth century. The arena changed throughout the decades and at times was threatened with extinction, but, affectionately known as "The Barn," it has continued as the home for Gopher basketball and other sports into the twenty-first century. One of its distinctive features has remained the elevated court, which has often been disconcerting to opposing players not accustomed to the arena floor.

Although the Gophers doubled their conference win total—from one to two—in MacMillan's first season, the team nevertheless finished in a last-place tie for the second year in a row. The Gophers improved and twice tied for second place in the Western Conference in 1931 and 1932 with a combined record of 28–7 (17–7 in the Big Ten). Upon the occasion of his second retirement in 1948, MacMillan selected his 1931 forwards, Earl Loose and Harold Schoening—the latter earning all-conference honors—as his best forward tandem ever. For his top guard tandem, he chose Mike Cielusak and Virgil Licht from the 1931 and 1932 teams. With the graduation of all four of Mac's favorite players, the team dropped back to the second division over the next four years. Then, in 1936 the Gophers were chosen to participate in a tournament for the right to represent the United States in the Olympic Games, despite a 5–15 regular season record. The Gophers defeated Carroll College and Drake in the tournament, before dropping two games to DePaul, 36–30 and 33–27.

That Championship Season

After the dismal 1935–1936 season, it was perhaps just as well that the Gophers returned few veteran players. Instead, for the 1936–1937 season, the team's hopes rested on John Kundla, a sophomore forward from Minneapolis Central High School. Kundla missed the

Minneapolis Edison grad Marty Rolek starred for the Gophers' 1937 conference champs and then earned All-America honors in 1938.

first month of the season with a foot injury, however, so another, much smaller sophomore, Gordie Addington, ably filled one of the forward positions. Hailing from a small Minnesota community, Addington—described by *St. Paul Pioneer Press* reporter George Christmas as the "migrating midget from Wahkon"—had not played freshman basketball and little was expected of him. Yet he earned a spot in the starting lineup and broke out with 13 points in a 49–16 nonconference win over Iowa State on January 2. That game was the first of the year for Kundla, who had 9 points. He doubled that total two nights later in a 34–25 upset of DePaul, despite having to leave late in the game after aggravating his bad foot.

Also moving into a key role was yet another sophomore, guard Marty Rolek, who had been a star at

The Gophers had a spirited rivalry with Carleton College throughout the 1920s and 1930s, the Carls defeating Minnesota in 1933 and 1935. The Gophers' eventual conference champs routed Carleton in December 1936, however, by a score of 41–11. Here, Carleton's Jackson (33) grabs a rebound as the Gophers' Bob Manly (23), Marty Rolek (18), and Dick Seebach (6) look on.

Minneapolis Edison High School. Rounding out the starting lineup as the Gophers prepared for their first conference game were center Bob Manly and guard Dick Seebach. The team was comprised mainly of Minnesota talent, though Gordie Spear and Guy DeLambert, who saw little action during the conference season, were from Montana. George "Butch" Nash, like Rolek, was from Edison, Seebach and Art Lillyblad from Red Wing, Paul Maki from Aurora, Grant "Spike" Johnson from Two Harbors, and Manly from Cretin High School in St. Paul.

The 1936–1937 season was the last in which the center jump was employed to establish possession after each basket. Though just six foot three, Manly gave the Gophers a distinct advantage in gaining possession of the ball in those all-important jump balls. When the ball was in play, however, Manly stayed outside with the guards, while Kundla and Addington hovered near the basket in the Gophers' "three-out and two-in" style of offense. "Usually, we didn't have a pivot man," Kundla recalled.

Like Addington, Rolek only moved into the starting lineup because of illness, as Seebach missed a couple of games with a bad cold. Seebach also had academic issues that forced him to sit out the Gophers' first Big Ten game, a 30–23 win over the Chicago Maroons on January 12. But with Rolek's emergence, it was Lillyblad—who had been Seebach's running mate both for Red Wing's 1933 state high school champs and for the 1936 Gophers—who took a seat on the bench. Rolek quickly established his value to the team. "The small blond Gopher guard was all over the floor hounding the ball, and

The 1936–1937 Gophers tied with Illinois for the Big Ten title—one of only two Gopher conference titles untainted by scandal since their 1919 national championship. Front row, left to right: Gordie Addington, John Kundla, Marty Rolek, Bob Manly, and Art Lillyblad; middle row: Dave MacMillan (coach), Ed Jones, Guy DeLambert, Gordon Spear, Grant "Spike" Johnson, Paul Maki, and Ellsworth Towle (manager); back row: George "Butch" Nash, Earl Halvorson, Ray Barger, and Al Sundberg (assistant coach); not shown: Dick Seebach.

The Big Game

Minnesota Gophers 34, Northwestern 33
March 1, 1937

The key game for the Gophers as they battled for the Big Ten championship in 1937 came in their next-to-last conference game against the Northwestern Wildcats. The Gophers had beaten Wisconsin at home two nights before, although they lost high-scoring John Kundla to an ankle injury late in the first half. Kundla was back against the Wildcats, and the Gophers needed him as Northwestern took control early in the game. Before a season-high crowd of more than 13,000 at the Field House, Minnesota held the lead only once during the first half and trailed 14–12 at intermission.

Kundla then gave Minnesota a 15–14 lead with a field goal and a free throw at the beginning of the second half. Bob Voigts put the Wildcats back on top with a basket, but Kundla came back again with a short-range field goal to give Minnesota the lead at 17–16. The Wildcats' Jean Smith scored the next 6 points with a basket and 4 free throws, however, and Northwestern had opened up a 5-point lead, its largest of the game.

Dick Seebach, playing his final home game for the Gophers, was doing an outstanding job guarding Mike McMichael, holding the Northwestern ace to only 1 field goal during regulation play. But the larger Wildcats, with their physical style, were keeping the Gophers from scoring as well. With slightly more than five minutes to play, Northwestern led the Gophers by a score of 30–25. Seebach, with a field goal, and Kundla, with a free throw, cut the lead to 2 points. Over the next two minutes, however, both Marty Rolek and Seebach were knocked out of the game as a result of Northwestern's rugged style of play. It was left to Gordie Addington to twist through a group of defenders and put up a shot that rolled in and tied the game with under ten seconds left in regulation play.

In overtime, Minnesota took the lead as Manly passed the ball to Paul Maki, who scored. Voigts made a free throw for Northwestern, but Kundla restored the Gophers' 2-point lead with a free throw of his own. With forty-five seconds left in overtime, McMichael unleashed a set shot from near midcourt that found its mark. The game was again tied. As the clock wound down, Manly drove toward the basket. He was knocked to the floor before he could shoot, earning him one free throw with five seconds left. Manly calmly made his shot, and the Gophers hung on for a 34–33 win. The win left the Gophers needing only a victory over the winless Chicago Maroons in their final conference game to clinch at least a share of the Big Ten title, their only such title over fifty-two seasons from 1920 to 1971.

setting up shots for his mates and leading the defense," reported the *Minneapolis Tribune* the next day.

The following Saturday at Ohio State, the Gophers blew a 21–15 lead in losing 23–22, despite strong defensive play by Rolek, who held the Buckeyes' All-America forward Jimmy Hull to 4 points. Rolek was part of the evolution of the guard position that had begun with Purdue great John Wooden a few years before. Guards had previously been defensive specialists, but now they were becoming an integral part of the offense. Kundla later described Rolek as a prototype for what eventually became known as the point guard position.

The Gophers won their next five games, including a 45–41 victory at home against Purdue in which Kundla scored 20 points. MacMillan's reputation was as a defensively oriented coach, but, Kundla said, he also liked to employ the fast break on offense. The Boilermakers were strictly a fast-breaking team, but the Gophers ran with them on this occasion. With a February 15 win at Iowa, the Gophers upped their conference record to 6–1, moving ahead of Illinois. Illinois was led by sophomore sensation Lou Boudreau, who went on to a Hall of Fame career as a player-manager for major league baseball's Cleveland Indians, but the Gophers did not play the Illini in 1936–1937. On February 20, the Gophers battled back from a 10-point halftime deficit at Purdue. Despite the late long-range shooting of Rolek, the Gophers still came up short, losing 34–33, their second 1-point loss in conference play.

Returning home to increasingly larger crowds, the Gophers also returned to their winning ways to keep pace with Illinois at the top of the Big Ten standings. Northwestern gave Minnesota a battle in the big game, but the Gophers emerged with a 1-point overtime victory. A win in the conference-season finale against Chicago would assure the Gophers at least a tie for the Big Ten title. The Maroons, 0–11 in the Big Ten, were on the verge of their second consecutive winless conference season. Yet Chicago led the Gophers by a point at halftime. Minnesota came out quickly in the second half, scoring 11 unanswered points in the first three and a half minutes on its way to a 33–23 win. Chicago's twenty-sixth Big Ten loss in a row was, for the Gophers, the victory that gave them a share of their first conference title in eighteen seasons—and their only title in the fifty-two seasons from 1920 to 1971. Illinois won at Northwestern that day to finish in a first-place tie with the Gophers with a 10–2 record.

Kundla was the team's leading scorer with 8.9 points per game in the Big Ten and a 9.1 average overall. The Gophers held their conference opponents to barely 27 points per game during the season, the lowest total in the Big Ten.

The Minneapolis City Conference All-Stars

The Gophers had another strong season in 1937–1938, starting and finishing well but losing their first three conference games. Over Christmas, they took their first eastern road trip since 1905 (other than a trip to Pittsburgh in 1933). MacMillan reveled in his old stomping grounds of New York and Madison Square Garden, and a smashing 56–41 win over highly regarded Long Island University added to his enjoyment. A 36–31 defeat of New York University (NYU) followed. After a 1–4 stretch (that included a nonconference loss to Notre Dame along with their first three conference games), Minnesota won its last nine games in the Big Ten and finished second by one game to Purdue. Rolek had another outstanding year and was named to the All-America team.

In those days, the conference schedule consisted of home-and-home series with six opponents but no games against the other three. For two straight years, Minnesota did not play its primary competitor for the Big Ten title. Whether matchups with Illinois in 1937 and Purdue in 1938 might have resulted in the Gophers winning more than just the one cochampionship, we will never know. On the other hand, in addition to Illinois, the 1937 conference champs did not play third-place Michigan, and the Premo Poll ranked Michigan and Illinois fourth and seventh in the nation, respectively, and the Gophers not at all. The 1938 team fared better in the rankings, checking in at number eight. Yet the 16–4 Gophers, with MacMillan's ball control offense, finished ninth in the conference on offense, scoring just 4 more points than last-place Chicago. The secret of their success came in leading the Big Ten in defense for the second straight year.

The following season, Minnesota won its first ten games, including three in the Big Ten, to extend its overall winning streak to nineteen. However, the Gophers lost five of their final nine conference games and

Gophers Annual Record, 1924–1942

Year	Overall Record	Big Ten Record
Coach Harold Taylor		
1924–1925	9–7	6–6 (6th)
1925–1926	7–10ª	5–7 (7th)
1926–1927	3–13	1–11 (9th)
Taylor Totals	19–30	12–24
	.388	.333
Coach Dave MacMillan		
1927–1928	4–12	2–10 (9th)
1928–1929	4–13	1–11 (10th)
1929–1930	8–9	3–9 (7th)
1930–1931	13–4	8–4 (2nd)
1931–1932	15–3	9–3 (2nd)
1932–1933	5–15	1–11 (9th)
1933–1934	9–11	5–7 (7th)
1934–1935	11–9	5–7 (7th)
1935–1936	7–17	3–9 (9th)
1936–1937	14–6	10–2 (1st)
1937–1938	16–4	9–3 (2nd)
1938–1939	14–6	7–5 (4th)
1939–1940	13–8ª	5–7 (7th)
1940–1941	11–9	7–5 (3rd)
1941–1942	15–7ª	9–6 (5th)
MacMillan Totals	159–133	84–99
1927–1942	.545	.459
Gopher Totals	179–163	96–123
1925–1942	.525	.438

ª Five different sources were consulted for the Gophers' early win-loss records, and there are discrepancies in these seasons. All of the records shown here are based on lists of actual opponents and game scores.

finished in fourth place in 1938–1939. The Gophers remained competitive in the early 1940s as they came to resemble nothing so much as the Minneapolis City Conference All-Stars. A 1942 news article noted that backup center "Red" Mattson, a four-year starter at Minneapolis Marshall High School, had played against eight of his ten teammates in high school.

MacMillan's teams won thirty games while losing twenty—and going 19–17 in the Big Ten—from 1939–1940 through 1942. But each year, the fans and the coach had expected more, and the highlights from those years were mostly lowlights. The Gophers gave up a Big Ten–record 34 points to Illinois center Bill Hapac in 1940, then lost in Madison Square Garden for the first time 54–51 to NYU in 1941. MacMillan resigned as Gophers coach, for the first time, after the 1941–1942 season. Just as Doc Cooke's retirement in 1924 had signaled the end of basketball's pioneering era, so too MacMillan's retirement after fifteen years as Gophers coach signified the end of the coaches' era. In the future, the focus of the game would more and more be on the fellows in the short pants out there on the court.

11 *The Heyday of Senior Men's Play*

THE ASCENSIONS WERE Minnesota's dominant senior men's team from their founding in 1907 right through the 1930s. In fact, it was the Ascension Catholic Church in north Minneapolis that founded the state amateur basketball tournament in 1927, and the tournament was held at the Ascension gym into the 1940s. But senior men's ball gradually became ultracompetitive and even the mighty Ascensions took their lumps from time to time. The Ascensions did not even win their first state title on their own home court until 1930. Their archrival at the time was the team from Holy Cross Church, which won the first state title in 1927 and finished as runners-up in 1929 and 1932. Holy Cross also won the city league title against most of the same opponents in 1931, 1932, and 1935 and the Catholic title in 1933.

Looming over all of the early competition was a group of players from Minneapolis Edison High School, some from the 1928 state runners-up, others from earlier editions of the Tommies. The star of Holy Cross's 1927 champions and 1929 runners-up was guard Mike Cielusak, whose career as a Minnesota Gopher still lay in his future. But in 1929, the entire 1928 Edison team, playing under the name of Minneapolis clothier Jesse M. Stasch and coached by Ray Parkins, defeated Cielusak's team in the final, 27–25.

Another early power was an unlikely collection of talent representing the small central Minnesota town of Foley. The team consisted of Harold Bauerly, who had played for St. Thomas College and previously for an Oregon state high school champion, and four former members of an Iowa state high school championship team from the town of Merrill, all of whom now lived in Foley. They lost to Holy Cross, 31–28, in the first tournament in 1927, then clobbered the Citizen's Club of Minneapolis, 40–15, in 1928. Citizen's was led by Art Tverra, star of Minneapolis South's 1927 state

champs. It would be a quarter century before another Greater Minnesota club would win the state amateur title.

By 1930, the Ascensions had recruited guard Dallas Ward away from Holy Cross and clobbered Skelly Oils of Owatonna, 52–21, in the final. By now the so-called Ascension Tournament was affiliated with the Amateur Athletic Union (AAU), and the Ascensions were the first Minnesota champion to participate in the national AAU tournament. They beat the Davis Hunt Club of Kansas City, 31–24, before losing in the second round, 15–10, to the Indianapolis Turners. Ward scored 32 points in these last three games, while forward Chuck Wagner led the way with 46.

The Ascensions repeated as state AAU champions again in 1931 and 1933. In 1933, they had the misfortune to draw the three-time defending champion, the Oh Henrys from Wichita, in the national tournament and quickly bowed out, 47–21. They made it back to the state championship game in 1936 but lost to the Rock Spring Sparklers from Shakopee, 29–24. In 1937, led by former Minneapolis North star Don Griffin, the Ascensions defeated Holy Cross, 38–24, for its third state title of the decade. One week later, however, the Sparklers clobbered the Ascensions, 58–31, to win the city league title. In 1938, the Sparklers took their second state title, while All Saints won the city park board league title and then shocked the Ascensions, 47–27, in the first round of the AAU.

The Ascensions were back on top in 1940, led now by former Gophers John Kundla, Gordon Spear, and Butch Nash. They trounced Holy Cross, 41–23, in the final as Kundla scored 15 points. For the first time in seven years, the Ascensions decided to play in the national AAU tournament again. For the nationals they beefed up their roster with more former Gophers: Gordie Addington, Marty Rolek, and Guy de Lambert.

Nevertheless, they lost to Kansas City Commerce College, 49–38.

They repeated as state AAU champs in 1941, beating the Sparklers, 41–25, as Kundla scored 12 points. This time they added former Gopher Willie Warhol to the roster and played an exhibition to raise funding for another trip to the nationals. The opponent was the so-called All-Stars, consisting of the very few former Gophers who were not already members of the Ascensions. The Ascensions won, 50–44, but apparently failed to draw the necessary crowd or funds, as the trip to the nationals was cancelled.

Rock Spring Sparklers Provide Some Fizz

The Sparklers had first achieved notoriety in 1934, losing to Dominion Electric (the Dominions) in the state AAU final, 27–20. Playing for the Dominions between his Edison High School and U of M careers was future Gophers All-American Marty Rolek. The star for the Sparklers was Hans Rortvedt of Henning's state Class B champions of 1927 and Augsburg College. In 1935, Rortvedt was joined on the Sparklers by Ray Buffalo, All-America center on DeLaSalle's 1931 national Catholic champions. The following year Rortvedt and Buffalo were gone, however, replaced by Gordon Ditz and Wally Zimmerman, formerly of Hamline's perennial MIAC champions. Both editions of the Sparklers won the state title; the latter was the group that defeated the Ascensions, 29–24.

The Sparklers won their third state title in 1938, beating the Coolerators from Duluth, led by former Duluth Teachers College star Lou Barle, 36–24, in the final. In 1939, the Sparklers were upset in the quarterfinals; the Gambles of Thorpe, Wisconsin, beat Old Dutch of Minneapolis, 55–41, for the title. Meanwhile, the Young Americans (from Young America, Minnesota) won the park title, beating Old Dutch, 38–33. Minnesota teams had participated in the national tournament only sporadically, but with Thorpe claiming the right to do so, the Minnesota-based teams objected. Thorpe was judged ineligible to represent Minnesota at the national tournament, so the Young Americans went. They defeated Denver Furniture, 39–36, in the first round, then lost to the Hollywood Metros, 49–25.

The Ascensions decided not to field a team after Pearl Harbor, so in 1942 the Ascensions all-star roster did what they had to do. They accepted the offer of the Rock Spring Bottling Company to don the Sparklers' uniforms. There was no state or national AAU tournament that year, but the Sparklers went unbeaten in city league play. Then they did the same in 1943, with a regular roster of former Gophers: Warren Ajax, Kenny Exel, Kleggie Hermsen, Kundla, Don Smith, and Warhol, all also Minneapolis high school products.

Then they beefed up their roster even more—with additional former college stars Barle, Tor Faxvog of St. Thomas, and Tony Jaros from the U—and entered themselves in the World Professional Basketball Championship in Chicago. The Sparklers beat the Chicago Studebakers, 45–44, in the first round as Jaros scored 15 points, Warhol 10, and Kundla 8. In the second round they drew the Washington, D.C., Bears, an all-black barnstorming team led by six-foot-four center Dolly King, who was among the earliest black players in major college basketball. He led Long Island University to the second National Invitation Tournament (NIT) title in 1939 and to a thirty-four-game winning streak over the 1938–1939 and 1939–1940 seasons. Later he was the first black person to play in the National Basketball League in 1946–1947. In 1943, he led the Bears to a 42–21 trouncing of the Sparklers, despite 11 points by Exel, and then to the World Professional Championship.

Nevertheless, these Sparklers—Jaros, Kundla, Warhol, Exel, and Smith, with Faxvog and future pros Hermsen, Ajax, and Barle coming off the bench—were probably the greatest assemblage of basketball talent ever to represent Minnesota until the advent of the Minneapolis Lakers and George Mikan some four years later.

Another grand tradition was the All-Nations Basketball Tournament. The same young men who played in the Minneapolis city league and the Minnesota AAU tournament formed ad hoc teams based on their national origins. The Germans, always a powerhouse, won the first All-Nations title in 1929 with a lineup that featured former Carleton star Joe Hutton and former Red Wing High and Hamline stars Chuck Hartupee and Butsie Maetzold. Leading their final opponents, the Swedes, were former Gopher Herb Wolden and Ruben Johnson, formerly all-city at Minneapolis South. Gophers coach Dave MacMillan played for the Scots, of course. A decade later, Don "Swede" Carlson, then between his Minneapolis Edison and Minnesota

Gophers careers, led the Swedes over the Poles, 41–31, in the final, scoring 14 points. The following year the Scots upset the favored Germans in the quarterfinals, as MacMillan failed to score but "gave an illustrated lecture on the fine points of basketball. . . . [The] coach's passing [was] superb," according to a report in the *Minneapolis Tribune.*

The Postwar Era

But after World War II, the prominence of the names involved in senior men's ball seemed to decline—with the exception of 1952. The AAU now was organized in Twin Cities and Greater Minnesota brackets. In a Twin Cities bracket semi, the Jerseys, featuring Jaros and Hermsen, defeated Hamline, with Oscar Haddorf, Dave Hegna, and Paul Smaagaard from its 1952 squad, 74–70. In the other bracket semi, Ives clobbered Pillsbury House, 72–44, despite Bud Grant's 20 points for the Pills. The Jerseys then won the bracket final, 78–60. The Greater Minnesota bracket final featured former St. Thomas College stars on both sides. Chaska, with Doug Shonka (and also Kerwin Engelhart of Hamline's 1951 national champions), defeated Faribault and Fax-

vog, 72–56. In the state final, Chaska—its stars being ten years younger than its opponents'—surprised the Jerseys, 64–54.

Two weeks earlier, the All-Nations semis had provided a similar collection of names. The Germans, featuring Laurie Balzer, formerly of Macalester; Gene Blau, formerly of St. Thomas; and Hermsen beat the Scotch, made up entirely of former Hamline players, 60–47. Meanwhile, the Poles and Jaros beat the Norse and Gophers center Maynard Johnson, 62–60. In the final Hermsen, with ten NBA games still in his future, outscored his more famous high school rival and Gophers teammate Jaros, 21–19, and the Germans defeated the Poles, 76–70.

But the heyday of senior men's play was over, as young men scattered more and more widely in search of economic opportunity—whether on or off the basketball court—and the media increasingly turned its attention to national and international events.

The Rock Spring Sparklers, sponsored by the Rock Spring Bottling Company, Shakopee, won state senior men's titles in 1935, 1936, and 1938. The 1943 Sparklers, consisting mostly of Minneapolis high school and U of M grads, played in the World Professional Basketball Tournament. The three Sparklers pictured are from ca. 1930.

The First Golden Age of Minnesota Basketball, 1942–1960

The end of World War II launched a dramatically new and different era in American life. An economic boom gave millions of Americans, many for the first time, the ability to provide for their basic needs and those of their families—and even for a few luxuries. One luxury was the opportunity to take up new leisure-time activities. So Americans swarmed over beaches, highways, ballparks, and basketball arenas. Whatever attendance gains the state high school tournament had enjoyed during the previous decade, for example, were dwarfed by a 25 percent increase in 1946 alone and almost 50 percent from 1946 to 1948. Is it coincidence or was it somehow inevitable that basketball matured or modernized at precisely this moment? That, suddenly, the game had more to commend itself to spectators as well as players—running, dribbling, passing, the low post game, the jump shot, the fast break—than ever before? Whatever the causes, the effect was clear. This was the golden age of basketball in Minnesota.

Yet the old "control" style of basketball refused to die. Ozzie Cowles at the University of Minnesota and Joe Hutton at Hamline University had learned it as teammates at Carleton College in the 1920s, and both continued to employ it with great success right into the 1950s. Even so, the modernists would not be denied. New scoring records were being set, it seemed, annually and at every level. And the greatest exemplars of modernism—heck, the greatest basketball team that had ever played the game—called Minneapolis home. Twice a week at the old Minneapolis Auditorium, Minnesotans could see all of the elements of the modern game—George Mikan working in the low post, Whitey Skoog shooting the jump shot, and Slater Martin leading the fast break—meshed into one devastating attack. Soon there would even be high school teams that could do it all.

Jim McIntyre was the first great big man in Minnesota basketball, leading Minneapolis Patrick Henry to two state titles.

12

The Low Post, the Fast Break, and the Jump Shot

For most Minnesotans, the first opportunity to see the modern game of basketball came at about 9 P.M. on March 24, 1944. It was then that big Jim McIntyre, all six feet seven and three-quarters inches of him, and his Minneapolis Patrick Henry teammates and coach Frank Cleve stepped on to the court at the St. Paul Auditorium for the school's first-ever appearance in the Minnesota state high school basketball tournament.

How They Played the Modern Game

What was new or modern was, at least in part, obvious at a glance. It was McIntyre's height. He was more than two inches taller than the tallest boy to previously play in the tournament—that being six-foot-five-and-a-half Lloyd Aanstad of Thief River Falls' 1932 champions. But there was more. As soon as the game began, fans saw Cleve's offense doing something that was quite unprecedented. They pounded the ball down to the big guy in the low post over and over again, and as often as not, it was McIntyre who would shoot the ball. Thus, there was something old about it as well, borrowed from Cleve's playing days as an all-state center at Minneapolis South and at St. Olaf College in the early 1920s—the concept of a designated shooter who took most of his team's shots. But now the designated shooter was not necessarily the best all-around athlete on the floor, just the tallest.

No wonder, then, that the old-timers scoffed at this ungainly young man and Cleve's new-fangled offense. Yet the results spoke for themselves. A year and a day after that first tournament appearance, McIntyre and his teammates became the third team to win two con-

So proficient was Myer "Whitey" Skoog as a jump shooter that some have asserted that he invented it. He did not but sank many of them for Brainerd High School, the Minnesota Gophers, and the Minneapolis Lakers.

secutive state championships, having steamrolled six straight tournament opponents by an average of 20 points apiece. McIntyre was the Babe Ruth of Minnesota high school basketball, demolishing the Minneapolis City Conference and state tournament record books for individual scoring. He took the tournament scoring record from less than 20 points per game to 28.7 and then 33.3 points per game. He increased the record for most points in a single game from 27 to 29 in his very first game, then to 36, and finally to the 43 points he scored against Ely in the final game of his high school career, the 1945 state title game. And at a time when fans were told that 20 percent was a good field goal percentage, McIntyre converted nearly half of his attempts.

From there McIntyre went on to the U, where he set school season scoring records and earned first team All–Big Ten honors as both a sophomore and a junior. He also earned All-America honors twice, and in 1949 he led the Gophers to a number six national ranking—still their highest since 1919 if, like the NCAA, you discount their 1997 record.

Further, the critics must have known even as early as March 1944 that McIntyre was not the only big kid in the low post. Rather, Bob "Foothills" Kurland of Oklahoma A&M, the first prominent seven-footer, and six-foot-ten George Mikan at DePaul were already gaining notoriety in the form of All-America honors (the first of three such honors apiece) in their sophomore seasons. Before Kurland was done, his Aggies (now Oklahoma State) would become the first team to win two consecutive NCAA titles, with Kurland winning two tournament MVP awards while scoring 21.7 and 24 points per game. As a senior, he was the only Aggie to score in double figures in any tournament game, and he scored 52 percent of their points overall. He also scored 58 points during an 86–33 regular season rout of St. Louis.

Meanwhile, Mikan led DePaul to a 62–12 rec-

63

Frank Cleve won all-state honors at Minneapolis South and at St. Olaf College and then coached Concordia (Moorhead) to its only MIAC title prior to 1982. Later, as Jim McIntyre's coach at Minneapolis Henry, he helped establish the low post as the modern offense of choice.

ord over three years, and he was the national scoring champion in both his junior and his senior years. After finishing second in the National Invitation Tournament (NIT) in 1944, DePaul clobbered Bowling Green, 71–54, in the 1945 final at a time when the NIT may have had a stronger field than the NCAA. Mikan scored 53 points against Rhode Island State in an NIT semifinal game.

The biggest game in college basketball history (to that time) followed. It was the Red Cross War Relief Fund benefit game at Madison Square Garden, matching NCAA and NIT champions A&M and DePaul—and, more to the point, Kurland and Mikan. Mikan fouled out after just fourteen minutes of play, having scored 9 points, with DePaul leading, 21–14. A&M came back to win, 52–44, as Kurland scored 14 points. From this time forward, for almost the next fifty years, coaches would dream about one day having the opportunity to coach a dominant low post player. They spent much of their time and energy trying to develop one. Failing that, they knew that they might have to face and defeat such a player in order to win a championship. Little by little at first, then gathering momentum in the 1950s as

a second generation of big men emerged—including players like Ron Johnson of New Prague and the University of Minnesota and Wilt Chamberlain on the national scene—the game came to revolve around the big guy in the low post.

This is not to say that Coach Cleve's low post offense was entirely unanticipated. Six-foot-five Arnie Johnson and six-foot-five-and-a-half Clint Wager had enjoyed great success at Bemidji Teachers and St. Mary's colleges, respectively, from 1938 to 1942. In 1941, six-foot-eight Jim Lewison of Owatonna High School led the Big Nine conference in scoring. But precious few fans had ever seen these players.

In 1939, six-foot-nine "Slim" Wintermute had led Oregon to an NCAA title by playing "goalie." He was no more than the fourth option on offense, instead focusing his efforts on defense and rebounding. The goalie position more often than not was the role of the big center in the brief interregnum between the end of the center jump after every basket in 1937 and the advent of the low post offense in the early 1940s. Then, in 1943, just one year before McIntyre's high school tournament debut, Alexandria coach Harry Falk put his best—and, at six foot three, his tallest—player, Hal Haskins, under the basket and told him to shoot the ball. Haskins missed the tournament scoring record by 1 point, scoring 57 points in three games.

A Roll Call of Great Centers

After Haskins and McIntyre, the history of the state tournament in the coming years became in large part a roll call of great, dominant low post players, continuing immediately in 1946 with six-foot-five-and-a-half Dick Ravenhorst of Austin's champion Packers.

Center Rudy Monson, later an all-state college player at Duluth Teachers College and now a member of the University of Minnesota Duluth Athletic Hall of Fame, led Duluth Denfeld to the 1947 title. Meanwhile Mountain Lake center Ray Wall, though just six foot three, led all scorers for the second consecutive year, becoming the second of only four boys ever to do so.

In 1948, center Wes Sabourin led Bemidji to the title, though he too was but six foot three. The presence of three six-foot-five players—Pete Castle, Anoka; Milan Knezovich, Hibbing; and Lawrence Krause, Waseca—was a first, however, and created a minor stir. Knezovich and Krause each enjoyed a 30-plus-point game.

Six-foot-six Jim Fritsche led St. Paul Humboldt to the 1949 title and was regarded as the best big man between McIntyre and Johnson. He went on to star for Hamline's third NAIA championship team in 1951.

In 1950, six-foot-nine Robbinsdale center Don Dale outplayed six-foot-seven John Stephan of Duluth Central, although Central emerged victorious in a thrilling 42–40 final.

In 1951, it was the Boots and Burdie show. "Boots" was six-foot-ten Bill Simonovich of Gilbert, and "Burdie" was six-foot-eight Burdette Haldorson of Austin. Theirs was the most anticipated matchup of big men before Steve Lingenfelter and Kevin McHale in 1976. Simonovich dominated Haldorson, as Boots scored 35 points and fouled Burdie out of the game with six and a half minutes left to go. Gilbert pulled away to an 11-point win and then won two more games and the Iron Range's final state title of the single-class era.

In the mid-1950s, the six-foot-seven Johnson dominated for a couple of years, breaking most of McIntyre's scoring records. Like Mac, Johnson went on to All-America honors as a Minnesota Gopher.

Meanwhile, Johnson was one of four low post centers to hold the high school career scoring record between 1945 and 1958. The others were six-foot-five Jim Korth of Mankato Loyola (class of 1945), six-foot-three Jim Smith of Brainerd (1953), and six-foot-five Norm Grow of Foley (1958). Grow's 2,852 points was the Minnesota record for both boys and girls for more than twenty years, and it was not broken for a second time for more than thirty seasons.

Resentment against the dominance of the big kids in the low post bubbled into public view in 1950. "Robbinsdale was built completely around Dale," Ray Moren, Central's coach, said. "Now don't get me wrong. I think [Robbinsdale coach] Ed Kernan had a fine team and *playing without Dale they may have been even more effective.* They were all good players, but in attempting to play through Dale all the time they injured their team play" (emphasis added).

Against Moren's team, Dale outscored an all-state opponent 22–15, and his team lost, 42–40. He outscored Rochester's center, Jim Larson, 37–14 in a 57–55 semifinal win. And he scored 21 points against another all-state center, Irwin St. John, in a first round 48–34 win over Bemidji. He finished his high school career with 1,162 points as the fifth boy to reach the 1,000-point mark. It's incredible that Moren thought that such a player should be sitting on the bench. But such were the philosophical debates of the time. Moren soon left the coaching ranks to sell insurance.

Simonovich, meanwhile, began his college career at Hamline and then transferred to the U of M. He helped the Gophers to a second-place Big Ten season in 1955, scoring 15 points per game. He lost his starting job to Jed Dommeyer the following year, however, and scored just 4 points per game. Haldorson, meanwhile, went to the University of Colorado, where he won All–Big Eight honors. Later he earned two gold medals as the only Minnesota native ever to play for the U.S. Olympic basketball team. In 1958, he broke Kurland's National Industrial Basketball League (NIBL) records by scoring 50 points in a single game and 26.7 points per game for the season while playing with the Phillips Oilers of Bartlesville, Oklahoma. Though he chose not to play in the NBA, his was the best postcollege career of any of these stars of the high school tournament.

And meanwhile the best low post center on earth was performing twice a week at the Minneapolis Auditorium.

The Lynd Panthers and the Fast Break

The low post offense—and the sudden emergence of tall yet athletic young men—was the most revolutionary innovation to hit the game since 1891. Yet it was not the only innovation that came to define the "modernization" of basketball in the postwar years. There were other strategies that the old-timers loved to hate, such as the fast break and the jump shot.

Ward "Piggy" Lambert had been running the fast break at Purdue since before 1920. But his adoption and development of the fast break was predicated on its rarity. So few teams ran it, in other words, that most did not know how to stop it. And with few running it, most fans had never seen it, or at least not an effective version.

Then in 1946, the Lynd Panthers made it the talk of Minnesota basketball circles. The Lynd legend began to take shape only with the tip-off of its quarterfinal game against perennial power and heavily favored Crosby-Ironton. The Panthers had been the subject of much pretournament reportage, but surprisingly little was said about their fast breaking style. Rather, Lynd was the smallest school from the smallest town ever to appear in the tournament. Shortly, they would be the smallest school from the smallest town ever to make it to the finals. Compared to Lynd, Edgerton's 1960 state champions—the smallest school from the smallest town ever to win a single-class title—represented a bustling metropolis. The Panthers were written up as the team that practiced in a hayloft, as "barnyard basketeers." It was still considered news in 1946 that the Lynd team was made up of the sons of farmers. Times were beginning to change, but many farm families still needed their kids to help with chores around the farm. That made it difficult for them to participate in sports and other extracurricular activities at school.

Crosby-Ironton (C-I) was appearing in its seventh tournament in fifteen years, had been runners-up to Minneapolis Patrick Henry in 1945, and would be runners-up again in 1947. Moreover, at number two, they were the top-rated team in the tournament, since top-ranked Mankato had been upset in Region 2. Austin, runner-up to Mankato in the Big Nine Conference, was rated number three.

All the signs pointed to an easy win for C-I. Instead, Lynd won what one sports writer called "the greatest game ever played" in the state tournament, 58–47. Its fast break was so devastating that C-I took three timeouts in the first period alone to catch its breath. Despite the pace, Lynd coach Chet Bisel made only one substitution throughout the entire game, proving, as center Duane Londgren said after the game, "We never get tired."

Lacking the element of surprise, Lynd struggled to beat Stillwater in the semifinals, 45–39, but there was a historic behind-the-back pass thrown by Caspar Fisher to add to the Lynd legend. Then, in the final against powerful Austin and its three-inches-per-man height advantage, Lynd ran out of gas. The Packers prevailed easily, 63–31, by controlling the rebounds and thus preventing Lynd from getting its fast break going. Lynd's experience in the finals probably explains why the fast break remained a selectively used weapon. Except for Lynd in 1946, Red Wing in 1953, Cloquet in 1963, and Wabasso in 1997, all of whom used the fast break more or less continuously, the fast break was situational. It's a tactic that was used to exploit a weak, slow, or inattentive opponent.

Wallace Fisher drives to the basket in Lynd's semifinal victory over Stillwater in the 1946 state tournament. Many observers have called Lynd's upset 58–47 win over Crosby-Ironton the previous day the greatest high school tournament game ever played.

According to John Kundla, Gophers coach Dave MacMillan liked to fast break even back in the 1930s. Yet he did so infrequently enough to field some of the Big Ten's lowest scoring teams. Austin coach Ove Berven said in 1946 that the Packers ran the fast break—loved to fast break, in fact—but would not attempt it against Lynd. In 1954, Brainerd coach Fred Kellett credited his championship game win over Bemidji to two fast break baskets that helped his team to an early 13–2 lead. After that, he told his team to slow it down, to protect its lead; it barely was able to do so at 49–47.

Brainerd in fact went into a stall with 4:04 left and survived three Bemidji steals to win.

The fact that Lynd's fast break was emulated so rarely perhaps explains why, as many as fifty years after 1946 (as long as the old-timers were still around), Lynd was still the most talked-about high school basketball team that did not actually claim a state championship.

Whitey Skoog and the Modern Jump Shot

The jump shot arrived on the scene at about the same time as the fast break, and over time it became the more potent offensive weapon. Unlike the fast break, the jump shot was a tactic teams expected to use throughout the game and against any opponent. Yet it only slowly worked its way into the repertoire of offensive tactics, almost without comment.

Hank Luisetti of Stanford is generally credited with popularizing the running one-handed shot, as it was called then, during a 1936 road trip to New York City. What's not generally known is where he learned it. Jack Friel, Washington State coach for thirty years, once said that future Gophers coach MacMillan brought the shot out to the University of Idaho from the East Coast. By the time Luisetti brought it back to the Big Apple, it had been forgotten there. (MacMillan seems to have forgotten it as well, as his Gophers were never known for using it.) But the fact is that the shot was not new in 1936. That's why it was able to make an appearance at the Minnesota state tournament just fifteen months after Luisetti's celebrated night in New York. According to a 1958 report, George Lee, who coached Thief River Falls to the 1938 state high school basketball championship, "wasn't too impressed with the play of Friday night's semi-finals. . . . *'I can't get excited over the jump shot . . . because we had it in 1938'*" (emphasis added). Lee's contention is clearly supported by photos from the 1938 tournament, which show players shooting while jumping into the air.

E. J. Gamm, who played for Marshall's 1942 runners-up, also confirmed Lee's recollections, though with a caveat. After watching his son Paul and his Park Rapids teammates get torched by jump-shooting South St. Paul, 97–61 in 1970, Dr. Gamm observed that they played more defense in 1942. Offense, he said, consisted mostly of two-handed set shots and that players only used the "jump shot closer in" to the basket. Fritsche,

The jump shot became popular in the late 1940s, but it already had been around for at least a decade. Here Stewart Skoglund of Hopkins High School shows his form in the 1942 state tournament. His 22 points against Moorhead in the third place game were the most in any state tournament game since 1921.

star of the 1949 tournament who later coached St. Paul Central to the "big show" in 1967, said the same thing in 1960: "When I was in high school, only the big guys went for the jump shot and then only when they were close to the basket."

The term "jump shot" was not used in high school tournament reporting until 1953, when Laker coach John Kundla was quoted as saying that Omar Larson of Granite Falls and Mike Marion of Hibbing had the best jump shots. (Larson finished his career as the number three scorer in state high school annals, with 1,401 points.) By 1957, the jump shot was clearly established, however, and Tommy Nordland of

Minnesota State High School Champions, 1943–1960

Year	Championship Game Score	W–L	Authors' Choice: Postseason MVPs
1943	St. Paul Washington 55 Alexandria 33	22–2	Hal Haskins, Alexandria, C
	Cretin 35 Winona Cotter 28[a]		
1944	Mpls. Pat. Henry 51 Crosby-Ironton 42	24–1	Jim McIntyre, Mpls. Patrick Henry, C
	DeLaSalle 32 Cretin 28[a]		
1945	Mpls. Patrick Henry 66 Ely 35	24–1	McIntyre
	Mankato Loyola 37 Cretin 31[a]		
1946	Austin 63 Lynd 31	22–3	Ray Wall, Mountain Lake, C
	DeLaSalle 48 Winona Cotter 30[a]		
	Shattuck 41 Minnehaha 27[b]		
1947	Duluth Denfeld 46 Crosby-Ironton 44	23–3	Rudy Monson, Duluth Denfeld, C
	St. C. Cathedral 55 Winona Cotter 44[a]		
	Concordia 36 Pillsbury 35[b]		
1948	Bemidji 38 Hopkins 29	28–3	Wes Sabourin Bemidji, C
	Cretin 38 St. Thomas 31[a]		
	Minnehaha 41 Shattuck 35[b]		
1949	St. Paul Humboldt 47 Mankato 35	19–5	Jim Fritsche, St. Paul Humboldt, C
	St. Thomas 63 Cretin 45[a]		
	Shattuck 29 Minnehaha 23[b]		
1950	Duluth Central 42 Robbinsdale 40	24–3	Buzz Bennett, Duluth Central, G
	St. Thomas 52 Winona Cotter 41[a]		
	Minnehaha 43 Shattuck 40[b]		
1951	Gilbert 69 Canby 52	26–1	Bill Simonovich, Gilbert, C
	St. Thomas 37 DeLaSalle 30[a]	29–0	
	Minnehaha 54 Concordia 35[b]		
1952	Hopkins 42 South St. Paul 29	25–1	Dave Tschimperle, Hopkins, F
	Winona Cotter 70 DeLaSalle 57[a]		
	Minnehaha 81 Shattuck 46[b]		
1953	Hopkins 58 Hibbing 49	23–0	Tschimperle, C
	St. Thomas 61 St. Cloud Cathedral 59[a]		
	Minnehaha 52 Blake 43[b]		
1954	Brainerd 49 Bemidji 47	23–3	Bob Anderstrom, Willmar, C
	DeLaSalle 34 Duluth Cathedral 25[a]		
	I Blake 60 Minnehaha 59		
1955	Mpls. Washburn 67 Austin 58	22–1	Ron Johnson, New Prague, C
	DeLaSalle 57 Duluth Cathedral 33[a]		
	Blake 51 Concordia 50[b]		
1956	Mpls. Roosevelt 101 Blue Earth 54	20–3	Johnson
	DeLaSalle 67 St. Thomas 48[a]		
	Shattuck 48 Breck 45[b]		
1957	Mpls. Roosevelt 59 Red Wing 51	27–0	Paul Lehmann, DeLaSalle, G
	DeLaSalle 67 Winona Cotter 41[a]		
	Concordia 60 Minnehaha 52[b]		
1958	Austin 68 Brainerd 63	20–3	Ray Cronk, Bemidji, C
	Austin Pacelli 44 Winona Cotter 43[a]		
	Minnehaha 69 Concordia 53[b]		
1959	Wayzata 55 Carlton 41	23–4	John Pierson, Carlton, F
	DeLaSalle 59 Cretin 46[a]		
	Minnehaha 69 Concordia 54[b]		
1960	Edgerton 72 Austin 61	27–0	Dean Veenhof, Edgerton, F
	St. Thomas 71 St. Cloud Cathedral 60[a]		
	Minnehaha 60 St. Paul Academy 48[b]		

[a] Catholic tournament.
[b] Independent private school tournament.

Minneapolis Roosevelt was hailed as the best outside shooter in tournament history. That same year, five-foot-ten forward Jon Hagen of tiny Belview broke Johnson's career scoring record by 2 points (with 2,192), largely as a "jump shooter with uncanny accuracy from almost any range."

The most famous Minnesota jump shooter was neither Hagen nor Nordland, however. It was Myer "Whitey" Skoog of Brainerd High School, class of 1944—not his brother Rod Skoog, who led Brainerd to the state title in 1954, but Whitey, who never had the chance to play in the state tournament. Whitey Skoog's Warriors upset heavily favored and state-tournament-bound Bemidji in both the 1943 and the 1944 seasons. But they could not get past the eventual state runners-up, Alexandria and Crosby-Ironton, in their own region.

Of course, the truth is that Whitey attempted pre-cious few jump shots—and made even fewer—during his high school career. It was at the University of Minnesota, after two years of navy ball, that he began to practice and perfect his signature move. He perfected it to the point of making one or another All-America team in 1950 and 1951. He then was drafted by the Minneapolis Lakers, for whom he played 341 games over six years. He was a regular throughout most of his career, though knee problems caused him to miss part of his rookie year and relegated him to a backup role in his second. He finished his career scoring 8.2 points per game while shooting a respectable 38.8 percent from the field. By comparison, outside shooters of that era who were able to shoot 40 percent or better—guys like Paul Arizin at 42 percent and Bill Sharman at 43 percent—are in the Basketball Hall of Fame in Springfield, Massachusetts.

13 *The March of the Pied Pipers*

THE LOW POST, the fast break, and the jump shot revolutionized basketball after World War II, but the old "control game" hung on. In fact, thanks to two of its leading practitioners—former Carleton teammates Ozzie Cowles, now coaching at the University of Minnesota, and Joe Hutton at Hamline University—it enjoyed quite a resurgence in Minnesota in 1949.

At one time in early 1949, Hamline was the last unbeaten college team and the number five rated team in the United States—and not just the number five small college team, but number five among all college teams after Kentucky, St. Louis, Oklahoma A&M, and Illinois. The Minnesota Gophers, then 13–1 and second in the Big Ten, were rated seventh at the time.

By the end of the year, the Pipers were 31–3 and champions of America's small colleges for the second of three times, and they boasted two All-Americans—again, not Little All-Americans but All-Americans—in "Sleepy Hal" Haskins and Vern Mikkelsen. These Pipers were so good that they ran up scores like 95–48 (against St. John's) and 71–42 and 82–37 (against Concordia) while running a ball control offense.

This was but one of Hamline's remarkable seventeen titles in twenty seasons of Minnesota Intercollegiate Athletic Conference (MIAC) competition from 1932 through 1953. Through 1957—excepting 1944 through 1946, when the Pipers played an independent schedule—the Pipers finished first or second in the MIAC twenty-three times in twenty-four seasons. Hutton's thirty-six wins at the National Association of Intercollegiate Athletics (NAIA, formerly the NAIB) tournament remain to this day the most by any coach. He retired in 1965 with 588 wins and 186 losses for a career winning percentage of .759.

The legend began to take shape in 1932. Hutton, a decade removed from a stellar athletic career at Carleton College, was in his third year as coach at the St. Paul

school. After a 2–15 record in 1929–1930, improvement had come rapidly. Now, Hamline completed an unbeaten 11–0 season to win its first MIAC title. The Pipers followed up with four more MIAC titles through 1936. From 1937 through 1940, the Pipers struggled to just two conference cochampionships in four years. A 1939 newspaper item claimed that Hutton "finds it more difficult with each succeeding year to win the title. Since the halcyon days of Wally Zimmerman, Gordon Ditz, Giffy O'Dell and Ken Fladager"—who among them won all-conference honors twelve times between 1932 and 1935—"Hutton has fallen heir to few great basketball players."

Hamline was also thwarted for two years by a great St. Mary's College team. St. Mary's tied and then won the MIAC outright in 1939 and 1940, respectively, thanks largely to the exploits of Minnesota's first great, big scoring center, Clint Wager. The six-foot-five-and-a-half Wager, a local boy from Winona High School, had the distinct advantage of learning pivot play from Ed "Moose" Krause, former Notre Dame All-American and St. Mary's coach from 1933 to 1939. (St. Mary's under Krause was the first squad in the United States to fly to a basketball game, as Krause's friend Max Conrad took the team to Notre Dame in 1936.) Wager set MIAC season scoring records in his sophomore and senior seasons of 162 points in twelve games (13.5 points per game) and then 189 points in just ten games (18.9 points per game). He went on to play seven years of pro ball in the National Basketball League (NBL) and the National Basketball Association (NBA) from 1943 through 1950, scoring 10 points per game as a rookie and 5 points per game in a career that consisted of 310 games. He was also a punter and end for the National Football League's Chicago Cardinals.

Meanwhile, the NAIB had set up shop in Kansas City in 1937, but no MIAC team participated until

1940. That year, St. Mary's won the MIAC, but Hamline went to Kansas City; in 1941 Hamline took conference honors, but St. Mary's took the train south. Both teams played well, Hamline winning three games and St. Mary's two.

Bemidji Teachers College won three Northern Teachers Conference titles from 1940 to 1942 and played in the national tournament each time, too. Six-foot-five center Arnie Johnson, the "big, blond . . . likable Swede," led Bemidji to its first NAIB victory in 1941 with 21 points, including all of his team's 14 first-half points. Then in 1942, Bemidji won two games and beat the defending champs from San Diego State, 41–32. Johnson scored 46 points in three games. After the war, he played seven seasons for

The Hamline Pipers under coach Joe Hutton (center) won their first national title in 1942 behind freshman forward Howie Schultz (left) and senior center John Norlander (right).

the Rochester Royals, main rivals of the Minneapolis Lakers during their glory years. He finished his career in 1953 with 3,391 NBL and NBA points in 421 games for an 8.1 scoring average.

These were the best teams that St. Mary's and Bemidji Teachers, now Bemidji State University, have ever had. But for Hutton and Hamline, the fun was just beginning.

Three Championship Seasons

The first national championship came in 1942. Hamline won the MIAC by just one game, at 10–1, yet placed three players on the first all-state team. They were Iron Rangers John Norlander from Virginia, Minnesota, a six-foot-three center; guard Glenn Gumlia from Crosby-Ironton High School; and six-foot-six freshman

forward Howie Schultz from St. Paul Central. The Pipers won four tournament games—including two victories over former NAIB champions Southwestern College of Winfield, Kansas, and Central State Teachers of Warrensburg, Missouri—to gain the finals. There, Hamline edged Southwest State of Durrant, Oklahoma, 33–31, as they rallied from a 28–25 deficit late in the game. Columnist George Barton wrote, "It is . . . a tribute to the coaching ability of Joe Hutton, who has developed a host of cage stars at Hamline, but always has a bunch of boys who function as integral parts of a team rather than as individuals."

The Pipers won the MIAC championship again in 1943, 1947, and 1948 with a combined record of thirty-five wins and one loss. They represented the MIAC at the NAIB each time, winning seven games and losing three. The 1948 squad went 24–2, losing prior to the NAIB only to Oklahoma A&M and Wyoming in a holiday tournament.

But the big excitement between the 1942 and 1949 national championship seasons was provided by the 1944–1945 team. Schultz was now the Pipers' big star. Eighteen months before, he had signed a professional contract to play baseball for the Brooklyn Dodgers; he batted .258 with twelve home runs in 183 games over two years. As a result of his professional contract, the Amateur Athletic Union (AAU) declared that any athlete or school who played with or against Schultz would be ineligible for its events. The NCAA gave such athletes a clean bill of health, but several MIAC opponents declined to play Hamline and Schultz. So Hamline

Hutton's greatest team won the NAIA championship in 1949. Front row, left to right: Bob Leiviska, Duane Meyer, Joe Hutton Jr., Kerwin Englehardt, Bill Wanamaker; back row: Coach Joe Hutton, Hal Haskins, Bob Lundsten, Vern Mikkelsen, Dave Hegna, Jim MacDonald, and Harold Montgomery.

played an independent schedule against any team that was willing to play them, and they remained independent in 1945–1946, even though Schultz's career was over by then.

Hamline was knocked out of the 1947 NAIB by the eventual champion, Marshall, 55–54. Meanwhile, Mankato Teachers made it all the way to the finals under coach Jim Withan, a former all-state player at Bemidji Teachers. Like Hamline, Mankato also was bounced by Marshall, 73–59. Center Hank Epp, now eight years removed from Mountain Lake High School's 1939 state champs, earned second-team Little All-America honors. Marshall coach Cam Henderson said of Hamline and Mankato, "The class of basketball played in Minnesota apparently ranks very highly with the rest of the country."

In 1949, Hutton's greatest team almost did not make it to the NAIB. The Pipers were upset by St. Thomas, 45–43, and the two colleges settled for a tie for the conference title. A play-off game was scheduled to break the tie, but then the presidents of the two institutions agreed to settle the tie with a coin flip. St. Thomas won the coin flip, then edged Mankato Teachers, 56–55 in overtime, for the right to play for the national title. Hutton let it be known that "Hamline [was] open to all offers. . . . The Pipers were interested in any tournament that [came] along."

Hamline's other two losses came in a pair of back-to-back games against the legendary Phillips Oilers, sponsored by the Phillips Petroleum company. Phillips gave full-time jobs and salaries to players like Kurland, who in college had been better than Mikan, and Oklahoma All-American Gerald Tucker. Their job, however, was to play basketball. In 1948, the Oilers' starting five had been selected, en masse, to play for the U.S. Olympic team, who easily won the gold medal. So the Oilers beat Hamline twice, 52–38 and 49–46, but Mikkelsen outscored Kurland in both games, 16–14 and 18–14.

On March 4, the NAIB announced that Hamline would play after all. They would "fill a vacancy" caused when the New York district failed to send a team. The Pipers started strong, hammering Arkansas State, 76–43, as Haskins scored 24 points. Hamline then beat Indiana Central, 83–66, as Sleepy Hal scored another 29. Texas Tech was the next victim, 80–56. This time Mikkelsen led the way with 28 points. Next Beloit and star

guard Johnny Orr, future coach of the Michigan Wolverines and Iowa State Cyclones, were dispatched, 52–43. Haskins and Mikkelsen each scored 18 points. "Haskins [gave a] masterful exhibition of ball handling and direction of the control game, [and] also proved the outstanding Piper in the defensive battle." It was Haskins who held Orr to just 8 points, all in the second half. The next night Orr scored 31.

In the final, Hamline beat Regis, which had knocked

Stars of Hamline's 1951 national champs. **Left to right: Dave Hegna, Jim Fritsche, Paul Smaagaard, and Lloyd Thorgaard. Thorgaard and Fritsche completed their eligibility in 1953 as the first- and third-ranking scorer, respectively, in NAIA tournament history.**

off St. Thomas in the second round, 53–52, by a score of 57–46. The Pipers took an early 21–5 lead, expanded it to 47–27 with seven minutes to go, then went into a "semi-stall." Haskins "directed the Pipers' floor play [with] clock-like efficiency," scored 21 points, and was named the tournament MVP.

Haskins returned for his final season in 1949–1950, and on March 6, he scored 35 points against the so-called Duluth Branch—now, of course, the University of Minnesota Duluth but then the newest member of the MIAC. This was reported at the time as giving him exactly 2,000 points for his career. He was said to be the fifth college player ever to score 2,000 points, and he was also named the best visiting player to perform at Madison Square Garden that year. Hamline records credit Haskins with only 1,985 points for his career, however. Still, the Pipers lost just two games during the 1949–1950 regular season, to Long Island University in the Garden and to Pepperdine. Over Haskins's four-year career, they were 106–13.

During the 1950 NAIB the Pipers won just one game, 74–66 over Regis. They then lost a huge upset to Missouri Central, 76–66, as Haskins fouled out with about fifteen minutes to play. Without Haskins in the second half, Hamline was outscored 44–24, and their chance to become the first repeat NAIB winner was over.

With Haskins gone, Hutton in 1950–1951 fielded his greenest team in fifteen years. Guard Kerwin Engelhart, from Red Wing, and forward Jim Fritsche, from St. Paul Humboldt, were returning starters, while

six-foot-five Dave Hegna from Granite Falls took over at center. Otherwise Hutton's team consisted of "fabulous sophomores" six-foot-two-and-a-half forward Lloyd Thorgaard from Minneapolis Washburn, back-up center Paul Smaagaard, and guard Bob Gussner. Thorgaard made the first all-conference team, but no other Hamline player earned even second-team honors. Still, the Pipers swept through the MIAC again with just one loss.

Little was expected of the Pipers in the national tournament. Instead, they routed four teams by almost 20 points apiece to gain the finals. The Pipers then defeated Milliken College, 69–61, in the final. Thorgaard and Fritsche made the first all-tournament team; Hegna, the second; and Milliken's Scott Steagall was named tournament MVP. Hamline never trailed in the second half of any game and won all of its games by at least 8 points. No team had ever dominated the tournament to this degree, and nine of the ten roster players would return to play the following season. Thorgaard clearly was the best of them—he was Hutton's "quarterback on the floor, [his] best feeder, best ball-handler, a tough defensive man, a strong rebounder," according to Hutton, and the team's leading scorer at 18 points per game to boot.

The Long, Slow Decline

This nucleus of players easily won two more MIAC titles with a combined record of 27–1. In 1952, they clobbered Bemidji Teachers, 104–75, to win the NAIB

Minnesota Small College Champions, 1943–1950

Year	MIAC	Northern Teachers Conference
1943	Hamline[a]	St. Cloud Teachers[a]
1944	St. Thomas[b]	no competition
1945	Gustavus[b]	no competition
1946	Augsburg,[a] St. Thomas	St. Cloud Teachers
1947	Hamline[a]	Mankato Teachers[a]
1948	Hamline[a]	Mankato Teachers[a]
1949	Hamline,[a] St. Thomas[a]	Mankato Teachers[c]
1950	Hamline[a]	Mankato State[d]

[a] Participated in the NAIB tournament.
[b] The MIAC no longer acknowledges the 1944 and 1945 conference championships, stating that there were "no championships," owing to World War II. St. Thomas and Gustavus championships were reported and acknowledged and were regarded as legitimate at the time.
[c] Played St. Thomas in the NAIC District 13 playoffs and lost, 56–55 (OT).
[d] Conference name changed to the Northern Conference.

Minnesota Small College Champions, 1951–1960

Year	District 13 Playoff Matchup
1951	Hamline 49 Bemidji State 35
1952	Hamline 104 Bemidji State 75
1953	Hamline 74 Mankato State 72
1954	Gustavus 64 Mankato State 61
1955	Gustavus 63 Mankato State 50
1956	Gustavus 80 Mankato State 58
1957	Hamline 71 St. Cloud State 59
1958	Duluth Branch 71 St. Cloud State 66
1959	Duluth Branch 67 St. Cloud State 65 (OT)
1960	Hamline 76 Mankato State 62

Note: All winners of the District 13 playoff games between MIAC and NCC from 1951 to 1960 participated in the NAIB or NAIA tournament. The National Association for Intercollegiate Basketball (NAIB) became the National Association for Intercollegiate Athletics (NAIA) in 1952.

District 13 title, as the Pipers shot 50 percent from the field and Fritsche poured in 38 points. Favored this time, they instead were shocked by Portland in the second round of the NAIB, 75–65. Portland "clowned out the final four minutes in Harlem Globetrotter fashion," which Hutton said was "humiliating and uncalled for."

Despite a 15–1 conference record, the 1952–1953 season was already regarded as a disappointment before the annual pilgrimage to Kansas City. The Pipers lost eight regular season games in all, the most for a Hutton team since 1931. "We didn't play good defense," Hutton said. Then the Pipers just squeaked past Mankato Teachers, 74–72. But once in Kansas City, they won four games by scoring an average of 88 points, about 25 of them by Fritsche. In the final, Springfield became the first team to win back-to-back championships, however, beating Hamline, 79–71, and holding Fritsche to just 4 points. The game was not that close, either, as Springfield had led at one time by 66–41. Thorgaard (283 points) and Fritsche (272) joined Haskins (276) as the top three scorers in NAIB history, while Mikkelsen was still fifth and Norlander eighth.

Hamline's decline began in earnest in 1954, shortly after Paul Henry Giddens came to Hamline as its new president and announced that athletics had assumed altogether too much prominence in campus life. Hamline was dethroned by Gustavus Adolphus and coach Verl "Gus" Young, yet another Carleton grad. The Gusties repeated in 1955 and 1956, defeating Mankato Teachers three times for the right to go to Kansas City. There they won a total of five NAIB games while losing three behind three Minneapolis products, center Ed Springer, forward Bill "Shorty" Patterson, and "dribbling magician" Johnny Patzwald.

Hamline bounced back in 1957 and 1960, winning the final MIAC championships of Hutton's illustrious career, this time with a total record of 30–2 in the MIAC. This was Hutton's "prairie phase," as two-time all-conference forward Lee Hopfenspirger, 1,000-point scorer from Morgan High School, and center Del McClure from Montevideo starred on both teams in their freshman and senior seasons. The 1957 and 1960 teams each won the NAIA district playoff and two NAIA tournament games. But there would be no more national titles for Hutton or the Pipers nor even

another conference title after 1960, as Hamline under the administration of President Giddens came back to the MIAC pack. After winning seventeen of twenty conference championships through 1953, Hutton won just two in his final twelve years on the job. Then, adding insult to injury, Giddens forced Hutton into retirement in 1965. Hamline's policies required faculty and staff retirement at age sixty-five, allowing the option of continuation through age seventy with the president's authorization. Hutton made it known that he, of course, wished to continue, but Giddens refused to give Hutton the necessary blessing.

Along with the 588 wins, Hutton's legacy consists of his remarkable production of successful high school coaches. Bob McNish coached Red Wing to the 1936 state tournament, then the Rochester Rockets in 1944, 1949, and 1950. Harry Falk coached Alexandria and Hal Haskins to the 1942 state finals. Art Stock coached Virginia to the 1943, 1944, and 1952 tournaments, and Weldon "Buzz" Gray, who played in the 1934 tournament for tiny Cass Lake, coached Appleton to the 1952 tournament. Then there was Ken Fladager, who brought South St. Paul to the 1952 and 1962 finals. McNish's successors at Rochester were both Hamline grads, too. Howie Tompkins and Englehart brought the 1957 and 1964 Rockets, respectively, to the state tournament. Fritsche coached St. Paul Central to the 1967 tournament. Gordie Hakes, class of 1950, coached Mankato and Mankato West to four state tournaments between 1968 and 1980. Fred Schmiesing brought Tartan in 1978 and North St. Paul in 1999 to the high school tournament. As late as 1972, three of the four Class AA semifinalists were coached by Hamline grads—Joe Hutton Jr. at Bloomington Lincoln, Oscar Haddorff at Austin, and Ziggy Kauls at champion Mounds View. And these are just the coaches who have brought teams to the state high school tournament.

No one who knew Joe Hutton was surprised that he did not go gently into that good night, but all were shocked when his final team in 1965 went 1–15 in the MIAC and 3–21 overall. There was "a scent of acid in his leave-taking," columnist Jim Klobuchar wrote. But on March 1, 1965, the Hutton era ended as it had mostly unfolded—with a win. Hamline trounced Concordia and coach "Sonny" Gulsvig, who reportedly appeared pleased to have lost, 89–72.

14 Ozzie Cowles Brings Back the Control Game

Tony Jaros was a great three-sport athlete at Minneapolis Edison High School. He played baseball and basketball for the Minnesota Gophers and then played both sports professionally. He was a member of three of the Minneapolis Lakers' world championship teams.

FOR THE MINNESOTA GOPHERS, the golden age began in 1948 and ran through 1955. In the first seven years of the Ozzie Cowles regime, the Gophers won 105 games and lost 48 (including a record of 61–37 in the Big Ten); they produced two Big Ten runners-up, two nationally rated teams, and four All-Americans. Otherwise, they continued to experience the ups and downs of the previous quarter century.

Dave MacMillan resigned as Gophers coach in 1942. The Gophers floundered for two years under Carl Nordly, yet another Carleton teammate of Cowles and Hutton—and the best basketball player of the three. They fared little better for another year under Weston Mitchell, who had been John Kundla's coach at Minneapolis Central. So MacMillan came back for three more seasons. MacMillan, first named Gophers coach way back in 1928, long had been known as favoring the then predominant ball control style of play. His only conference champions, from 1937, finished fifth in the Big Ten in scoring but first in defense. His 1938 team, which at 16–4 compiled the best overall win-loss record of his career, was ninth in the conference in scoring. Now he came back in the fall of 1945 a new man. His first two teams finished second and fourth in scoring but eighth and ninth in defense. The difference? He had big Jim McIntyre to play the pivot.

An early highlight of Mac's second term was a matchup with defending NIT champ DePaul and George Mikan at the Field House in December 1945. The Gophers trailed by scores of 15–5 and 22–13 in the first half, but before a roaring crowd of more than 11,000 fans, they came back to win, 45–36. Ed "Punky" Kernan, a freshman from Two Harbors, led Minnesota with 17 points, but McIntyre was the Gophers' key player. McIntyre held Mikan to 2 field goals and 3 free throws, though big George also scored 4 points off Mc-Intyre's backup, "Red" Mattson. Mikan's 11 points, however, were his lowest regular season total ever.

By this time, MacMillan had adopted the pivot play, particularly with the emergence of McIntyre. In an article entitled "Man in the Hole and the Pivot Play," MacMillan wrote, "Nearly every team has a tall man who is not suited to play any spot other than the 'hole' because of physical limitations in speed, agility, and deftness." MacMillan cited McIntyre as an example of such a player who initially "had the fault of feeding the ball too hard, too soon, or too late. To perfect this fault we had to work continuously, with both teacher and pupil employing lots of patience. . . . During this process Jim improved his footwork, which is so essential to good 'hole' play." MacMillan added that he recommended folk dancing to help his players with their footwork. The folk dancing seemed to work, as McIntyre led the Big Ten in scoring and earned first team all-conference honors in his sophomore and junior seasons. Moreover, he twice set a school record for most points in a season and also set a new record for points in a single game, with 36 against Iowa on January 19, 1948.

McIntyre won All-America honors in 1948, while newcomer Harry "Bud" Grant of Superior, Wisconsin, did an outstanding job rebounding. Yet the best any of Mac-Millan's Gophers could do during his second stint was fourth place in the Big Ten. After a seventh-place finish in 1948, MacMillan requested that he be relieved of his duties again, citing poor health as the reason. The 10–10 record, MacMillan's first nonwinning season since 1936, represented a disappointing way to close out his career. But in his final game as Gophers coach, his squad defeated Wisconsin at Williams Arena, 46–41.

Browns Valley, Minnesota, native Ozzie Cowles returned to his home state in 1948 to coach the Minnesota Gophers. He had coached Dartmouth to the 1942 NCAA final, where he was beaten by Stanford and Coach Everett Dean, who had been Cowles's own coach at Carleton College.

Cowles Arrives and Mac Departs

On two separate occasions in March 1949, the *Minneapolis Tribune* noted a resurgence of the "so-called control style of basketball"—the old-time, slow-down, ball control, defensive-oriented style of play popular in the 1920s and 1930s. Exhibit A was the success of the Minnesota Gophers under first-year coach Ozzie Cowles. The Gophers had a great start under Cowles, winning their first thirteen games, including five in the Big Nine to move to the top of the conference standings. As a senior, McIntyre was averaging 16.9 points per game,

Minnesota Mysteries and Myths

John Wooden and the Minnesota Gophers

As short as Dave MacMillan's second coaching tenure was, it encompasses one of the great mysteries of Golden Gophers basketball. It concerns the search for his successor in 1948, which immediately focused on Hamline's Joe Hutton and the Lakers' John Kundla. Both quickly turned down the offer from Gophers athletic director Frank McCormick, and over the next month almost a dozen more candidates were mentioned in *Minneapolis Tribune* reports. None of the names mentioned was John Wooden, who was coaching basketball and baseball at Indiana State Teachers College at the time.

In his autobiography, *They Call Me Coach*, Wooden wrote that he had visited both Minnesota and UCLA, was considering coaching offers from both, and had promised to give McCormick and Wilbur Johns, the outgoing coach and new athletic director at UCLA, his answer on an agreed-upon evening. In fact, "I had decided to take the Minnesota job," Wooden wrote—because, according to reporter Sid Hartman, Wooden was a midwesterner at heart. But there was a sticking point. The Gophers wanted their new coach to retain MacMillan as an assistant, since they had to pay Mac for another year anyway. Wooden objected.

"Even though I liked Mr. McMillan [sic]," Wooden wrote, "I wanted my own man, Eddie Powell. Minnesota had to get approval from its board that was meeting that particular day for me to bring Powell and not keep McMillan [sic]. As it was set up, McCormick was to call me for my answer at 6:00 P.M. and Johns would call at 7:00.

"There was a snow storm raging in Minneapolis that day," Wooden continued, "and Frank got snowed in and couldn't get to a phone on time. I didn't know of the problem so when Mr. Johns called, right on time, I accepted the UCLA job. When McCormick finally reached me about an hour later, he told me everything was 'all set.'

"'It's too late,' I told him. 'I have already accepted the job at UCLA.'"

But there are a few problems with Wooden's story. First, it seems unlikely that Wooden could have slipped into and out of the Twin Cities unnoticed by the local press. Researcher Joel Rippel believes, however, that Wooden may have met with McCormick and Johns at the National Association of Basketball Coaches convention in New York on March 22–24. Both athletic directors were there, and Rippel adds, "I can't imagine that Wooden would not have been at this convention. I think that's when the initial 'offers' came to Wooden."

Second, no snowstorm hit Minneapolis during the period in question. Based on this information, some have speculated that McCormick perhaps fabricated the snowstorm story in order to save face concerning the disagreement about keeping MacMillan as assistant coach. But a major snowstorm did hit South Dakota on April 7, and telephone lines were damaged by high winds. McCormick was from South Dakota, still operated a business there, and often returned to his home state on weekends. So maybe the snowstorm story holds up after all, although Wooden writes that one of the reasons he would not renege his acceptance of the UCLA job was that they had "already released the news of my appointment to the press in Los Angeles." The new release did not appear in Los Angeles newspapers until April 21, two weeks after the snowstorm in question. It is also true that when MacMilllan's successor finally was hired another month later, MacMilllan was not retained as his assistant. So maybe, as Wooden says, "everything was," indeed, "all set."

On balance, how close the Gophers came to hiring the man who became the Wizard of Westwood may never be completely known. Nor will we ever know precisely how the Gophers finally hired Ozzie Cowles as MacMilllan's successor. Finally, of course, we can never be certain whether Wooden would have had more success than Cowles at the U.

A Browns Valley, Minnesota, native and Carleton College grad, Cowles had led Dartmouth to seven Ivy League titles in eight years. His 1942 squad was NCAA tournament runner-up to Stanford and coach Everett Dean, his predecessor at Carleton. Then, in just two short years he had taken the Michigan Wolverines, a team that had not had a winning conference record since 1937, to a Big Ten title. But when his championship team returned from New York and the National Invitation Tournament (NIT), he recalled years later, Fritz Crisler, then the Michigan athletic director and head football coach, "stuck his head in my office and asked me where I'd been. That was when I decided that Michigan was no place to coach basketball." Yet Cowles was never mentioned as a candidate until a month after the infamous delayed phone call is supposed to have occurred. Perhaps the Gophers simply believed that Cowles was not interested in leaving Michigan, that Crisler would never let him out of his contract to coach the Wolverines, or that such an experienced coach would cost too much money. And perhaps they also simply preferred Wooden, younger by a decade and already a legend as a player at the high school, college, and professional levels. But the fact is that Cowles enjoyed considerable success, including two conference runners-up and top ten nationally ranked teams in 1949 and 1954. Of the men who coached the Gophers in one hundred Big Ten conference games or more, Cowles's winning percentage of .558 (86–68) is the second best ever.

his lowest total since his freshman year. Sophomore Whitey Skoog averaged more than 14 points while sharing the front court with Bud Grant.

Minnesota went to Illinois to play the Big Nine's only other undefeated team on Saturday, January 29, 1949. The Gophers held a 27–16 lead late in the first half. The Illini scored the final 4 points of the half, however, and then the first 8 points of the second half to take the lead. Minnesota twice got the lead back in the second half, but troubles at the free throw line doomed the Gophers, along with their inability to stop the Illinois fast break. Minnesota was also outrebounded for the first time that season, and the Illini won the game, 45–44, to take possession of first place.

Minnesota won five of its next six games and still had a shot at catching Illinois for a share of the conference title as the Gophers finished their season at Wisconsin. The Badgers took a 45–38 lead late in the game, but Minnesota closed to within 2 points and got the ball back with fifteen seconds left. Skoog tried to tie it but was wide with a jump shot. Grant got the rebound and passed it back to Skoog in the corner. This time Skoog's shot hit the rim, bounced high in the air, and appeared to be coming down straight for the basket. Instead, it rimmed in and out, ending the Gophers' hopes. The 45–43 loss to Wisconsin rendered insignificant a loss by Illinois two nights later. The Illini won the conference title with a 10–2 record, a game ahead of Minnesota.

The Gophers could not quite recapture the magic of 1948–1949. Skoog was back, averaging 17 points per game, but McIntyre was gone, and, early in the season, so was Bud Grant. In mid-December, Grant was declared ineligible because of what was described by reporter Sid Hartman as a "scholastic deficiency." Grant left school and within days signed a contract to play professional basketball with the Minneapolis Lakers. The Gophers, after winning eight of their first nine nonconference games, won only four of twelve in the Big Ten.

The following year, Maynard Johnson, a native of Plainview, Minnesota, who began his college career with two years at Macalester College, inherited McIntyre's spot at center. On December 27, 1950, Johnson broke McIntyre's school record for points scored in a game. The Gophers were playing in the Big Seven Tournament in Kansas City, and Johnson scored 38 points in a 74–68 win over Colorado. Skoog also had a big game against Colorado, scoring 20. He was again Minnesota's leading scorer, averaging 14.4 points per game his senior season, and was named to several All-America teams in 1951. The Gophers split their conference games to finish fourth in the Big Ten.

The season concluded with Williams Arena hosting the third-place and championship games of the NCAA basketball tournament. On March 27, 1951, before a crowd of more than 15,000, Illinois beat Oklahoma A & M for third place, and Kentucky beat Kansas State, 68–58, for the national title. The following December, the defending champions came back to Williams Arena to play the Gophers. Ed Kalafat, a six-foot-six center from Anaconda, Montana, scored 30 points for the Gophers as Minnesota beat Kentucky, 61–57. Meanwhile, guard Chuck Mencel of Eau Claire, Wisconsin, began his Gophers career in that rare season when freshmen could play varsity ball. He used his extra year of eligibility to become the Gophers' leading career scorer and remained as such until Mychal Thompson came along more than twenty years later.

Cowles Picks Up the Pace

Led by Kalafat and Mencel, the Gophers finished third in 1952 and tied for third in 1953. Surprisingly, even Cowles was now picking up the pace, as the Gophers' scoring jumped from 51 points per game in 1949 to 73 points, third best in the conference, in 1953. "I guess all of us—even Ozzie at Minnesota—are falling victim to the general trend of basketball," Hamline coach Joe Hutton said. "Everybody thinks only of offense today."

Over the next two years, the roster was bolstered by a pair of stars from Minnesota's Mesabi Iron Range, forward Dick Garmaker and center Bill "Boots" Simonovich, and the scoring continued to rise, to 76 and then 79 points per game. Of course, the Gophers would also give up more than 70 points per game, as scoring stars like Don Schlundt of Indiana and Robin Freeman of Ohio State continued to push the scoring envelope, too.

Minnesota Mysteries and Myths

Was Jim McIntyre Really Any Good?

Jim McIntyre's fabulous Minnesota basketball career ended on a surprising note—one of disappointment. His final game was an upset loss at the hands of the Wisconsin Badgers that cost the Gophers a possible share of the 1949 Big Ten title. Moreover, he was supplanted as the first-string All–Big Ten center by Wisconsin center Don Rehfeldt. Within the week, *Minneapolis Tribune* columnist Joe Hendrickson wrote, "We might agree that McIntyre was not a great basketball player. . . . He failed to make full use of his natural physical attributes. . . . He didn't enjoy rugged contact and frequently permitted himself to become discouraged. Aggressive defensive men could stop him in key games. . . . He wouldn't consistently get off his feet."

Critics also noted that McIntyre's scoring average had dropped in his senior season, but they failed to acknowledge that this was primarily because he took fewer shots in new coach Cowles's slow-down offense. He set a new Big Ten record with a .396 shooting percentage and outplayed and outscored Rehfeldt in his final Big Ten game. Still, fifty years later, McIntyre's stock had dropped to the point that Tony Jaros, all of whose Minneapolis City Conference and Gopher scoring records McIntyre had broken, was chosen to represent the 1940s on the U's all-century team. McIntyre was not mentioned.

It has become fashionable to suggest that coach Dave MacMillan erred in recruiting McIntyre instead of Vern Mikkelsen in 1945. Mikkelsen went on to a Hall of Fame professional career with the Minneapolis Lakers, while McIntyre was not even drafted by an NBA team. The inference now is drawn that McIntyre wasn't good enough. This (it must be said) is revisionist hogwash.

In their sophomore years, McIntyre was first-team All–Big Ten. Mikkelsen was second-team all-MIAC. As a junior, McIntyre was an All-American, while Mikkelsen was not even a Little All-American. It was only in their senior seasons that it occurred to anyone that Mikkelsen might be as good as or better than Mac. The Rochester Royals were set to pick McIntyre in the first round of the NBA draft, until he turned down the opportunity to play professionally. A year later, the Milwaukee Hawks purchased his rights and made a similar offer. McIntyre again said no.

Why? Jim McIntyre wanted to be a minister. He was ordained by the Presbyterian Church in 1960 after earning a

Jim McIntyre twice won All-America honors at the University of Minnesota, but he declined opportunities to play in the NBA. Instead, he played two years for the Goodyear Wingfoots of the National Industrial Basketball League and then attended Princeton Theological Seminary, where he was ordained as a minister.

masters of divinity degree at Princeton Theological Seminary. He served congregations in Pennsylvania and Wisconsin and Long Lake, Crosby-Ironton, St. Paul, and Golden Valley, Minnesota, over a period of thirty-two years. But first he worked and played basketball at the Goodyear Tire and Rubber Company from 1952 to 1954 to earn tuition money to attend Princeton. The Goodyear Wingfoots played in the National Industrial Basketball League (NIBL), which continued to draw some of the country's best basketball talent throughout the 1950s. In two seasons he scored 14.6 and 14.3 points per game, which made him the sixth leading scorer in the

NIBL in 1952–1953. By comparison, Clyde Lovellette, who the following year succeeded George Mikan as the Minneapolis Lakers' center and who scored as many as 23.4 points per game in his best NBA season, scored 15.3 playing for the Phillips Oilers. The previous year, McIntyre scored 26 points in a 69–64 upset of the legendary Oilers.

Finally, in fairness to coach MacMillan, it should be noted that he had tried to recruit Mikkelsen. Mikkelsen, however, envisioned himself sitting on the bench behind McIntyre for four years and politely demurred. So it came to pass that during the summer of 1945 Hamline professor Al Holst was on his way to the Mesabi Iron Range to check out a basketball pros-

pect for coach Joe Hutton. Fate intervened in the form of a flat tire in the tiny town of Askov. As Elmer Morgenstern fixed Holst's flat, Holst told him that he was a basketball recruiter. Morgenstern said, "We've got a pretty good ballplayer here in Askov, too. As long as you're here, you might as well check him out." Holst found Mikkelsen working in neighbor Chris Hendricksen's rutabaga field, and he gained an invitation to dinner at the Mikkelsens'. When Mikkelsen's father, a stout Lutheran, heard that Hamline would pay his tuition and room and board, his father "quickly overlooked the fact that Hamline was a Methodist school," Vern recalled.

The sharpshooting Garmaker transferred from Hibbing Junior College, whom he had led to the junior college Final Four, and played two years for Minnesota. In his first season he set a new individual season scoring record with 475 points. A 37-point performance against Illinois on January 2, 1954, also set a Minnesota record for the most points in a conference game. In 1954–1955, Garmaker upped his season total to 533 points, or 24.2 points per game in twenty-two games. Simonovich, a six-foot-ten (some said seven-foot) center who had led Gilbert to the state high school title in 1951, joined the varsity in the 1954–1955 season and averaged 15.3 points per game. Meanwhile, Mencel completed his college career by scoring more than 24 points per game.

Led by this high-scoring trio, the Gophers nearly became the first nonsouthern team to win the Dixie Classic in December 1954. Playing in Raleigh, North Carolina, the Gophers reached the championship game with wins over Wake Forest and Duke. Their opponent in the title game was second-ranked North Carolina State, coached by Everett Case. Simonovich scored 24 points and had 20 rebounds in the game. Garmaker also had 24 points, including a tip-in with seventeen seconds left to put the Gophers ahead, 84–83. Mencel added 22 points, but John Maglio scored for the Wolfpack with nine seconds left to give State an 85–84 win.

Not only did the Gophers set school records for points in the conference and overall, they also topped 100 points twice early in the Big Ten season. One of those games was a 102–88 win over Purdue at Williams Arena. However, when the teams met at Purdue two weeks later, on January 29, 1955, it was a different kind of battle. The Gophers used a zone defense, keeping Si-

monovich camped under the basket. So Purdue played deliberately on offense, often holding the ball for long stretches in the second half without taking a shot. At the end of regulation time, the score was 47–47. Purdue controlled the jump at the start of the five-minute overtime period. The Boilermakers held on to the ball for the entire period, opting to either win it on a last-second shot or send it into another overtime—which is what happened. The situation was repeated in both the second and third overtime periods. The Boilermakers got the tip, held the ball for nearly five minutes, and missed a shot as time ran out. Finally, the Gophers got the jump ball to start the fourth overtime. However, Joe Sexson of the Boilermakers promptly stole the ball from Gophers forward Dave Tucker, and Purdue held the ball for a final shot. Once again, they missed.

There was scoring at last in the fifth overtime, as each team got a basket. After that, though, Purdue resorted to its earlier form by holding the ball and trying to win it on a shot at the end. Sexson took the shot, but it was blocked by Simonovich. Purdue coach Ray Eddy screamed that Boots had put his hand through the bottom of the net and that goaltending should have been called, but the official underneath the basket called it a clean block. Finally, in the sixth overtime period, the teams started putting up some shots. The Gophers were down by 3 with just over three minutes left when they scored four straight baskets. Guard Buck Lindsley's field goal with a minute and a half to go put the Gophers ahead, 55–54. Dave Tucker increased the Minnesota lead by adding two more baskets before the Boilermakers scored at the buzzer—finally converting on a last-second shot, though it did them no good. The final score was Minnesota 59, Purdue 56. The six overtimes tied a college record, which has since been broken. Garmaker, Simonovich, Mencel, and Lindsley played the entire seventy minutes, while Tucker was spelled for just three minutes by the sole Gophers reserve to see action, Doug Bolstorff.

The Gophers survived another multiple overtime game two weeks later, beating Illinois in double overtime for their fourth straight win. And Minnesota kept winning, getting three victories on the road the following week to up its record to 10–2 in the conference and set up a showdown with Iowa.

The Gophers and Hawkeyes were tied for first place as a record crowd of 20,176 filled Williams Arena on Saturday night, February 28, 1955. The score remained close throughout the game with neither team having larger than a 5-point lead. The Gophers had a 2-point edge at halftime, but the Hawkeyes got hot in the second half, making two-thirds of their field goal attempts. Iowa led, 67–64, but Mencel scored 6 straight points to put Minnesota ahead, 70–67. The Hawkeyes hit two quick baskets to retake the lead by a point, survived a missed shot by Mencel, and then stalled. The Gophers had to foul, and Iowa's

Gophers Annual Record, 1942–1959

Year	Overall Record	Big Ten Record
Coach Carl Nordly		
1942–1943	10–9	5–7 (6th)
1943–1944	7–14	2–10
Coach Weston Mitchell		
1944–1945	8–13	4–8 (6th)
Coach Dave MacMillan		
1945 1946	14–7	7–5 (5th)
1946–1947	14–7	7–5 (4th)
1947–1948	10–10	5–7 (7th)
MacMillan Grand Totals		
1927–1942 and	197–157	103–116
1945–1948	.556	.470
Coach Ozzie Cowles		
1948–1949	18–3	9–3 (2nd)
1949–1950	13–9	4–8 (6th)
1950–1951	13–9	7–7 (4th)
1951–1952	15–7	10–4 (3rd)
1952–1953	14–8	11–7 (3rd)
1953–1954	17–5	10–4 (3rd)
1954–1955	15–7	10–4 (2nd)
1955–1956	11–11	6–8 (6th)
1956–1957	14–8	9–5 (3rd)
1957–1958	9–12	5–9 (8th)
1958–1959	8–14	5–9 (9th)
Cowles Totals		
1948–1959	147–93	86–68
	.612	.558
Gopher Totals		
1942–1959	210–153	116–110
	.579	.513

Dick Garmaker played high school and junior college ball in Hibbing. He twice set new season scoring records for the Minnesota Gophers and then joined the Minneapolis Lakers in 1955.

Deacon Davis made 1 of 2 free throws, leaving Minnesota with a chance to tie the game. The Gophers did not score again and lost, 72–70. For Iowa, the win clinched a share of the Big Ten title, and any chance the Gophers had of catching the Hawkeyes ended when they lost to Wisconsin in their final game of the season. Two nights later, Iowa lost its final conference game to finish at 11–3, a game ahead of Minnesota and Illinois.

Garmaker and Mencel were both named All-Americans in 1955, their final season at Minnesota, and went on to play for the Minneapolis Lakers. The Gophers team the next year featured two new players— Jed Dommeyer from Slayton, Minnesota, and George Kline from Dyer, Indiana—who filled much of the scoring burden left with the departure of Garmaker and Mencel.

Kline and Decline

In his junior season, Kline set a new school record by scoring 40 points in a 102–81 win over Iowa on February 25, 1957. Cowles substituted for his starters with about three and a half minutes left and Kline just 2 points short of Johnson's record of 38. Informed of the situation, he put Kline back into the game. Kline missed his next 2 shots but scored on his third try and then added another basket to give him 40 points and sole possession of the Gophers' single-game scoring record.

"One thing about George Kline," recalled Ray Christensen, who broadcast the Gophers on radio from 1955 to 2001. "He had a cowlick. I swear that you could tell when George had his shooting touch because his cowlick *bristled*. It was like an antenna. I got the feeling that when his cowlick activated, every shot he took was going to go in. It was kind of a silly feeling, but there seemed to be something to it."

Kline and sophomore Ron Johnson, who had starred at New Prague High School, both averaged more than 17 points per game in 1957–1958. But the Gophers finished in a tie for eighth place with a conference record of 5–9, as their defense slumped to only eighth best. Cowles finally put his foot down, and the Gophers defense jumped all the way back up to number one in the conference in 1958–1959. Another 5–9 record and another ninth-place finish, however, were the result. Cowles then announced his retirement, forty years after he had entered Carleton College as a freshman. It was the end of a frustrating era in Golden Gophers basketball, one characterized more than anything by the near miss. The two losses to Wisconsin in the 1949 and 1955 season finales had cost the Gophers two Big Ten cochampionships, and these were Badger teams that both finished seventh with a combined 10–16 record in the conference. Still, Cowles finished with the best winning percentage in Big Ten conference games of any Gophers coach to date—better, at 86–68 (.558) even than Cooke's 105–100 (.512), not to mention MacMillan's 103–116 (.470). Overall, Cowles won 147 games and lost 93 for a .612 percentage, better again than MacMillan's 197–157 (.556).

Williams Arena could hold as many as 20,000 basketball fans in the 1950s. Its capacity was reduced in ensuing decades because of remodeling, and today its capacity is under 15,000.

15 *The Greatest Show on Earth*

A HEADLINE ON THE FRONT PAGE of the December 1, 1946, *Minneapolis Tribune* read, "Jane Russell Wins London Battle of Bulging Bodice." Wedged well inside the sports section was a much smaller headline announcing, "5,000 to See Pros Play Here." The "pros" were the Oshkosh All-Stars and the Sheboygan Redskins of the National Basketball League (NBL), who would be playing at the Minneapolis Auditorium that evening. Their appearance was the brainchild of an enterprising twenty-six-year-old Minneapolis sportswriter, Sid Hartman. Hartman had convinced his friend Ben Berger, a local businessman who owned restaurants and movie theatres, to sponsor an NBL game to test the interest of Twin City fans in professional basketball.

More than 5,500 people poured into the Minneapolis Auditorium that night to see Oshkosh beat Sheboygan, 56–42. The experiment was encouraging enough to prompt Hartman to push Berger to acquire a team of his own for Minneapolis. In July 1947, Berger and ice-show promoter Morris Chalfen purchased the Detroit Gems of the NBL for $15,000. Soon Minnesotans would see the "modern" game of basketball at its very best.

Three Years, Three Leagues, Three Titles

For their $15,000, however, Berger and Chalfen acquired little more than a few old basketballs, some useless uniforms, and a piece of paper saying they now owned a franchise in the National Basketball League. The Gems had been on the verge of collapse after having won only four of forty-four games the year before, and the NBL had already divided up the club and assigned the players to other teams in the league. The start of the 1947–1948 NBL season was less than three months away, and Berger and Chalfen had to build

from scratch. They hired Max Winter, a Minneapolis café owner and former fight manager, to run the operation and take a financial interest, and then they looked for a coach.

Joe Hutton, who had been at Hamline University in St. Paul since 1929 and had built the Pipers into a national small-college power, turned down the job. So Winter turned to thirty-one-year-old John Kundla, the former Gopher star, then in his first year as coach at St. Thomas College.

The Lakers still had no players until mid-August when they purchased Tony Jaros and Don "Swede" Carlson from the Chicago Stags of the rival Basketball Association of America (BAA). Both men had been stars at the University of Minnesota and Minneapolis Edison High School before that. But the real prize for the Lakers came a few days later with the signing of Jim Pollard, who had been a member of the Stanford University team that had won the 1942 NCAA title. At six foot five, Pollard was a noted leaper who went by the nickname "The Kangaroo Kid" and was the tallest of the original Lakers.

As the Lakers' inaugural season was launched, there were two pro basketball teams in the Twin Cities. The night before the Lakers' debut, the St. Paul Saints, managed by Phil Gallivan and led by player-coach Bruce Hale, played their first home game in the newly formed Professional Basketball League of America. The Saints lost to the Chicago Gears, led by George Mikan, 59–49, before 3,100 fans. The League of America folded after only a few weeks, however, and Mikan, the league's top player, ended up with the Lakers. (Players from the disbanded league became subject to an NBL draft. The Lakers, by virtue of having the worst record in the league the previous year as the Detroit Gems, were given the first choice.) Mikan soon became the most dominant player in the game, to the point that a few years later the marquee over Madison Square Garden in New York read, "TO-NITE: MIKAN VS. KNICKS."

Because of Mikan, the eyes of the professional basketball world were on the Lakers, who did not disappoint. Minneapolis completed its first regular season with a 43–17 record, best in the Western Division. Its biggest game of the year did not count in the standings, however. The Harlem Globetrotters are known today as the "clown princes" of the basketball world. But from their founding in 1927 through the early 1950s, they were a legitimate, competitive basketball team first and entertainers second. As a result, Winter and Globetrotters owner Abe Saperstein arranged for a game between the two teams to be played at Chicago Stadium on February 19, 1948. Interest was such that the game produced a crowd of 17,823, a record for the stadium.

The Lakers held a significant height advantage, with several players taller than the Trotters' six-foot-three center Reece "Goose" Tatum. But the star of the Globetrotters was Marques Haynes, acknowledged as the world's greatest ball handler.

It became apparent early that Tatum would be no match for Mikan. The Lakers jumped to an early 9–2 lead and held a 32–23 edge at the half. Mikan had pumped in 18 points while holding Tatum scoreless. With their 103-game winning streak in jeopardy, Saperstein's men tried some new tactics in the second half. Playing a much more physical game, the Trotters held Mikan to

George Mikan (99) and the Minneapolis Lakers battle the Fort Wayne Zollner Pistons at the Minneapolis Auditorium. Mikan led the Lakers to six league championships in the NBL, BAA, and the young NBA and led the league in scoring for four seasons. In 1950, he was voted the greatest basketball player of the half century.

The Lakers won league championships in their first three years of existence. Front row, left to right: Arnie Ferrin, Kevin O'Shea, Slater Martin, and Tony Jaros; second row: Bob Harrison, Joe Hutton, Jr., Vern Mikkelsen, Ed Beach, Jim Pollard, Bud Grant, George Mikan, and Herm Schaefer.

only 6 points the rest of the way. Meanwhile, the fast-breaking Globetrotters battled back to tie the score at 42 as the third quarter ended.

With a minute and a half left, the Trotters tied the game again, 59–59, and then got the ball back. It was time for Haynes to display his talents, as the Trotters' magician kept the ball and dribbled down the clock. With seconds remaining, he flipped the ball to Ermer Robinson, who unleashed a long set shot as the final buzzer sounded. The ball swished through the basket, but did he get the shot off in time? One timer said yes, the other said no, but the final ruling went against the Lakers, and the Globetrotters had pulled out an incredible 61–59 victory.

The Lakers were the best in the NBL's Western Division, while the Rochester Royals finished 44–16 to win the Eastern Division title by two games over the Anderson Packers. Both Minneapolis and Rochester advanced to the final round of the playoffs, but the championship series was delayed, as the Lakers ac-

cepted an invitation to play in the World Professional Tournament in Chicago, which was in its tenth and final year.

The Lakers crushed the Wilkes-Barre Barons, champions of the Eastern League, 98–48 in the opening round and then squeaked by the Anderson Packers by 3 points. Their opponents in the title game would be the winner of the very first tournament in 1939, the New York Rens, an independent all-black team that was inducted as a team into the Basketball Hall of Fame in 1963. Led by Mikan, who set a tournament record with 40 points, Minneapolis defeated the Rens, 75–71, to capture the World Pro Crown.

The Lakers had one day to rest before opening their best-of-five series with Rochester at the Minneapolis Armory. The Minneapolis Auditorium, their normal home, was under contract during part of the spring for the Sportsman's Show, and the Lakers had to find another floor for the playoffs. The Armory was jammed as the Lakers took the first two games.

The series shifted to Rochester for the remaining games, and the Royals stayed alive with a 74–60 win, despite 32 points by Mikan. In Game 4 the Lakers, with no desire to face a do-or-die fifth game, grabbed an early lead and held it the entire game. Mikan scored 27, and Pollard added 19 as the Lakers, with a 75–65 win, took the NBL championship in their first year in the league.

From the NBL to the BAA
and from the BAA to the NBA

The Lakers' first year in the NBL would also be their last. The Basketball Association of America (BAA) had completed its second year of operations and controlled the large population centers and big arenas in the East. BAA president Maurice Podoloff persuaded Rochester, Fort Wayne, and the Indianapolis Kautskys—who would change their name to the Jets—to jump from the NBL to the BAA. The Lakers had little interest in making such a move initially, since they were on the verge of creating an NBL dynasty. But finally they decided that if the other top NBL teams were going to break ranks, they would join them.

Of the old BAA clubs, only the Washington Capitols, coached by Arnold "Red" Auerbach, appeared to be in the Lakers' class. With six-foot-nine Bones McKinney at center and a backcourt consisting of Bob Feerick, a superb ball handler, and hot-shooting Fred Scolari, the Capitols won their first thirteen games of the 1948–1949 season to open a big lead in the Eastern Division. Meanwhile, the Lakers fought with Rochester and the St. Louis Bombers for the top spot in the Western Division.

On November 24, Minneapolis set a single-game league scoring record when it defeated the Providence Steamrollers, 117–89. A few weeks later, Mikan scored 47 points in a game to tie another BAA mark. On January 30, 1949, he scored 48 to set a new record. That record was short-lived, however, as less than a fortnight later, Philadelphia's Joe Fulks scored 63 points in one game. Fulks and Mikan battled the rest of the season for the scoring lead, with Mikan emerging as the league champion with 28.3 points per game. Seven times during the season Mikan scored more than 40 points in a game. Twice he topped 50.

The Lakers also continued their rivalry with the Harlem Globetrotters. They were handicapped in their game at the Chicago Stadium on February 28, as both Jim Pollard and Swede Carlson were nursing injuries and missed the game. So the Trotters again roared back from a half-time deficit to win 49–45. The Trotters felt comfortable enough in the fourth quarter to perform some of their crowd-pleasing antics, including a dazzling dribbling routine by Haynes. The Lakers were at full strength for the return engagement March 14 before 10,122 fans, the largest basketball crowd ever at the Minneapolis Auditorium. This time Minneapolis rolled to a 68–53 win, and now it was the Lakers' turn to clown. Don Forman delighted the crowd with a dribbling act of his own.

The Lakers' rivalry with the Rochester Royals, their nemesis from the NBL, not only continued but intensified. Minneapolis finished with a 44–16 record, in second place in the Western Division, one game behind the Royals.

In the playoffs, the Lakers beat both the Chicago Stags and the Rochester Royals in two-game sweeps to advance to the championship, best-of-seven series against the Washington Capitols. The Lakers won the first three games but lost the next one. Mikan also chipped a bone in his right hand early in the fourth game. With Mikan in a cast, the Capitols won Game 5 to pull within one game. The Lakers rolled to an easy 77–56 win in Game 6 at the St. Paul Auditorium, however, and the defending NBL champions were now the champions of the BAA.

During the off-season, seven more teams—the Anderson Packers, Denver Nuggets, Indianapolis Olympians, Sheboygan Redskins, Syracuse Nationals, Tri-Cities Blackhawks, and Waterloo Hawks—left the NBL. This time they were not simply absorbed into the BAA; rather, the two leagues were merged into a new one, the National Basketball Association (NBA). Meanwhile, the Lakers added two more players and came back stronger than ever. They were Slater "Dugie" Martin, an outstanding playmaker, outside shooter, and defender from the University of Texas, and six-foot-seven center Vern Mikkelsen, who had earned All-America honors at Hamline.

Mikkelsen saw little playing time as an understudy to Mikan for the first third of the season. But by Christmas time, Kundla had conceived of a "double pivot" offense. He moved Mikkelsen to a forward spot, creating basketball's first "power forward." With Pollard, Mikan, and Mikkelsen, Minneapolis now had the most formidable front line in the NBA.

In 1949–1950 the Lakers played two more games against the Harlem Globetrotters and handled them easily, winning 76–60 at the Chicago Stadium in February and 69–54 at the St. Paul Auditorium the next month. But the Lakers could not shake the Rochester Royals in the new NBA Central Division. Both finished with 51–17 records, forcing a tie-breaker playoff game in Rochester. The Royals led by 6 points with three minutes to play, but the Lakers battled back and tied the score. With three seconds left, Tony Jaros let fly with a long set shot that dropped through the basket to give Minneapolis a 78–76 win.

The Lakers then won six straight games to sweep past Chicago, Fort Wayne, and Anderson in the preliminary playoff rounds and earn another berth in the championship round. In the finals, they met the Syracuse Nationals, the only team with a better winning percentage than Minneapolis. The Nationals had the home court advantage in the best-of-seven series, and the Nats were just as tough on their home court as the Lakers were. Like Minneapolis, they had lost only one game at home all year. But the Lakers would have to win at least one game in Syracuse's State Fair Coliseum if they were to retain their world title.

They got that win in the very first game, as Bob Harrison unleashed a set shot from forty feet out. The ball dropped through the basket as the buzzer sounded to give the Lakers a 68–66 win. From there, the home teams prevailed. Minneapolis held a three-game-to-two lead and had a chance to finish off the series at home in Game 6, a wild affair that featured several fights between the teams. In between the fisticuffs, Mikan connected for 40 points, while Pollard added 16 to go with 10 assists. The Lakers rolled to an easy 110–75 victory and their third consecutive championship.

With three titles in three different leagues in three years, the supremacy of the Lakers now was unquestionable. And twenty-six-year-old George Mikan, studying law in the off-season, was carrying pro basketball to new levels of prestige.

Dethroned

Following the NBA's first season, teams in three of the league's smaller cities—Sheboygan, Waterloo, and An-derson—withdrew. Denver, because of its distance to other cities in the league, also dropped out. These cities joined a new league, the National Professional Basketball League, a circuit that included the St. Paul Lights, coached by former Hamline star Howie Schultz. Like the earlier professional St. Paul team, this one was short-lived, however. The Lights folded less than two months into the season.

The 1950–1951 season marked the first time that the Lakers finished with the best record in their league. In fact, it was the first time they fashioned a better record than their archrival, the Rochester Royals. Yet this was the only season among their first seven in which they failed to win the league championship.

Mikan beat out Alex Groza and Boston's Easy Ed Macauley to win another scoring title with 1,932 points, averaging 28.4 per game. But in the second-to-last regular-season game, Mikan broke a bone in his ankle and was hobbled as the Lakers prepared for the playoffs. Still, Minneapolis got by Indianapolis, two games to one, in the opening round. Even with a broken ankle, Mikan scored 41 in the series opener, but in the second game, a 108–88 loss at Indianapolis, he was held to a career-low 2 points, as he played only fifteen minutes in the game. Mikan came back with 30 points in the final game of the series, which Minneapolis won, 85–80.

The Lakers then beat Rochester by 3 points in the opening game of the best-of-five semifinal series at the Minneapolis Armory, but they dropped the second game, 77–66. The Royals won the next two games at Rochester to take the series. Rochester went on to defeat the New York Knicks in seven games to capture their first and last NBA championship. The franchise later moved to Cincinnati, then Kansas City-Omaha, and finally to California, where they play today as the Sacramento Kings.

Three More Titles

In 1951–1952 the NBA doubled the width of the foul lane, where the three-second rule prevented an offensive player from taking a stationary position, to twelve feet. This move was aimed at big men in general—and George Mikan in particular, because Mikan did most of his scoring by setting up his pivot play as close to the basket as possible. Mikan adjusted to the new rule, although his scoring average dropped to 23.8 points per

The Big Game

Fort Wayne Zollner Pistons 19, Minneapolis Lakers 18
November 22, 1950

The 1950–1951 season was the only one of their first seven seasons in which the Minneapolis Lakers failed to win their league's championship. Yet it was in that season that they played their most famous game. It had been nearly a year since the Lakers had lost at home, so coach Murray Mendenhall and his Fort Wayne Zollner Pistons decided to try a different approach.

The tempo of the game became apparent very early. Fort Wayne controlled the opening tip, and George Mikan, flanked by Jim Pollard and Vern Mikkelsen, lumbered into defensive position. But as the trio turned around, they saw Pistons center Larry Foust standing at midcourt with the ball on his hip. And that's where Foust—and the ball—stayed. Foust was under strict orders from Mendenhall to do nothing until the Lakers came out to play man-to-man defense. The stall continued through most of the first quarter and into the second. There were brief flurries of action, however—just enough to give the Lakers a 13–11 edge at the half.

The Lakers held the lead throughout the second half, but Fort Wayne continued its tactics. Minneapolis had scored only 1 point in the fourth quarter, but it still held an 18–17 lead, as Fort Wayne inbounded the ball with nine seconds left. With six seconds on the clock, Curly Armstrong fed the ball to the breaking Foust, who tried to put one over Mikan's outstretched arms. Mikan got a piece of the ball, according to Vern Mikkelsen. But it still dropped through the hoop to give the Pistons a 19–18 lead. Minneapolis roared back down the floor, but guard Slater Martin's shot hit off the rim as the final horn went off, ending the lowest-scoring game in the history of the NBA.

After the game, sportswriter Charlie Johnson called the exhibition a "sports tragedy." But *Minneapolis Tribune* columnist Dick Cullum defended the stall as Fort Wayne's best chance to win. "Therefore, it cannot be criticized for using it," Cullum wrote. "It is a low conception of sports to say that a team's first duty is to give you a lot of senseless action instead of earnest competition."

Jim Pollard concurred. "Maybe Mendenhall was smart in not playing a regular type of game," Pollard recalled years later. "Anytime the Lakers and Pistons played an ordinary type of game, we beat them because we had that much more talent. So he decided he wanted to do something different and make it a more competitive game, and he certainly did."

"The name of the game is to win," added Mikkelsen, "particularly when you're playing on the road. That may have been the key to it. Since the game was in Minneapolis, Mendenhall had nothing to lose. After all, he wasn't alienating his fans." But alienating the fans was something that concerned NBA Commissioner Maurice Podoloff. "It seems to me that the teams showed complete disregard for the interest of the fans by the type of game they played," Podoloff said the next day.

Many people remember the shot clock being introduced shortly after this game. In reality, it was not until the 1954–1955 season, nearly four years later, that such a system was implemented. Nevertheless, it was reported that a "gentleman's agreement" was reached among NBA teams not to resort to such tactics in the future. A full-game stall was never again witnessed in the NBA, although stalling tactics remained common toward the ends of games until the shot clock was finally implemented.

game, and he failed to win the scoring title for the first time. Instead, the crown went to a young Philadelphia sharpshooter, Paul Arizin.

The Lakers were bolstered by the addition of Whitey Skoog, Minnesota's first great jump shooter, who went right from the Minnesota Gophers into the Lakers' starting lineup. The Lakers' front line all topped the 1,000-point mark, Mikkelsen and Pollard both reaching that level in the final game of the regular season. Minneapolis finished second in the West, however, with a record of 40–26, one game behind Rochester.

The Lakers easily handled Indianapolis in the open-ing playoff round, then headed to Rochester for the start of the best-of-five semifinal series against the defending NBA champion Royals. Rochester won the series opener by 10 points despite a 47-point performance by Mikan. The Lakers won Game 2 in overtime and had the road victory they needed. Back in Minneapolis, the Lakers won the third game but were tied in the closing seconds of Game 4. If they lost, they would have to go back to Rochester for the decisive fifth game. Instead, Pollard stuffed in a missed shot by Mikan with two seconds left to give Minneapolis an 82–80 win and another berth in the championship finals.

The New York Knicks, with Max Zaslofsky, Sweet-

Clyde Lovellette, who succeeded George Mikan as the Lakers' center, tries a hook shot over the Philadelphia Warriors' Neal Johnston. Lovellette scored 23 points per game in his best season and is a member of the Basketball Hall of Fame.

water Clifton, Vince Boryla, Harry "The Horse" Gallatin, Connie Simmons, Ernie Vandeweghe, and the McGuire brothers, Al and Dick, were the Lakers' opponents. The series opened at the St. Paul Auditorium, and it was Jim Pollard with the hot hand, scoring 34 points. Of more significance, however, was a basket by New York's Al McGuire that wasn't counted. Late in the first period, McGuire drove in, got off a shot, and drew a foul. But what the officials, Stan Stutz and Sid Borgia, did not see was that the shot McGuire took went in—even though ten thousand other people in the arena clearly saw it drop. The Knicks raved, coach Joe Lapchick protested the game, but the basket remained uncounted. McGuire made 1 of the 2 free throws, so the

failure of the officials to see his field goal cost the Knicks at least 1—and possibly 2—points. Those points turned out to be decisive as the game was tied at 71 at the end of regulation play. The Lakers went on to win the game in overtime, 83–79.

The teams traded wins the rest of the way, setting up a Game 7 showdown. The Lakers won the final game, 82–65, the most one-sided game of what was otherwise a nip-and-tuck series, to capture their fourth championship in five years.

In 1952–1953, the race in the Western Division again came down to a contest between Minneapolis and the old rivals from Rochester. The Lakers finished with a 48–22 record, four games ahead of the Royals, the largest margin between those two teams in their four years in the NBA. But while the Lakers cruised by Indianapolis in the first round of the Western Division playoffs, the Royals lost to Fort Wayne. The Lakers then defeated the Pistons, three games to two, in the division finals, while the Knicks again emerged victorious in the East.

New York won the first game at Minneapolis, 96–88, and nearly took the second game as well. The Lakers barely held on to salvage a 73–71 win. It was a jubilant group of Knicks that headed East for the next three games. But the Knicks would not be playing on their home court, as a circus had taken over Madison Square Garden. So they were relegated to playing those three "home" games in the five-thousand-seat Sixty-Ninth Regiment Armory.

Vince Boryla and several other Knicks boldly predicted that the series would end in New York and there would be no need for a return trip to Minneapolis. As it turned out, they were right, but not in the way they had hoped. In the third game Skoog and Harrison handcuffed Ernie Vandeweghe, while Slater Martin stuck to Dick McGuire and held the Knick playmaker to 2 points. Meanwhile, Mikan hit for 20 points, Pollard added 19, and the Lakers went one up in the series with a 90–75 win.

Game 4 came down to the wire. Mikan fouled out with under two minutes left and the score tied. But Skoog untied the score, driving and slanting through a wall of Knicks to drop in a two-pointer. A few seconds later Skoog grabbed the rebound on Jim Holstein's missed free throw, put in another field goal, and the Lakers held on to win 71–69.

There would be no trip back to Minneapolis for the Knicks, as predicted, when the Lakers also won the fifth game, 91–84. For the Lakers, this was their fifth championship in six years. Whitey Skoog, still recovering from knee surgery during the regular season, came alive in the finals. After the championship series, Joe Lapchick pointed at Skoog and said, "There's the fellow who beat us. We had no way of stopping him."

The 1953–1954 Lakers team included five players who would eventually be inducted into the Basketball Hall of Fame—George Mikan, Vern Mikkelsen, Jim Pollard, Slater Martin, and newcomer Clyde Lovellette, a six-foot-nine graduate of Kansas. Lovellette led Kansas to the NCAA championship in 1952, then spent a year in AAU competition, and now was being groomed as Mikan's successor.

During this season the Lakers took part in a game against the Milwaukee Hawks at the Minneapolis Auditorium that was played with experimental rules. The Lakers arrived home from a road trip on March 7, 1954, to find the baskets at the Auditorium two feet higher than normal. The game was to be played with twelve-foot-high baskets, and it was closely watched by many parties. The colleges were considering raising the height of the baskets—Kansas coach Phog Allen had been campaigning strenuously for such a move for many years—and were scheduled to vote on the matter in the next few weeks. A larger-than-expected crowd showed up for the game.

Advocates of raising the baskets contended that it would deprive the tall man of some of the advantage resulting from his height. Dick Cullum of the *Minneapolis Tribune* disagreed and wrote before the game, "Seems to me the higher basket will hurt the little fellow more than the tall one." Cullum proved prophetic. After the game, Mikan commented, "It just makes the big man bigger." Mikkelsen added, "It was a horrible flop. It didn't help the smaller guy. It helped me, the big, strong rebounder, because it gave me another tenth of a sec-

Slater "Dugie" Martin was a great guard out of the University of Texas. He played seven seasons for the Minneapolis Lakers, averaging about 10 points and 4 assists per game, and is now a member of the Basketball Hall of Fame.

Vern Mikkelsen spent his entire basketball career in Minnesota. He was a center at Askov High School and at Hamline University but moved to forward after he joine the Minneapolis Lakers. He played for the Lakers for ten seasons, averaging 14.4 points and 8.5 rebounds per game.

Minneapolis Lakers' Annual Record, 1947–1960

Year	Regular Season	Rank	Playoffs	Playoff Result	Coach
1947–1948	43–17	1st in Western Division	8–2	NBL Champions	John Kundla
1948–1949	44–16	2nd in West	8–2	BAA Champions	Kundla
1949–1950	51–17	1st (tie) in Central	11–2	NBA Champions	Kundla
1950–1951	44–24	1st in West	3–4	Lost Division Finals	Kundla
1951–1952	40–26	2nd in West	9–4	NBA Champions	Kundla
1952–1953	48–22	1st in West	9–3	NBA Champions	Kundla
1953–1954	46–26	1st in West	9–4	NBA Champions	Kundla
1954–1955	40–32	2nd in West	3–4	Lost Division Finals	Kundla
1955–1956	33–39	2nd (tie) in West	2–2	Lost Division Semifinals	Kundla
1956–1957	34–38	1st (tie) in West	2–4	Lost Division Finals	Kundla
1957–1958	19–53	4th in West	N/A	N/A	George Mikan; Kundla
1958–1959	33–39	2nd in West	6–7	Lost NBA Finals	Kundla
1959–1960	25–50	3rd in West	5–4	Lost Division Finals	John Castellani; Jim Pollard
Kundla Totals	466–319 (.594)		70–38 (.648)		
Lakers Totals	500–399 (.556)		75–42 (.641)		

ond to get set after a shot." The Lakers shot only 28.6 percent from the field in the game, but still managed to beat the Hawks, 65–63. Even so, the idea of higher baskets did not get rave reviews from the participants.

In that same game, an attempt was made to address another problem, that of the parades to the free throw lines that too frequently interrupted the action. In the first and third quarters of the game, no foul shots were taken during the regular playing time. Instead, they were held "in escrow" and shot at the end of the period. Like the higher baskets, this experiment was not repeated.

The Lakers finished the regular season with the NBA's best record at 46–26 and again finished four games in front

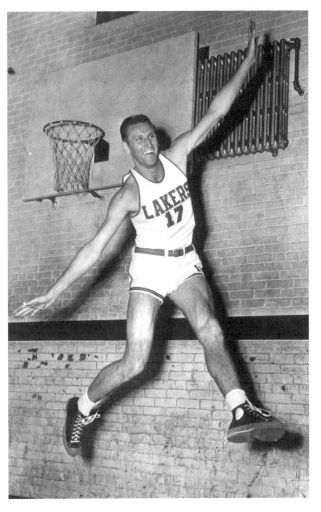

Jim Pollard was a great athlete and was known as the "Kangaroo Kid" for his leaping ability. He scored more than 13 points per game in eight seasons with the Minneapolis Lakers.

of Rochester in the Western Division. Since there were only four teams in the Western Division, the NBA tried a new playoff format. Three teams in each division advanced to the playoffs, and the three teams engaged in a round-robin series to determine two survivors in each division.

Minneapolis and Rochester were the survivors in the Western Division. The Lakers then knocked off the Royals, two games to one, to advance to the championship round against the Syracuse Nationals. It would be a rematch of the 1950 championship series for Al Cervi

and Dolph Schayes of the Nats and George Mikan, Jim Pollard, Vern Mikkelsen, and Slater Martin of the Lakers, although it would be played with different supporting casts.

The Nats entered the series without a completely healthy starting five. Playing with a cast on a broken right wrist, Dolph Schayes was in the first game for only four minutes; the Lakers won, 79–68. The second game, in Minneapolis, was televised nationally and won by Syracuse, 62–60, as the Nationals' Paul Seymour hit a shot from just beyond the midcourt line in the final seconds.

The Lakers then won two of the three games played in Syracuse and came back to the Twin Cities needing only one more win to wrap it up. But the Nats pulled another upset in Game 6. Jim "Rebel" Neal dropped a shot from twenty-seven feet out in the closing seconds to give Syracuse a 65–63 win.

There were 7,274 fans at the Minneapolis Auditorium for the seventh game, and the Lakers, behind Pollard's 21 points, got off to a fast start and cruised to an 87–80 win. The Lakers had won their sixth league championship in seven years—four in the NBA, one in the BAA, and one in the NBL.

But change was in the air.

16 *Shooting Stars of the Golden Age*

THE MINNEAPOLIS LAKERS were the greatest basketball team on the planet, and Hamline was a small college powerhouse. The Minnesota Gophers fielded two of their best teams since the 1919 national title. But when Minnesotans called the post–World War II years the golden age of Minnesota basketball, they were referring to one thing and one thing only: the state high school tournament, which was for a generation or more the most popular sporting event and the toughest ticket of any kind in the state. With the possible exception of the State Fair, more Minnesotans cared passionately about the high school tournament than any other event.

What made the tournament special was that every town had a stake in the game. In dozens of towns—including many that no longer even have a high school of their own—kids, parents, and fans could dream of being the next Gaylord, the next Lynd, the next "Hoosiers" to wear Cinderella's slipper, to win their way to "the big show" in Minneapolis and to shine the spotlight on their little town. In the first twenty years after World War II, at least three teams—Gilbert in 1951, Edgerton in 1960, and Luverne in 1964—added their names to the list of Cinderella state champs. Failing that, even a district championship would provide the thrill of a lifetime, as in Arlington (1943), Hendrum (1944), Morton (1945), Deephaven (1946), Echo (1948), East Chain (1949), Wanamingo (1952), Lamberton (1953), Hanley Falls and Starbuck (1954), Garden City (1955), Belview (1956), Olivia (1957), Jasper (1959), and Dodge Center (1960).

The popularity of the high school game was enhanced by the new styles of play. Where their father's skills and personalities were constrained by the strategies of the day, now boys and young men were able to express themselves more freely—specifically, by running, jumping, and putting the ball in the basket with vastly greater frequency than the previous generation had ever done.

The 1,000-Point Club

The first member of Minnesota's 1,000-point club was six-foot-five center Jim Korth, who led Mankato Loyola to its only state Catholic title in 1945. Korth was judged by at least one observer to be the best high school player in the state, though this was the same year that Jim McIntyre and Vern Mikkelsen completed their high school careers. This judgment surely was wrong, but not entirely without basis. McIntyre's Patrick Henry High School team lost just one game that year—to a DeLaSalle team that tied for the Catholic Conference title at 9–3 with Cretin and St. Thomas. The Islanders lost to St. Thomas in their region, and Loyola beat St. Thomas, 42–39, and Cretin, 37–31, at state, as Korth scored 54 points in the two games (76 in three). In 1949, Korth at Mankato Teachers College, like Mikkelsen at Hamline, was the starting center for a Minnesota small college conference champion.

In December 1945, George Borgerding of Belgrade became the first modern Minnesota high school player to score 50 points in a game in a 100–10 rout of Murdock. Oddly, it was the only time in three years on the Belgrade varsity that Borgerding, who later played at St. John's College, scored even 20 points. It would be more than seven years before his total of 55 points would be exceeded, though probably no one knew at the time that Jonas Holte of Starbuck had scored 58 in 1919, in a 92–2 win over Barrett.

The next 1,000-point scorer was another six-foot-five center, Dave Hegna at Granite Falls, in 1947. Hegna was Mikkelsen's backup at Hamline in 1949 and then started at center and made the all-NAIB second team for the Piper's 1951 national champions. Over the next ten years another forty-five boys scored 1,000 points or more, and 1956 saw the first and also the second 2,000 point scorer. Many of the big scorers were low post centers in the McIntyre, Korth, and Hegna mold. In 1950, it was six-foot-seven Don Dale of Robbinsdale's state runners-up and six-foot-five Pete Castle, who had led Anoka to the 1948 state tournament. In 1951, six-foot-ten Bill Simonovich of Gilbert's state champs joined the 1,000-point club. Several smallish low post centers were soon club members as well—including six-foot-three Jim Smith of Brainerd in 1951 and, in 1952, Ervin Mikkelson of Canby and Vern "Moose" Baggenstoss of Albany, both six foot two. Baggenstoss later led St. Cloud State to three Northern Intercollegiate Conference (NIC) titles and earned Little All-America honors in 1958.

Gilbert's Tom Richardson scores on a driving layup in their 69–52 win over Canby in the 1951 state title game. This was the sixth and final championship by a team from the Mesabi Iron Range in the high school tournament's single-class era.

Just so critics could not miss the emergence of the low post, Simonovich, Smith, and Mikkelson all played in the 1951 state tournament. Smith credited Whitey Skoog with teaching him the hook shot as his grade school coach (apparently while Skoog was still in high school), and Smith finished his high school career with a new state record of 1,376 points. Simonovich led his team to the state title. Mikkelson led Canby to a semifinal victory over Smith and Brainerd, but Gilbert clobbered Canby, 69–52, in the final, as Simonovich outscored Mikkelsen, 17–10. Mikkelsen was then a junior and had not yet scored 1,000 points, so the first showdown between 1,000-point scorers was still a year or two away—and nine years away in the state tournament.

Six-foot-five Bob Anderstrom led Willmar to the 1954 state tournament and then finished his career in 1955 with 1,364 points. That same year, six-foot-five Jerry Olson of Austin played in his fourth state tournament and also was the first boy of his size to play a forward spot in the tournament. His team was the first with at least two (in this case, three) boys of that size, and Olson was the more agile of the group. He finished his career with 1,014 points in the toughest conference in the state. Ron Johnson took New Prague to the state tournament in 1955 and 1956, broke most of Jim McIntyre's scoring records, and, like Mac, earned All-America honors at the University of Minnesota. He shattered the scoring record by a staggering 500 points, finishing his career with 2,190.

But not all the big scorers were centers. Neil Fedson of Lyle was an old-fashioned, smallish forward who broke Korth's career record with 1,303 points in 1949. His specialty was the old-time set shot from the corner. Six-footer Jim Akason of Halstad broke Smith's record with 1,640 points in 1952. Omar Larson of Granite Falls was one of the first great jump shooters, according to no less an authority than John Kundla, at the 1953 state tournament. He finished his career with 1,401 points.

Also in 1953 the first pair of teammates, Leroy German and Paul Olson of Madelia, reached the 1,000-point mark. In fact, both scored more than 1,200—1,277 and 1,267, to be exact—in leading Madelia to its only state tournament ever. And in 1953, another Ron Johnson brought the single game scoring mark back to Starbuck with 69 points in a 104–50 rout of Kensington.

Foley star Norm Grow's 2,852 career points remained the Minnesota boys high school record for more than twenty years, and he holds the career rebounding record to this day. He went on to a reserve role with the Minnesota Gophers.

That same year, Red Wing set a playoff record of 92 points, defeating Braham, 92–73, in a regional final. The 165 points also broke the two-team record by more than 30 points.

The Prairie Game

By 1960, membership in the 1,000-point club had almost tripled from 45 to 129. More than half of them came from small prairie towns in the western half of the state where, to be honest, the competition wasn't all that tough. An eighth or ninth grader with good athletic abilities could earn a spot on the varsity and start filling

up his résumé. Jim Akason was such a player and by the time of his senior season, he was not even regarded as the best player on Halstad's state tournament entry.

For many of the tiniest towns, where even a district title was out of the question, a high scoring individual brought notoriety to the town. In some towns 1,000-point scorers became almost routine. Brownton, Madelia, Rush City, Walnut Grove, and Wood Lake— and one larger city, Anoka—led the way with three each before the end of the 1950s. In Walnut Grove, it was Rich Wichman in 1955, Bill Nordstrom in 1957, and Jack Litfin in 1958. Nordstrom retired as the number seven scorer to that time, and he and Litfin combined to bring Walnut Grove all the way to the state semifinals in 1957. In 1961 Bruce Nordstrom made Walnut Grove the first school with four members of the 1,000-point club. Meanwhile, Ken Abram and Dick Peik, not yet 1,000-pointers, led Brownton to the 1958 state tournament in their junior seasons. In Anoka, 1957 teammates Dick Erickson and Chuck Wennerlund joined Castle in the 1,000-point club. Wennerlund went on to start at guard on Joe Hutton's last MIAC champs at Hamline in 1960.

In 1959, the first pair of brothers scored 1,000 points. Donald Frye of Cotton was the fourth boy to do it way back in 1949, and ten years later Larry finished with 1,041. The following year, Lyndon Sonju of Hawley, just a junior, joined big brother Virgil, who played at Finlayson and Kennedy, in the 1,000-point club. Another six years later, little brother Larry did the same.

One of the great early jump shooters, Jon Hagen of Belview, broke Johnson's career record by the skin of his teeth. Belview had won its only district title ever the previous year, but in 1957, Hagen's team was upset by Gibbon in the second round, 43–41. Hagen scored 32 points and broke Johnson's record by 2. He went on to play at Mankato State, where he still holds the school record with 50 points in a single game. He twice led the nation in free throw percentage and his career 90 percent is still third best all-time in the NCAA Division II. Yet he made only two of seven free throw attempts in the 2-point loss that ended his high school career.

His record of 2,192 was broken, in turn, almost as soon as it was set. Norm Grow of Foley had already become the fourth boy to score 2,000 points, and he had another season left to play. And play he did until he had scored 2,852 points, a record that would stand for both boys and girls for more than twenty years (and for the boys for more than thirty years). His record of 70 points in a single game stood as the boys record for more than forty-five years. And Grow remains to this day the number one career rebounder among Minnesota boys despite the fact that rebounds were not tabulated until his sophomore season. His final three seasons are the number one, four, and five rebounding seasons ever.

Greatest Teams of the Golden Age

It was only about this time that even the best high school teams could do it all—the low post, the jump

Ron Johnson scored a then state record of 2,190 points for New Prague High School and then earned All-America honors at the University of Minnesota in 1960.

shot, and the fast break. In 1955, one newspaper columnist asked rhetorically, concerning Minneapolis Washburn's champions: "What past champions could do more things well . . . could beat you so many different ways . . . had an answer for so many opposing moves?" Perhaps Washburn's 1955 champions would have beaten most earlier championship teams, perhaps not. But in its time, Washburn was probably only a very good team, not a great one. In part, this was the conclusion of fans who, the very next season, willingly promoted Minneapolis Roosevelt's champions in the same terms—"best ever." And who could argue the point, as the Teddies indeed put all the game's weapons on display in an unprecedented 101–54 rout of Blue Earth in the 1956 championship game?

Then, in 1961, these same fans proclaimed Duluth Central's champions "best ever," except maybe, they said, for Hopkins's 1953 team or maybe Roosevelt in 1956. Washburn had fallen from favor. By 1961, the simple ability to do a lot of different things well was taken for granted. Maybe this defined the maturity of the modern game of basketball among Minnesota high schools.

The Big Game
Edgerton 63, Richfield 60 (overtime)
March 25, 1960

Edgerton is remembered as Minnesota's "Hoosiers," as the Cinderella of Cinderellas, as the smallest school from the smallest town ever to win a Minnesota single-class state championship. It was the Flying Dutchmen, more than anyone, who put the gold in the golden age of Minnesota basketball. But in 1960 there was another story—actually, two—that since have been forgotten.

One is that Edgerton's semifinal matchup with Lake Conference powerhouse Richfield marked the first ever state tournament face-off of two members of Minnesota's 1,000-point club. Six-foot-five Bill Davis of Richfield entered the game with 1,138 points to his credit and added 28 against Edgerton and 40 in the third-place game against Granite Falls for a career total of 1,206. Four years later, he was not only a starting forward but also captain of the Minnesota Gophers. Meanwhile, Edgerton's Dean Veenhof, also six-foot-five, had already scored his 1,000th point in his junior year. He added 70 more, including 20 against Davis and Richfield and another 26 against Austin, with the state championship on the line. A year later, he finished his high school career as the (then) fifth highest all-time scorer in Minnesota with 1,887 points.

The other forgotten story is this: Edgerton was the greatest free throw machine in Minnesota high school history. "Field goals are important," read one newspaper report. "But Edgerton wins without them."

In its thrilling semifinal win over Richfield, Edgerton made just one field goal in the final eleven minutes—the fourth quarter plus overtime. Fifteen times in the game, Edgerton went to the free throw line for a one-and-one opportunity. Twelve times they came away with 2 points.

"I've never seen such free throw shooting in all my life," Davis said. Teammate Mac Lutz added, "We had to foul near the end, but we kept fouling the wrong man. They never missed."

"I kept looking at [Edgerton guards] Leroy Graphenteen and Darrell Kreun to see how nervous they were while shooting those free throws," Veenhof said. "But they never moved a muscle or batted an eye." Graphenteen later offered, however, that "I'd rather not have to shoot those free throws again."

Edgerton coach Richie Olson summed it up when he said, "[The Richfield victory] came the same way our other triumphs had—at the free throw line." Indeed, Edgerton was outscored from the field in all three of its state tournament victories. Its three opponents—Chisholm, Richfield, and Austin—scored 71 field goals, while Edgerton scored just 59, for a deficit of 24 points. But in each game they made more free throws than their opponents attempted, making 82 free throws in all while their opponents only attempted 54. Edgerton enjoyed almost a 50-point margin from the line.

And this was no accident, for the Dutchmen had done exactly the same thing in four of their six subdistrict, district, and regional games as well. Overall, in nine district, region, and state tournament games, Edgerton outscored its opponents by 44 points from the field. From the line the margin was 104.

Edgerton's 35-for-43 performance against Richfield was a near-record performance, and their 82 free throws in 116 attempts over 3 games is in fact *more than the state record*. The MSHSL record book (2005–2006 edition) inexplicably lists Hibbing's 75 free throws made in 1957 and Duluth East's 101 attempted in 1966 as the tournament records.

Darrell Kruen calmly sinks one of Edgerton's 35 free throws against Richfield in 1960. The Dutchmen made only one field goal in the game's final eleven minutes—the fourth quarter plus overtime—yet held on to win 63–60. Fifteen times in the game, Edgerton went to the free throw line for a one-and-one opportunity. Twelve times they came away with two points.

Minnesota High School 1,000-Point Club, 1945–1956

Year	Player	Total Points
1945	Jim Korth, Mankato Loyola	1,300
1947	Dave Hegna, Granite Falls	1,025
1949	Neil Fedson, Lyle	1,303
	Donald Frye, Cotton	1,087
1950	Don Dale, Robbinsdale	1,162
	Pete Castle, Anoka	1,170
1951	Jim Smith, Brainerd	1,376
	Bill Simonovich, Gilbert	1,012
	Roger Krienke, St. Paul Park	1,004
1952	Jim Akason, Halstad	1,640
	Ervin Mikkelson, Canby	1,365
	Dave Schneider, Appleton	1,105
	Vern Baggenstoss, Albany	1,011
	Ron Hood, Paynesville	1,007
1953	Jim Longlin, Marshall Central	1,510
	Omar Larson, Granite Falls	1,401
	Leroy German, Madelia	1,277
	Paul Olson, Madelia	1,267
	Neil Bennett, Walker	1,231
	Ev Christenson, New Ulm Cathedral	1,081
	Don Kuelbs, Sleepy Eye	1,051
	Leslie Trehus, Spring Grove	1,043
1954	Norris Stenson, Starbuck	1,272
	Warren Jeppeson, St. Louis Park	1,236
	Jerry Eye, Wood Lake	1,189
	Bob Robinson, Bird Island	1,182
	Milan Wehking, Buffalo Lake	1,095
	Marvin Miller, Wheaton	1,063
	Art Johnson, Thief River Falls	1,012
1955	Charles Benson, Roseau	1,607
	Bob Anderstrom, Willmar	1,364
	Sherman Moe, Ada	1,309
	Rich Wichman, Walnut Grove	1,215
	Gene Polzin, Jeffers	1,205
	Roger Krause, Ivanhoe	1,199
	Jim Colosimo, Eveleth	1,198
	Alden Kieske, Chisholm	1,081
	Jerry Olson, Austin	1,014
	Ken Schultz, Pelican Rapids	1,007
1956	Ron Johnson, New Prague	2,190
	Virgil Sonju, Finlayson, Kennedy	2,008
	Chuck Lierman, Kerkhoven	1,425
	Ron Eickoff, Wykoff	1,356
	Gene Voltz, Janesville	1,291
	Lee Hopfenspirger, Morgan	1,171
	Dwight Johnson, New London	1,033
	Warren Bloomquist, Hanska	1,031
	Jerry Olson, Glenwood	1,027

17 *The Lakers after Mikan*

FOLLOWING THE CLOSE of the 1953–1954 season, the NBA adopted two changes in the playing rules in an attempt to curb the ever-rising number of fouls. The first was a limit on the number of fouls a team could commit in any one quarter. If a team exceeded the limit, the opposing team would receive a bonus free throw. On a nonshooting foul, a team in the bonus would receive two shots instead of one; on a shooting foul calling for two shots, the shooter would have three chances to make two.

The other rule, more revolutionary, was the idea of Syracuse owner Danny Biasone—a time limit on ball possession without taking a shot at the basket. Set at twenty-four seconds, the time limit made it unnecessary for the trailing team to foul deliberately, thus eliminating the steady procession to the free throw line in the closing minutes.

Many wondered how the faster-paced game brought about by the shot clock would affect the Minneapolis Lakers and, in particular, George Mikan. Mikan, never a racehorse to begin with, was now thirty years old. The Lakers style had been a deliberate one—clearing the boards, then making their way downcourt slowly, waiting for Mikan to lumber into position.

But the question of how Mikan would react to the clock became moot on September 24, 1954. Just three days prior to the opening of the Lakers' practices, George Mikan announced his retirement. By this time, Mikan had passed the bar exam in Minnesota and planned to open his own law practice.

At the time of his retirement Mikan had scored 11,764 points as a professional, topping the next closest player, Joe Fulks, by more than 3,700 points. He led the league in scoring four times and was named to a postseason All-Star team for seven consecutive years. Mikan missed only two games in his years with the Lakers, and in 458 regular-season games he was the team's leading scorer 348 times. In 1950, the Associated Press had voted Mikan the Greatest Basketball Player of the Half Century.

Eleven days after his retirement, Mikan returned to the Lakers in a new capacity. Max Winter, wanting to concentrate on securing a professional football team for the area (he would eventually be granted the Minnesota Vikings franchise), resigned and announced that Mikan had purchased his stock and would succeed him as vice president and general manager of the Lakers.

The Lakers without Mikan were still a good though no longer a championship team. After the retirement of Jim Pollard a year later, the team began to truly decline, and even a half-season return of Mikan as a player could not stop the slide.

New Owners, a New Coach, and a New Superstar

By 1957, the future of the franchise was in doubt. With Lakers' attendance dropping at the Minneapolis Auditorium, Ben Berger was ready to sell the team to a pair of Missouri men who planned to move the Lakers to Kansas City. But local investors, headed by trucking magnate and political maverick Bob Short, were able to raise the funds necessary to buy the Lakers and keep them in Minneapolis—at least for the time being.

In addition to new owners, the Lakers had a new coach in 1957–1958, as Mikan and Johnny Kundla, the only coach the Lakers had ever had, swapped jobs. The Lakers got off to their worst start ever, losing their first seven games. In January, with the team's record at 9–30, Bob Short fired Mikan as coach and Kundla returned to his customary role.

The Lakers improved slightly, but they still ended the season at 19–53, fourteen games behind the next-worst record in the league. While the Lakers had great difficulty in beating anyone else, they still had little trouble in defeating the Harlem Globetrotters. When these exhibition contests had begun in 1948, the Globe-trotters were a legitimate challenger for the right to claim themselves as the world's greatest team. But with the integration of the NBA, the Trotters no longer had a monopoly on the best black players. Relying more and more on their comedy routines, the Globetrotters, as they do to this day, remained a great attraction.

The Lakers-Globetrotters game at Chicago Stadium on January 3, 1958, was the first meeting between these teams since 1952 and the final game of what had been a great rivalry. The Globetrotters had won the first two games they played, but the Lakers won the final six including this one, 111–100.

Having the worst record in the league gave the Lakers the top pick in the 1958 college draft. They invested the pick in Elgin Baylor, a forward from Seattle University whom John Kundla called "the greatest find since Jim Pollard."

The Lakers improved by fourteen games in 1958–1959, finishing with a record 33–39. That was good for second place in the West, although still sixteen games behind the division-champion St. Louis Hawks. The resurgence clearly was due to the spectacular play of Baylor, who missed just two games during the season. One was because of illness; the other was for an entirely different reason.

The Lakers played many games that year in neutral cities south of the Mason-Dixon line. The three black players on the team—Baylor, Boo Ellis, and Ed Fleming—were not allowed at hotels where the Lakers normally would have stayed. Bob Short insisted that the Lakers stay together on the road; the entire team would find lodging that allowed blacks. In Charleston, West Virginia, however, Baylor became upset when he was refused service at a restaurant, and as a result he would not dress for the Lakers' game that evening against Cincinnati. Without Baylor, the Lakers lost to the Rochester Royals, 95–91. The Charleston American Business Club, who had sponsored the game and had counted on Baylor as a gate attraction, asked league president Maurice Podoloff to discipline Baylor and the Lakers. Podoloff sided with the Lakers, and Bob Short stood behind Baylor. "That shows there's a guy who believes in principle," said Short of Baylor. "I don't argue with principle."

The two best teams in the NBA that year were Boston and St. Louis, and fans anticipated the third

In his rookie season of 1958–1959, Elgin Baylor helped the Minneapolis Lakers get back to the NBA finals for the first time since 1954. He had two spectacular years in Minneapolis before the team moved to Los Angeles.

straight meeting between those teams in the championship round. But the Hawks never made it to the finals. In the Western Division finals, St. Louis won two of the first three games, but the Lakers shocked the Hawks and the NBA by winning the final three games. First, the Lakers evened the series at two games apiece by winning 108–98 at home. The Hawks could not have been too concerned at that point, however. They still had the home court advantage, and they had demolished the Lakers in St. Louis, 124–90 and 127–97. Instead the Lakers won a dramatic fifth game, 98–97, in overtime. Then they won again at home, 106–104, to close out the series.

The prognosis for Minneapolis in the finals was not good. Baylor now was slowed by a severe bruise on his left knee, and the Lakers' opponent, the Boston Celtics, had won the last eighteen games between the two teams. Only a month before, in fact, the Celtics had humiliated the Lakers, 173–139, their 173 points remaining to this day the NBA record for points in a regulation game. Indeed, the Lakers could not break the Celtic hex in the playoffs. Boston swept the championship series in four games, the first time a sweep had ever occurred in the final round. This would be the first of eight straight NBA championships for the Celtics. Even so, for the Lakers there was cause for great optimism. In two of their four wins, the Celtics' margin of victory was 5 points or fewer.

The Lakers had high hopes for the coming year, but they would open the 1959–1960 season with a new leader. The day after the playoff series with Boston ended, Kundla announced his resignation to accept the head coaching job with the Minnesota Gophers. Kundla had been with the Lakers from the beginning and had compiled a 466–319 record in his eleven years as coach. In 1995 he was inducted into the Basketball Hall of Fame along with another Minnesota and Lakers legend, Vern Mikkelsen, who also retired in 1959 after ten seasons.

To succeed Kundla as coach, Short hired thirty-two-year-old John Castellani, who had been Baylor's coach at Seattle University. And there were other changes as well. The Minneapolis Auditorium had always been the Lakers' primary court, but in 1959, Short spruced up the Minneapolis Armory—adding new seats and a new floor, as well as other improvements—and the Lakers had a new home. Their first game in the renovated Armory was the season opener, a 106–105 loss to Detroit despite 52 points by Baylor. He topped that total three weeks later against Boston, as the Lakers ended their twenty-two-game losing streak, 136–113. Baylor scored 64 points to set a new league record.

But the Lakers needed more than Baylor. On January 2, 1960, the Lakers had an 11–25 record, and Castellani resigned as coach. Jim Pollard, back in the Twin Cities after coaching LaSalle College for three years, was hired to coach the Lakers the rest of the season. A little more than two weeks later, a groggy Bob Short picked up the phone around one in the morning on January 18, 1960. At the other end of the line was an official of the Civil Air Patrol. "Are you the owner of the Minneapolis Lakers?" Short was asked. "Yes." "Your plane is missing."

Lakers Narrowly Avert Disaster

The private airplane carrying the Minneapolis Lakers basketball team and several other adults and children had left Lambert Field in St. Louis the night before. The DC-3, a converted World War II cargo plane that Short had purchased for the team, had yet to reach its destination in Minneapolis and its whereabouts were unknown.

Pilot Vern Ullman, a retired Marine pilot who had seen action in both World War II and the Korean War, and copilot Harold Gifford had been watching a severe weather system, and the Lakers' departure had been delayed for several hours. Finally, at 8:30, the plane took off. As soon as they were airborne, some of the players hauled out their makeshift card table and placed it in the aisle. No sooner had the first card been dealt, however, than the lights went out. The plane's two generators had failed, and the battery was drained of its remaining power immediately. The power outage left the crew with no guidance instruments except for a compass, which soon failed as well. They were without heat, defrosters, lights, or a radio, which precluded an attempt to return to the St. Louis airport. Instead, Ullman pointed the aircraft in the general vicinity of Minneapolis and tried to climb above the storm to pick up the North Star.

It took nearly five hours for the plane to escape the storm, and it had also drifted off course. With the gauges dead, Ullman and Gifford had no way of knowing how much fuel was left. "We thought we better find a place to land," Gifford said. Through the blowing snow they could see the lights of a town—Carroll, Iowa—below. They first flew past the water tower, hoping to find the name of the city. Snow had obliterated most of the name, and all the crew could make out were the final letters, "O-L-L." They then began buzzing the town in desperate search of an airport.

Because of the frost on the windshield, Ullman and Gifford had to keep the small cockpit windows on each side open. Parts of their faces were frostbitten from sticking them out the window. The pair finally gave up hope of finding an airport and began debating their other options. They considered putting the plane down on the highway, but then they spotted a cornfield on a farm north of the city. Both Ullman and Gifford had been raised on farms and knew that a cornfield would be free of rocks and ditches. Ullman jammed his head out the side window as far as he could and began the descent. Not only did Ullman put the plane down in a perfect three-point landing, but he inadvertently hooked the tail wheel on the top strand of a barbed-wire fence. "The barbed-wire helped bring us to a stop," said Gifford. "It was just like landing on an aircraft carrier."

The passengers took a bus back to the Twin Cities the next day, but the pilots stayed behind. "They were going to have someone else fly it out," Eva Olofson, Ullman's widow, said, "but Vern wouldn't let them. He said, 'I put it in there. I'm going to take it out.'" Ullman became a folk hero of sorts to the people of Carroll, Iowa. He returned two months after his emergency landing to be the keynote speaker at the annual convention of the Flying Farmers of Iowa.

Minneapolis finished in third place with a 25–50 record; then, as always seemed the case, they came to life just in time for the playoffs. First, they upset the Detroit Pistons in the opening round. They nearly pulled off another upset of the heavily favored Hawks in the second, winning three of the first five games. But the Hawks easily won the final two games to take the series.

There was drama beyond the outcome of the games, however. Once again it began to look as though the Lakers, continuing to have attendance problems, would not be in Minneapolis much longer. The NBA had given Bob Short permission to move the Lakers. No specific city was mentioned, but it was no secret that Los Angeles was his first choice. Short had even transferred a couple of home games to Los Angeles to test the interest of West Coast fans. No official announcement regarding the team's future had been made when the season ended, but the Minneapolis fans could sense that this was the end.

About two months after their forced landing, the Minneapolis Lakers played their final game. Again they were in St. Louis, and again they lost to the powerful Hawks. The locals back home paid little attention. Their interest instead was riveted on the final game of the state high school basketball tournament, played that same evening, in which the Cinderella team from tiny Edgerton completed its season with still another upset to capture the state championship.

On April 28, it became official as Short announced he was moving the team to Los Angeles. Charlie Johnson was not shy with his opinions regarding the Lakers' failure in Minneapolis. "The downfall of the Lakers," he wrote in the *Minneapolis Tribune*, "can be summarized as follows: lack of professional leadership and management; mistakes in draft choices, trades, player deals, selection of coaches"—he was not referring to Pollard, but undoubtedly he had Castellani in mind—"and unwise expenditures; too much switching of games and far too much talk of moving." Fingers were pointed, the buck was passed, and just as anticipated, Minnesota did get major league baseball and football within the next year, but professional basketball was going to take a vacation from the Twin Cities. The winning tradition of the Lakers would continue, but Minneapolis was left behind.

Authors' Choice:
Minnesota All-Stars, 1942–1960

Center George Mikan, Minneapolis Lakers. Mikan was nicknamed "Mr. Basketball," and why not? He led the NCAA in scoring twice and won an NIT title at DePaul. Then he led three different pro leagues in scoring a total of four times while winning seven league championships in his first eight seasons as a pro. In 1950, he was voted the greatest basketball player of the half century.

Center Jim McIntyre, Minneapolis Patrick Henry High School and University of Minnesota. McIntyre was Minnesota's first great, big low post center. He rewrote the state tournament record book in leading Henry to two consecutive titles, then earned All-America honors at the U.

Forward Vern Mikkelsen, Askov High School, Hamline University, and Minneapolis Lakers. As one of the few who played high school, college, and pro ball in Minnesota, he had arguably the greatest all-Minnesota basketball career ever. He (and coach John Kundla) virtually invented the modern power forward position in supporting Mikan and the Laker dynasty.

Forward Hal Haskins, Alexandria High School and Hamline University. Haskins missed the high school tournament scoring record by 1 point, then played the "point forward" spot for Joe Hutton's Hamline dynasty. He teamed with Mikkelsen to win the 1949 NAIA national championship and holds Hamline's career scoring record to this day.

Guard Whitey Skoog, Brainerd High School, University of Minnesota, and Minneapolis Lakers. Whitey did not invent the jump shot, as has been claimed, but he was its leading practitioner in the state of Minnesota during basketball's first golden age. He was named an All-American twice at the U, then scored an average of 8 points per game (11.6 in 1955) in 341 NBA games.

SECOND TEAM *Center* Ron Johnson, New Prague High School and University of Minnesota; *center/forward* Jim Fritsche, St. Paul Humboldt High School, Hamline University, and Minneapolis Lakers; *forwards* Don "Swede" Carlson, Minneapolis Edison High School, University of Minnesota, and Minneapolis Lakers; Dick Garmaker, Hibbing High School, Hibbing Junior College, University of Minnesota, and Minneapolis Lakers; *guard* Slater Martin, Minneapolis Lakers.

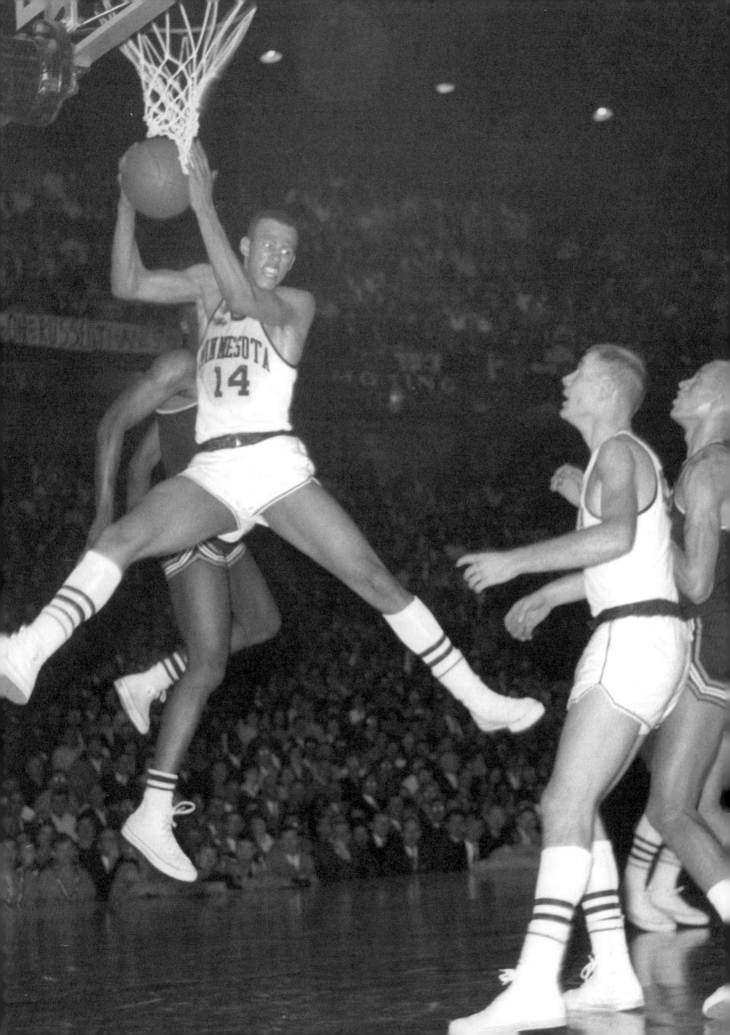

Some Are More Equal
than Others, 1960–1983

The 1960s are remembered as a time of dramatic and rapid change in America. So it was in the world of sports, including Minnesota basketball. Beginning in the 1960s and continuing for more than twenty years, change blanketed the Minnesota hoops landscape like a state tournament blizzard. And most of the changes shared one simple theme: they meant that a vastly more diverse collection of individuals would share the basketball spotlight in the Gopher state. But even if the main theme of the day was a more equal distribution of opportunity, it was true that some were more equal than others.

In other words, it was only in the mid-1970s that the most obvious of the changes—the emergence, after three-quarters of a century of disappointments, of girls and women's basketball—took place. But in the late 1960s and early 1970s, the focus was still squarely on men's and boys basketball. As the Minnesota State High School League (MSHSL) grappled with the introduction of girls sports, for example, most fans were more interested in the possibility of splitting the boys high school tournament into two classes. After forty years of debate, the tournament was finally split in 1971, giving more boys (at first) and girls (later on) the chance to showcase their skills at the statewide level. In 1975 private schools became eligible for the boys MSHSL state tournament, too.

But more important, this also was a time when black athletes first began to make a significant impact on Minnesota basketball. The Gophers program was integrated in 1962, but it would be 1976 before a mostly black high school team would win a state championship.

The controversies of the golden age had concerned the game on the court: Did the low post game represent good, winning basketball? Was the "control game" boring? Now, increasingly, the spotlight shifted off the court to administrative, regulatory, and disciplinary matters. And looming above it all was a nagging concern, expressed more openly than ever before, that maybe Minnesota basketball wasn't very good after all.

A new era in Golden Gopher basketball was launched in 1962 when coach John Kundla recruited Lou Hudson (shown here), Archie Clark, and Don Yates. They were the first blacks recruited to play basketball at Minnesota, and their recruitment also marked a transition to nationwide recruiting for the Gophers.

18 *Good, Natural Basketball Talent?*

THE STATE TOURNAMENT was the most popular and exciting event on the Minnesota sporting calendar throughout the postwar years. Of this there is no question. But how good was the caliber of play, really? This debate was joined, perhaps inadvertently, by Carleton College coach Mel Taube in 1952. Recently transplanted from basketball-mad Indiana, Taube said that Indiana kids had more poise and better ball-handling skills, though Minnesota kids were just as good as shooters.

The following year, *Minneapolis Tribune* columnist Charles Johnson wrote, "One no longer hears the cry of a few years back that Minnesota doesn't produce good natural basketball talent. This year's field was loaded with outstanding players." Well, in fact, one did continue to hear over the following decade that "Minnesota doesn't produce good, natural basketball talent." Almost annually, one newspaper columnist or another would report hearing just such talk and then would invariably quote a Minnesota college or high school coach to the contrary. They could be excused, perhaps, for thinking the debate was over, because in 1953 Minnesota basketball was still at or near a high-water mark. But shortly after Johnson's column, that wave would break. Over the following decade, the Lakers left town, Gopher and Hamline fortunes faded, and fingers would again point out a lack of homegrown talent.

By 1958 and 1959, it was noted that the state tournament suddenly lacked tall players. In 1960, the tournament was said to lack college prospects. Yet Jim Fritsche, star of the 1949 state tournament and of Hamline's last national champions in 1951 and at the time an assistant coach in the St. Paul system, said that "the

Archie Clark was a backcourt star for the Gophers' basketball team, as well as an outfielder on the Gophers' baseball team that won the NCAA championship in 1964.

present day team would win 9 out of 10 games" against teams from his day. "Better yet," he added, "make it 19 out of 20 games. That would be more like it." Why? "The game is definitely faster and the shooting improved so much." The inescapable conclusion was that the game had improved even more rapidly in neighboring states.

In 1961, Gophers assistant Bob Griggas reported that the Illinois high school tournament featured eight teams that would have won the Minnesota tournament, and forty Big Ten prospects. Minnesota had only one obvious prospect, guard Terry Kunze of Duluth Central's state champs. In 1962, Gophers coach John Kundla called for a longer high school season, protesting that "Minnesota high school basketball is just as good as that played in Illinois, Indiana and Iowa, except that those states have the jump on us starting earlier." In 1963, Kundla noted that there were "very few outstanding big seniors" in Minnesota, and in 1964, *Minneapolis Tribune* columnist Dick Cullum said there were "fewer outstanding players likely to succeed in big time basketball." So the Gophers basketball program finally arrived at the same conclusion the football program had reached five years earlier, that you could not win with homegrown talent. The Gopher hoopsters would recruit on the national market.

Things had not improved by 1969, according to new Gophers coach Bill Fitch, who said, "The first thing I've noticed about the [state high school] tournament is the lack of outside shooting. Most of the teams have tried to work the ball in close to the basket and it's hard to tell if there is a good outside shooter or not. . . . Because of the lack of a big man to control the boards, none of the teams fast break." Under Fitch and his (not quite) successor Bill Musselman, the national recruiting initiated by Kundla was continued and intensified. The immediate impact was positive. One of the greatest recruiting classes in Gophers history found its way to campus in 1962, and from 1963 through 1965, they won thirty-six games, the most ever in a two-year period. In 1972, the Maroon and Gold won their first Big Ten title in thirty-five years. But in that same year and continuing longer term, recruiting nationally would have consequences that no one could have foreseen in 1962.

To some the source of the problem seemed to be the Minnesota State High School League (MSHSL) itself. In the 1940s and early 1950s, many high schools had played up to thirty games in a season. Then, in 1958, the MSHSL dictated a maximum of sixteen regular season games. And not only would in-season play be limited, but summer camps and summertime coaching by the school staff were outlawed—all in the interest of maintaining "balance," both in student-athletes' lives and in terms of competition. Minneapolis Washburn's 1955 state champions had played summer league ball under the direction of the school's coaching staff, which, it seemed, might have given them an unfair advantage. The league's new rules drew protests. State representative Henry Basford of Wolf Lake introduced a bill into the legislature that read, in its entirety, "No public high school shall refuse to permit any student enrolled therein to compete in high school athletic events and contests because such student may have engaged in post season amateur athletic events." The bill went nowhere, though there was widespread support for its sentiment. "The State High School league dictates the athletic activities of boys throughout the summer vacation, and even after graduation, without, itself, offering any beneficial vacation program," *Minneapolis Tribune* columnist Dick Cullum wrote. "If the state league has the right to control kids during the vacation it also has the obligation to do something for them."

John Kundla Takes Charge

John Kundla, six-time world champion as coach of the Minneapolis Lakers, left the professional ranks in 1959 to return to collegiate coaching at his alma mater. The Kundla era at the University of Minnesota began with great optimism, as the 1959–1960 squad boasted three Minnesota schoolboy legends. Ron Johnson averaged 21.1 points per game in his senior season and earned All-America honors. And it was the first varsity season for Ray Cronk and Norm Grow. Cronk had scored almost 1,500 points and played in three state high school

Minnesota Mysteries and Myths
Black Basketball in a Very White State

It is no surprise that black basketball players are almost invisible in Minnesota history prior to 1962, when the University of Minnesota Gophers program became integrated. One factor is the size of the black population in the state, which increased only very slowly from 0.3 percent of the total in 1900 to about 0.5 percent in 1950. In real numbers, we're talking about black populations of 5,000 at the turn of the century and still only 15,000 in 1950. But basketball was embraced as enthusiastically by Minnesota's small black community as by the predominant white population.

Throughout those years, Minnesota's black population was very much concentrated in Minneapolis's near north side and the Rondo neighborhood of St. Paul. For many, the Phyllis Wheatley House in Minneapolis and the Hallie Q. Brown Center in St. Paul were at the heart of community life. By 1930, at the latest, boys, girls, men, and women were playing basketball in both of these community centers. Also in the 1930s, the first integrated basketball games in Minnesota—games between all-black and all-white teams—featured barnstorming black teams like the famous Harlem Globetrotters, among others. Local fives would face the Globetrotters, or in major markets "Moose Krause and His Minnesota All-Stars," "Moose Krause and the All-Minnesota Coaches," or however they would be billed on a given evening, sometimes opposed them. Duluth Teachers College appears to have upset the Trotters in a 1935 contest.

It is also likely that black teams from Wheatley and Brown played against white teams, perhaps as early as the 1930s and certainly by 1946. In 1946, an all-black team, the Negroes, played for the first time in the All-Nations Basketball Tournament. The Negroes lost to the Norse, 68–51, in the first round, as former Minneapolis Marshall and Gophers player Red Mattson scored 19 points for the Norse. No Negroes player was mentioned by name in the news report, and no mention of the game could be found in the black-run *Minneapolis Spokesman*. By 1960, at the very latest, the Brown center sponsored basketball tournaments that drew white, black, and integrated teams.

Where and when the first integrated basketball teams appeared is unknown, though one can guess that it was Minneapolis Central High School around the turn of the twentieth century. Bobby Marshall "excel[led] in sports" there, and he later played football at the University of Minnesota and pro-

For several decades, the Hallie Q. Brown and Phyllis Wheatley centers were at the heart of the black communities in St. Paul and Minneapolis, respectively, and boys and girls and men and women of all ages played basketball at both centers. Here, men's teams from the two centers are seen in action in 1958.

fessional baseball for black teams. What is not known for certain is whether Marshall played hoops at Central High.

Unlike states with larger black populations, Minnesota never had segregated schools or a black high school league. So surely there were other black players on Minnesota high school teams over the years. But, of course, their numbers were extremely small, and it is likely that racism prevented many from participating in sports and other extracurricular activities.

The first black player known today to have participated in the MSHSL state tournament was Bob Wagner of Hopkins in 1951 and 1952. Hopkins won the state championship in the latter year, and Wagner won all-tournament honors. There was not another black all-tournament player until 1965, however, when LeRoy Gardner of St. Paul Central won the honor. Jim Hill, also of St. Paul Central, was in 1967 the only other black all-tournament player before the end of the single-class era.

Given Minnesota's small black population, it is no surprise that the Gophers' first black players came from places like Ecorse, Michigan; Greensboro, North Carolina; and Uniontown, Pennsylvania. Gardner was the first Minnesota black person to win a basketball scholarship to the U, and while to-

day it may be difficult to believe, Dave Winfield, yet another St. Paul Central grad, was only the second black Minnesota native to contribute prominently to the Gophers' program.

Black players suddenly became vastly more visible with the advent of the two-class state tournament in 1971. Now Minneapolis and St. Paul schools did not have to compete with the bigger suburban schools to reach the tournament, and so more of them made it. Such players as Emanual Rogers, Minneapolis Central (1971); Randy Washburn, Minneapolis Washburn (1974); Elmer Bailey, St. Paul Mechanic Arts (1975); and Percy Wade, DeLaSalle (1975), were among eight black all-tournament players during that period.

The dam broke in 1976 when the Minneapolis Marshall-University High School boys and St. Paul Central girls both won state championships behind the exploits of Ronnie Henderson, Linda Roberts, Lisa Lissimore, and other talented black players. It was about this time that basketball, nationally, would begin to be described as "the city game," almost entirely dominated by black players. Basketball in Minnesota would never become so dominated, but black players and "the city game" were now, at last, a factor of which no fan could be unaware.

tournaments for Bemidji. He was a strong rebounder who could also score. Grow, meanwhile, had started playing on the varsity team for Foley High School when he was in eighth grade and went on to set state high school records for most points and most rebounds in a career.

Minnesota finished in a three-way tie for third place with an 8–6 record but with a disappointing overall record of 12–12.

For the first few years under Kundla, the Gophers continued to consist primarily of Minnesota players. Cronk, unfortunately, became academically ineligible during the 1960–1961 season (although he averaged better than 14 points per game in the years before and after this), and Grow was never able to get it going for the Gophers. Meanwhile, a less heralded recruit picked up some of the slack.

Coach John Kundla (center) moved over from the Minneapolis Lakers to the University of Minnesota in 1959 and is best remembered for expanding the Gophers' recruiting efforts beyond the Upper Midwest and integrating the program at the same time. He is pictured here with players Bob Jensen (left) and Bill Davis (right).

Eric Magdanz, six-foot-six forward from Minneapolis South High School, joined the varsity as a sophomore in 1960–1961 and became a regular in the lineup the following year. He capped his junior season with a record-breaking performance against Michigan in the final game of the season. Magdanz had 10 points in the first half, as the Gophers built a 19-point lead. In the second half, Minnesota held its margin as Magdanz poured in the points. With two minutes to play in the game, he connected on a jumper to give him 40 points, tying George Kline's school record. Soon after, he was fouled and went to the free throw line, where he hadn't missed all night. He remained perfect, sinking both to give him 42 points to go with 18 rebounds.

This was not, however, the biggest individual offensive performance the Gophers had seen that year. That had come five and a half weeks earlier, in a game against Indiana on January 27, 1962. The Gophers had already beaten the Hoosiers 104–100, setting a school record for the most points in a game. In the return match, at Indiana, the Gophers again scored 104 points. This time, however, it wasn't enough: an outstanding performance by Jimmy Rayl made the difference. "Rayl was built like his name—a rail," recalled Ray Christensen. "When he pulled up for a jump shot he looked like a pencil. When he was hitting, he was impossible to stop. This night he was hitting."

The game was tied, 93–93, at the end of regulation. In overtime Tom McGrann scored all 11 of the Gophers' points. His 2 free throws with seven seconds left gave him 37 points for the game and the Gophers a 1-point lead, but the Hoosiers raced back downcourt, and Rayl threw up a desperation twenty-foot jump shot that dropped through the basket as the buzzer sounded. Indiana won the game, 105–104, and Rayl finished the evening with 56 points, a new Big Ten record. Rayl made twenty baskets from the field, and Christensen estimated that "at least half his field goals were from beyond today's three-point arc, but in those days, of course, they only counted for two."

The Gophers finished in the upper half of the Big Ten standings in three of the first four years under John Kundla. But the team had yet to post an overall winning record in any of those seasons.

The Gophers Go National

That changed after Kundla and the Gophers went nationwide in their recruiting. Football star Bobby Bell had played two minutes of a Gophers basketball game in January 1961, but the program became truly integrated with the addition of three black sophomores from out of state—Archie Clark, Lou Hudson, and Don Yates—to the 1963–1964 roster.

Kundla was able to land Hudson because of his acquaintance with Horace "Bones" McKinney, who had been a star in the National Basketball Association while Kundla was coaching the Lakers. McKinney became the coach at Wake Forest University in Winston-Salem, North Carolina, and wanted to recruit Hudson from nearby Greensboro. But Wake Forest and southern colleges generally were not yet integrated. So he recommended Hudson to Kundla, who was able to recruit him.

Meanwhile, Clark was playing ball at Andrews Air Force base in Virginia, where the coach was Duluth Central and U of M graduate "Buzz" Bennett. Previously, Bennett was best remembered for inadvertently "mooning" fans at Xavier University in Cincinnati, Ohio, in the fall of 1953, when he forgot to put his game shorts on under his warm-up pants. Now he would also be remembered as the man who brought Clark and Kundla together.

Finally, Yates was discovered playing high school ball in territory that was well-known to Gophers football recruiters. Gophers All-America quarterback Sandy Stephens had previously come to Minnesota from Yates's hometown of Uniontown, Pennsylvania.

The trio had an immediate impact on the Gophers, though the squad also was bolstered by such local talent as Mel Northway, a center from Minneapolis Patrick Henry; guard Kunze; and Bill Davis of Richfield. (Clark and Davis were also members of the Gophers baseball team that won the national championship in 1964.) Hudson, Davis, Yates, Northway, Kunze, and Clark all averaged in double figures in scoring; Hudson was scoring leader, with 18.1 points per game. The Gophers finished with a 17–7 overall record, and in the Big Ten they finished at 10–4, only a game behind Big Ten cochampions Michigan and Ohio State.

All but Davis were back when the Gophers won their first four games of the 1964–1965 season and found themselves ranked fourth in the country. The team suffered a serious blow on December 15, however, when Kunze was suspended for the 1965 calendar year. A December 17 newspaper report revealed that "Dean of Students Edmund G. Williamson confirmed a report that the suspension . . . was because Kunze cheated on an exam."

In 1962, Eric Magdanz, from Minneapolis South, set a Gopher men's record that still stands—though it was later tied by Ollie Shannon—by scoring 42 points in a single game.

Kunze could have come back in January 1966 but did not. Dennis Dvoracek, a forward from Eau Claire, Wisconsin, moved into the starting lineup, and Minnesota kept winning, finishing its nonconference schedule with a record of 8–2. In the Big Ten the Gophers won eight of their first nine games. On February 23, they hosted Michigan, which was undefeated in the conference, with a chance to tie the Wolverines for the Big Ten lead. The game was tied at halftime, but All-American Cazzie Russell led a second half surge that gave Michigan a 91–78 win.

The teams met again at Michigan a week and a half later. Despite 31 points from Hudson, the Gophers lost 88–85. Minnesota then wrapped up its season with an

LeRoy Gardner from St. Paul Central was the first black Minnesotan to earn a scholarship to play basketball at the University of Minnesota.

overtime win over Iowa to finish with an 11–3 record and second place in the Big Ten. The Gophers finished in the top ten in the national polls for the first time since 1949. Their nemesis, Michigan, went on to the NCAA Final Four for the second year in a row, reaching the championship game before losing to UCLA.

The Gophers suffered their first setback of the 1965–1966 season before the first game, when Yates was de-

clared scholastically ineligible. Then, in the fourth game of the year against Creighton, Hudson was undercut and crashed to the floor, injuring his right wrist. Hudson played the rest of the game, finishing with 32 points, but X-rays after the game showed he had broken a bone in his wrist. With Hudson out of action, Clark stepped up beginning in the very next game at Detroit University. Clark was a native of Ecorse, Michigan, and with many of his family and friends in the stands, he scored 38 points in a 4-point win.

Hudson returned to the lineup in mid-January, four weeks after he had been injured, but he did not start a game until mid-February and had to play the rest of the season with his right hand and wrist in a cast. "Even though this hampered his play," Ray Christensen said, "I've often felt that the injury turned out to be a fortunate break for Hudson. It forced him to use his left hand more. Hudson was able to gather in some rebounds with his right hand and even put some shots back up with that hand, but basically he became a left-handed player, and a good one. As a result, when he went into the pros, he shot equally well with either hand and thus became virtually impossible to stop."

The Gophers finished the 1966 Big Ten season with a disappointing 7–7 record, in a fifth-place tie with Northwestern. They experienced an even bigger drop off following the graduation of Clark and Hudson, finishing 9–15 overall and 5–9 in the Big Ten during the 1966–1967 season. One bright spot that year, though,

was the play of Tom Kondla, a center from Brookfield, Illinois. As a junior, Kondla led the Big Ten in scoring, the first Gopher to do so in the modern era, with 28.3 points per game. He also was named to some All-America teams. Kondla had another great season for the Gophers in his senior year of 1967–1968, but the Gophers, with a 4–10 conference record, finished in a tie for last place in the Big Ten in what was John Kundla's last year as coach.

The Kundla era will always be remembered for the entrance of the Gophers into the national recruiting market and for the team's successful integration. Arguably, it was Kundla's leadership that provided the foundation for the Gophers' Big Ten titles of 1972 and 1982. But his own squads never quite put it together. Hudson's injury was a factor—though injuries are, of course, a natural part of the game. The academic problems of Cronk, Kunze, and Yates were perhaps more critical in keeping the Gophers from delivering on their considerable potential.

Authors' Choice:
Minnesota All-Stars, 1960–1983

Center Randy Breuer, Lake City High School, University of Minnesota, and Minnesota Timberwolves. In 1982, Breuer joined Red Wing's Dick Seebach as the only player ever to lead his high school to a state title and then the Gophers to a Big Ten title. His tournament scoring record of 113 points in three games in 1979 still stands, and later he scored 40 points in an NBA game.

Forward Kevin McHale, Hibbing High School and University of Minnesota. McHale did not enjoy the team success in high school or as a Gopher that other big men (Breuer, Olberding) did, but his Hall of Fame NBA career with the Boston Celtics is unquestionably the greatest pro career of any Minnesota native or U of M grad.

Forward Mark Olberding, Melrose High School and University of Minnesota. Arguably the best of a string of great big Minnesota high school kids in the 1970s, Big Mark set state high school tournament records (since broken) with 112 points in 1974 and 228 career points. He went on to a twelve-year professional career, scoring more than 8,000

points with an NBA high of 13.8 points per game in 1982.

Forward Lou Hudson, University of Minnesota. "Sweet Lou" scored more than 23 points per game and earned All-America honors as a junior; he then broke his wrist early in his senior season. He scored more than 20 points per game in a thirteen-year NBA career, including a high of 27 in 1973.

Guard Terry Kunze, Duluth Central High School, University of Minnesota and Minnesota Muskies. One of the quickest Minnesota high school guards before Khalid El-Amin, Kunze led Duluth Central to the 1961 state title. Unfortunately, his U of M career was cut short by academic problems. Later, he played one season as a backup guard with the Minnesota Muskies of the ABA.

SECOND TEAM *Center* Mychal Thompson, University of Minnesota; *forwards* Jim Brewer, University of Minnesota; Bill Davis, Richfield High School and University of Minnesota; Eric Magdanz, Minneapolis South High School and University of Minnesota; *guard* Archie Clark, University of Minnesota.

19 The Decline and Fall of the Single Class

THE STATE HIGH SCHOOL basketball tournament in the 1960s and early 1970s presented a variety of themes—two of which are directly contradictory to one another. The first was the dominance of the Lake Conference, encompassing the new, booming suburban communities to the south and west of Minneapolis, with its six state titles between 1959 and 1968. The smaller schools, people said, just could not compete anymore.

The second was that the smaller schools were competing as successfully as ever. Prairie Cinderellas from Edgerton, Marshall, Luverne, Sherburn, St. James, and Melrose won a remarkable six state titles in fifteen years—and wannabes from Carlton (in 1959), Danube, Cloquet, and Henning came close.

Had Carlton defeated Wayzata for the 1959 title—which they of course did not, losing, 55–41—they would have been the smallest school ever to do so. After Edgerton successfully won that distinction in 1960, Danube was the smallest school in the 1961 field. They bowed out quickly. But in 1962 they returned with tourney experience, a 22–1 record, one of Minnesota's greatest athletes ever in Bob Bruggers, and legitimate championship hopes. After a first-round win, they met favored St. Louis Park in the semis. Bruggers scored 36 points, but it wasn't enough. Park won, 66–62, then

Confetti, Cheers... And Tears

Cloquet guard Dave Meisner weeps on the shoulder of opponent John Nefstead, Marshall forward, after Marshall upset Cloquet, 75–74, in the 1963 state title game. Some fans still call it the greatest state championship final ever played.

defeated South St. Paul, 62–57, for its only state title. Bruggers completed his high school career as the second leading scorer in Minnesota high school annals with 2,364 points. He played freshman hoops at the U but concentrated on football after that, playing for the Gophers in college and the Miami Dolphins and San Diego Chargers in the pros.

That same year, it was Cloquet's turn to get some tourney experience, winning the consolation title. They came back in 1963 rated the number two team in the state. Unfortunately, they drew number one Bloomington in the first round, and nobody gave them a chance against what one scribe described as "the greatest defensive team I have ever seen." The "greatest defensive team" gave up 87 points to the Lumberjacks, who now became the favorites. Nonetheless, Marshall pulled another surprise in the final, winning, 75–74, in what some still regard as the greatest final ever. Terry Porter led Marshall with 22 points and scored 1,311 for his high school career. Then he set a St. Cloud State career scoring record (since broken) with 1,694 points.

Edgerton had provided the script for Cinderella success: make free throws. But Danube and Cloquet had missed that part of the script. Bruggers made just 10 of 23 free throw attempts in Danube's 4-point loss

Minnesota Mysteries and Myths

Minneapolis Roosevelt Not Singled Out in 1961

Minneapolis Roosevelt had cruised to the Minneapolis City, the Twin City, and the Region 5 championships with a 22–1 record in 1961, and they entered the state tournament as cofavorite with unbeaten Duluth Central. Then, just one day before the tournament began and without even a hint of prior warning, came the stunning headline, "Roosevelt Cagers Ruled Ineligible for State Tourney." This late-breaking story appeared on the front page of the *Minneapolis Tribune*. Meanwhile, on the sports page was the usual tournament preview prominently featuring the favorites from Roosevelt High.

It turned out that two of Roosevelt's deep reserves had played in DeMolay League games, and such "independent" play by varsity athletes was prohibited. As fate would have it, one of the games had been against a Mound DeMolay team, and Roosevelt had ended up playing Mound High School for the Region 5 title, winning 62–55. One of the Mound players had officiated the DeMolay game and recognized the Roosevelt boys. Fate, in fact, had to intervene twice to bring Roosevelt to its denouement. Two Mound athletes, golfer Dave Eiss and tennis player Roger Nelson, had been declared ineligible the previous spring for playing in the 1960 state DeMolay basketball tournament. But for this cruel twist of fate, Mound might not have known that the two Roosevelt players were ineligible or might have been inclined to look the other way. As it was, they filed a protest.

At 10 P.M. on the Tuesday night after the Region 5 title game—only forty hours before the opening of the state tournament—the MSHSL Board of Control convened an emergency meeting. Roosevelt coach Wayne Courtney was then notified at 1:30 A.M. Wednesday morning that his team had been barred. A coin was flipped to determine whether Mound or Royalton would be invited to represent Region 5, and the coin landed with the Royalton side up. Legend has it that Mound was not invited so that it would not benefit from its own protest, but such was not the case.

Immediately upon learning of the ban, Hennepin County district court judge Leslie Anderson ordered league officials into court to explain their decision. At the same time, two bills were introduced into the state legislature to ban league restrictions on summertime activities. Neither effort was successful. The following day, judges Anderson and Levi M. Hall ruled that the league was within its rights to bar Roosevelt from the tournament. The league, they said, could have been lenient within the law, however, and they added, "There is of course a serious question in the minds of many whether high school boys engaged in competitive sports should be precluded from Boy Scouts, church, YMCA and DeMolay games."

The league apparently felt that it could *not* be lenient, and it protested that it had tried to find a way to allow Roosevelt to compete in the state tournament. Columnist Sid Hartman quoted Kermit Alexander of the league saying, "I've never seen men try harder to find a loophole." League director B. H. Hill said that there had been twenty-five previous rulings this year and that the league could not distinguish this one case from the others just because of its unfortunate timing.

The MSHSL had banned teams from the state basketball tournament before. In 1915, the Rochester team, along with one Red Wing player, was banned because they had attended a beer bust after a game at Red Wing the weekend before the tournament. In 1917, St. Paul Humboldt got the boot because it played too many games against non-MSHSL members. And in 1928, Minneapolis South was banned for reasons that do not survive. Then in 1933, Bemidji beat Thief River Falls for the Region 8 title, but Thief protested that Bemidji had used an ineligible twenty-year-old player. The MSHSL upheld Thief's protest but found that the Prowlers also had used a twenty-year-old player. So both were banned, and Ada, winner of the third-place game, went in their place.

But the times and values were indeed changing. There is no record of any particular remorse concerning these earlier disqualifications. But now the adult leadership at the MSHSL thought the penalty in this case was unfortunate, if not unfair. So late in 1961 the penalty for this infraction was changed to disqualification of the ineligible players instead of the entire team.

---

to St. Louis Park. Cloquet, meanwhile, came into the 1963 tournament with a remarkable 53 percent field goal percentage, but the Lumberjacks barely shot free throws any better than that. They shot a mediocre 64 percent for the tournament and just 57 percent in their title game defeat. Marshall shot 68 percent in the title game and got their game-winning points when Dennis Schroeder sank a pair of free throws with 15 seconds left. Cloquet's tournament-leading scorer Mike Forrest shot just 3-of-7 in the final and 52 percent in three games. Cloquet's experience also seemed to demonstrate that it is hard to win three games in three days while running a fast-breaking offense. Lynd could not do it in 1946, Red Wing could not do it in 1953, and Cloquet appeared too exhausted to do it in 1963.

The following year, Luverne came in at 17–5 against mediocre competition, though a few fans noted that the Cardinals had won twelve straight games, ever since coach Ray Merry had inserted six-foot-five sophomore John Beyer into the starting lineup. Still, each of their three tournament victories was considered an upset. Like Marshall the year before, they had the advantage of a fatigued opponent in the final, as Rochester John Marshall needed an overtime to upset favored Edina, 76–71, in the late Friday night game. So Luverne was able to pull away from that 55–55 tie with 6:34 remaining to lead 69–59 with a minute left. The final was 72–66.

After an interregnum of five years, Sherburn, St. James, and Melrose would duplicate the success of Edgerton, Marshall, and Luverne. But first came a half-dozen years when neither the smaller schools nor almost anybody else could compete with the mighty Lake Conference. So complete was the dominance of the suburban powers that most observers were certain the smaller schools would never be able to compete again.

The Lake Takes Control

The Lake's ascendancy had been foreshadowed by Wayzata's state title in 1959 and St. Louis Park's in 1962. Then in 1965, Minnetonka got the ball rolling in earnest. As if to underscore the Lake's awesome power, 'Tonka, like Wayzata in 1959, had only finished third in the conference during the regular season. But they got hot at the right time and won all three tournament games by double-digit margins. Faribault was their final victim, 71–60.

History largely has forgotten how difficult the first championship of Edina's 1966, 1967, and 1968 three-peat was. The Hornets edged Windom, 60–59, in the first round but then needed four overtime periods to defeat Henning and Duluth East. Henning was led by the six-foot-five Peterson twins, Bob and Dick, who scored more than 3,000 points in their high school careers and finished up as the highest scoring teammates and the highest scoring pair of brothers in Minnesota history to that time. Forwards Jay Kiedrowski and Kurt Schellhas and guard Jeff Wright won all-tournament

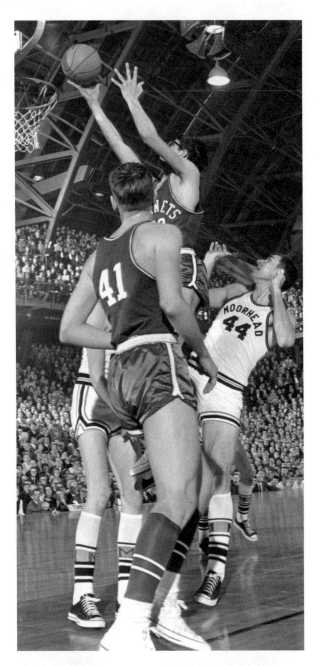

Edina center Bob Zender scores 2 of his 22 points against Rich Isaman (44) and Moorhead in the 1967 state title game. The Hornets dominated three tournament opponents by an average of more than 20 points per game and placed four players—Zender, Jay Kiedrowski (41, in foreground), Kurt Schellhas, and Jeff Wright—on the all-tourney team.

honors for Edina, and all three returned in 1967. Center Bob Zender was now the Hornets' star, however, and the second title came much more easily than the first. No Edina margin was closer than 13 points, and all four players made the all-tournament team.

Only Zender returned in 1968, but it did not matter. This time, the Hornets' closest game was a 63–49 win over Hayfield in the first round. Moorhead was vanquished in the final for the second straight year, and Zender made all-tournament for the second time.

Then in 1969, Minneapolis South shocked the District 18 and Lake Conference representative Bloomington Lincoln in the Region 5 tournament, winning for the Minneapolis City Conference its first state tournament berth in a dozen years. But the two largest schools in the field, Rochester John Marshall and Duluth Central, swept to the finals. In the seven championship-round games, not one was decided by fewer than 10 points. Rochester won the final, 58–42. Central would win its third of four state titles two years later, beating Melrose in the first two-class overall title game, 54–43.

Not only was competitive balance perceived to be a problem, but tournament attendance had dropped almost 6 percent since the high-water mark of 1962. Many reasons were advanced. One was the new competition from major league professional sports—first the Twins and Vikings in 1961, followed by NHL ice hockey and ABA basketball. No longer was the state basketball tournament almost the only game in town. And not only did professional sports compete for the sports fan's entertainment dollar, it competed for the attention of the media—newspapers, radio, and television.

Then there was the rise of the state high school hockey tournament to rival the basketball tournament as the premier high school sporting event. By 1969, the Edina-Warroad hockey final, probably the greatest hockey final ever, produced a frenzy of interest like that surrounding Edgerton's basketball title of 1960. For the first time, the hockey tournament clearly and decisively eclipsed the level of interest in the state basketball tournament.

Others blamed declining attendance on the perceived competitive imbalance—two kinds of imbalance, in fact. First was the familiar complaint that the smaller schools could not compete with the larger schools, particularly those of the Twin Cities area. Second was the imbalance in the structure of the districts and regions. A large percentage of the state's population (student or otherwise) was clustered in two of the eight regions—Regions 4 and 5 representing the Twin Cities area. The schools, after all, were grouped into regions such that approximately the same number of schools was placed in each. But the Twin Cities schools tended to be much larger on average; Region 5, in particular, had about four times the student population as, say, Region 3 or Region 6. Not that these were new complaints. Both had been heard for forty years.

The Class System

After the demise of the old Class B tournament of 1923–1927, a return to a two-class system was first proposed in 1936 but rejected by the MSHSL assembly. The following year, a slight wrinkle was proposed in hopes of generating some support: district and regional tournaments would be in two classes, but the playoffs would culminate in a single sixteen-team state tournament. This proposal was adopted, but not until sixty years later (for the Sweet Sixteen tournaments of 1995 and 1996). In 1937, it was rejected.

Not to be discouraged, partisans of a two-class tournament returned again in 1938 with a new proposal. H. B. Gough, superintendent of St. Cloud schools, suggested that big and small district champions be crowned, then combined in eight regional playoffs. The state tournament would continue to have just eight entrants. Opponents noted that a two-class tournament was "not working" in Wisconsin and other states. Proponents noted that 38 percent of Minnesota high schools had an enrollment under two hundred, and no such school had ever appeared at the state tournament. Gough's proposal was voted down every year through 1942.

Finally, in 1943, there was a breakthrough, as the assembly voted to allow each region to decide whether to have A and B district playoffs. If so, an eight-team regional tournament would follow, with one state tournament entry per region and continuing with an eight-team state tourney. Only Regions 1 and 8 ever adopted the proposal, Region 8 for its 1944 through 1946 tournaments, Region 1 in 1948.

The MSHSL refused in 1948 by a 27–5 vote to adopt a mandatory two-class tournament right through the state level. They also voted 18–14 not to mandate the two-class format through the district and region. It was not until 1955 that a Class B tourney was proposed again. This time, the assembly voted 24–8 in favor of holding a referendum of league members. Off the record, the assembly expressed confidence the proposal would be voted down. It was.

In 1957, the clamor for two classes took on a new as-

Bob Bruggers (32) of Danube scored the first basket of the 1962 state tournament and went on to score 29 points in Danube's 65–63 win over Ada. For the tournament Bruggers led all scorers with 31 points per game, still the seventh-highest average in boys tournament history.

MSHSL cannot be affected by this ruling," he wrote. "Instead, it takes one-fourth as many students in one region to send a team to the state tournament as it takes in another region."

The debate continued in 1966, and it seemed that momentum was finally on the side of change. An informal survey revealed that twenty-two of the thirty-two districts and 294 of 395 schools favored redistricting. Yet nothing happened. Newspapers made no mention of redistricting again until 1969, when the assembly voted down a proposal to redistrict based on total school enrollment rather than the number of schools.

The MSHSL seemed in 1970 to be no closer than before to making a radical change. Five different scenarios were being studied, but B. H. Hill, executive secretary of the MSHSL, said, "It will be some time before any decision is made by our committee." So it came as a shock when it was announced just a few weeks later that the 1971 tournament would feature play in two classes. Nevertheless, behind the scenes, another critical factor was at work. By the late 1960s, the growth of the hockey tournament meant that for the first time the MSHSL did not need to rely on the basketball tournament alone to support its other activities. So after forty years of debate and discussion, the climate for experimentation with the basketball tournament format was finally ripe.

The Last of the Cinderellas

Just when the idea that the smaller schools could not compete became institutionalized, the smaller schools once again competed. Sherburn reversed the recent trends in the last of the single-class tournaments. They were the antithesis of Edgerton, a tall team but one that did not bother much to work the ball inside. Instead, they embraced the jump shot and rarely got to the free throw line.

pect. Previously, support for two-class ball seemed to come primarily from the smaller schools. Now representatives of the Minneapolis and St. Paul areas joined the bandwagon for change. In 1960, for the first time in five years, a specific proposal was advanced to the MSHSL assembly. Class L would consist of the 128 largest schools organized into sixteen districts. The other 362 schools would play in thirty-two Class S districts. The two classes would still be combined in single-class regions, however. The vote on this proposal was not reported, but it was not approved.

In 1963, *Tribune* columnist Dick Cullum addressed "That Touchy Subject Again," noting the Supreme Court's "one man, one vote" ruling. "Too bad the

First, they defeated Melrose, 65–54, as Tom Mulso delighted the fans with a graceful 29-point effort. In the semis Sherburn demolished Marshall, this time with rugged Jeff McCarron leading the way with 37 points and 24 rebounds. In the final, the team from South St. Paul was of course favored. But the Packers—who twice before, in 1952 and 1962, had made it to the final without winning a championship—once again fell short. Mulso startled even himself with a 39-point effort, then the second highest total ever in any championship round game, and Sherburn won easily, 78–62. He set a record of 81 field goal attempts for the tournament that stands to this day, and he finished his high school career with 1,192 points.

Then in 1972, St. James played the role of Cinderella. In the Class A final, Melrose and St. James were nip-and-tuck throughout. Finally, it was 55–55 when Saints guard Jeff Nessler swished a desperation shot from half-court as the horn sounded. (The following year, Melrose and Mark Olberding would lose another Class A final at the buzzer, 53–52, to Chisholm.) St. James took a 20–10 first period lead in the Class A-Class AA playoff against Mounds View, then held on to win, 60–52. Nessler outscored Mounds View star Mark Landsberger 22–17 to finish his high school career with 1,239 points. He went on to a stellar small college career at Augsburg.

Mark Olberding (53) of Melrose broke two of Ron Johnson's most prominent state tournament scoring records with 112 points in 1974 and 228 points for his tournament career. After losing on a pair of buzzer-beaters in 1972 and 1973, Olberding's Flying Dutchmen took the Class A and the overall championships in his senior season.

Anoka defeated Chisholm in the 1973 playoff, but Olberding was the big story—and was again in 1974. Melrose played in their fourth straight Class A championship game in 1974, and this time they annexed both the Class A and the playoff titles. Olberding scored at least 24 points in every game over the two years and became the fourth player to twice lead the boys tournament in scoring. His 228 career points demolished Ron Johnson's career record. Olberding went on to play just one season as a Minnesota Gopher, then a dozen years in the NBA.

Finally, 1975 saw the last of the playoffs between the Class A and Class AA champions. For the second consecutive year, both champs came from central and northern parts of the state. And for the second time in three years, Chisholm was the Class A champ and was defeated in the overall final. In 1973, Anoka had defeated the Bluestreaks, 63–56, with the tallest lineup in tournament history. This time Little Falls knocked off Chisholm, 54–50.

The Return of the Big Fella in the Low Post

Along with the small-town Cinderellas, the early 1970s also saw the sudden reemergence of the big fella in the low post. Como Pontliana of Duluth Central was the first, leading the Trojans to the 1971 Class AA and overall titles by scoring 26, 34, 18, and 26 points in four victories. He then packed up his six-foot-ten frame and moved out to Colorado State on a basketball scholarship.

Next, Landsberger took the spotlight. He led Mounds View to a surprise Class AA title in 1972 and brought them back to the 1973 field as favorites for the overall crown. Instead, Anoka won the title with six-foot-eight twin towers Loren Erickson and Greg Kettler and six-foot-five forward Bryan Rohs.

Olberding dominated in 1973 and 1974, but coach Bob McDonald's son Paul (six foot five) also helped put Chisholm back on the map in 1974 and 1975. He won all-tournament honors in both years and a Class A title in 1975, finishing his high school career in 1976 with 1,425 points and 1,134 rebounds. The latter stood as a state record for twenty-three years—until it was discovered that Norm Grow had gathered in 1,417 of them almost twenty years before.

In 1975, six-foot-five Frank Wachlarowicz led the Little Falls Flyers to the state title; he scored 1,330 points in his high school career. He went on to St. John's University, where he became the top men's college scorer, at any level, in Minnesota history with 2,357 points.

In 1978, it was Jimmy Jensen of Bemidji who went absolutely wild, scoring 50 points, with 22 rebounds, in a consolation semifinal victory over Woodbury. (This tournament record stood for almost thirty years until 2006, when Cory Mountain of AlBrook scored 51 points and made 10 three-pointers, also a new record, in a first-round loss to Maranatha Christian.) Jensen finished the 1978 tournament as the fourth boy ever to score 100 points, and his 33.3 average tied Jim McIntyre's for the second best ever to that time. He also completed his high school career as the number thirteen scorer of all time with 1,763 points.

In that same tournament Randy Breuer, a seven-foot junior (who would eventually reach seven foot three) from Lake City, led the Lakers to the Class A title, scoring 68 points, including 36 in a semifinal win over Butterfield-Odin. The following year Breuer outscored Duluth Morgan Park all by himself, 42–39 in the first round—the game's score was 77–39—and then followed up with 30 and 41 more points for a tournament record 113 points that still stands. For his career Breuer

scored 1,599 points, number twenty-six on the all-time list (at that time).

The 1983 tournament matched six-foot-ten Tom Copa of Coon Rapids and seven-footer Paul Van Den Einde of Willmar. Van Den Einde won their Class AA semifinal battle, outscoring Copa, 24–23, while Coon Rapids won the war, 59–50. But there were a couple of party crashers: One was six-foot-seven Keith Hasselquist of Chisago Lakes, who tied Van Den Einde for tournament scoring honors with 72 points (Copa scored 69). The other was unbeaten but unsung Woodbury, who shocked the Cardinals, 56–50, in overtime in the final.

Bicentennial Bash

The greatest of all the two-class tournaments occurred in 1976. It is best remembered for the most anticipated matchup of big men since Bill Simonovich and Burdie Haldorson in 1951. Of even greater historical significance, however, was the emergence of Minneapolis Marshall-University as the first mostly-black state champions (in Class A).

Five-foot-six point guard Ronnie Henderson was Marshall-U's sparkplug, while Ronnie Hadley and Rodney Hargest did most of the scoring. Starters Steve Newby and Jim Ludgate also won all-state honors, making Marshall-U the only team—boys or girls—ever to place all five starters on the all-tourney team. Among the five only Ludgate was white.

Meanwhile, the 1976 Class AA final is remembered, accurately enough, as Kevin McHale's coming out. What is often forgotten is that, until this very game, it was not at all obvious that Jefferson's Steve Lingenfelter and even McHale's teammate, guard John Retica, were not better ballplayers. Lingenfelter, in fact, had badly outplayed McHale in the 1975 consolation championship game. Both Jefferson and Hibbing lost close first-round games in 1975, the Jaguars to Lake Conference rival Robbinsdale, 55–53, and the Bluejackets to eventual tournament champion Little Falls, 48–46, as Wachlarowicz outplayed McHale. Both then won fairly easily in the consolation round, setting up Jefferson's embarrassment of Hibbing, 59–35, in the consolation championship game. Retica, a six-foot-five thoroughbred with point guard skills and son of coach Mario, led all scorers in all three Hibbing games with a total of

Randy Breuer (52) was already over seven feet tall when he was in high school in Lake City, and he kept on growing. He scored a state tournament record 113 points in 1979 and then led the Minnesota Gophers to the Big Ten title in 1982. He also played eleven seasons in the NBA, including three seasons with the Minnesota Timberwolves.

66 points. Retica earned all-tournament honors, while McHale did not.

The following year, Jefferson was the clear tournament favorite, while Hibbing was no more than a toss-up to get past defending champion Little Falls, in part because Retica was playing injured. It was immediately apparent, however, that McHale was vastly improved: he led all scorers in Hibbing's 64–41 first-round rout of Minneapolis North. Then in the semifinal, McHale again led all scorers, as Hibbing came from way behind, 35–26 after three periods, to beat Falls, 41–39.

The final was like two different games. Hibbing

shocked Jefferson by winning the first half, 32–25, but the Jaguars came back to win the second half and the game, 35–19, for a final score of 60–51. It is easy to forget that Lingenfelter again outscored McHale, 26–21. But McHale set a tournament record for field goal percentage that still stands, making a remarkable twenty-seven of thirty-four attempts (79.4 percent) in three games. Never in state tournament history had two unbeatens squared off for a state title. In a final irony surrounding the MSHSL's formatting decisions, Bloomington Jefferson and Minneapolis Marshall-U were both unbeaten in 1976, but this was the first year that the Class A and Class AA champions did not play for the overall title.

Steve Lingenfelter of Bloomington Jefferson (airborne, left) and Kevin McHale of Hibbing (airborne, right) battle in the 1976 Class AA championship game. Lingenfelter outscored McHale, 26–21, and Jefferson won the title game, 60–51. It was McHale, however, who went on to a Hall of Fame career with the Minnesota Gophers and the Boston Celtics.

Minnesota State Boys High School Champions, 1961–1983

Year	Championship Game Score	W–L	Authors' Choice: Postseason MVPs
1961	Duluth Central 51 Bemidji 50 DeLaSalle 74 Duluth Cathedral 58[a] Blake 55 Concordia 49[b]	27–0	Terry Kunze, Duluth Central, G
1962	St. Louis Park 62 South St. Paul 57 DeLaSalle 67 St. Thomas 40[a] Minnehaha 44 Shattuck 43[b]	22–2	Bob Bruggers, Danube, F
1963	Marshall 75 Cloquet 74 Benilde 32 St. Thomas 29[a] Minnehaha 50 Blake 46[b]	25–1	Mike Forrest, Cloquet, F
1964	Luverne 72 Rochester John Marshall 66 Benilde 52 Austin Pacelli 49[a] Minnehaha 65 Wessington Springs (South Dakota) 42[b,c]	20–5	Greg Thone, Luverne, G
1965	Minnetonka 71 Faribault 60 Austin Pacelli 86 Winona Cotter 56[a] Blake 68 Fergus Falls Hillcrest 53[b]	22–4	Dave Lobb, Austin Pacelli, C
1966	Edina 82 Duluth East 77 (OT) Rochester Lourdes 64 DeLaSalle 43[a] Shattuck 60 Concordia 36[b]	26–0	Kurt Schellhas, Edina, F

Year	Championship Game Score	W–L	Authors' Choice: Postseason MVPs
1967	Edina 72 Moorhead 55	27–0	Jim Hill, St. Paul Central, F-G
	Rochester Lourdes 67 Cretin 64[a]		
	Edgerton SW Christian 61 Prinsburg Central Christian 51[b]		
1968	Edina 70 Moorhead 45	26–1	Bob Zender, Edina, C
	Rochester Lourdes 67 St. C. Cathedral 64[a]		
	Shattuck 86 Mayer Lutheran 68[b]		
1969	Rochester J.M. 58 Duluth Central 42	23–1	Tony Jenkins, Shattuck, C
	St. Cloud Cathedral 64 Benilde 47[a]		
	Shattuck 85 Mayer Lutheran 65[b]		
1970	Sherburn 78 South St. Paul 62	26–0	Tom Mulso, Sherburn, F
	St. Thomas 63 Benilde 38[a]		
	Shattuck 47 Minnehaha 30[b]		
1971	A Melrose 64 Red Wing 53	24–3	Como Pontliana, Duluth Central, C
	AA Duluth Central 54 North St. Paul 51		
	Duluth Central 54 Melrose 43[d]	23–1	
	Cretin 52 Shattuck 50[e]		
1972	A St. James 57 Melrose 55		Jeff Nessler, St. James, G
	AA Mounds View 62 Austin 54	21–5	
	St. James 60 Mounds View 52[d]	29–0	
	Fridley Grace 63 DeLaSalle 42[e]		
1973	A Chisholm 53 Melrose 52		Loren Erickson, Anoka, C
	AA Anoka 58 Richfield 54	27–1	
	Anoka 63 Chisholm 56[d]	24–2	
	Rochester Lourdes 47 SW MN Christian 46[e]		
1974	AA Melrose 38 Mound 32		Mark Olberding, Melrose, C
	A Bemidji 52 Richfield 50	22–3	
	Melrose 58 Bemidji 42[d]	27–0	
	Cretin 50 Rochester Lourdes 33[e]		
1975	A Chisholm 44 St. P. Mechanic Arts 33	27–1	Frank Wachlarowicz, Little Falls, C
	AA Little Falls 54 Robbinsdale 49		
	Little Falls 54 Chisholm 50[d]	26–1	
1976	A Marshall-U 64 Mankato Wilson 59 (OT)	28–0	Steve Lingenfelter, Jefferson, C
	AA Bloomington Jefferson 60 Hibbing 51	27–0	
1977	A Winona Cotter 60 Pelican Rapids 47	25–2	Brian Pederson, Prior Lake, C
	AA Prior Lake 52 Duluth Central 49	24–3	
1978	A Lake City 60 Breckenridge 44	25–1	Jimmy Jensen, Bemidji, C
	AA Prior Lake 44 St. Louis Park 33	24–1	
1979	A Lake City 63 Howard Lake-Waverly 50	26–0	Randy Breuer, Lake City, C
	AA Duluth Central 62 St. Paul Central 54	22–3	
1980	A Bird Island 78 Lk of the Woods 74 (2 OT)	23–3	Redd Overton, Mpls. North, C
	AA Mpls. North 60 St. Cloud Tech 53	23–2	
1981	A Bird Island 49 Winona Cotter 47 (2 OT)	15–10	Barry Wohler, Bird Island-Lk. Lillian, G
	AA Anoka 61 Austin 53	21–4	
1982	A Winona Cotter 48 Chisholm 46	23–2	John Lynch, Bloomington Jefferson, F
	AA Jefferson 59 Duluth East 51	23–1	
1983	A Barnum 53 Luverne 47	26–0	Bill Schiffler, Woodbury, G
	AA Woodbury 56 Coon Rapids 50 (OT)	24–0	

[a] Catholic school tournament.
[b] Independent school tournament.
[c] The independent tournament was open to a few schools from outside the state of Minnesota.
[d] Overall championship (Class A v. Class AA).
[e] Combined private, Catholic, and independent school tournament.

20 *From John Kundla to Bill Musselman*

WITH THE RETIREMENT of John Kundla, a total of five head coaches had served the Minnesota Gophers for a period of forty-one seasons. Now, counting forward from Kundla's final year, the Gophers would have five coaches over a period of just nine seasons. Succeeding Kundla was Bill Fitch, who had just come off a very successful year as head coach at Bowling Green State University. Prior to that, Fitch had spent five seasons at the University of North Dakota.

A first-class character, Fitch tried to recruit an in-state athlete, Paul Presthus of Rugby, when Fitch was at North Dakota. Presthus instead decided to attend the University of Minnesota, where he played in the front court on Kundla's final teams. When Presthus called Fitch to tell him he would be attending Minnesota, he recalled Fitch saying, "Wait a minute," and putting the receiver down. A few seconds later, Presthus heard a gunshot, and then the phone went dead.

Fitch had not killed himself but survived long enough to coach two seasons at Minnesota, with the team finishing fifth in the Big Ten each year. He then moved on to the National Basketball Association. He needed his perverse sense of humor there to keep him going as the first coach of the expansion Cleveland Cavaliers, a team that lost its first fifteen games. Fitch had more success with other teams, winning the NBA title as coach of the Boston Celtics in 1980–1981, and coached a total of twenty-five years in the league.

Fitch was succeeded by George Hanson, one of his assistants who had also played for Minnesota in the 1950s. Under Hanson, the Gophers lost their first six Big Ten games in 1971, and it did not appear that the freshman team he had recruited was going to provide much hope for the future. Hanson had given most of the scholarships available to players who had just performed in the Minnesota high

school tournament, and none of these players ever played for the Gophers varsity.

One star Hanson did have on his team that year was sophomore and Fitch recruit Jim Brewer, an outstanding rebounder from Maywood, Illinois. The team's backcourt had a pair of holdovers, Eric Hill, from Indianapolis, and Ollie Shannon, who was from Brooklyn but had played junior college ball at Metro State Junior College (now Minneapolis Community and Technical College). Shannon tied Eric Magdanz's school record by scoring 42 points in the Gophers' final home game, a 104–98 win over Wisconsin in March 1971. Even with these players Minnesota finished 11–13 overall and 5–9 in the Big Ten, and Hanson was fired as coach.

The Bill Musselman Show

The Gophers hired Cal Luther, the athletic director and basketball coach at Murray State University in Kentucky, in April. Fewer than twenty-four hours after agreeing to coach Minnesota, however, Luther changed his mind. The next day he resigned as Gophers coach, citing personal reasons. The coaching job instead went to thirty-year-old Bill Musselman, setting off a period that was as turbulent as it was exciting. Musselman had been the head coach at Ashland College, Ohio, where he stressed defense, a trait he brought to Minnesota along with a personal intensity that was soon reflected in his team.

A couple of people from Ashland accompanied him in his move to the Gophers. One was an assistant coach, Jimmy Williams, who had played for Musselman at

Dave Winfield, better known as a Hall of Fame baseball player, was invited to join the Minnesota Gophers after an assistant coach saw him playing intramural hoops. He went on to become one of the Iron Five who brought the Gophers to the 1972 Big Ten championship.

The Big Game
Ohio State 50, Minnesota Gophers 44
January 25, 1972

The Ohio State Buckeyes and Minnesota Gophers, both undefeated in Big Ten conference play, were scheduled to meet at Williams Arena on January 25, 1972. Four days earlier, at a meeting of the Rebounders Club in Columbus, Ohio, Indiana coach Bobby Knight presented Buckeye coach Fred Taylor with a mock survival kit, including earmuffs, for dealing with the frenetic atmosphere at Williams Arena. As it turned out—survival kit or not—neither Coach Taylor nor anyone else could have been prepared for what would happen that night.

The Buckeyes were led by seven-foot center Luke Witte, who was averaging more than 18 points and 15 rebounds a game, and guard Alan Hornyak, who was leading the Big Ten in scoring. In the first half, Witte was overly aggressive with his elbows when rebounding, the Gophers thought, and he went even farther at the end of the half.

The Gophers had tied the game at 23–23 with an 11–1 run. When the Buckeyes missed a last-second shot that would have given them the lead at intermission, Bob Nix of the Gophers raised his fist in jubilation. As he walked by on his way to the locker room, Witte slammed his elbow into Nix. Film replays clearly show Nix's head being jolted backward as he was hit by Witte. Ron Behagen started after Witte but was restrained before he could reach him.

Nix was the squad's only white starter and had not been well accepted by some of his teammates. A few weeks before the game, the other regulars in the lineup expressed unhappiness with Nix and a preference for another black player, Keith Young, as their point guard. Following Witte's attack, those differences were forgotten, at least momentarily.

Midway through the second half, Ohio State pulled away from the Gophers. They held a 50–44 lead with under a minute left in the game, when Witte drove in for a layup. As he went up, he was hit by Corky Taylor and Clyde Turner and knocked to the floor. Turner was called for a flagrant foul and ejected from the game, though it had been Taylor, not Turner, who had delivered a blow to Witte's head on the play.

Taylor's next blow was lower—literally and figuratively. Taylor extended a hand to help Witte up. Instead, as he pulled Witte off the floor, Taylor kneed him in the groin. Witte fell back to the floor and lay there, helplessly. Behagen, who had fouled out earlier, came off the bench and stomped on

Witte's head and neck until he was finally pushed away by Coach Taylor. Other fights broke out, and even fans got involved. Dave Winfield pummeled an Ohio State player, and another Buckeye was injured when he was slugged by a fan. When order was finally restored, athletic director Paul Giel announced he was calling off the remaining thirty-six seconds of the game. Ohio State was declared the winner. Three Buckeyes—Witte, Mark Wagar, and Mark Minor—were taken to University Hospital. Witte and Wagar were hospitalized overnight.

It was perhaps the ugliest incident in the history of Minnesota sports and one with racial overtones. Benny Allison, a black Ohio State player, said that he and black teammate Wardell Jackson thought the Gophers were trying to single out the white Ohio State players. "Wardell and I were right out in the middle of it, just like everybody else, but nobody swung on us," Allison said. "They just passed us up and went for the other guys."

Harsh words flew between Minnesota and Ohio over the next few days. Coach Taylor blamed Musselman and the Gophers' pregame routine for inciting the Gophers' players and their fans. He described the Gophers' behavior to reporters as "bush—plain bush." Witte's father—Wayne Witte, a professor at Ashland College, where Musselman previously had coached—added some strong words of his own, stating, "Musselman's intent seems to be to win at any cost. His players are brutalized and animalized to achieve that goal." Ohio governor John Gilligan chimed in with a description of the incident as a "public mugging."

The brawl became the subject of a four-page article in *Sports Illustrated* by William F. Reed, which painted a one-sided and inflammatory picture of the events. Witte's elbow to Nix at halftime, a contributing factor, was described by the article's author as an attempt by Witte to "shove the fist out of his way with the elbow" that "clipped Nix lightly on the jaw." Reed also noted a sign that Musselman had in the locker room that stated, "Defeat is worse than death because you have to live with defeat."

Giel responded with a lengthy letter to the magazine. While stating that he did not "condone the acts of physical violence and crowd reaction that led to early termination of the Ohio State-Minnesota basketball game," Giel added, "I must, however, strongly protest the reporting of William F. Reed. Any reaction from Minnesota fans in the waning moments of the game is far overshadowed by the nationwide reaction he has precipitated by his highly inflammatory rhetoric and strongly biased editorializing to the discredit and detriment

Luke Witte of Ohio State (34) and Jim Brewer of Minnesota (52) fight for a rebound in a game between the Big Ten leaders in January 1972. A bigger fight broke out in the final minute of the game with Witte receiving the worst of it. After being kneed in the groin by Minnesota's Corky Taylor, Witte was stomped by Minnesota's Ron Behagen (11).

of the university, its athletic department, its basketball program, and Coach Bill Musselman."

Minnesota suspended Taylor and Behagen indefinitely, and the Big Ten followed up by suspending them for the remainder of the season. Winfield was not suspended, to the dismay of some, including *Minneapolis Star* sports editor Max Nichols, who wrote, "He [Winfield] was only about three feet from me when he was slugging Ohio State's Mark Minor, who was on the floor. Winfield, like Behagen, had come off the bench to get in his licks. Evidently, Winfield was not on film and therefore was not 'caught.'" (Other sources claim that the player beaten by Winfield was Mark Wagar, not Mark Minor.)

Minneapolis Tribune columnist Sid Hartman, in his 1997 autobiography, revealed that he had also seen Winfield's as-

sault. "Someone from the [Big Ten] conference called and asked me about Winfield. I lied. I said, 'I didn't see Winfield hit anyone.' They did not have videotape and replay to check. So, Winfield escaped."

Three and a half years later, Musselman left the University under a cloud that, some say, has followed the Gopher men's basketball program from January 25, 1972, right up to the present day.

Ashland. Another was a player, George Schauer, who played very little for Musselman at either Ashland or Minnesota. His primary function was to lead the pregame warm-up. Musselman had started the routine, with Schauer as the centerpiece, at Ashland the year before. At Minnesota, Schauer developed a slick ball-handling and passing routine that the players participated in, an entertaining pregame show similar to that of the Harlem Globetrotters. For the introduction of the starting lineup, the lights were lowered with only a spotlight on a wooden cutout of a seventeen-foot-high Gopher. Each player emerged as he was introduced through the curtains that covered an opening in the giant Gopher.

Fans came back to Williams Arena in numbers not seen in more than a decade. By Musselman's second season, tickets were so scarce that the university showed the games on a large screen in the hockey side of the arena for fans who were unable to get seats on the basketball side.

Musselman made it clear that he had no plans for a rebuilding season. His goal was to win the Big Ten title. Joining Brewer, who would play at center, were junior college transfers Ron Behagen, Bob Nix, and Clyde Turner. Another newcomer was sophomore Keith Young. And along with Brewer, holdovers from the previous season included forward Marvin "Corky" Taylor and guard Bob Murphy. Soon after the season started, the Gophers added another player, David Winfield. Winfield had played on the freshman team two years before. He then quit basketball, other than intramural ball, to concentrate on baseball, in which he was a star both as outfielder and as pitcher. While playing intramural ball, however, he was spotted by assistant coach Williams and persuaded to join the varsity. Winfield, of course, became a baseball All-American and went on to a lengthy career in the major leagues. He was elected to the Baseball Hall of Fame in 2001.

The Gophers won six of nine nonconference games and, in the process, averaged nearly 11,000 fans at home. More than 19,000 people jammed into Williams Arena for the conference opener against Indiana, the team's first sellout in twelve years and their second-largest crowd ever at Williams. This was the first Big Ten game for Musselman and also for Bobby Knight, a longtime acquaintance of Musselman who was in his first year as head coach of Indiana. Like Musselman at Minnesota, Knight had transformed Indiana's basketball program. The Hoosiers had been picked to finish somewhere in the middle of the Big Ten standings, but with an 8–2 nonconference record they came to Minnesota ranked fifth in the entire nation.

Indiana took the lead late in the first half and held it through much of the second half. But with seventeen seconds to play, Bob Nix made 2 free throws to put Minnesota ahead 52–51. A few seconds later, Brewer blocked an Indiana shot to preserve the victory.

The Gophers won their next three games and were on top of the Big Ten. Ohio State, at 3–0, was the only other team with an undefeated conference record. The Buckeyes were ranked sixth in the nation, while the Gophers had risen to a ranking of sixteenth when Ohio State came to Minnesota for a matchup of undefeated teams. Ohio State beat the Gophers, 50–44, but the night is remembered for the horrible brawl that caused the game to be called early, with thirty-six seconds still left to play. Behagen and Taylor were suspended for the remainder of the season as a result of their roles in the brawl, and so Winfield and Keith Young moved into the starting lineup. With Turner, Brewer, and Nix, they formed the "Iron Five" that carried on for the Gophers.

Play-by-play broadcaster Ray Christensen said, "We could feel the tension as Minnesota played on the road the rest of the season. The Gophers were not popular in opposing arenas because of what had happened. I remember the fans on the road as still being very fair. The next game after the brawl was in Iowa, which could be an unfriendly place for visitors even under normal circumstances. As the Gophers came on the floor and the Iowa public-address announcer made his usual announcement, 'Let's give a warm welcome to our guests from the University of Minnesota,' the fans applauded. It was not a standing ovation by any means, but they were very polite." Minnesota won that game, along with a rematch with the Hawkeyes at Williams Arena a week later. The Gophers lost two games on the road in February, but at the end of the month they were tied with the Buckeyes for first place in the Big Ten.

On Saturday, March 4, in their final home game, the Gophers beat Illinois, while Ohio State was losing. The Gophers had clinched a tie for the Big Ten title and could capture the Big Ten championship with a win the next week at Purdue. If they lost and finished in a first-place tie, a playoff game at a neutral site would have to be held to determine the Big Ten representative to the

Jim Brewer (52) was an outstanding rebounder and an intimidating player in the low post. His number was retired by the Minnesota Gophers.

NCAA tournament. (At that time, only twenty-five conference champions went to the national tournament.)

The Gophers appeared to have the game easily in hand as they opened up a 15-point lead midway through the second half. Then, for the final eight minutes, Minnesota did not get off a shot from the field, and the Boilermakers whittled away at the lead. The Gophers finally clung to a 49–48 lead, but Purdue had the ball with thirteen seconds left. The Boilermakers got off 3 shots before time ran out; all missed the mark. The Gophers had their first outright Big Ten title since 1919 and would make their first-ever appearance in the NCAA tournament.

The Gophers did not last long, however, losing in

their first game 70–56 to the Florida State Seminoles. The loss was considered an upset, but the Seminoles made it all the way to the NCAA title game before losing to UCLA. Two days later, the Gophers beat Marquette University for third place in the Mideast Region, finally ending a tumultuous season. The tumult continued, however, as NCAA rules violations uncovered over the next few years caused Minnesota's participation in the 1972 tournament to be voided.

An Embarrassment of Riches and an Embarrassment

With Behagen and Taylor back, along with all members of the "Iron Five," Minnesota had an embarrassment of riches in 1972–1973. The Gophers had a perfect non-conference season, capped by three victories in the Far West Classic, leaving them ranked fifth in the nation. Minnesota then won ten of its first twelve conference games to put them on the verge of another Big Ten title. Their final two games were against the bottom two teams in the conference, Iowa and Northwestern. Wins in both games would clinch the championship. One win would clinch a tie and at least force a playoff for the NCAA tournament spot.

Meanwhile, Musselman was being considered for the head coaching job at the University of Florida, and he even traveled to Florida to interview for the position. Less than a week later, the Gophers faced Iowa in what was also their final home game of the season. Holding a 46–33 lead at halftime, the Gophers brought Jim Brewer back onto the court to retire his number 52. Brewer closed his remarks by saying, "I've got to get back to my teammates in the locker room, because this one isn't over yet."

Indeed, the Hawkeyes cut into the Minnesota lead throughout the second half and finally took the lead in the closing minutes. Brewer hit an outside shot to put Minnesota back up by a point, and Iowa called a time-out with thirty-six seconds to play. When play resumed, the Hawkeyes ran the clock down, looking to win on a shot in the final seconds. Guard Rick Williams spotted Iowa's seven-foot center, Kevin Kunnert, open underneath the basket. Kunnert took the pass from Williams and put up a shot, only to have it blocked by Brewer. But the ball came back down to Kunnert, who laid it in while getting fouled by Brewer with five seconds left. Kunnert

made the free throw, and Iowa pulled out a 79–77 win.

The loss to the Hawkeyes meant the Gophers would have to win at Northwestern the following Saturday to at least finish in a first-place tie. The Wildcats had won only one game all year. But the Gophers started cold in the long-range shooting department, and Northwestern built an early 14-point lead. Minnesota compounded its problems by getting into foul trouble in the second half, and the Wildcats held on to beat them 79–74. As this was happening, Indiana was winning its game against Purdue to capture the Big Ten title.

Much was made of Minnesota's final-week meltdown, including suggestions that Musselman had distracted his troops by interviewing with another school. Whatever the reason, the Gophers had let an almost-sure conference title slip away and would instead play for the first time in the National Invitation Tournament (NIT).

Brewer had 8 rebounds and blocked 6 shots as Minnesota beat Rutgers in its opening NIT game to advance to a quarterfinal game against Alabama. The Gophers built a 12-point halftime lead and led by 8 points with just over eight minutes left to play. But the Gophers went the next seven and a half minutes without scoring, while Alabama scored 16 points. With a collapse much like the one they had experienced against Iowa, the Gophers lost 69–65, ending their brief NIT run.

Musselman Rebuilds

Musselman had made it known that he did not believe in rebuilding, but that is what he did in 1973–1974. Most of the starters from the previous season had completed their college careers, and several other players chose not to return, the start of a disturbing trend of transfers, with many of them citing Musselman as their reason for leaving.

One player who left after the 1972–1973 season was Greg Olson. His departure was accompanied by a charge that Musselman had tried to punch him during a practice. Musselman downplayed the incident as a "shoving match." Then in May 1973, Olson admitted that he had twice sold the complimentary season tickets each player received for $50 a pair to Harvey Mackay, a prominent Gophers booster. The sale of these tickets for more than their face value was a violation of NCAA rules. Olson's allegations prompted an NCAA investigation, and additional allegations involving Mackay and other boosters dribbled out.

On the court, the Gophers finished the 1973–1974 season with an overall 12–12 record, 6–8 in the Big Ten, and more player transfers followed. They included Keith Young; Tommy Barker, who sometimes is noted as the Gophers' first seven-footer, although his height has often been listed by some sources, including *Total Basketball*, as six foot eleven; and Rick McCutcheon, who had started at guard and was the team's second leading scorer.

Yet the Gophers came back strong in 1974–1975. Musselman had recruited an outstanding group of freshmen, who now were eligible to play varsity ball. They included two players from the Bahamas who had played high school ball together in Miami and won the Florida state title their senior year. They were guard Osborne "Goose" Lockhart and six-foot-ten center Mike (later Mychal) Thompson.

The Gophers also had a pair of Minnesota Marks in the front court. Mark Landsberger, a standout at Mounds View High School, had transferred to Minnesota from Allan Hancock Junior College in California. He was joined by freshman Mark Olberding, who had just led Melrose to the state championship. The two were the leading scorers and rebounders for the Gophers in what would be their only season at Minnesota. The Gophers finishing the season tied for third in the Big Ten with an 11–7 record (18–8 overall).

Landsberger transferred again, this time to Arizona State, along with more players who were disillusioned playing for Musselman. Olberding left for a different reason. In July 1975, Musselman resigned to become head coach of San Diego in the American Basketball Association. The following month, Olberding signed a contract to play for Musselman on his ABA team. Although many players had left the Gophers because they had trouble dealing with Musselman, Olberding had chosen to stay close to him. "He's an excellent coach, at least college-wise," Olberding said in a 1976 interview. "In the pros, in San Diego, he stressed hard work and defense." Their time together in San Diego was brief, however, as the Sails disbanded after just eleven games. After that, Olberding's and Musselman's paths diverged.

Musselman's departure from the university followed charges by the NCAA of more than one hundred violations during Musselman's tenure. The charges, which were not made public until more than six months later, included the selling of complimentary tickets by players and improper practice sessions. The more serious charges included direct payments to players along with free airline tickets for team members and their families. Two days after resigning as Gophers head coach, Musselman admitted to the *Minneapolis Star* that he had given rent money to Ron Behagen and transportation money to Rick McCutcheon and McCutcheon's family. The charges of payments and improper aid to players extended to a number of supporters of the basketball team, most notably Mackay. On his way out of town, Musselman said, "The investigation is of the university, not a single individual. And I am no longer a member of the University of Minnesota."

21 *Small Colleges Achieve Parity*

WITH THE DEMISE of the Hamline dynasty, no fewer than seven Minnesota small colleges enjoyed their greatest success ever (to that time) over the following quarter century. Meanwhile, the Northern Intercollegiate Conference (NIC) slowly moved toward parity with the historically dominant Minnesota Intercollegiate Athletic Conference (MIAC).

The first mini-dynasty was the Duluth Branch (now the University of Minnesota Duluth [UMD]) under coach Norm Olson. The Bulldogs won four MIAC championships in five years, sandwiched around Hamline's last title in 1960. The 1958 and 1959 teams fashioned a combined record of 41–7 and defeated St. Cloud State, 71–66 and 67–65 in overtime, in the National Association of Intercollegiate Athletics (NAIA) District 13 playoffs. Dave Baker led the Bulldogs scorers in both St. Cloud games and retired in 1961 as the highest scorer in Duluth history. Bill Mattson, six-foot-seven center from Virginia, Minnesota, and UMD class of 1962, and Mike Patterson, six-foot-six forward from Mahtomedi and class of 1965, also contributed mightily to the Bulldogs' success. Both are still among the school's top five career scorers.

St. Cloud turned the tables in 1962 with a vengeance, beating Duluth 63–42. Remarkably, this was the first District 13 playoff victory ever for an NIC team. The Huskies were in the midst of winning thirteen NIC titles in fifteen years from 1956 to 1970, nine of them under coach "Red" Severson. But the 1962 squad was one of just two to make it to the NAIA tournament. The second was in 1968, when St. Cloud beat Gustavus two games to none (41–38 and 79–54) in the first best-of-three playoff. St. Cloud stars during their great fifteen-year run included Vern "Moose" Baggenstoss, six-foot-two forward from Albany, who earned Little All-America honors in 1958; six-foot-eight Izzy Schmiesing from Sauk Centre, who did the same in

St. Thomas coach Tom Feely is dwarfed by seven-foot-three center Bob Rosier. Rosier completed his career in 1974 with four straight MIAC titles and 2,133 career points, still the Tommies' record today.

132

1966; and guard Terry Porter from Marshall, who set the Huskies' career scoring record (since broken) in 1968.

In 1963, 1964, and 1965, Augsburg eliminated St. Cloud each time by 1-, 5-, and 5-point margins, respectively, behind six-foot-nine center Dan Anderson. Hailing from Portland, South Dakota, he went on to play 140 games in the ABA, scoring 12.2 points per game. The 1965 squad was one of the few Minnesota entrants to win two games at the NAIA national tournament, defeating Central Connecticut, 107–87, and Hastings, Nebraska, 66–65, before losing to unbeaten Central State, Ohio, 66–57.

St. Thomas succeeded the Duluth Branch and Augsburg as the class of the MIAC, winning seven championships (and six NAIA District 13 titles) in nine years from 1966 to 1974. The 1966 squad was the first un-

beaten MIAC champ other than Hamline since Concordia in 1931. But only the 1972 team won more than one game at the NAIA tournament, defeating Tri-State, Indiana, 78–61, as Jack Tamble scored 20 points, then Ouachita Baptist, 93–87, behind Bob Rosier's 30 points. The seven-foot-three Rosier finished his career in 1974 as the top scorer in Tommies history with 2,133 points. Also among the Tommies' top all-time scorers are Steve Fritz (class of 1971) from Rochester Lourdes and Dennis Fitzpatrick (class of 1973) from St. Thomas Academy. Coach Tom Feely was at the helm throughout this period and retired as coach in 1980 with a 417–269 record and a .608 winning percentage.

Winona State shared the NIC title (its first in eighteen years) with St. Cloud in 1968 and did the same again in 1969. The Warriors then followed up with four straight outright championships from 1972 through

Frank Wachlarowicz (shooting) led Little Falls High School to the state championship in 1975 and then led St. John's to its second and third ever MIAC titles in 1978 and 1979. He also completed his college career as Minnesota's top male scorer at any level with 2,357 career points.

1975. In 1973, as the district playoff switched to a four-team, single elimination format, they joined the Huskies as only the second NIC team to win its way to the NAIA. Herschel Lewis was the NIC MVP in 1973; Roscoe Young scored almost 25 points per game in 1974; and Gus Johnson was NIC MVP in 1975. Lewis and Johnson remain the Warriors' number three and five all-time scorers, respectively.

In 1978 and 1979, behind the exploits of six-foot-five forward Frank Wachlarowicz, St. John's won only its second and third MIAC titles. The Johnnies had had only twelve winning seasons in the previous fifty-three years—and only three in coach Jim Smith's first eleven years at the helm. But beginning with Wachlarowicz's freshman year, St. John's would enjoy fifteen consecutive winning seasons and nineteen out of twenty. Wachlarowicz completed his Johnnies' ca-

reer as the top male scorer in Minnesota college history, with 2,357 points, including 89 in his last three District 13 and NAIA tournament games. St. John's won twenty-seven games in a row before bowing to Southwest Texas, 79–75.

Finally, Moorhead State's best teams in its history went to the NAIA in 1980 and 1982. Kevin Mulder from Renville became the Dragons' all-time scoring leader (to that time) with 1,797 points, and Dave Schellhase set a record for coaching wins with 137 in an 82–75 victory over Catawba in the 1982 NAIA tournament.

By 1980, there were more competitive small college programs than ever before. But the wide distribution of the state's small college basketball talent made it difficult for MIAC and NIC teams to compete nationally. It had now been thirty years since a Minnesota team had won more than two games at the NAIA.

Minnesota Small College Men's Champions, 1961–1983

Year	District 13 Playoff Games	MIAC/NIC Winner
1961	Gustavus[a] 61 Mankato State 60	Duluth Branch (MIAC)
1962	St. Cloud State 63 Duluth Branch 42	
1963	Augsburg 56 St. Cloud State 65	
1964	Augsburg 72 Duluth Branch[a] 71	St. Cloud State (NIC)
1965	Augsburg 65 St. Cloud State 60	Moorhead State (NIC, tie)
1966	St. Thomas 50 St. Cloud State 48	
1967	St. Thomas 73 Bemidji State 64	
1968	St. Cloud State 41–79 Gustavus 38–64	Winona State (NIC, tie)
1969	St. John's 53–66 Winona State 50–61 (OT)	St. Cloud State (NIC, tie)
1970	St. Thomas 62 St. Cloud State 60 (OT)	
1971	St. Thomas 64 Augsburg[a] 63	Moorhead State (NIC)
1972	St. Thomas 66 Winona State 65 (OT)	
1973	Winona State 74 St. Thomas 70	
1974	St. Thomas 63 Winona State 53	
1975	Winona State 79 Augsburg 73	Gustavus (MIAC, tie)
1976	Gustavus[a] 64 Augsburg 60	St. Cloud State (NIC)
1977	Augsburg 97 Moorhead State[a] 76	Minnesota Morris (NIC)
1978	St. John's 98 Moorhead State[a] 85	Minnesota Morris (NIC)
1979	St. John's 84 Mankato State 82 (OT)	
1980	Moorhead State[a] 77 Mankato State[a] 58 (OT)	Augsburg (MIAC); Michigan Tech (NIC)
1981	Macalester defeated Moorhead State	St. Thomas (MIAC, tie)
1982	Moorhead State 82 Concordia 76	Minnesota Duluth (NIC, tie)
1983	St. John's[a] 84 Concordia 70	Minnesota Duluth (NIC)

Note: From 1961 to 1969, the District 13 playoff, in theory, matched the champions of the MIAC and the NIC. In practice the regular season champion or cochampion often failed to appear in the playoff final. Beginning in 1970, both the first- and second-place teams from each conference competed in the playoff, so more teams appeared in the playoff final without winning a conference title. Regular season champions who failed to make it to the playoff are identified in the third column.
[a] These teams played in the playoff final but did not win the regular season title.

22 *The Red, White, and Blue Ball*

SEVEN YEARS AFTER the Minneapolis Lakers left for Los Angeles, Minnesota had another professional basketball team. It would not compete with the likes of the Lakers, Celtics, or Knicks, however. Its opponents would be the New Jersey Americans, Anaheim Amigos, and New Orleans Buccaneers, among others.

The Minnesota Muskies became charter members of a new league when, following years of planning, the formation of the American Basketball Association (ABA) was announced in February 1967. In addition to having a team in the Twin Cities, the ABA would have its headquarters in Minneapolis, since the league had selected George Mikan, the former Minneapolis Lakers great, as its commissioner.

The ABA borrowed an idea from the defunct American Basketball League (ABL), which had operated briefly earlier in the 1960s, when it adopted a three-point field goal for shots from beyond twenty-five feet. They would also differ from the NBA with a thirty-second shot clock, rather than the NBA's twenty-four-second limit.

While it was unlikely that anyone would confuse the two leagues, just to make sure, the ABA came up with a red, white, and blue ball. "They should put that ball back on the nose of a seal where it belongs," said veteran coach Alex Hannum. This, of course, was before he left the NBA's Philadelphia 76ers and became coach of the ABA's Oakland Oaks.

The NBA still had Wilt Chamberlain, Elgin Baylor, and Oscar Robertson, but the ABA would feature stars of its own, although their biggest name would spend the first season on the bench. The ABA had persuaded Rick Barry, who had dethroned Wilt Chamberlain as the NBA scoring champion the year before, to play out his option with the San Francisco Warriors and join the new league. Even though Barry would have to sit out his option year, his signing gave the ABA credibility. Mean-while, the league could showcase another star, Connie Hawkins, of the Pittsburgh Pipers. The "Hawk" had been barred from playing in the NBA because of alleged involvement with the college betting scandals earlier in the decade. Hawkins, who had been a legend on the playgrounds of New York City, had played in the ABL and then spent some time with the Harlem Globetrotters after the ABL folded. Two other players who had been tainted by the betting scandals and not allowed in the NBA, Roger Brown and Doug Moe, also hooked up with the ABA.

The Muskies made headlines in the spring of 1967 when they signed Lou Hudson, who had averaged 18.4 points per game during his rookie year with the NBA St. Louis Hawks. Hudson had starred for three years at the University of Minnesota and was an All-American in 1965. Unfortunately, Hudson also signed a contract to play another season with the Hawks, and the courts enjoined him from performing in Minnesota.

They might have missed on Hudson, but the Muskies landed a legitimate star in Mel Daniels, one of the most sought-after players coming out of college that year. Daniels, a six-foot-ten center who had set several scoring records at the University of New Mexico, was the Muskies' first pick in the college draft. Daniels was also a first-round choice of the NBA Cincinnati Royals, but Minnesota won the bidding war, and Daniels became a Muskie.

The Muskies' home was the recently built Metropolitan Sports Center in Bloomington, which they shared with the Minnesota North Stars, who were beginning their first season in the National Hockey League. The Muskies opened the season at home against the Kentucky Colonels on October 22, 1967. An impressive crowd—8,104—turned out as the Muskies fell to the Colonels, 104–96. A month later, the Muskies drew nearly eight thousand in a win over the Indiana Pacers, a matchup of the top two teams in the Eastern Division at that time, but attendance figures at other Muskies home games more commonly hovered between one and two thousand.

Despite performing before a sea of empty green, gold, and white seats at the Met Sports Center, the Muskies, coached by former Lakers star Jim Pollard, kept winning. But the Pittsburgh Pipers, after a slow start, got hot and took over first place in the division, finishing the regular season four games ahead of Minnesota. The Muskies, at 50–28, had the league's second-best record. Mel Daniels led the league with 15.6 rebounds per game and was named the ABA Rookie of the Year.

Their first playoff opponent would be either Kentucky or New Jersey, starting on March 24. The Colo-

nels and the Americans had finished in a fourth-place tie and were to meet in a tie-breaker game for the final playoff spot. The game was to be played at an ancient arena in Commack, New York, since the Americans' regular arena was unavailable. But it was discovered that the arena floor was marred by breaks and holes and was deemed unfit to play.

Assistant commissioner Lee Meade said that both teams agreed to move the tie-breaker game to the Met Sports Center and that, if New Jersey won, all playoff games with the Muskies would be played in Minnesota. The Colonels arrived in Minnesota at five o'clock

Ron Perry sets a pick for Don Freeman in an ABA game at the Met Sports Center. The Minnesota Muskies played in front of mostly empty seats and moved to Florida after one season. Their successors, the Minnesota Pipers, didn't do any better and also left after only one year of play.

Sunday morning expecting to play New Jersey that afternoon. Commissioner Mikan, however, had already forfeited the tie-breaker game to Kentucky, who now would be playing the Muskies in the opening round of the playoffs. A bitter Art Brown, the Americans' owner, said he would file suit to have the ABA playoffs declared illegal. He did not follow through on that threat but later said he would seek Mikan's ouster as commissioner.

The Muskies beat Kentucky but then fell in the division finals to Pittsburgh. The series against the Pipers also marked the Muskies' final games representing Minnesota. Despite being the second-best team in the league, the Muskies averaged only 2,400 fans per game. The league average was barely four hundred fans per game more than that, but, even so, the team moved south and became the Miami Floridians for the 1968–1969 season.

The ABA felt compelled to maintain a team in the Twin Cities, however, since the league was headquartered in Minneapolis. The void was filled on June 28, 1968, when Gabe Rubin, owner of the Pittsburgh Pipers, announced he was moving the team to Minnesota. Rubin remained chairman of the board and continued to operate the team even though he sold a controlling interest in the club to Bill Erickson, a Northfield, Minnesota, lawyer and former legal counsel for the ABA. Vern Mikkelsen, another former Lakers star who had served as general manager of the Muskies in its final month, was hired to perform the same job with the Pipers.

The Pipers, like the Muskies, had played before a near-empty arena in Pittsburgh even though they had won the ABA title and produced the league MVP in Connie Hawkins. They would open the season in Minnesota with a new leader. Vince Cazzetta, who had coached the Pipers to the championship, resigned after Erickson and Rubin refused to give him a raise to cover moving his wife and six children to the Twin Cities. Hired to replace Cazzetta was thirty-nine-year old Jim Harding, who had compiled a 93–28 record in five seasons at LaSalle College in Philadelphia. Harding had been equally successful in coaching tenures at two other colleges, but he left behind a trail of NCAA violations and endless turmoil, the latter a pattern that followed him to the professional ranks.

In an attempt to establish regional support, a deci-

sion was made for the Pipers to play only twenty-five of their thirty-nine home games at the Met Sports Center. Ten games were to be played in Duluth, and the remaining four were to be scheduled in other Upper Midwest locations. The experiment was aborted, however, when the team averaged barely 1,500 fans in eight games at the Duluth Arena. The remaining two games scheduled for Duluth were instead played at the Minneapolis Armory and the St. Paul Auditorium, and no games ever did take place other than in the Twin Cities and Duluth.

The crowds at the Met Sports Center were barely any larger. Only 1,943 showed up to watch the Pipers crush Miami, 126–94, in the season opener. Led by Hawkins, the Pipers jumped to the top of the Eastern Division standings and opened up a comfortable lead over the second-place Floridians. On November 27, Hawkins set an ABA record with 57 points in a 110–101 win over the New York Nets. Eight days later he poured in 53 against the Denver Rockets to raise his season average to 34.4.

Finally available to play in the ABA, Rick Barry was performing similar heroics as he led the Oakland Oaks, who had been the league's worst team the year before, to a 16–2 start. The Oaks would eventually win their division by fourteen games. Barry and Hawkins were battling for the league scoring lead, and fans were looking forward to the first head-to-head meeting of these stars, scheduled for December 13 in Oakland. Two nights before, however, Hawkins ruptured a blood vessel in his arm and sat out the Oakland game. With Hawkins on the bench, the Pipers blew an 8-point lead in the closing minutes and lost, 127–122. Barry scored 45 for the Oaks, but this would be his only appearance of the season against the Pipers. Injuries shelved Barry for a significant part of the season, and the much-heralded matchup between Barry and Hawkins never materialized.

Hawkins remained out of the lineup for a week, but in the meantime the team found itself dealing with a problem that had been brewing all season. Tension between Harding and the players came to a head after an altercation between the coach and center Tom Hoover. Unhappy that the incident was reported in the newspapers, Harding ordered his players not to talk to sportswriters and closed all practices to the press. The Minnesota management, in turn, refused to back Harding, and all restrictions on the press were lifted.

During the next week, Harding began experiencing chest pains and underwent an electrocardiogram. Just before the team was to fly to Houston for a December 20 game, it was announced that Harding would not be making the trip. Concerned by the coach's chest pains and dangerously high blood pressure, doctors ordered Harding to take an indefinite leave of absence.

Mikkelsen assumed the coaching duties in the interim. The Pipers won only six of thirteen during that time but still maintained the lead in the division. Originally, Harding was to be gone for six weeks, and the Pipers said Mikkelsen would take his place as coach of the East squad in the all-star game. Harding, however, returned three weeks early and was back on the bench in mid-January.

Only three days after Harding's return, though, disaster struck. Hawkins suffered a cartilage lock in his right knee in practice. He sat out the game the following night but was back in the lineup against Oakland two days later. Early in the second half, Hawkins had already scored 21 points. But a few minutes later, he came down with a rebound, and his knee locked again. This time the injury required surgery, and Hawkins missed the next twenty-five games, including the all-star game.

Art Heyman, nursing a groin injury, also missed his chance to play for the Eastern All-Stars. The Pipers representatives for the game instead were Tom Washington and Charlie Williams, as well as Coach Harding. Harding was angered, however, by Washington's and Williams's absence at a banquet the night before the all-star game and attempted to fine them $500 each. His anger increased when he was overruled by team officials, and he sought out part-owner Rubin. The result was a bloody midnight confrontation that left Rubin with a welt on his temple and Harding with a scratched face. Harding was immediately relieved of his All-Star duties by Commissioner Mikan. Two days later, he was fired as coach of the Pipers.

Verl "Gus" Young, the team's director of special promotions and a former coach at Gustavus Adolphus, replaced Harding. Without Hawkins, though, the team lost five of its first six under Young. By the middle of February, they had been knocked out of first place, relinquishing the top spot for the first time that season. They made a couple of forays back into first, but the slide continued even after Hawkins's return. They finished in fourth place with a 36–42 record. They were then eliminated in the opening round of the playoffs by the former Minnesota Muskies, now the Floridians, four games to three.

The Pipers suffered equally at the gate, averaging only 2,300 fans per game despite reducing the ticket prices to only $2.00 a game with five weeks left in the season. Even promotions through supermarkets, at which fans could purchase two tickets for 29 cents, failed to fill the seats.

The Pipers and the entire league had been hurt by the injuries to Hawkins and Barry that prevented the two from appearing against each other. Still, there was hope for the future, as the ABA teams banded together in an attempt to lure UCLA star Lew Alcindor (who later became Kareem Abdul-Jabbar) for the following season. Erickson, anticipating the huge crowds that would flock to see Alcindor, even announced that the Pipers would stay in Minnesota if the ABA could acquire him. Five days later, Alcindor announced that he was signing with the NBA Milwaukee Bucks, despite a claim by Mikan that the ABA had offered him a five-year, $3.25 million contract to play for the New York Nets (formerly the New Jersey Americans) of the ABA.

The failure to land Alcindor prompted a disillusioned Erickson to leave the sport. The ABA over time lured other young stars away from the NBA, including Julius Erving, Spencer Haywood, Artis Gilmore, George McGinnis, and David Thompson, and after the 1975–1976 season, the four leading ABA teams—the Denver Nuggets, Indiana Pacers, New York Nets, and San Antonio Spurs—were absorbed by the NBA.

The Pipers were sold to an eastern group who moved the team back to Pittsburgh for the 1969–1970 season. Both of Minnesota's former ABA teams disbanded in 1972 without ever again posting a winning record.

23 The Triumphs and Trials of Jim Dutcher

When Bill Musselman left his post as Minnesota Gophers head basketball coach in July 1975, he left his successor the double whammy of sharply higher expectations and an NCAA investigation that would make it fiendishly difficult to meet those expectations. About three weeks after Musselman's resignation, Jim Dutcher became that successor. Dutcher had been an assistant coach for the Michigan Wolverines for the past three seasons and head coach at Eastern Michigan University for six years before that. He would serve the university for almost eleven years. During that time he produced perhaps the Gophers' greatest achievement since the 1919 national championship: the 1982 Big Ten title, untainted (unlike the 1972 and 1997 conference championships) by scandal. Unfortunately, his tenure is also remembered for a pair of scandals that were not Dutcher's own doing.

On the very day Dutcher was hired, Tommy Barker—once known as the Gophers' first seven-footer, but now just another kid from out of town who had bailed out of Musselman's program—charged that Musselman had given him money in an attempt to lure him back to Minnesota. On the previous day, Mark Olberding had signed a professional contract to play for Musselman and the San Diego Sails. Along with Musselman and Olberding, star forward Mark Landsberger was

Jim Dutcher (right) took over a scandal-ridden program in 1975 and coached the Minnesota Gophers to their only Big Ten Conference title untainted by scandal since 1937. Assistant coach Terry Kunze (left) led Duluth Central to the state high school championship in 1961 and started for the Gophers in the 1960s.

also gone, having transferred to Arizona State. But the cupboard was not bare—in the front court were Mike Thompson, Dave Winey, and Ray Williams, while Phil "Flip" Saunders and Osborne Lockhart made up the backcourt.

Dutcher's team got a big win early in the 1975–1976 season when on December 18 the Gophers pulled out an upset, overtime victory over Marquette, the number-two-ranked team in the nation. Thompson had 29 points and 16 rebounds in the game. That same day, the university's faculty-student Assembly Committee on Intercollegiate Athletics (ACIA) presented to the NCAA the results of its investigation of wrongdoing during the Musselman era. The university's internal probe acknowledged a number of violations of NCAA rules by current team members.

The most serious charge was against Thompson for selling his complimentary tickets for greater than face value. Winey had also sold his tickets, though only for face value, but he also had been an overnight guest at the cabin of a booster. Saunders, while helping assistant coach Kevin Wilson make calls to recruits on a wide area telephone service (WATS) line, had used the free long-distance line to call his parents in Ohio. And Saunders had used a car belonging to Wilson's mother-in-law to deliver materials to Musselman's basketball camp in St. Peter, Minnesota, and

had stayed overnight in the dormitory being used by students at the camp.

The ACIA deemed the violations by Winey and Saunders to be too minor to merit action against the players. Regarding Thompson's sale of complimentary tickets for more than face value, the ACIA noted that this kind of an infraction would normally result in a player being declared ineligible. The committee said that in this case it did not believe such discipline would be necessary or fair, citing a climate at the university "in which selling was commonplace and even allowed by coaches."

NCAA procedures called for a university or college to declare an athlete ineligible and then appeal to the NCAA for restoration of eligibility. In mid-January, the university declared Thompson, but not Winey or Saunders, ineligible for fourteen games—the number of games the Gophers had left in the season. Thompson sat out one game, which the Gophers lost. The next day, Thompson appeared at an NCAA hearing to appeal the penalty. The NCAA turned down the appeal. Thompson then went to court and obtained a restraining order in Minnesota's Hennepin County District Court that allowed him to keep playing.

Back in the lineup, he showed why his presence was so important. He had 29 points and 17 rebounds in a win at Wisconsin the following Saturday. A week later Thompson scored 34 points and blocked 12 shots as the Gophers beat Ohio State. Minnesota finished the 1975–1976 season with a 16–10 record—8–10 in the Big Ten, good for a sixth-place finish.

Meanwhile, Thompson and Lockhart, who had been high school as well as Gophers teammates, were affected by a decision of the Florida High School Athletic Association. The Association was considering whether to declare a forfeit of the Class 4A state title won by Jackson High School of Miami in 1973–1974 because it had played four ineligible players from the Bahamas. The players, all starters who averaged in double figures in scoring, were Thompson, Lockhart, and two of Thompson's cousins. Ultimately, the board did not strip Jackson of the title. Instead, it voted to "taint their title into perpetuity" by placing an asterisk next to their

Mychal Thompson (43), considered the all-time best Gophers basketball player by many, was a consensus All-American in 1978. Jim McIntyre and Dick Garmaker are the only other Gophers to win consensus All-America honors.

entry in the record book, footnoting the use of the ineligible players.

On March 4, 1976, two days before the 1975–1976 season ended, the university agreed to NCAA penalties for the other violations that had been investigated. The Gophers were put on probation for three years. For the first two years, the team was prohibited from participating in any postseason tournament and also from appearing on NCAA-sanctioned telecasts. In addition, the team had its number of scholarships cut in half for two years. Moreover, the NCAA ordered the university to sever relations with a number of "representatives of the University's athletic interests," most notably Harvey Mackay. Mackay was named in more than twenty infractions, many of them among the most flagrant. Mackay, who admitted to thirteen of the violations, characterized the regulations he broke as "technical and minor in nature." While Minnesota accepted the overall penalties, it balked at the insistence of the NCAA to declare Thompson, Winey, and Saunders ineligible. After holding its own due-process hearing regarding the players, the university refused to take action against them. As a result, all three played in 1976–1977. However, the deteriorating situation with the NCAA placed a cloud of uncertainty over the season.

The university had become engaged in what is called a "defiance case" against the NCAA. The only other known defiance cases had taken place in the previous five years, by the University of California, Denver University, and Centenary College of Shreveport, Louisiana (the Centenary case involving Robert Parish, who became a star in the NBA). In all three cases, the NCAA had responded by placing the entire school's men's athletic department on probation, meaning no NCAA-sanctioned telecasts nor postseason appearances for any of the teams. With such a history, the prognosis for Minnesota was not good. In addition, the school's decision to fight the NCAA was not universally supported by players and coaches of some of the other men's teams at the university. A group of nonbasketball players formed the Committee of Concerned Athletes and campaigned the university to drop its protest so that they and other nonbasketball players could get off probation. A number of coaches also indicated their displeasure at the university's action; hockey coach Herb Brooks and baseball coach Dick Siebert were the most outspoken. As expected, in October 1976 the NCAA took the same action against Minnesota that it had against other defiant schools, placing all of the men's teams at Minnesota on indefinite probation.

University president C. Peter Magrath remained adamant in his support of the basketball players, announcing the formation of a "Fairness Fund" to be financed by public contributions to challenge the NCAA policy to refuse athletes a hearing before they are declared ineligible. Magrath called the NCAA enforcement procedures a "Rube Goldberg contraption gone mad" and said that he would not engage in "lifeboat ethics" by throwing Thompson, Winey, and Saunders to the sharks in order to save the rest of the men's teams.

While Magrath's stand was unpopular with some, it was supported by other coaches, including Musselman's former assistant, Kevin Wilson, who by this time was the head basketball coach at Metro State Community College (formerly Metro State Junior College and later Minneapolis Community and Technical College). "The big spenders, the Ron Behagens, the Tommy Barkers, the Rick McCutcheons are free," Wilson told Chan Keith of the *Minneapolis Star*. "They broke most of the rules. They got most of the money. But they're gone, leaving these three kids holding the bag." As for the current players, Wilson said it was Musselman, not the players, who was responsible for the violations. Regarding Dave Winey staying at the cabin of a booster, Wilson said, "Yes, Dave did it, but he had nothing to do with setting it up. Before the holidays, Musselman went around to a lot of the program's supporters, enlisting guys to take players for the holiday. He said he'd send three players to this guy's house, two more to this fellow's house, another one to some other booster's home. Bill never asked the kids if they wanted to go. He told them they were going. And that was that. If Winey or anyone else would have refused, Bill would have taken it out on him in practice. He would have run the kid to death or thrown him in the middle of a loose-ball drill or something."

On Saunders's use of Wilson's mother-in-law's car to bring items to Musselman's camp in St. Peter, Wilson said, "He [Musselman] told him [Saunders] to do it and told him to use my car," adding that since Saunders was tired, instead of driving back that night, he slept in a vacant dorm room. Regarding Thompson selling tickets, Wilson said, "Not only did he [Musselman] en-

courage his players to sell their tickets, in most cases he arranged for their buyers. To show you what kind of guy Musselman was, he took George Schauer's tickets and sold them for his own profit."

The cloud over the university lifted somewhat in December 1976, when U. S. District Judge Edward Devitt issued an injunction that directed the NCAA to lift its probation on the entire men's athletic department. This enabled the Gophers baseball team—led by Paul Molitor, who went on to a long major league career that put him into the Baseball Hall of Fame—to play in the College World Series (for the last time) in 1977.

Twenty-four Wins, or None?

The basketball team remained ineligible for postseason play, but the Gophers challenged for the Big Ten title in 1976–1977. They were bolstered by the addition of Kevin McHale. Both McHale and his high school rival, Steve Lingenfelter of Bloomington Jefferson, joined Dutcher's program. But while Lingenfelter and Jefferson had gotten the best of McHale's Hibbing squad in both the 1975 and 1976 tournaments, it was McHale who became the star at the university. After four outstanding years with the Gophers, McHale went on to a Hall of Fame career with the Boston Celtics. Thompson might be considered the greatest Gopher of all time, but McHale had the greatest pro career of any former Gopher.

The U won all of their nonconference games plus their first two in the Big Ten in 1976–1977. After an overtime loss at Purdue, Minnesota won five more before losing to Michigan. The Gophers then won eight of their final nine games, with only another loss to the Wolverines. Their 15–3 conference record was good for second place. Under normal circumstances, the finish would have earned a berth in the NCAA tournament, which had expanded to thirty-two teams, making it possible for more than one team from a conference to make the tournament. However, with the probation preventing Minnesota from postseason competition, the tournament bids went to Michigan and third-place Purdue.

Kevin McHale (44) had the greatest professional career of any Minnesota Gophers player. He averaged nearly 18 points and more than 7 rebounds per game in his thirteen seasons with the Boston Celtics. McHale was elected to the Basketball Hall of Fame in 1999.

It was thought that the basketball team would be eligible for the tournament following the next season, as the restriction on postseason play was set to expire on March 4, 1978. However, the saga of Thompson and Winey continued. (Saunders had completed his college eligibility after the 1976–1977 season, making him no longer a part of the case.) The issue heated up again in August 1977, when the Eighth U.S. Circuit Court of Appeals dissolved Judge Devitt's injunction from the previous December, putting all of the university men's teams back on probation. Magrath announced that the university would take the case to the U.S. Supreme Court. It was thought that it would take three to five months before the high court would even decide whether to hear the case.

In the meantime, the dissatisfaction of some athletes and coaches became more vociferous. Then, on October 22, the Gophers football team upset Michigan, the number one ranked team in the country. The 16–0 shocker put Minnesota's win-loss record at 5–2, spawning talk of an invitation to a postseason bowl game, one that would not be possible if the men's program were still on probation. Two days later, the university's Assembly Committee on Intercollegiate Athletics declared Thompson and Winey ineligible. Although the ACIA declared that its action was not prompted by the football team's win over Michigan, it said it hoped that this would end the probation on all the men's teams and that the NCAA would decide to end, or at least shorten, the ineligibility of Thompson and Winey.

Their wishes were granted on both counts. On November 7, the NCAA lifted the probation on the other men's programs. However, in doing so, the NCAA extended the postseason restriction on the basketball team, due to end on March 4, 1978, until October of that year, meaning that the basketball team would not be eligible for postseason tournaments for the upcoming season. A week later, the NCAA declared Thompson ineligible for the first seven games of the 1977–1978 season (including an exhibition game against the Cuban national team) and Winey ineligible for the Cuba game as well as the first two nonconference games.

Thompson expressed regret about not turning pro when he had the chance the previous summer, passing up a chance to sign a contract worth more than a million dollars with the Buffalo Braves of the NBA. Thompson had decided to remain at Minnesota, in part because of a chance to play in the NCAA tournament, a quest that was now gone because of the extension of the restrictive probation. In addition to the other actions, the NCAA ultimately ruled that Minnesota would have to forfeit all of its games in 1976–77. In its media guide, the Gophers still list their season record as 24–3 (15–3 in the Big Ten) while noting that the Big Ten lists its records as 0–27, 0–18. Thompson told Jon Roe of the *Minneapolis Tribune*, "One thing I've learned out of all this is that when you're under investigation, the best thing to do is to be dishonest," adding, "I'm glad it is finally over."

Without Thompson, the Gophers beat the Cubans but lost four of six nonconference games. Thompson returned for the Pillsbury Classic, in which the Gophers beat Air Force and Florida State to win the tournament. Minnesota posted a 12–6 conference mark that was good for a second-place tie with Indiana, three games behind the champion Michigan State Spartans and freshman sensation Earvin "Magic" Johnson. Thompson scored more than 22 points per game and earned All-America honors for the second time. Later that year, he became the first player taken in the 1978 NBA draft; he was chosen by the Portland Trail Blazers.

Dutcher Treats

The Gophers had all their scholarships back by the summer of 1978, and Dutcher made good use of them, recruiting one of the Gophers' best freshman classes ever. Among the new players were forward Leo Rautins from Toronto, forward/center Gary "Cookie" Holmes from Miami, forward/guard Trent Tucker from Flint, Michigan, and guards Mark Hall from Springfield, Massachusetts, and Darryl Mitchell from West Palm Beach, Florida. It was a rebuilding year, although the Gophers still had Kevin McHale back for his junior year. The Gophers finished the 1978–1979 season in an eighth-place tie with a 6–12 record in the Big Ten.

Rautins, who had scored 31 points in a nonconference double-overtime win over Chicago Loyola, left after one year to transfer to Syracuse University. But the Gophers added another notable player the next season, seven-foot-two (later seven-foot-three) center Randy Breuer from Lake City, Minnesota. The Gophers finished in a fourth-place tie in the Big Ten in 1979–1980 and went to the National Invita-

Darryl Mitchell, seen here scoring on a driving layup, teamed up with Trent Tucker and Randy Breuer to bring the Gophers the Big Ten title in 1982. Mitchell was selected as the conference MVP.

tion Tournament (NIT). They won their first four games to make it to the championship game against a Virginia team with an even taller freshman center, seven-foot-four Ralph Sampson.

At Madison Square Garden in New York, Minnesota opened up a 9-point lead in the first half with Darryl Mitchell having the hot hand. But then the Gophers missed eight consecutive shots from the field, two of them being blocked by Sampson. Virginia rallied dur-

ing the Minnesota drought, and the game was tied at halftime. The score remained close throughout the second half. A pair of free throws by Sampson put the Cavaliers ahead, 54–53, with just over a minute and a half left. A turnover gave Virginia the ball back and turned the final minute into a fouling contest. Jeff Lamp made 2 free throws to give Virginia a 3-point lead. At the other end of the court, McHale converted 2 free throws. Down by 1 point, the Gophers fouled Lamp, who again made both of his free throws with two seconds left. The final score was 58–55 in favor of Virginia.

Minnesota made it back to the NIT in 1981 but lost in the third round. The following season, 1981–1982, would be the final year for Dutcher's heralded freshman class of 1978. Hall, Holmes, Mitchell, and Tucker remained with the Gophers, though Hall missed the first part of the season because of academic problems. He regained his eligibility following a decision by U.S. District Court judge Miles Lord in early 1982, but he also faced charges of billing personal phone calls to university phone numbers. On February 23, the day before he was to appear at a hearing before the university's Student Behavioral Committee, Hall resigned from the team. After having been a key member of the Gophers in his first three seasons, Hall scored only 38 points in eleven games in his final season. (Another sad note on Hall is that six years later, at the age of twenty-eight, he died of what was later determined to be "acute cocaine intoxication.")

With Hall gone the remaining seniors—along with juniors Breuer and Zebedee Howell, sophomore Jim Petersen, and freshman Tommy Davis—kept the Gophers in contention for the Big Ten title. A big win came at Purdue on Saturday, February 13. The Gophers trailed, 52–51, when Purdue's Curt Clawson missed a pair of free throws with nine seconds left. Petersen got the rebound and fired an outlet pass to Mitchell, who was fouled with one second left. Mitchell stepped to the free throw line for the first time in the game and, in between a pair of Purdue time outs, calmly made his shots, giving the Gophers a 53–52 win.

Mitchell found himself at the line in another key situation two weeks later at Iowa. Coming into the game, the Hawkeyes were in first place with a 12–3 record. The Gophers at 11–5 were in second. The game went into overtime after Breuer blocked an Iowa shot in the final seconds of regulation play. The Hawkeyes again missed potential game-winning shots in the waning seconds of the first two overtime periods. Minnesota and Iowa had swapped field goals in the first thirty-seven seconds of the first overtime, which was the last of the scoring for either team until the end of the third overtime, when Mitchell launched a jumper from the top of the key. The shot missed, but Mitchell was fouled. No time remained on the clock as he stepped to the line and sank both free throws, giving the Gophers a 57–55

Gopher Men's Annual Record, 1959–1986

Year	Overall Record	Big Ten Record
Coach John Kundla		
1959–1960	12–12	8–6 (3rd tie)
1960–1961	10–13	8–6 (4th tie)
1961–1962	10–14	6–8 (7th)
1962–1963	12–12	8–6 (4th tie)
1963–1964	17–7	10–4 (3rd)
1964–1965	19–5	11–3 (2nd)
1965–1966	14–10	7–7 (5th tie)
1966–1967	9–15	5–9 (9th)
1967–1968	7–17	4–10 (9th tie)
Kundla Totals	110–105	67–59
	.512	.532
Coach Bill Fitch		
1968–1969	12–12	6–8 (5th tie)
1969–1970	13–11	7–7 (5th)
Fitch Totals	25–23	13–15
	.521	.464
Coach George Hanson		
1970–1971	11–13	5–9 (5th tie)
Hanson Totals	.458	.357
Coach Bill Musselman		
1971–1972	18–7	11–3 (1st)
1972–1973	21–5	10–4 (2nd)
1973–1974	12–12	6–8 (6th)
1974–1975	18–8	11–7 (3rd)
Musselman totals	69–32	38–22
	.683	.633
Coach Jim Dutcher		
1975–1976	16–10	8–10 (6th)
1976–1977	24–3	15–3 (2nd)[a]
1977–1978	17–10	12–6 (2nd, tie)
1978–1979	11–16	6–12 (8th)
1979–1980	21–11	10–8 (4th)
1980–1981	19–11	9–9 (5th)
1981–1982	23–6	14–4 (1st)
1982–1983	18–11	9–9 (6th)
1983–1984	15–13	6–12 (8th)
1984–1985	13–15	6–12 (8th)
1985–1986	13–7	3–4
Dutcher Totals	190–113	98–89
	.617	.524
Gopher totals	405–246	221–194
1959–1986	.622	.533

Note: Dutcher resigned January 25, 1986. Records shown are through that date.
[a] The NCAA lists the Gophers record as 0–27 and 0–18.

triple-overtime win, a share of the conference lead, and an appearance on the cover of *Sports Illustrated*. It was later revealed that the Gophers had been under police protection in Iowa after a call to the Minnesota athletic department with a death threat against Breuer, who did not let the threat affect his performance: he scored 12 points against the Hawkeyes.

Iowa then lost its final two Big Ten games to drop out of the race. Meanwhile, the Gophers beat Michigan State at Williams Arena to clinch a tie for first place. Their final game was against Ohio State, which trailed Minnesota by a game. A win would mean an outright title; a loss would mean a first-place tie with the Buckeyes. Led by Randy Breuer with 32 points and Trent Tucker with 23, the Gophers beat the Buckeyes by 12 points to win the conference title. Mitchell was named the Big Ten's MVP.

In the NCAA tournament, Minnesota beat Tennessee-Chattanooga by a point, then lost by 6 points to Louisville to end their season and the college careers of Mitchell, Tucker, and Holmes.

For the 1982–1983 season, Petersen and Davis joined Breuer in the starting lineup, along with newcomers Roland Brooks and Marc Wilson, but the Gophers dropped to a sixth-place tie in the Big Ten. They dropped even further over the next two years, but the poor performance on the court was about to be overshadowed again by events off the court.

Voices of the Gophers

Left, *Julius Perlt's distinctive voice was familiar to basketball fans at Williams Arena as he did the public address announcing for Gophers games for more than fifty years. Center, Dick Jonckowski succeeded Perlt in 1985. Right, Ray Christensen called the action over the airwaves for nearly fifty years.*

"Women Could No Longer Be Ignored," 1971–1983

The impact of Title IX on the development of girls and women's basketball can hardly be overstated, and yet, paradoxically, it has been somewhat overstated. It is often said, for example, that we have girls and women's basketball because of Title IX. True enough. Yet it is equally true that we have Title IX because of girls and women's basketball.

Title IX is nothing more than the ninth section of the federal education bill, the Education Amendments, of 1972. It prohibits discrimination on the basis of gender at schools and colleges that receive federal funds and applies not only to athletics but to all of the schools' programs.

To say that it came about in a roundabout fashion would be an understatement. Representative Howard W. Smith of Virginia proposed inserting the word "sex" into the Civil Rights Act of 1964 so that it would prohibit discrimination against women as well as blacks. He did so in the belief that this would generate a firestorm of opposition and would result in the defeat of the Civil Rights Act. Instead, the Civil Rights Act was passed, and it prohibited gender as well as racial discrimination.

By 1983, girls and women's basketball in Minnesota was well established. As with the men, Minnesota had even seen a professional league come and go. But Title IX is not the whole story. From the very beginning of the game in 1891—and continuing right up to the pivotal years of the early 1970s—girls and women played the game with as much enthusiasm as their brothers. Institutional support for the girls and women's play was missing, however, because of Victorian attitudes and medical myths about female bodies and social roles.

Of course, the lack of institutional support—principally, facilities and funding was a huge barrier. But a generation of women from the end of World War II through the 1960s and into the early 1970s protested this lack of gender equity. In Minnesota, Belmar Gunderson, Eloise Jaeger, Dorothy McIntyre, and Sue Tinker were among the most important voices; they worked toward achieving equity for girls and women. Title IX unlocked the door to girls and women's basketball, but only because Gunderson, McIntyre, and countless more had made their way to that door and were demanding entry.

The impact of Title IX in overcoming institutional inequities was immediate, and it was huge. But the idea that Title IX fundamentally changed American values is another overstatement. Rather it reflected beliefs that, by 1972, most Americans had come to support.

Janet Karvonen (45) shows what observers called her "picture perfect" jump shot form. Karvonen put girls basketball on the map in Minnesota, leading New York Mills to three straight state championships in 1977, 1978, and 1979 and completing her high school career with 3,192 points.

24

The MSHSL and Fans Embrace Girls Hoops

I_N 1965, the Minnesota Association for Health, Physical Education and Recreation (MAHPER) formed a study committee to develop a position statement on girls interscholastic sports. It recommended in 1967 that the Minnesota State High School League (MSHSL) undertake the administration of girls athletics. The MSHSL, by a unanimous vote, adopted bylaws to that effect in the spring of 1969. Many wanted to know when the League would be initiating a girls basketball tournament. But it was only in 1976, under the apparent impetus of Title IX, that the first "official" girls state roundball tournament was held.

The first girls state tournament of any kind had been a track meet in the spring of 1972. Gymnastics, tennis, and volleyball followed in 1974–1975. There was no girls cross-country until the fall of 1975, however, so in 1973 several courageous young women made the news by entering boys meets. Karen Keyport and Sandy Rose of Visitation High School, Mendota, ran in the independent school state meet. Meanwhile, Ruth Harris of Henry Sibley finished sixty-sixth in the St. Paul Suburban Conference meet.

The biggest news in girls sports in 1973 was a set of guidelines for high school athletics published by the Minnesota chapter of the National Organization for Women (NOW)—at least, it was the only girls sporting news to make the first sports page of the *Minneapolis Tribune* during the entire year. NOW suggested what sports should be offered, including coeducational play in swimming and tennis. Girls would compete against girls, and boys, against boys; but the scores would roll up together. NOW also suggested that girls should have as many sports to choose from as boys and that their

budgets should be equal. A public hearing was scheduled to debate the issues.

It was a chaotic time for girls athletics. Schools introduced new girls sports rapidly, and the League scrambled to keep up. In this environment many schools, especially smaller ones and those in rural communities, launched girls basketball as a fall sport. There were concerns about scheduling both girls and boys basketball in the same facilities in the same season. In a poll of interested parties in Region 6 in west central Minnesota, 800 of 801 respondents preferred fall ball. But most larger schools and most of those in the Twin Cities area scheduled volleyball in the fall and basketball in the winter.

The Legends of the Fall

The first MSHSL girls basketball tournament was held in the fall of 1973. It was implemented only at the district and regional levels, with no state tournament. About a dozen districts in old Region 1 (southeastern Minnesota), old Region 3 (southwestern Minnesota), and old Region 6 (west central Minnesota) played district championships. Only Region 6 had a full complement of four district champs and played off to a regional championship. Thus, the first girls regional basketball champion in state history was future Cinderella New York Mills, which knocked off Breckenridge, 44–36, for that honor.

There were two state tournaments in 1974. In March, there was a first and last independent school tournament won by St. Margaret's Academy, 41–26, over St. Bernard's. The champions, led by ninth grader Joan Kowalsky, finished with a 20–3 record. St. Margaret's and fellow tournament entries Hill-Murray and Mayer Lutheran would be prominent players in the first several official tournaments, as the private schools gained admittance to the MSHSL in 1975. Holy Angels

Kay Konerza of Lester Prairie (right) drives against Annie Adamczak of Moose Lake (25, left) in a 1982 Class A first round game. Moose Lake won 67–47 en route to the state title, but Konerza scored 31 points and completed her career with 2,715.

returned to win the unofficial MSHSL state tournament of 1975.

Two unofficial tournaments were held in the 1974–1975 school year—the MSHSL sanctioned both a fall and a winter state tournament, though it refused to designate either as "official." The tournaments were played with little fanfare, so only about six thousand fans saw each of them.

Glencoe clobbered Wadena, 46–29, to win the fall tournament and finish the season 21–0 and with a fifty-four-game winning streak overall. Sue Wacker led the winners with 14 points and 12 rebounds. Both fall finalists would return to the first official tournament the following year. Mayer Lutheran came into the winter basketball tournament as the top-rated girls team in the state. But Mayer had settled for consolation honors in the 1974 independent tourney against some of these same opponents. Indeed, Holy Angels edged Mayer, 36–33, then won two 2-point games over Crookston and LeSueur to finish its season 21–3. Jen Savage of LeSueur was the top individual, however, with 32 points in the first round, 18 in the championship game, and 60 overall. For runner-up LeSueur, the defeat was their first ever after winning twenty-five straight games over two seasons.

The Holy Angels victory confirmed that the best girls basketball in the state was played among the Catholic high schools of the Minneapolis area. The Angels had beaten Regina by just 1 point in the Region 5 final, after taking third place in the independent tournament of 1974. The 1974 independent champion, St. Margaret's, had defeated Regina, 48–42, in that region final and would return as Benilde-St. Margaret's to claim a second-place and a third-place finish in the official tournaments of 1976 and 1977. Regina took runner-up honors in Class AA in 1978.

At the conclusion of the 1975 winter tournament, it was announced that there would be only one state tournament the following year—in the winter—thus sounding the death knell for girls fall ball.

The Girls Bicentennial Bash

The significance of 1976 is that, along with being the year of the first official girls tournament, it was also the year of the first tournament in which black star players and mostly black teams—girls or boys—claimed state championships. Among the boys, Minneapolis Marshall-University, with four black starters, won the Class A (small school) title.

Girls High School Champions, 1974–1983

Year	Championship Game Score	W–L	Authors' Choice: Postseason MVP
1974	Glencoe 46 Wadena 29	20–3	Sue Wacker, Glencoe
	St. Margaret's Academy 41 St. Bernard's 26[a]	21–0	
1975	Holy Angels 39 LeSueur 37	21–3	Jen Savage, LeSueur
1976	A Redwood Falls 41 Glencoe 28	21–1	Isabella Ceplecha, Redwood Falls, C
	AA St. Paul Central 49 Benilde-St. Margaret's 47	17–3	
1977	A New York Mills 40 Mayer Lutheran 39	25–1	Joyce Detlefson, Burnsville, F
	AA Burnsville 46 St. Cloud Apollo 41	25–1	
1978	A New York Mills 64 Redwood Falls 55	25–1	Laura Gardner, Jefferson, F
	AA Bloomington Jefferson 53 Regina 40	24–0	
1979	A New York Mills 61 Albany 52	25–1	Janet Karvonen, New York Mills, F
	AA St. Paul Central 55 Northfield 46	20–3	
1980	A Albany 56 Austin Pacelli 25	26–0	Kelly Skalicky, Albany, G
	AA Little Falls 50 Hill-Murray 42	24–1	
1981	A Heron Lake–Okabena 62 Moose Lake 46	26–0	Kelly Skalicky, Albany, G
	AA Coon Rapids 60 St. Paul Harding 42	25–0	
1982	A Moose Lake 52 East Chain 49 (OT)	26–0	Annie Adamczak, Moose Lake, F
	AA St. Cloud Apollo 53 Rochester Mayo 44	25–0	
1983	A Henderson 52 Lake City 31	26–0	Janice Streit, Eden Valley–Watkins, C
	AA Albany 41 Edina 39 (OT)	23–2	

[a] Independent school tournament.

Among the girls, it is doubly noteworthy that the Class AA (big school) champ was St. Paul Central, led by two black cousins—sophomore Lisa Lissimore and junior Linda Roberts. Lissimore would play in the first three girls tournaments, helping Central to hardware each time—a consolation championship in 1977 and third place in 1978 to go along with its 1976 championship. (Central would claim a second Class AA title in 1979 behind Stacy Durand, Jean Tierney, and Dana Watts.) At the end of her junior season, Lissimore was the girls career scoring leader with a total over two tournaments of 87 points. This was one more point than Kowalsky of Benilde-St. Margaret's, not counting her performance in the independent school tourney in the fall of 1974. The following year, Lissimore would return to the state tournament but relinquish her career scoring record to Laura Gardner of 1978 champion Bloomington Jefferson, who also played in the first three tournaments and finished with 141 points to Lissimore's 130. In 1979, Janet Karvonen of New York Mills blew them all away.

Meanwhile the first Class A tournament featured another star black player, crowd favorite and eighth grader Melanie "Squirt" Moore of Marshall-University High School of Minneapolis. Moore in fact held the single-game scoring record for a day, scoring 20 in a first round 63–31 rout of Esko. Like Lissimore and Gardner, she returned to play in the 1977 tournament, by the end of which she had 76 career points. Unfortunately, she and Marshall-U High never made it back after her freshman season.

The first girls tournament drew about 34,000 fans—fewer than one-third as many as the boys. But the girls quickly built a following, and by Karvonen's biggest year in 1979, attendance at the girls tournament increased to 59,000, or more than 60 percent of the attendance at the boys tournament.

For all the changes inaugurated in that historic year of 1976, what followed was the second longest period of stability in tournament history. The girls tournament format was unchanged through 1997, when the four-class format was introduced. As a result of this stability

St. Paul Central's Deb Krengel signals "two points" as she scores on a layup against Wadena's Vicki Hutson during Minnesota's first official girls state basketball tournament, in 1976. Central defeated Wadena, 42–34, and then took the first Class AA championship with wins over Austin and Benilde-St. Margaret's.

Joan Hopfenspirger (22) of Redwood Falls drives to the basket against Glencoe in the first girls Class A high school championship game, in 1976. Redwood Falls won, 41–29, as Hopfenspirger handed out a tournament record 26 assists. Defending is Steph Torgerson (43) of Glencoe.

in the tournament format, several great statewide rivalries were able to develop.

The Mills, Albany, and Who?

Albany and New York Mills were the dominant small town teams in the tournaments' early years. But Austin Pacelli beat them both—in their primes. Because the Shamrocks never won a state title of their own, however, their accomplishments have been largely forgotten.

The girls from the Mills became Minnesota's team, winners of the 1977 and 1978 Class A championships behind Karvonen's exploits. Then in 1979, they became the second team overall and first girls team to three-peat, beating Pacelli, 50–36, in the first round and Albany, 61–52, in the final. Karvonen outscored Albany star Kelly Skalicky, 38–23, in the final and finished with 98 points overall in her most productive tournament.

The final was not as close as it sounds, either, as the Mills led 49–30 after three quarters.

Then in 1980, the Mills and the Pacelli Shamrocks collided again, this time in the semis. New York Mills, if only from habit, was heavily favored, but Pacelli shocked Minnesota fans with a 55–43 win, after falling behind 16–8 after the first period. Pacelli held Karvonen to 21 points and outscored the Mills 47–27 after that slow start. The Shamrocks ran out of gas the next night against Albany, however, as Skalicky scored 21 to lead Albany to a 56–25 romp.

After closing out the 1980 tournament, Pacelli and Albany opened the next one. This time Pacelli got revenge, 48–44, but fell victim to eventual champion Heron Lake–Okabena the following night and settled for third place. Meanwhile, New York Mills was upset in the first round by Mankato Loyola, 55–51. So Albany and the Mills played for the consolation championship instead of the real one. Albany won one of the most

Evolution of Girls State Tournament Records

Points in a Single Game

Year	Name	Points and Game
1976	Isabella Ceplecha, Redwood Falls	26 vs. SW Christian (semifinals)
1977	Janet Karvonen, New York Mills	29 vs. Buhl (first round)
1978	Karvonen	31 vs. Fertile-Beltrami (first round)
1978	Karen Swanson, Mountain Iron	34 vs. Albany (consolation semifinals)
1979	Karvonen	34 vs. Brady (semifinals)
1979	Karvonen	38 vs. Albany (championship game)
1980	Karvonen	40 vs. KMS (first round)
1981	Kelly Skalicky, Albany	45 vs. Bagley (consolation semifinals)

Rebounds in a Single Game

Year	Name	Rebounds and Game
1979	Liz Wolf, Brady	22 vs. Redwood Falls (semifinals)
1979	Cammy Matuseski, Moose Lake	24 vs. Brady (third-place game)
1982	Dana Patsie, New York Mills	25 vs. Howard Lk-Waverly (first round)
1983	Janice Streit, Eden Valley-Watkins	27 vs. Waubun (consolation semifinals)

Assists in a Single Game

Year	Name	Assists and Game
1979	Kim Salathe, New York Mills	10 vs. Austin Pacelli (first round)
1979	Joan Hopfenspirger, Redwood Falls	12 vs. Brady (first round)
1979	Kelly Skalicky, Albany	17 vs. Moose Lake (semifinals)

Tournament Points

Year	Name	Points/Games	Average
1976	Isabella Ceplecha, Redwood Falls	53/3	17.7
1977	Janet Karvonen, New York Mills	59/3	19.7
1978	Laura Gardner, Bloomington Jefferson	78/3	26
1979	Karvonen	98/3	32.7
1981	Kelly Skalicky, Albany	102/3	34

Tournament Rebounds

Year	Name	Rebounds/Games	Average
1982	Dana Patsie, New York Mills	58/3	19.3
1983	Janice Streit, Eden Valley-Watkins	64/3	21.3

Tournament Assists

Year	Name	Assists/Games	Average
1979	Joan Hopfenspirger, Redwood Falls	26/ 3	8.7
1979	Kelly Skalicky, Albany	26/3	8.7
2001	Jackie Radunz, St. Michael–Albertville	26/3	8.7

Career Points

Year	Name	Points/Games	Average
1976	Isabella Ceplecha, Redwood Falls	53/3	17.7
1976–1977	Lisa Lissimore, St. Paul Central	87/6	14.5[a]
1976–1978	Laura Gardner, Bloomington Jefferson	141/8	17.6
1977–1980	Janet Karvonen, New York Mills	329/12	27.4

[a] Lissimore returned to the tournament again in 1978 and finished with 130 points.

entertaining games in tournament history, 76–70 in overtime, behind Skalicky's 35 points.

The Albany legend, though never a match for the Mills, was substantially enhanced by a second state title in 1983—this one in Class AA, despite Albany's being one of the smallest AA schools in the state. Two Carols—Thelen and Oehrlein—led Albany to a thrilling 41–39 overtime win over Edina in the final.

Pioneers

Entering the first official tournament of 1976, the girls record book was a blank slate. At the time, no one knew that it would be inscribed with the names Gardner, Jean Hopfenspirger (Redwood Falls), Karvonen, Kay Konerza (Lester Prairie), Moore, Skalicky, and Janice Streit (Eden Valley–Watkins), among others. Nor could anyone know that by 1983 the list of girls individual records would be virtually complete. After 1983, hardly a single one of the most prestigious records would be rewritten.

As great as Karvonen and Skalicky and the others were, the fact is that they just did not face the caliber of competition that Minnesota girls would face a few years later. Like the boys of the 1920s, the girls after 1976 would get more and more court time and more and better coaching at younger and younger ages. As a result, the skill levels would increase rapidly, and quickly it became more difficult for girls to dominate in the way that the great pioneer players did. So the girls individual records, which have changed so little since 1983, may not see many more changes any time soon.

Known mostly for her scoring, Janet Karvonen (left) also knew how to box out on the boards as she demonstrates here in the celebrated 1979 Class A final against Albany. New York Mills won, 61–52, to complete their three-peat.

The Big Game
New York Mills 61, Albany 52
March 24, 1979

Janet Karvonen burst on the Minnesota basketball scene on March 24, 1977, but it was exactly two years later that she made her legacy.

In her first state tournament game as just a ninth grader, Karvonen hit 14 of 16 field goal attempts and scored a record 29 points as New York Mills hammered Buhl, 68–43. But only the seven thousand or so fans at Williams Arena saw her debut. Accessible for the first time to a television audience in the semifinal, she needed a last-second bucket to score 15 points against Minneapolis Marshall-U, and then she scored 15 more in a 40–39 win over Mayer Lutheran for Mills' first state title. It was teammate Tina Ruttan whose basket and free throw provided the Eagles with their margin of victory. Still, Karvonen's 59 points was a girls tournament record.

The next year, the pretournament buzz was all Karvonen all the time, and she fearlessly announced that she would score 3,000 points in her high school career. "I'm a better all-around player [this year]," she said. "I can play outside or inside, and I bring the ball up the court against the press. . . . I'm playing facing the basket. I shoot from up to 20 feet now."

She delivered in the first game with 31 points, tying the state record of Morton's Beth Bidinger for career points (1,453) with two more years of high school still ahead of her. Everybody agreed that she was "awesome." On television again, she was only great—but not quite awesome—scoring 24 points in each of Mills' remaining games as they cruised to their second state title. Her total of 79 points was a new tournament record.

But there was still work to do. In 1979, Karvonen scored 26 points in a 50–36 first round win over Austin Pacelli and 34 more in a 70–50 win over Brady. The *Minneapolis Tribune* did not even print a report on the Pacelli game, but in its place published a "Q & A" with reporter Bruce Brothers doing the Q and Karvonen supplying the A. The headline after the Brady game read, "Karvonen Scores 34, Ho-Hum, to Propel New York Mills." She hit 16 of 26 shots, and her 34 points tied the tournament record.

In the final Karvonen had the very good fortune to meet Albany and guard Kelly Skalicky. They say that you've got to beat the best to be the best, and Skalicky's legacy— by the time of her graduation in 1981—would be as the second-best girl (among the pioneers, anyway). Mills raced to a 33–17 halftime lead as Skalicky "tried to do too much." After three periods, it was 49–30. Albany settled down in the fourth quarter and sliced 10 points off Mills' lead, but the game was not as close as the final score of 61–52 suggests. Skalicky tied the tournament record with 26 assists but hit only 10 of 30 shots in the championship game. Meanwhile, Karvonen hit 15 of 28 shots and scored a record, yet again, of 38 points, along with 13 rebounds. For the third year in a row, she set a tournament record, now with 98 points. Albany coach Nancy Way was "in awe. She's something else," she said.

Mills and Minnesota basketball fans were shocked in 1980 when Austin Pacelli beat the Eagles, 55–43, in a semifinal, thereby depriving Mills and Karvonen of an unprecedented four straight titles. Moreover, Albany won the state title, and Skalicky outscored Karvonen, 102–96, breaking her tournament scoring record. Yet none of this dulled the luster of Karvonen's earlier achievements. When Karvonen and Skalicky went head-to-head, it was clear which was the Best Girl Ever.

25 *A Good Start for Gopher Women*

Women's intercollegiate basketball officially reemerged at the University of Minnesota in 1973–1974, after a lapse of more than sixty years. Letters were first awarded in 1973, but it was only in 1973–1974 that the team played a published schedule of games. The squad, under coach Linda Wells, posted a 3–10 record. (It was only in 2005 that win-loss records for 1971–1972 and 1972–1973 were added to the Gophers' media guide, but the opponents and game scores have not been published. Those teams, under coaches Joan Stevenson and Deb Wilson, respectively, posted 5–3 and 8–8 records.) Over the next three seasons, from 1975 through 1977, behind the leadership of coach Jenny Johnson and two-time MVP Denise Erstad, the Gophers posted a 36–37 record.

Not surprisingly, the initial environment was vastly different from the environment in which the Gopher men competed. The governing body of men's college athletics, the National Collegiate Athletic Association (NCAA), showed little interest in managing women's sports. So a new organization, the Association for Intercollegiate Athletics for Women (AIAW), was formed in 1971. It would be more than a decade before the NCAA and the Big Ten would get involved in women's basketball.

Recruiting also was severely limited, and scholarships were unknown. Colleges with a strong pool of local talent had an edge, and initially it was some very small schools that flourished. Immaculata College, drawing from the Catholic high schools of Philadelphia, won the first three AIAW titles, from 1972 to 1975. Their run was stopped as Delta State of Cleveland, Mississippi—led by in-state players Debbie Brock, Ramona Von Boeckman, and Lusia Harris—won the national championship for the next three years.

The 1977 AIAW tournament was held at the University of Minnesota. As the host team, the Gophers received an automatic bid, which gave them a first-round game against Delta State. Minnesota was no match for the Lady Statesmen, who beat the Gophers, 87–43, on their way to another championship. Most of the tournament was played at Williams Arena, but one of the opening-round games was at the Bierman Building, a complex of offices mixed in with small courts. For many years, one of those small courts was the regular home of the women's team. The Gophers occasionally made it to the bigger stage of Williams Arena as a preliminary to a men's game and eventually made Williams their regular home. One such event was in January 1976, when the women faced Grandview College of Des Moines, Iowa, prior to the men's game against the Iowa Hawkeyes. Grandview beat the Gophers, 69–36, with a team that featured a pair of Iowa high school stars, Rhonda Penquite

Ellen Mosher (later Ellen Mosher Hanson) talking to her players. Hanson coached the Gopher women's team from 1977 to 1987, and her 177 career victories, against 119 losses, remains the most in the program's history.

Elsie Ohm (33) played for the Minnesota Gophers for three years before transferring to Mankato State, where she played her final season of college ball.

of Ankeny and Molly Van Venthuysen of Moravia.

These teams played again, in Iowa, two years later, in January 1978. By this time Van Venthuysen had a new name, along with a child and husband, Dennie Bolin. Molly Bolin would soon become the best known player in the Women's Basketball League, which started play in late 1978. The Gophers fared better in this rematch with Grandview, winning by a score of 64–62. The victory was indicative of the progress the Gophers were experiencing under a new coaching tandem.

Ellen Mosher Arrives

Ellen Mosher and Chris Howell had arrived at Minnesota for the 1977–1978 season, Mosher as head coach and Howell as her assistant and recruiting coordinator. They had coached together the past two years at UCLA,

leaving behind future Hall of Famers Ann Meyers and Denise Curry and a team that would go on to win the AIAW title in 1978. Meyers was the first big-name scholarship player in women's basketball, and by that point the era when small institutions such as Immaculata and Delta State were able to dominate the sport had come to an end.

The 1977–1978 Gophers were led by Elsie Ohm, Brenda Savage, Rachel Gaugert, and Linda Roberts. But Diane Scovill, then a senior, credits the transformation of the program to Mosher and Howell. Scovill says she "learned the game" from Mosher. "I didn't even know how to box out [before that]. . . . They proceeded to teach us how to walk, how to turn, how to stop. She built us." Other players remember Mosher as an intense coach whose confidence rubbed off on them. (A story cited by many players regarding Mosher's confidence

involves the coach getting out of the team van and personally directing traffic to get them through a traffic jam and to their game on time.)

For the purpose of the national AIAW tournament, the country was broken into nine regions with each region being further divided by individual states. Minnesota was in Region 6 along with Iowa, Kansas, Missouri, Nebraska, North Dakota, and South Dakota. In 1978, the Gophers beat St. Cloud State to win the state tournament for the first time. They lost, 96–81, to Kansas State in the Region 6 tournament, but the progress of the team was evident, as barely more than two months before it had lost to Kansas State by a score of 70–30.

Minnesota ended its season by winning one of three games in the National Women's Invitation Tournament (NWIT) to finish with an overall record of 24–10. Ohm led the Gophers with an average of 16.5 points per game, a new record that would stand for five years. Freshman Roberts, from St. Paul Central, was third in scoring and set a team rebounding record that stands to this day. Joan Kowalsky, from Benilde-St. Margaret's, led the team in assists and steals.

Minnesota hosted the Region 6 tournament in 1979, and the Gophers lost to Kansas State again. This time the score was closer yet, at 84–80, as the Gophers battled back after trailing at halftime by 14 points. They even took a short-lived 78–76 lead with three and a half minutes to play. Once again, the Gophers accepted an invitation to the NWIT and finished fifth, winning their game with Mississippi, as freshman Laura Gardner scored 26 points and had 12 rebounds. Gardner had been the state's first Ms. Basketball; she led Bloomington Jefferson to the state Class AA high-school championship in 1978. She had an outstanding year with the Gophers in 1978–1979, starting all thirty-two games—of which the Gophers won fifteen—and averaging nearly 15 points and 8 rebounds per game. She suffered a serious knee injury in the summer of 1979, however, and missed the next season.

The Gophers in 1979–1980 were also missing Ohm, who transferred to Mankato State University for her final season. Mary Manderfeld transferred from Mankato to Minnesota, however, and combined with

Laura Gardner (23) scores for the Gopher women. Before coming to the University of Minnesota, Gardner led her Bloomington Jefferson team to three state tournaments and the 1978 Class AA title. It was her state tournament career scoring record that Janet Karvonen broke in 1979.

Deb Hunter was generally regarded as the greatest guard in Gopher women's history until Lindsay Whalen came along. She scored 1,361 points and remains the Gophers career leader in assists and steals.

Roberts to give the Gophers a fierce rebounding duo. In the backcourt, a freshman from Cloquet, Deb Hunter, provided balance and leadership in helping the Gophers to an 18–11 record.

During the late 1970s and early 1980s, the most prominent high school players, such as Janet Karvonen of New York Mills and Kelly Skalicky of Albany, were leaving Minnesota to play college basketball elsewhere, but the Gophers were successful in recruiting Hunter, Martha "Marty" Dahlen of Mabel, and Mary Dressen of Browerville. In fact, it was because of Hunter that Mosher and Howell failed to make a strong recruiting pitch to Skalicky. Skalicky chose Louisiana State, in part because a southern school afforded better opportunities for her other passion, golf. Mosher later said she did not think Skalicky would have taken Hunter's job away, and "she's not the type of player who would be happy to sit on the bench."

For the first time in 1981, the Gophers won the Big Ten tournament, beating Wisconsin, Ohio State, and Northwestern for the title. Minnesota was also nationally ranked when it ended its regular season, making it as high as number fifteen in the polls. The Gophers hosted the Region 6 tournament for the second time in three years. They made it to the championship game before falling, 67–61, to Kansas, which was led by Lynette Woodard, who went on to become the first female player on the Harlem Globetrotters and is now a member of the Basketball Hall of Fame.

Although they did not win the regional tournament, the Gophers received an at-large bid to the 1981 AIAW tournament. The national tournament was no longer being held at a single site—the 1977 tournament in Minneapolis had been the last time that happened. So the Gophers hosted their opening-round game, playing Jackson State. Despite having three players—Roberts, Manderfeld, and Dahlen—in double figures in rebounds, the Gophers lost, 68–65, as Jackson State went on a 13–0 run during the second half.

It was the final college game for Roberts and Manderfeld. Less than a week later, both were playing for the Minnesota Fillies of the Women's Professional Basketball League after the regular Fillies players walked out because they had not been getting paid. Roberts ended her Minnesota career with 1,856 points, a school record at the time that has since been surpassed. Her career rebounding average of 11 per game remains a Gophers record, however.

A quarter century later, the entire 1980–1981 women's basketball team was inducted into the Gopher Women's Basketball Hall of Fame. Three members of that team—Roberts (who also had her jersey retired), Hunter, and Coach Mosher—were also inducted individually.

The NCAA and the Big Ten Take Over

The NCAA took on the administration of women's basketball in 1981, and colleges had a choice of affiliations during the 1981–1982 season. The Gophers remained in the AIAW and reached its national tournament by beating Central Missouri, 76–71, for the Region 6 championship, as freshman Laura Coenen had 28 points and 15 rebounds.

Coenen had another double-double—20 points and

Linda Roberts (21) scored more than 1,800 points in her four-year college career at the U of M, and she remains a top-five career point scorer a quarter century later. Her jersey was retired in 2006.

13 rebounds—as Minnesota beat St. John's, 68–56, in their opening game in the national tournament. They then lost to Rutgers, 83–75, and were stopped one game short of making the AIAW Final Four. Theresa Grentz, who as Theresa Shank had played on the Immaculata championship teams in the 1970s, coached Rutgers, which went on to win the championship. Grentz later became the head coach for Illinois, where she continued to coach against the Gophers for many years.

Coenen, a six-foot-one forward and center from Neenah, Wisconsin, averaged more than 16 points and 11 rebounds per game as a freshman. Although her rebounding total dropped, she increased her scoring average to 24.2 points in 1982–1983, which was also the first season in which the Big Ten officially sanctioned women's basketball. (The Gophers and all other women's intercollegiate basketball teams were by this time under the jurisdiction of the NCAA, as the AIAW had disbanded in 1982.) Coenen had her biggest game of

Laura Coenen (44) set Gopher women's records—since broken—when she scored 42 points in a game in 1984 and completed her career with 2,044 points.

the season on February 18, when she scored 41 points in a game at Wisconsin. The Gophers finished in a tie for third place with a 13–5 conference record. Coenen and Deb Hunter were named to the All–Big Ten first team, while Coenen was also named the Big Ten Player of the Year.

As the 1983 season drew to a close, the Gopher women's basketball program looked to be in terrific shape. They were now members of the Big Ten and the NCAA. They had won about six of every ten games—or,

to be exact, they had won 177 games while losing 119, for a winning percentage of .598—while Mosher had won more than two-thirds of her games over a six-year period. But appearances were deceiving. After winning at least seventeen games in seven of her first eight seasons as head coach, Mosher would never again win even ten. The Gophers themselves would win ten games only four times over the following sixteen seasons. The promise the program had showed through its first decade would go unfulfilled for almost another twenty years.

Minnesota Mysteries and Myths

Women's Basketball Not an Immaculate Conception

The Department of Intercollegiate Athletics for Women became a part of the University of Minnesota scene in 1975, though the more or less official records of intercollegiate play date from 1971–1972. But neither intercollegiate play nor the new department was born of an immaculate conception. Rather, participation in intercollegiate sports by the female students at the university date from 1895, when a tennis tournament was sanctioned by the Ladies Tennis Association. Basketball was begun in 1900, though the U put a stop to intercollegiate play in 1908.

Initially such activities were run by the students themselves under the Women's Athletic Association (WAA). The WAA became part of the Department of Physical Education for Women in 1913 and remained as such through the 1950s. In the 1920s the WAA sponsored archery, basketball, baseball, field hockey, golf, horseback riding, ice hockey, tennis, and swimming. It was only in 1936, however, with the construction of the Norris Gymnasium, that the WAA, women's

Dayton's women's basketball team ca. 1943. Women's basketball never vanished completely from Minnesota life. Dayton's and other employers sponsored women's teams in the Minneapolis Park and Rec League throughout the decades after the game disappeared from the schools.

physical education classes, and women's intramural athletics had a dedicated facility including a large sports area, swimming pool, racquetball court, shower and locker space, and a board room and faculty lounge.

Programming had dwindled, however, due to a lack of funding and staff. Then, as the U faced a massive influx of students in the post–World War II years, the WAA found new buildings being constructed on the sites of its two outdoor fields. In 1949, after thirty years of debate, the Department of Physical Education for Women was allocated $300 from the Student Fee Fund for WAA activities.

Golf and tennis clubs were re-established in the 1950s, but there was little opportunity for actual play. The University Golf Course and tennis courts were controlled by the Department of Intercollegiate Athletics for Men and were very rarely available to the women.

In 1964, a new department was created—the School of Physical Education, Recreation and School Health Education—encompassing men's and women's physical education and intramurals, women's extramurals, and other disciplines. University women were incredulous that no woman had been named to the committee that conducted the feasibility study of the new school that included women's physical education and athletics. But Belmar Gunderson took over the administration of women's intramural and extramural athletics, and slow progress was made. Most of the supervision of extramurals was done voluntarily, on an overload basis, by faculty, teaching assistants, and part-time instructors.

Gunderson has been referred to as "the mother of women's intercollegiate athletics" at the university. It is not clear that Gunderson herself has claimed the title, and it is probably true that her boss, Eloise M. Jaeger, and her predecessor Sue Tinker are equally deserving of such recognition. What is clear is that the philosophy and administrative personnel were in place in the early 1970s to take advantage of the opportunity afforded by Title IX and that no one person could have accomplished this by herself.

In 1970, the Department of Intramurals for Women participated in a pair of intercollegiate tournaments—a golf tournament that it hosted at the University Golf Course and the Tri-State Tennis Meet held in Madison, Wisconsin. In 1972–1973, the university approved $5,000 "for funding of the Women's Intercollegiate Program," but the program remained under the Department of Intramurals. For 1973–1974, the operating budget was increased to $35,595 and

the following year to $129,781, or $333,406 if renovation and remodeling of new spaces for women's intercollegiate athletics were included. In 1975, the university's new president, C. Peter Magrath, and Minnesota Lieutenant Governor Rudy Perpich were instrumental in securing $380,000 in additional legislative funding.

Jaeger said the funding was "adequate if not fully equal." "There is no question," she added, "that Title IX, passed by Congress in 1972, had a significant impact on the financial support made available for women's athletics. . . . Women could no longer be ignored. Money had to be found somehow, and from someplace it came pouring out."

Gopher Women's Annual Record, 1971–1983

Year	Overall Record	Big Ten Record
Coach Joan Stevenson		
1971–1972	5–3	
Coach Deb Wilson		
1972–1973	8–8	
Coach Linda Wells		
1973–1974	3–10	
Coach Jenny Johnson		
1974–1975	7–12	
1975–1976	14–11	
1976–1977	15–14	
Johnson Totals	36–37	
1974–1977	.493	
Coach Ellen Mosher Hanson		
1977–1978	24–10	
1978–1979	17–15	
1979–1980	18–11	
1980–1981	28–7	
1981–1982	18–11	
1982–1983	20–7	13–5
Mosher Hanson Totals	125–61	13–5
1977–1983	.672	.722
Gopher Totals	177–119	13–5
1973–1983	.598	.722

26 "They Were Concerned about Being Basketball Players"

OF ALL THE PIONEERS of girls and women's basketball, perhaps none experienced a roller-coaster ride like that of the Women's Professional Basketball League (WBL), including the Minnesota Fillies, from 1978 to 1981. And yet in Minnesota, the WBL provided an opportunity not just for women but also for a man in search of a new career.

Gordy Nevers had been an outstanding pitcher who spent several seasons in professional baseball in the late 1950s and early 1960s. As he was winding up his pro career, he entered the funeral home business operated by his in-laws. By 1976, he was back in sports. His company, International Sports Management, had helped to launch the Pillsbury Holiday Classic basketball tournament, hosted by the Minnesota Gophers. Along with former Gophers player Paul Presthus, Nevers had also tried to break into business as a player's agent. Nevers explored other possibilities but was still trying to find the right path when, in the spring of 1978, he learned of the WBL's formation by Bill Byrne, who had been involved in the short-lived World Football League in 1974 and 1975. Nevers contacted Byrne and ended up with one of the original franchises, the Fillies, who began play in December 1978.

Nevers hired Dee Hopfenspirger as coach. As DeMaras "Dee" Mercie, she had coached Redwood Falls to the 1976 Class A title in the first Minnesota girls state high school basketball tournament. Hopfenspirger never made it to the regular season for the Fillies, however. She resigned in November during training camp.

"Coaching professional athletes, as I realized, was a little different," she said. "There were some very fine players there, but they were very individual," she explained. "They were very good, all of them, competitive, but I didn't think that the work ethic was especially what I would have expected it to be at that level. I didn't think they were in good condition. . . . So I wasn't as en-amored with coaching at that level as I was with my own high school athletes."

Nevers then hired Julia Yeater, who was about to start her third season as head coach of the women's team at Western Kentucky University. One of the players Yeater had coached in college was Brenda Chapman, now a Fillies player (and receptionist), and it was on Chapman's recommendation that Nevers hired Yeater.

Yeater said she left Western Kentucky because of a desire to see more female head coaches in the WBL. Lynnette Sjoquist, one of the original Fillies, credited Nevers for his efforts in hiring women coaches. "This was 1978, six years after Title IX," she said, "and there really weren't a lot of women coaches at the collegiate level even. [But] there was a lot more security at that point if you were a woman coaching at the collegiate level, certainly . . . more security than going with the WBL." Sjoquist, a native of Cannon Falls, Minnesota, had played at Golden Valley Lutheran College in the Twin Cities and then spent four seasons with the All-American Redheads, a female barnstorming basketball team. Sjoquist started the season as the Fillies' center and was in the starting lineup opening night, jumping against the Iowa Cornets' Doris Draving on December 15, 1978.

Iowa won the game, 103–81, as Chapman led all scorers with 23 points while Joan Uhl was high for Iowa with 22. Molly Bolin played little in the game for Iowa and scored 3 points. As Monna Lea "Molly" Van Venthuysen, she had been a great scorer for Moravia High School. In Iowa, girls still played a six-player version of the game that featured separate three-on-three matchups in the front court and the backcourt. Bolin did not make an immediate impact in the WBL. The reason often cited is that it took her some time to adjust to the five-on-five game. However, Bolin had played this style during her two seasons on the basketball team at Grandview College in Iowa, where she twice played against the Minnesota Gophers. Regardless of the reason for her slow start, Bolin soon became a top scorer and, dubbed "Machine Gun Molly" by the *Washington Post*, became the league's best-known player.

The crowd at the Met Center for the Fillies' first game was announced as 4,102. *Minneapolis Tribune* reporter Gary Libman covered the game but spent some of his time surveying groups in the stands to see if they had actually paid their way in or had received complimentary tickets. Nevers was frustrated with the focus of Libman's story and became increasingly agitated in the ensuing years as the Minneapolis and St. Paul newspapers largely ignored the Fillies.

The Fillies lost again two nights later, despite 43 points from Chapman as well as the debut of Marie Kocurek for the Fillies. Nevers made a trade with Houston for the draft rights to Kocurek, flew her to Minnesota for a tryout, and had her play that night. Kocurek gave a one-word answer when asked why she signed with Minnesota after turning down Houston: "Money." Kocurek said the Fillies paid her $8,000 for the season, $3,000 more than the Houston Angels had offered her. She also said, however, that she was used to first-class treatment and accommodations in college and felt that the Fillies and the WBL were a step down.

The addition of Kocurek gave the Fillies and their prime rival, the Cornets, the top two centers in the league. Both Kocurek and Draving made the WBL All-Pro Team in each of the first two years. Draving said Kocurek was "one of my least favorite players to play against. She had this ability to shoot over me, which really made me mad. She was a great player. She was so technically sound."

Two weeks later, the Fillies also acquired Marie "Scooter" DeLorme as the team's point guard. In February, there were more changes: Nevers fired Yeater, saying he had become disenchanted with her after watching her refuse to take a time out in a game against Iowa during a surge by the Cornets. Yeater characterized her departure as the result of "a lot of issues (some personal) about the direction the team was going" with Nevers and that she was to be reassigned as the director of scouting for the league office. Instead, she took the head coaching job in Milwaukee. Nevers coached one game himself before hiring Lou Mascari, who lasted only seven games. Nevers coached the Fillies again be-

fore turning over the reins for the final two games of the season to Trish Roberts. Roberts had been the team's top draft pick, but she played little that first season after injuring her knee during training camp.

The game of musical coaches was not confined to Minnesota. Yeater was the Milwaukee Does' fourth coach. Her predecessor in Milwaukee, George Nicodemus, had already been fired by another team, the Iowa Cornets, after some of his players had complained about him. Player complaints also were commonplace. Several Does complained about their general manager turned coach, Gene DeLisle. Among the complaints were that DeLisle had encouraged the players to break training rules, that he and other front-office staff came to practice with liquor on their breath, and that DeLisle was "close to a player." Two of the Does who had complained, Kathy DeBoer and Marguerite Keeley, were traded to Minnesota. The trade was controversial in Minnesota, too: one of the players the Fillies gave up was Chapman, who was leading the league in scoring. She held the league scoring lead through the rest of the season, but the players the Fillies got in return were great contributors to the team. With Minnesota, Keeley and DeBoer increased their scoring, and both averaged nearly 10 rebounds per game.

Minnesota finished the season with a 17–17 record, in third place in the four-team Midwest Division. Kocurek, Keeley, and Donna Wilson had represented the Fillies in the all-star game in March, and Kocurek was named to the league's all-pro team.

Home attendance was averaging barely more than a thousand, however, far below what would be needed for the team to survive. Nevers looked forward to better times. But first he had to deal with the coaching situation again, which was causing problems with the team's star player, Marie Kocurek. Of the coaches the Fillies had their first year, Kocurek said, "None of them were competent. They were all stupid. None of them knew basketball." At the end of the season, she said she told Nevers she would not play again if "you do not have competent coaching. Trade me."

The Second Season

Instead of trading Kocurek, Nevers hired Terry Kunze, the former star at the University of Minnesota and Duluth Central High School, as coach. Following college,

Brenda Chapman (right) is hounded by Iowa's Joan Uhl in the Minnesota Fillies' first game, December 15, 1978. Chapman led the Women's Basketball League in scoring that year, although the Fillies traded her to the Milwaukee Does midway through the season.

Kunze played one year for the Minnesota Muskies but otherwise played in Europe, where he said he could make more money. After his playing days were over, he coached a year at Mora High School and served as a Gophers assistant coach under Jim Dutcher in the mid-1970s and as an assistant at Eastern Carolina University before taking the job as the Fillies' head coach.

Kocurek said Kunze "did know basketball. He was a man's coach all his life, but he knew basketball. He knew his stuff." Kocurek had trouble with some of Kunze's methods, however, particularly his language. Asked about his language, Kunze said, "I treated them as athletes, not girls or women."

The Fillies were better, challenging Iowa for the division title. Six-foot-five center Katrina Owens, the team's top pick in the college draft, provided help in the front court as did Roberts, who was back from an injury after playing in only four games the season before. But the Fillies again played before mostly empty seats at the Met Center. And the league as a whole was

struggling—barely a month into the season the Philadelphia and Washington franchises folded.

The WBL had a bona fide star in 1979–1980, when Ann Meyers agreed to play with the New Jersey Gems. Meyers had been a four-time All-American at UCLA and was drafted by the Indiana Pacers of the NBA. Meyers was not the first woman drafted by an NBA team, but she became the first to go to training camp. After being cut by the Pacers, Meyers signed to play in the WBL. Sjoquist, by this time the Fillies' public relations director after being waived as a player, commented, "That's what the league needed . . . talent—all the talent we could find."

Several teams decided that another way to draw fans was to promote the physical appearance and attractiveness of certain players. Iowa promoted Bolin, producing and selling posters of her in a couple of different poses. The Chicago Hustle promoted Janie Fincher, though somewhat less aggressively. The glamour focus produced some publicity for the league, but it alienated some of the players. "They thought the heavier audience would be male," Sjoquist said, "and I think that was a mistake. I was pretty vocal at the time that I didn't agree with it. I thought we could promote a game for the game itself." Owner Gordy Nevers thought otherwise. "Makeup was something that was very resistant to our team. We had very, very nice people. They were good people, but they were so concerned about being basketball players, they didn't want you to know they were women."

The Fillies finished the season with a 22–12 record and made the playoffs. The playoff games were moved to Williams Arena because of scheduling conflicts with the Minnesota North Stars at the Met Center. Nevers also announced that the team would not return to the Met Center and instead would play its games for the 1980–1981 season at the Minneapolis Auditorium.

Minnesota lost its first playoff game in the best-of-three series to the New Orleans Pride before four hundred fans at Williams Arena. Three nights later, in New Orleans, the Fillies trailed and were on the verge of elimination when Owens scored to tie the game with four seconds remaining in regulation play. Minnesota then won in overtime. The deciding game, also played in New Orleans, was tied until the Fillies scored 6 points in the final minute for a 97–91 win. Kocurek broke the tie with a layup and later added a pair of free throws.

The Fillies next faced the Cornets in another best-of-three series. Minnesota got off to a fast start and cruised to a 108–87 win in the first game at Williams Arena. In the second game, Molly Bolin was at her best, scoring 50 points, as Iowa won to tie the series. Iowa built a 17-point lead in the third game, but the Fillies came back and cut the lead to a point. Denise Sharps had a chance to put Minnesota ahead but missed a shot in the final seconds. Iowa won, 95–92, earning a trip to the league's championship series.

The Cornets had lost to the Houston Angels, three-games-to-two, in the 1979 final. This time they lost to the New York Stars in four games. But the championship series marked the end for both the Stars and the Cornets. The demise of the Cornets was somewhat surprising, since the team was among the leaders in attendance. Draving blamed the collapse on the sale of the team from George Nissen to Dick Vance, whom she said "dragged the team under."

Two other teams—the Milwaukee Does and Califor-

nia Dreams—also did not return for the 1980–1981 season, although the owner of the Dreams ended up with a new franchise in the league, the Nebraska Wranglers. While Meyers refused to return to the New Jersey Gems after not receiving her full salary, the team survived and was one of only three original teams to make it through a third season. The Chicago Hustle and Minnesota Fillies were the other two.

Turmoil in the Final Season

The WBL ended up with a couple of other stars who had been hanging on to their amateur status so they could play in the Olympics. Those Olympic dreams evaporated when the United States boycotted the 1980 Games in Moscow, so Carol Blazejowski signed with the New Jersey Gems. Nancy Lieberman, who had led Old Dominion to the national college championship in 1979 and 1980, joined the Dallas Diamonds.

The addition of great college players like Blazejowski and Lieberman did not help attendance, however. In fact, the league struggled more than ever. A new team, the New England Gulls, was having trouble paying its players. On January 15, 1981, the Gulls refused to play, causing the team to disband.

Nevers was also experiencing problems meeting payroll, and this nearly resulted in a strike by the players in mid-February. "By the middle of my third year, we were not getting checks—half checks, no checks, bouncing checks," recalled Kocurek. "We were tripling up on roommates. We had a team meeting before practice and all decided not to play, including the coach." Kocurek said Kunze called Nevers, "who came and gave a 20-minute speech about how he's doing us a favor by giving us a job that we love and that we should want to do for free.

"After he left, I—the big mouth that I am—spoke up and said until we get paid we will not practice or play anymore, expecting my teammates to also speak up and back me up. Not one did."

When Kocurek got home from practice, she received a call from *Minneapolis Star* sports columnist Doug Grow. Kocurek was highly critical of Nevers, and the day after her comments appeared in the paper, she was traded to the Nebraska Wranglers. Grow responded with a column that began sarcastically, "The uppity wench deserved it. . . . She grumbled about not

Authors' Choice:
Minnesota All-Stars, through 1983

Center Linda Roberts, St. Paul Central High School, University of Minnesota, and Minnesota Fillies. Roberts helped lead Central to the 1976 Class AA state championship and its 1977 consolation title. Then she scored 1,856 points as a Gopher and set school rebounding records that still stand. More importantly, the Gophers' eighty-seven wins during her four-year career were the most ever until 2001–2005.

Forward Janet Karvonen, New York Mills High School. Karvonen almost single-handedly put Minnesota girls high school basketball on the map while leading Mills to a championship three-peat in 1977, 1978, and 1979. She broke the single-game scoring record four times and set a tournament scoring record with 98 points in 1979. A 38-point outburst came in the 1979 final, a 61–52 win over Albany and Kelly Skalicky, which remains one of the greatest girls finals ever. Most of her scoring records have now been broken, but her career turnabout total of 329 probably will never be matched.

Forward Laura Gardner, Bloomington Jefferson High School and University of Minnesota. Gardner led the Jaguars to each of the first three girls high school tournaments and the 1978 Class AA title. It was her career tournament scoring record of 141 points that Karvonen broke the following year. She scored 15 points per game as a freshman at the U and earned all-tournament honors at the National Women's Invitation Tournament (NWIT). She blew out her knee the following summer, however, and was never the same player again.

Guard Debbie Hunter, Cloquet High School and University of Minnesota. Hunter played her high school career in Karvonen's and Skalicky's shadow but blossomed into the best guard the Gopher women had ever had, until Lindsay Whalen came along. Though not primarily a scorer, she scored 1,361 points as a Gopher and set season and career records for free throw percentage, assists, and steals.

Guard Kelly Skalicky, Albany High School. Albany gave as good as it got in a rousing rivalry with Karvonen and New York Mills, taking second-place and then first-place honors in 1979 and 1980. In 1981, after Karvonen's graduation, Skalicky broke her game and tournament scoring records with 45 and 102 and then closed out her high school career with 35 points in a 76–70 overtime win over archrival Mills for fifth place.

SECOND TEAM *Center* Marie Kocourek, Minnesota Fillies; *forwards* Annie Adamczak, Moose Lake High School, and Elsie Ohm, Rochester John Marshall High School, University of Minnesota, and Mankato State; *guards* Scooter DeLorme, Minnesota Fillies, and Joan Kowalsky, St. Margaret's Academy, Benilde-St. Margaret's High School, University of Minnesota, and Mankato State.

---

being paid on time and he [Nevers] had her on the next bus to Nebraska."

Kocurek went to a team that was reeling over the murder of one of its players, Connie Kunzmann. A native of Everly, Iowa, not far from the Minnesota state line, Kunzmann had played two seasons with the Cornets. When the team disbanded, she went to Nebraska to play for the Wranglers. On February 6, 1981, Kunzmann was at an Omaha bar with some teammates and later got a ride with an acquaintance, Lance Tibke. The next day, Kunzmann was late for practice, and she was reported missing. Three days later, Tibke turned himself in to the police. The two had had an argument, he said. He stabbed her, hit her with a tire iron, and threw her body into the half-frozen Missouri River. Kunzmann was presumed dead, although her body was not recovered for more than a month.

The confession by Tibke came the day after the league's all-star game. Rosie Walker of Nebraska led the Central Division with 13 points, but the next night Nebraska postponed its game. The Wranglers went on to win the WBL title, beating Nancy Lieberman and the Dallas Diamonds in the championship series.

Meanwhile, the Fillies won only one more game. Their roster was down to eight players, and they were now traveling to games in the Midwest in a van rather than a bus. On March 21, Kunze and the Fillies drove to Chicago for a game against the Hustle. At the hotel, they found that the credit card Nevers had given them to pay for the rooms was rejected. Accounts vary as to what happened from there. Nevers said he had arranged with the management of the Chicago team to help out if needed and that Kunze was to have called them if there was a problem with the credit card. Kunze does not remember any issues over payment for the hotel, although a newspaper story two days later said

Kunze produced his own credit card for the rooms after the one from Nevers was rejected.

Scooter DeLorme remembers the incident with the credit card, which, combined with salaries being in arrears, resulted in a team meeting to decide whether to play the game that night. DeLorme, who was an assistant coach on the team in addition to being a player, said she opposed walking out, as did Nessie Harris, a college teammate of hers, and Donna Wilson, the only original member of the Fillies still with the team. However, they agreed to abide by the majority opinion, and the other players—Angela Cotman, Kim Hansen, Nancy Dunkle, Anita Ortega, and Coco Daniels—voted not to play. They decided that Chicago, where the league office was located, was the place to make a statement. In addition, the WBL commissioner, Sherwin Fischer, was on the Hustle's board of directors.

The Fillies still took the floor before the game, not even wearing their normal uniforms under their warm-up attire, and then left just before the starting lineups were to be introduced. They exited through the locker room and got into their van. DeLorme recalls that the van was held up for about fifteen minutes while the referees and Chicago management came out to talk to them. Kunze said he had no idea what the players had planned until they left the floor, but Nevers expressed anger at his coach. "Had I had a little more stable leadership, they never would have walked out," Nevers said nearly twenty-five years later. "I can't believe what Terry did. He was a ringleader. He actually supported it."

Now the Fillies got the newspaper coverage they had always hoped for. As Nevers had remarked a month earlier, "The only time we get any ink is when one of our players gets killed or when our players don't get paid."

The WBL suspended Kunze and the players. Nevers had to postpone a game at home the next night, but he was determined to have the Fillies finish their schedule. He came up with a coach named Mark DeLapp and cobbled together a roster that included former Fillies Sue Wahl-Bye and Cheryl Engel along with several college players who had just completed their senior seasons—Linda Roberts and Mary Manderfeld of the University of Minnesota, Lynn Peterson of Mankato State, and Elsie Ohm, who had played at both schools.

On March 23, the fill-in Fillies lost 128–80 to the St. Louis Streak. With a slightly different cast, the Fil-

lies lost badly to St. Louis again the following night. Minnesota finished the season on the road, and Sjoquist took over coaching duties while bringing along a uniform so she could also play. After a 44-point loss in Dallas, the Fillies played their final game in San Francisco on March 31, and it was another embarrassing loss, 122–61.

Despite the tumultuous end of the season, Nevers was optimistic. He envisioned Lynn Peterson as a star for the team and a possible gate attraction because of her looks. "She was beautiful, number one. And she could play," said Nevers, adding that Peterson could "have been our Molly Bolin, our Janie Fincher. She was a very beautiful girl and a lovely person." The Fillies, having the league's worst record (7–28), would also be able to bolster their roster with the top pick in the college draft, which probably would have been used to select Lynette Woodard of Kansas. But the draft was postponed, and the entire league was finally disbanded.

The following February, Nevers filed for Chapter 7 bankruptcy, claiming assets of $1,525 and liabilities that totaled more than a million dollars. Despite the financial devastation, he is not sorry that he tried. "It was a part of my life that was very positive. I enjoyed it," Nevers said, then added, "You can live your life like you're jumping on a train. You're not worrying about the destination, but you just enjoy the ride. That's a good philosophy of life as far as I'm concerned."

Among Nevers's creditors were Kocurek and DeLorme, former roommates who remain friends to this day. Neither got her full pay, but DeLorme—now Scooter Barnette, former coach, and current faculty member at her alma mater, the College of Charleston—called her time in the league "a great adventure and a great opportunity." Kocurek went back to her hometown of Corpus Christi, Texas, and got a job with Valero Refinery. On November 8, 1989, Kocurek was riding her bike outside of town when she was hit by a car, dragged seventy feet, and, in her words, "left for dead." She was in a coma for eight days, in intensive care for two weeks, and out of work for nearly a year and a half. She returned to Valero after recovering from her injuries and still works there. She harbors resentment over some of her experiences but said, "The pro league, it can be bitter and sad, but the friendships we made were lasting, and I'll thank them for that."

Rebuilding Years for Minnesota Basketball, 1983–1997

Minnesota basketball seemed to be on the rise in the late 1970s and early 1980s. Minnesota girls and women finally got the opportunity to play, and fans quickly fell in love with Janet Karvonen and the girls game. Meanwhile, Minnesota high schools turned out a series of great, big men, two of whom—Kevin McHale and Randy Breuer—went on to outstanding careers with the Minnesota Gophers.

The period from the mid-1980s through the mid-1990s, however, was one of almost unrelieved frustration for Minnesota basketball fans. The Gopher men stumbled from scandal to scandal with but a few real high points in between. The achievements of its 1997 team—its greatest since its unbeaten national champions of 1919—turned out to be dependent on an elaborate academic fraud. Later, its achievements were vacated by the Big Ten and the NCAA. Meanwhile, the Gopher women fell from twenty wins in 1982–1983 to just eight by 1985–1986, and they would win as many as just ten games only four times over a period of sixteen years.

Attendance at the boys and girls high school tournaments stabilized in the 1980s, but then both declined suddenly by about one-third by 1994. So debate about the tournament format, which had consumed so much time and energy during the 1960s, flared again. And the next generation of Breuers, Karvonens, and McHales failed to materialize at Minnesota high schools.

The return of the NBA to Minnesota after an absence of almost thirty years provided a breath of fresh air, at first. But the Minnesota Timberwolves quickly became a laughingstock and remained so until the arrival of two Kevins—Garnett and McHale—along with coach Flip Saunders in 1995.

The one bright spot on the landscape was the success of women's small college teams—particularly those at Anoka-Ramsey Community College, Concordia (Moorhead), St. Benedict's, and St. Thomas.

Jessica Beachy (24) led Concordia (Moorhead) to the 1988 NCAA Division III national championship and was named the Division III Player of the Year. In 2006, she was named to the Division III twenty-fifth anniversary all-star team and also coached Concordia to the MIAC postseason title.

27 *New Patterns in Girls Hoops*

THE GIRLS HIGH SCHOOL tournament settled into middle-aged respectability as of 1984. Enough girls now had sufficient court time and coaching to become fundamentally sound basketball players, so it became harder for single individuals to dominate in the way that Janet Karvonen and Kelly Skalicky and the other great pioneers had dominated. Team play became the thing. And the best teams and the best programs—which, generally, were those with the best coaches—were now able to achieve repeated success despite the graduation of a star player or two.

Class A Powerhouses

After New York Mills, Albany, and Austin Pacelli from 1977 through 1981, the history of the Class A tournament revolved for a decade around another round-robin rivalry among New London-Spicer (NLS), Rochester Lourdes, and Tracy/Milroy. In fact, the Lourdes girls, under the leadership of coach Myron Glass, were (and are) the undisputed queens of girls basketball with five state titles between 1987 and 1995 and three more since then. Meanwhile, NLS, under long-time coach Mike Dreier, became the unquestioned leaders in near misses and tears and disappointment.

Lourdes played in five title games, NLS four through 1995. Lourdes won them all, while NLS lost a remarkable four in a row to Lourdes in 1991 and 1993, and Tracy/Milroy and Blake in 1992 and 1994. What's remarkable, of course, is that they played in four consecutive title games, something only one other team—boys or girls—had ever done before. Also to their credit, the 1991, 1993, and 1994 championship game losses came at the hands of the greatest teams ever among Minnesota girls—as measured by their win-loss records, at

least—as Lourdes (twice) and Blake each finished with a record of thirty victories and no defeats.

NLS finally captured a pair of state titles, in 1997 and 2002.

Meanwhile Tracy/Milroy appeared in four finals under a series of different names and won championships in 1988, 1992, and 1996. The 1992 title came under the name Tracy Area, while the 1985 title game loss was actually suffered by tiny Milroy. Still another tournament appearance was made by Tracy-Milroy/Walnut Grove. The 1988 title was under coach Shorty Engel, and the two titles in the 1990s were under Terry Culhane, who would return in the twenty-first century to win two more titles with Marshall High School.

Overall, NLS appeared in nine tournaments in thirteen years (1985–1997), Lourdes in eight tournaments in ten years (1986–1995), and Tracy, Tracy Area, Milroy, Tracy/Milroy, Tracy-Milroy, and Tracy-Milroy/Walnut Grove in ten tournaments in sixteen years (1981–1996). Along the way, these three powerhouses played seven games among themselves, though Lourdes and Tracy/Milroy somehow managed to avoid one another.

In this way all seven games involved NLS, and NLS's fate was sealed by losses in six of those seven games. NLS went 13–8 in championship round games, and six of its eight losses—in fact, every one of the first six losses—was to Lourdes or Tracy/Milroy. NLS was 12–2 against all others.

Lourdes and Tracy/Milroy overlapped three times. But in 1987, Tracy/Milroy was overwhelmed by Wheaton in the first round. Lourdes later edged Wheaton in the final, 33–31, for its first title. In 1989, it was Lourdes's turn to bow out early to the eventual champion Storden-Jeffers, who also beat Tracy-Milroy/Walnut Grove in the semifinal. The two came closest to a dream matchup in 1995, when both earned first-round victories. But while Lourdes won handily against Christ's Household of Faith in the semis,

Ann Ogren of Mankato East (34) shoots over Jodi Anderson (51) of Little Falls in the 1985 girls Class AA final as Mary Agnew (42) of East looks on. Little Falls prevailed, 48–41, to become the second girls team to win a third state title.

Archrivals New London-Spicer (NLS) and Rochester Lourdes battle in the 1991 Class A final. Lourdes won, 53–28, for their third of eight state titles. NLS lost in four straight state championship games, plus a fifth in 2001, but the Wildcats won two titles in 1997 and 2002. Identifiable Lourdes players are Stacy Sievers (32) and Leslie Whiting (4); for NLS are Tracy Hanson (52), Angie Sampson (43), and Lisa Oman (14).

Tracy-Milroy lost an overtime heartbreaker to St. James. Lourdes then trounced St. James in the final for its fifth state title.

Lourdes in 1991 and 1993 and Blake in 1994 closed out a string of ten unbeaten Class A champions in the fifteen years from 1980 through 1994. The first four all finished 26–0. In 1980, it was Albany and Kelly Skalicky crushing Austin Pacelli, 56–25, in the final. The following year, Pacelli shocked Albany in the first round but lost to Heron Lake–Okabena in the semis. Heron Lake then defeated Moose Lake, 62–46, to complete its unbeaten season.

Moose Lake returned the following year to edge East Chain, 52–49, in overtime in the final. Annie Adamczak led the Lakers to a sweep of the volleyball, basketball, and softball titles; she then went on to win All-America honors in volleyball at the University of Nebraska. In 1983, it was Henderson, defeating Chisholm and Lake City to win its championship. Henderson's Lisa Walters went on to play with Heron Lake's Pat Burns at what is now Minnesota State Mankato. Walters earned All-America honors and played professional ball in Sweden.

Chisholm returned in 1984 and finished 27–0 with wins over Staples, Glencoe, and Eden Valley–Watkins, 55–41, in the final. Judy McDonald, daughter of the Bluestreaks boys coach Bob McDonald, scored 69 points. It was Staples' turn in 1985 to become the sixth unbeaten Class A champ in a row at 28–0, knocking off Milroy, 49–39, in the final.

Finally, Storden-Jeffers (S-J) played in three straight finals in 1988, 1989, and 1990—and in six tournaments in seven years through 1994, though with a new name, Red Rock Central, in 1994. After losing to Tracy/Milroy, 47–35, in the 1988 final, S-J turned the tables, defeating Tracy-Milroy/Walnut Grove, 57–41, in a 1989 semi. Eden Valley–Watkins was the twenty-seventh and final victim of the year in a 76–52 rout. In 1990, S-J lost to the Lourdes girls, 52–45, in the final, but Darci Steere won all-tournament recognition for the third time. Steere went on to win NCAA Division II All-America honors at North Dakota State, while teammate Tracey Pudenz won all-conference honors at the University of North Dakota.

Along with Mills and Lourdes, any listing of girls Class A dynasties would have to include the Oistads of Fertile-Beltrami (F-B). Four daughters of assistant coach Rod Oistad played at F-B, three made it to the state tournament, and all three won all-tournament honors. Shelley played in the 1977, 1978, and 1979 tournaments, scoring 23, 25, and 31 points in her highest scoring games. She won all-tournament honors twice, and her 1,270 point total was a school record for a decade. Kristi, unfortunately, never made it to state. Missy made it to state in 1982, scoring a high of 14 points in a game, although F-B lost both tournament games. Marie finally got to state in her senior year of 1988. She scored a high of 20 points as F-B had its best showing, clobbering Kenyon, 57–36, for the consolation title. The trip to state also enabled Marie to squeeze in just enough scoring to edge Shelley's school record for most career points.

We'll never know whether the Oistads, even with dad Rod on the floor, could beat the Miller sisters of Milroy five-on-five, however. Mary Jo, three-time all-stater—first for Milroy's runners-up in 1985, then for Tracy-Milroy's consolation champions and state champions of 1987 and 1988—told how she developed her devastating jump shot. "I've got five older sisters," she

Mary Jo Miller (21) celebrates Tracy/Milroy's state Class A title in 1988, after leading all scorers in the final with 23 points. She also earned all-tournament honors for a third time, having been previously honored while playing for runner-up Milroy in 1985 and for Tracy-Milroy's consolation champions in 1987.

Minnesota Girls High School Champions, 1984–1996

Year	Championship Game Score	W–L	Authors' Choice: Postseason MVPs
1984	A Chisholm 55 Eden Valley–Watkins 41	27–0	Lea Blackwell, Edina, G
	AA Little Falls 45 Burnsville 43	22–4	
1985	A Staples 49 Milroy 39	28–0	Mary Jo Miller, Milroy, G
	AA Little Falls 48 Mankato East 43	22–4	
1986	A Midwest Minnesota 54 East Grand Forks 38	25–1	Jennifer Hall, Burnsville, G
	AA St. Louis Park 61 St. Paul Highland Park 55	24–2	
1987	A Rochester Lourdes 33 Wheaton 31	26–2	Shirley Ethen, Rocori, C
	AA Mankato East 50 Cold Spring Rocori 47	25–1	
1988	A Tracy/Milroy 47 Storden-Jeffers 35	25–2	Mary Jo Miller, Tracy/Milroy, F-G
	AA Edina 41 Rosemount 33	25–1	
1989	A Storden-Jeffers 76 Eden Valley–Watkins 52	27–0	Jessica Fiebelkorn, Osseo, C
	AA Osseo 54 Little Falls 50	24–2	
1990	A Rochester Lourdes 52 Storden-Jeffers 45	27–1	Shannon Loeblein, St. Paul Harding, F
	AA St. Louis Park 60 Elk River 50	22–4	
1991	A Rochester Lourdes 53 New London–Spicer 28	30–0	Shannon Loeblein, St. Paul Harding, F
	AA Burnsville 59 St. Paul Harding 54 (OT)	23–5	
1992	A Tracy Area 61 New London–Spicer 52	27–1	Tricia Wakely, Burnsville, F
	AA Burnsville 53 Mounds View 36	25–2	
1993	A Rochester Lourdes 48 New London–Spicer 43	30–0	Colleen Polzin, Jefferson, C
	AA Bloomington Jefferson 42 Roseville Area 34	26–1	
1994	A Blake 39 New London–Spicer 36	30–0	Leah Klaassen, Willmar, C
	AA Bloomington Jefferson 73 Osseo 50	26–2	
1995	A Rochester Lourdes 65 St. James 39	30–1	Coco Miller, Rochester Mayo, F-G
	AA Rochester Mayo 74 St. Cloud Apollo 49	27–1	Kelly Miller, Rochester Mayo, F-G
1996	A Tracy-Milroy 40 Blake 38		Erin Ditty, Hastings, F
	AA Hastings 54 Osseo 52	26–3	

said, "so I always had to jump over them to shoot. . . .
Coaches were always showing my sisters the right way
to shoot, so they'd come home and show me."

Meanwhile among the Big Schools . . .

Little Falls (in 1985), Burnsville (1992), and Bloomington Jefferson (1994) became the first Class AA schools
to win three state titles. This is a perfect reflection of the
shift in the balance of power among the big schools toward the metro area. The metro and Greater Minnesota
areas split the first twelve titles right down the middle, with St. Cloud Apollo (1982), Albany (1983), and
Mankato East (1987) joining the Falls Flyers in the winners' circle. But the metro won seven in a row from 1988
to 1994, with Burnsville and Jefferson winning four in
a row, two apiece, through 1994. The rapid growth of
youth basketball in the metro area—that is, of club play
outside of the schools and outside of the school year—is
too obvious an explanation to ignore.

The Flyers' first title came in their first tournament
appearance in 1980. Center LeeAnne Grosso was the
best player in Class AA—and she was again in 1981, but
Falls fell to eventual champion Coon Rapids by 1 point
in the semis. The Cardinals then clobbered St. Paul
Harding, 60–42, in the final to close out their unbeaten
season. Falls returned to the tournament in 1984 and
edged Burnsville for the title, 45–43, behind future Gophers guard Deb Hilmerson. With Hilmerson gone in
1985, the successful title defense was a complete surprise, but Sue Lies and Julie Cool, daughter of coach
Jerry, led the Flyers over Mankato East, 48–41, in the final. East returned with Kristin Maschka and Kendra
Carter to win the title two years later. The Flyers made
it to their fourth title game another two years later, in
1989, but lost to Osseo and center Jessica Fiebelkorn in
a 54–50 thriller.

Osseo's win, coupled with Edina's state title the previous year, began the period of metro dominance. St.
Louis Park, which had won in 1986, repeated in 1990.
Burnsville, which had won in 1977, then took the 1991
and 1992 titles. The Braves edged future Gophers
Shannon Loeblein and Cara Pearson and St. Paul Harding, 59–54, in overtime in 1991; they then won easily
in 1992, behind Tricia Wakely, who would go on to win
All-America honors at Drake, and Chelsea Schwankl.

The last unbeaten AA champion—after Jefferson

*Caroline Moos of Blake challenges a shot by New London-Spicer's
Heather Mayhew as Blake's Kinesha Davis (4) and Tiffany Willard (54)
and the Wildcats' Trisha Olson (43) look on. Blake won its first of three
state titles in 1994 and finished 30–0 by defeating NLS in the Class A
final, 39–36.*

in 1978 and Coon Rapids in 1981—had been St. Cloud
Apollo way back in 1982, reflecting the improvements
in girls hoops over the years. Still, the greatest of the
girls champions through 1996 was surely Jefferson's
1993 and 1994 champs. The 1993 squad, led by Missy
Kane, Kiersten Miller, and Colleen Polzin, won three
games by an average of 11 points to finish 25–1. The
1994 team squeaked past Apple Valley, 55–52, in the
semifinals, then hammered Osseo, 73–50, in the final
as Kane, Miller, and Maren Walseth starred.

The two-class era closed out with another runner-
up finish for Osseo. The Orioles were heavily favored
to win the 1996 Class AA title, but Hastings shocked
the Orioles in a 54–52 thriller as Erin Ditty scored 23
points.

By the mid-1990s, girls hoops in Minnesota featured the same patterns as the boys. The metro suburbs
dominated, but Minnesota overall was not producing
many Division I caliber players and the Minnesota Gophers were struggling with a roster filled with Minnesota high school graduates. But all of that was changing,
thanks largely to a couple of girls from Rochester Mayo.

28 *Living in the Past*

W ITH THE ADVENT of two-class play in 1971, the boys state tournament came to be dominated by a series of great rivalries. Between 1979 and 1999, Duluth Central, Bloomington Jefferson, Chisholm, Minneapolis North, and DeLaSalle each tied Red Wing's longstanding record of four state titles. Jefferson's dynastic status depended on its success against archrivals Hibbing (in 1975 and 1976) and Duluth East (in 1981 and 1982), and Chisholm's came in spite of a pair of heartbreaking losses to Winona Cotter in 1981 and 1982. Yet none of these was the greatest rivalry of the two-class era. That, instead, would be the 1984 and the 1985 championship matches between the unbeaten Bears and the unbeaten Bears. Through it all was a persistent theme of decline. By 1994, attendance was barely two-thirds of what it had been in the golden age—despite two classes featuring twice as many teams and twice as many games. Old-timers lamented the passing of the days when the boys high school tournament was the highlight of Minnesota's sporting year.

In 1984, the Polars of Minneapolis North, led by guard Brett McNeal, came into the tournament as prohibitive favorites. The equally unbeaten Bears of White Bear Lake came in as unsung as an unbeaten, second-ranked team can be, despite a six-foot-five, six-foot-five, and six-foot-four front line and a 67–42 average margin of victory. The Bears' success was attributed to the recent consolidation of White Bear Lake and Mariner high schools, which provided them with a deep, nine-player rotation.

Sure enough, the (White) Bears won their first two games by 9 and 21, while giving up just 37.5 points per game and putting nine boys in the scoring column. North was unimpressive in its two victories, winning by 6 and 5. The Bears' defense was the difference in the final; they held the Polars' vaunted offense to just 1 field goal in the final thirteen minutes. Even so, the Bears

Doug Carter of Minneapolis North tries to find a way to score as White Bear Lake's Larry Ogden (45) and Tom Nilsen (25) defend. The Minneapolis North Polars and White Bear Lake Bears both came into the 1984 and 1985 Class AA tournaments unbeaten and met in the title game both times. White Bear Lake won both finals.

were only able to pull ahead on a pair of Larry "Hot Shot" Parker free throws with five seconds left. Parker, it turns out, had won a statewide "Hot Shots" shooting contest as an eighth grader. The final was 51–47.

The following year, the roles were almost exactly reversed. Both teams were unbeaten, but it was the (White) Bears who were favored yet performed unimpressively in the first two rounds. Meanwhile, North scored more than 75 points per game and then forced the tempo by taking an early lead in the final. The Bears showed unexpected flexibility, however, outplaying the Polars in a fast-paced second half to win, 67–62.

North's Doug Carter led all scorers across the six games at 17 points per game, but in the two finals the Bears' Joe Regnier led the way with 39 points. Carter, McNeal, and Regnier all made the AP five-player all-state team, and McNeal went on to play major college ball for Clem Haskins at Western Kentucky. Regnier earned all-conference honors twice at North Dakota State.

Jefferson matched the Bears' back-to-back titles in 1986 and 1987 behind the exploits of Kevin Lynch and Tom Batta. And as in 1982, they had to go through Duluth to get there. In 1986, the Jaguars edged Duluth Central in a 52–51 championship game thriller, denying the Trojans the opportunity to become the state's first five-time champ. Then in 1987, Jefferson defeated East, 44–39, before disposing of Blaine, 54–37, in the final, after Blaine had beaten Moorhead, 62–56, in a record five overtimes in their semifinal.

Cretin, under coach Len Horyza, won the 1991 Class AA title in an exciting overtime matchup against Minneapolis Roosevelt and then waltzed into the 1992 finals heavily favored after a pair of easy wins. But Anoka, 1973 and 1981 champion, had other ideas. The Tornadoes ground the pace down to a near-halt, flexed the muscles of Matt Adler, Bryan Doughty, and Dan Novotny in the paint, and came from behind to win, 50–47. Cretin's Arvesta Kelly Jr., however, was the game's and tournament's leading scorer with 14 and 67 points.

In 1993, the final was regarded as a toss-up, since Cretin had just one loss all year long but struggled to a double-overtime win over Elk River and Skipp Schaefbauer in the semis. Meanwhile, Anoka had cruised by Duluth Central, 66–54. In the final Cretin took an early lead, forced the pace a bit, and won easily, 56–44. This is the only case in tournament history of a championship

Kevin Lynch led Bloomington Jefferson to state Class AA titles in 1986 and 1987 and then starred for the Gophers through their great NCAA tournament runs of 1989 and 1990.

rematch that produced a different result. Kelly became the third player ever to win boys all-tournament honors a third time. Cretin also made history by becoming just the fourth boys team ever—after Moorhead in 1928–1930, Edina in 1966–1968, and Melrose in 1971–1974—to play in three or more straight finals.

When we think of suburban powers, we think of the west metro Twin Cities and the Lake Conference. But the slower-growing east metro suburbs, clustered in what had been Region 4 during the single-class era, began flexing their muscles in 1972 and 1973. That's when Mounds View and Anoka won back-to-back Class AA titles. In fact, between 1968 and 1997, only Bloomington Jefferson of the Lake Conference won a state title—though, of course, the Jaguars won four. Meanwhile, five different east metro schools won titles: Anoka won three, White Bear Lake a pair, and Mounds View, Woodbury, and Simley one each.

If there was an east metro style, it was classic smash-mouth basketball emphasizing the big guy, the low post, defense, and ball control—just the style of play that some observers blamed for declining interest in the state tournament. None of the east metro champions scored as many as 60 points per game in the tournament. East metro stars were most likely to be built along the lines of six-foot-six Mark Landsberger (Mounds View, 1972), Anoka's twin six-foot-eight towers Loren Erickson and Greg Kettler (1973) and six-foot-seven Tryg Johnson (1981) and two-time champion six-foot-six Joe Regnier (White Bear Lake 1984 and 1985). The average scoring margin from Mounds View in 1972 through Simley in 1997 was 55–45.

Landsberger was the top individual, and the top coach was Ziggy Kauls, who led the Mustangs to that 1972 title and then returned twenty-seven years later for another. But the top single team was surely White Bear Lake. It is just a question of whether you prefer the nine-deep rotation of the 1984 squad or the more experienced 1985 team. The east metro also produced the top father-son combo of coach Del and guard Bill Schiffler, who led Woodbury to the 1983 title in a huge upset. Woodbury knocked off the favored metro power, Coon Rapids, and six-foot-ten Tom Copa in a thrilling overtime battle of unbeatens, 56–50.

Then, as had occurred in the 1960s, there was after Copa a sudden shortage of tall, low post players. It would be six years before six-foot-nine Chad Kolander led Owatonna in scoring in five of their six consecutive tournament victories in 1989 and 1990. Their 1989 win was a huge upset, 45–43 in overtime, over defending state AA runner-up Armstrong. In 1990, the Huskies won more easily in a record-breaking 72–24 rout of Minneapolis North. In this case the big scare came in the semis, when Owatonna held Chaska to 2 fourth-quarter points in a 35–34 win.

The other new powers were the Catholic schools that only became eligible to play in the Minnesota State High School League (MSHSL) tournament in 1975. Winona Cotter, under Hall of Fame coach John Nett, was the first to break through in 1977—and again

Minnesota Boys High School Champions, 1984–1996

Year	Championship Game Score	W–L	Authors' Choice: Postseason MVPs
1984	A Pelican Rapids 57 Winona Cotter 55	24–2	Joe Regnier, White Bear Lake, C
	AA White Bear Lake 51 Mpls. North 47	26–0	
1985	A DeLaSalle 56 Winona Cotter 46	26–2	Larry Ogden, White Bear Lake, F-G
	AA White Bear Lake 67 Mpls. North 62	26–0	
1986	A LeSueur 55 Staples 43	26–2	Tim Radosevich, Duluth Central, C-F
	AA Bloomington Jefferson 52 Duluth Central 51	23–4	
1987	A Norman County West 70 Crosby-Ironton 58	26–2	Kevin Lynch, Jefferson, F-G
	AA Bloomington Jefferson 54 Blaine 37	26–0	
1988	A DeLaSalle 58 Russell-Tyler-Ruthton 36	26–1	Jeff Voit, Cold Spring Rocori, F
	AA Cold Spring Rocori 66 Armstrong 56	26–0	
1989	A Rushford-Peterson 64 Russell-Tyler-Ruth. 52	26–2	Chad Kolander, Owatonna, C
	AA Owatonna 45 Armstrong 43 (OT)	24–1	
1990	A Lake City 52 Mankato Loyola 51	26–2	Mike Broich, Owatonna, F
	AA Owatonna 72 Mpls. North 26	23–2	
1991	A Chisholm 77 Westbrook-Walnut Grove 61	29–1	Joel McDonald, Chisholm, G
	AA Cretin 74 Mpls. Roosevelt 62 (OT)	27–1	
1992	A Austin Pacelli 68 DeLaSalle 62	19–11	Arvesta Kelly Jr., Cretin, F
	AA Anoka 50 Cretin 47	25–3	
1993	A Maple River 33 Faribault Bethlehem 29	29–1	Skipp Schaefbauer, Elk River, G
	AA Cretin 56 Anoka 44	28–1	
1994	A St. Agnes 78 Morris Area 71	25–5	Byron Suttles, Mpls. Washburn, G
	AA Mpls. Washburn 66 Hopkins 65	27–1	
1995	Mpls. North 54 Staples-Motley 52[a]	30–0	Blaine Joerger, Staples-Motley, F-G
1996	Mpls. North 80 Fertile-Beltrami 47[a]	29–1	Khalid El-Amin, Mpls. North

[a] Sweet Sixteen format tournaments.

in 1982. In fact, the Ramblers played in five Class A title games in nine years, winning two and losing three.
Cotter returned to the class A final in 1984 to face Peli
can Rapids, whom they had defeated, 60–47, in 1977
for their first title. Now it was the Vikings' turn to edge
the Cotter Ramblers, 57–55, as Pat Westby scored 22
points. Cotter also lost the 1985 Class A final to Minneapolis DeLaSalle, 56–46, to become the fourth of
six boys teams to lose successive championship games.
The Islanders repeated in 1988, beating Russell-Tyler-
Ruthton, 58–36. They also played for the state title in
1992 and 1997, losing to Austin Pacelli and Caledonia,
respectively, then won two more in 1998 and 1999.

Then came Cretin-Derham Hall with its big school
titles in 1991 and 1993. Three of the four finalists in
1992 were Catholics, as Pacelli beat DeLaSalle and Cretin lost to Anoka. St. Paul St. Agnes took the Class A title
in 1994, while Mankato Loyola in 1990 and Faribault
Bethlehem in 1993 also made it to the small-school final. The success of Catholic and other independent
schools accelerated after 1997 with two champions in
1998 (DeLaSalle and St. Thomas Academy) and 1999
(Southwest Christian and DeLaSalle, again) and three
finalists each in 1999 and 2001. Some suggested that
the private schools ought to go back to holding their
own separate but equal tournament.

Other than White Bear and Jefferson, there were
but two other unbeaten champions in the entire decade of the 1980s. One was 1983 Class A champ Bar-
num, who defeated Luverne, 53–47, despite 22 points
by the Cardinals' Gordie Hanson. The other was 1988
Class AA champion Cold Spring Rocori, who surprised
Robbinsdale Armstrong, 66–56, in the final as Jeff Voit
scored 21 points.

Chisholm won its fourth state title in 1991 behind the exploits of Joel McDonald, youngest son of
Hall of Fame coach Bob. Joel scored an incredible
1,156 points in 1991—38.5 per game—to break older
brother Tom's 1982 state record. That also gave him
an all-time record 3,292 points for his career, breaking the thirty-five-year-old record of Norm Grow of
Foley. More importantly, the 'Streaks blitzed three
tournament opponents by an average of 18 points to
win Coach Bob his third Class A title. Bob McDonald
continues to coach the Bluestreaks through 2006, and
he holds a state record himself with more than eight
hundred career victories.

Minnesota Mysteries and Myths
Sweet Sixteen Expected to Bring Back Glory Days

The idea of a Sweet Sixteen state tournament format was
first proposed in 1937. The MSHSL had rejected the idea
of a two-class tournament, so backers proposed the Sweet
Sixteen as a watered-down version that they hoped would
gather some support. It did not. It was never discussed as an
option prior to the initiation of two-class play in 1971. It was
next discussed only in 1972, when MSHSL executive director
Murrae Freng told the *Minneapolis Tribune* that some more
tinkering with the tournament format was possible.

In 1975, Anoka coach Bill Wanamaker expressed frustration that the coaches did not have much to say about the
tournament format. "Most would like a sixteen team tournament," he added. As if to prove Wanamaker's point, Freng was
quoted the following year saying that the only chance for a
change in the tourney format was if attendance should fall to
the point that the MSHSL experienced financial trouble.

It was another decade before the Sweet Sixteen format
was again discussed seriously, but new MSHSL executive director Orv Bies said in 1985, "The [Sweet Sixteen format] has
little support among Class A coaches. The majority apparently favor the present system." But the coaches' association
sponsored a fifteen-member committee, chaired by Staples
coach Lynn Peterson, to study the tournament format, and
Peterson's committee recommended the Sweet Sixteen format. Rather than adopting the committee's recommendation, however, twenty-five MSHSL region representatives and
board members agreed only to hold sixteen regional meetings. "If there is a strong consensus for the proposed plan at
the regional meetings," Peterson said, "[the] committee will
take it to the MSHSL for approval."

That did not happen, and so the next change to the tourney format, for both the boys and the girls, was a switch to a
four-day schedule in 1993. Previously, both A and AA quarterfinals were played on the same day. The *Minneapolis Tribune* reported that the switch was a success but noted that
attendance was down by 2,000.

So in 1994, the Sweet Sixteen was finally approved by the
MSHSL Board of Directors for implementation for the boys
1995 and 1996 tourneys, but never for the girls. The result
was a tremendously exciting and competitive tournament
featuring six David and Goliath matchups. David won three
by a total of 22 points, and Goliath won three by a total of 35.
The final was another David meets Goliath story and one of

the great finals of recent memory. Unbeaten Minneapolis North claimed the title, 54–52, over Staples-Motley on a last-second put-back by Kavon Westberry. Blaine Joeger scored 28 points for the losers.

The 1996 Sweet Sixteen tournament was just as good until the final, which again matched Minneapolis North against a David. In fact, David (Class A) beat Goliath (Class AA) in their first two meetings—a pair of quarterfinal upsets of Staples-Motley over Cold Spring Rocori and Minnehaha Academy over Eden Prairie—before the larger schools asserted themselves. Unfortunately, Cinderella threw a shoe in the one game that anybody remembers. North hammered Fertile-Beltrami, 80–47, in the final as Jabbar Washington scored 28 for the Polars.

On the court, the Sweet Sixteen worked, as the smaller

schools won five of eleven David and Goliath games. But the small schools never really liked the idea, and the lack of response to all of this by the Minnesota sporting public was fatal. Not only did the Sweet Sixteen fail to "bring the basketball tournament back to its glory days," as newspaper columnist Sid Hartman had predicted it would, but attendance dropped from that of the last two-class tournament in 1994. *Minneapolis Tribune* columnist Pat Reusse wrote, "This is a noble effort. . . . [But] if the goal is to bring back huge crowds and huge media coverage of the basketball tournament, that time is long past and will never be duplicated."

Now, finally, the MSHSL, the coaches, and the fans of the boys tournament would have to let go of the past and appreciate the modern tournament for what it is rather than lamenting what it no longer was.

Chisholm's Joel McDonald (44) shoots over Jason Bakke (35) and Stephen Jensen (14) of Westbrook-Walnut Grove in the 1991 Class A final. Chisholm won the game and the title, 77–61, as McDonald, the fourth son of coach Bob McDonald to play in the state tournament, scored 30 points.

Blaine Joerger (21) of Staples gets off a shot against Minneapolis North in the first Sweet Sixteen boys final, in 1995. North won, 54–52, despite Joerger's 28 points.

29 *Small College Women Overachieve*

THE BRIGHTEST SPOT on the Minnesota basketball landscape throughout the second half of the 1980s and through the 1990s was women's small college play. Specifically, the Minnesota Intercollegiate Athletic Conference (MIAC) powers Concordia (Moorhead), St. Benedict, and St. Thomas made it all the way to the NCAA Division III Final Four eight times in fourteen years—with Concordia (in 1988) and St. Thomas (in 1991) bringing national championship trophies back to the Gopher state.

MIAC began women's play in 1982, when the NCAA also first began the administration of women's athletics. Concordia College won six of the first nine conference championships. In 1987, the Cobbers under coach Duane Siverson were just 4–3 at Christmastime, but then their three-guard offense—led by five-foot-six junior Jessica Beachy, from Staples; five-foot-seven senior Karen Hanson, from Bismarck, North Dakota; and five-foot-six junior Mary Lee Legried, from New York Mills—caught fire. Concordia stormed through the MIAC with a 21–1 record, as Beachy was named conference MVP and first-team Division III All-American. She then scored 28 and 29 as Concordia turned the tables on their previous postseason nemeses Bishop (Texas), 77–64, and Pomona-Pitzer, 68–46, to win their first regional title. In the Elite Eight, they dispatched the nation's top-ranked team from Rust College (Mississippi), 72–62, as Beachy scored another 24 points. Kean College (New Jersey) was the next victim, 74–69, but the Cobbers fell short against Wisconsin-Stevens Point, 81–74, in the final and finished with a record of 26–5.

Then, in 1988, with Beachy and Legried back, Concordia took the MIAC title with another 21–1 record and was selected as host of the Division III Final Four. There they defeated unbeaten St. John Fisher (New York), 65–57, to claim Minnesota's first college basket-

ball national championship of any kind in thirty-seven years.

Concordia won another MIAC title in 1990 and won eighteen games or more twelve times in the next thirteen years. But the focus of power in the MIAC shifted southward to St. Thomas and St. Ben's. The Tommies had always been competitive, with just one losing season on their record. But it was in 1991 that they asserted themselves as the MIAC's leading power, and over a twelve-year period beginning in 1991, St. Thomas won eight MIAC titles, made four Final Four appearances, and posted a 217–22 (.908) conference record.

The big highlight for the Tommies and coach Ted Riverso came right at the start—a national championship in 1991. St. Thomas hammered Eastern Connecticut, 91–55, and Muskingum, 73–55, in the Final Four to complete its dream season at 29–2.

The following year, St. Thomas waltzed through the MIAC undefeated, built its undefeated streak to forty games, and earned a number one national ranking. Junior forward Lauie Trow, from Rochester John Marshall, was named the Player of the Year by the Division III coaches. But Luther College (Iowa) shocked the Tommies, 61–60, in the postseason.

In 1993, it was St. Ben's turn to go 20–0 in the MIAC, though Trow finished her career at St. Thomas as the second-leading scorer in Minnesota basketball history (men or women, small college or large) with 2,607 points. The Bennies, led by coach Mike Durbin and All-America guard Kelly Mahlum, from Sacred Heart, Minnesota, made it all the way to the Final Four before losing to Central College (Iowa), 60–59, in the semis.

In 1995, the Bennies again won the MIAC, at 19–1 (27–2 overall), with the Tommies second at 17–3 (25–6 overall). The two were placed in different regions for the Division III playoffs, and both made their way to the Elite Eight. There, St. Thomas surprised St. Ben's,

The Big Games
Concordia (Moorhead) 65, St. John Fisher 57
March 19, 1988

St. Thomas 73, Muskingum 55
March 16, 1991

I f women's small college ball was the bright spot on the Minnesota hoops horizon in the period from the mid-1980s through the mid-1990s—and it was—then the brightest spots of all were the NCAA Division III national titles won by the women from Concordia (Moorhead) and St. Thomas in 1988 and 1991, respectively.

Concordia was led by five-foot-six senior guards Jessica Beachy from Staples and Mary Lee Legried from New York Mills. The Cobbers stormed to the MIAC title with a 21–1 record and hammered Wisconsin-LaCrosse, 85–68, to win the West Regional title. Then Concordia was chosen as the site of the Division III Final Four. Playing on their home court, the Cobbers won easily over North Carolina-Greensboro, 103–66, in the semifinal and then faced unbeaten St. John Fisher (New York) in the final.

The Cobbers led 26–23 in the first half and then went on a 19–4 run to increase their lead by halftime to 45–27. They shot 51 percent from the field in the first half. Concordia then had to survive a two-for-twenty shooting drought in the second half to win, 65–57. Beachy led all scorers with 20 points, including 6 during that spurt at the end of the first half, and was named the Division III Player of the Year. Duane Siverson was named Coach of the Year; Legried, second-team All-American; and Jillayn Quaschnick and Michelle Thykeson, to the all-tournament team. Concordia finished up at 29–2, while St. John Fisher ended its season with a 31–1 record.

In 1991, St. Thomas began a run of eight MIAC titles in twelve years, winning nineteen of twenty conference games and earning a number two national ranking. The Tommies then bounced St. Benedict and MIAC second-place Concordia, 75–62 and 76–62, in the first two rounds of playoff action. Wisconsin-Oshkosh was the next victim in the Great Lakes Region, as sophomore forward Laurie Trow, from Rochester John Marshall, scored 35 points.

Now in the Final Four, St. Thomas clobbered Eastern Connecticut, 91–55, despite Trow sitting out twelve minutes of the first half with foul trouble. Center Suzy Bouquet, from Wabasha, filled the void, scoring 24 points. In the final, the Tommies soundly defeated Muskingum, 73–55, as Trow scored

Laurie Trow (50), formerly of Rochester John Marshall, led St. Thomas University to the 1991 NCAA Division III national championship. She completed her college career as the number two women's scorer with 2,607 points.

33 points on fourteen-of-sixteen shooting. Point guard Tonja Englund, from Hill-Murray, added 8 points, 7 assists, and 15 rebounds.

Trow completed her sophomore season averaging 22 points and 10 rebounds per game. Two years later she completed her career with 2,607 points, second best among Minnesota women. Like the 1988 Cobbers, St. Thomas finished its dream season at 29–2.

67–65, behind 15 points by freshman forward Kirsten Vipond, from Barrett, Minnesota, and West Central High School. The Tommies were then defeated in the national semifinal, 68–59, by Capital (Ohio).

The following year, the MIAC's top two teams—the Tommies and Bethel, under coach Debbie Hunter—were again placed in separate regions and again met in the Elite Eight. St. Thomas prevailed once more, 65–57, and then lost to another Ohio team, Mt. Union, 71–57, in the semis despite Vipond's 21 points. They then beat Salem (Massachusetts) State, 82–79, in overtime for their second straight national third-place finish.

St. Thomas completed a second consecutive unbeaten season in the MIAC in 1996–1997 and this time clobbered the Bennies, 96–67, in a regional final, with all five starters scoring in double figures. Again, Capital (Ohio) ended the Tommies season, this time in the Elite Eight. In 1998, St. Thomas and St. Ben's tied for the MIAC title at 21–1, and they both lost to

Ted Riverso coached the St. Thomas women for fifteen years, winning 337 games and the 1991 NCAA Division III national championship. His final season of 1999 marked the thirteenth consecutive year that the Tommies qualified for the NCAA Division III tournament.

Mt. Union in the regional tournament. Vipond completed her career as the Tommies' number two scorer, with 1,700 points.

The Bennies returned to the top in 1999, going 21–1 in the conference and 28–2 overall behind "super strong" point guard Molly Mark from St. Cloud Apollo. Center Laura Wendorff from Fulda, then in her junior season, later finished as the Bennie's all-time leading scorer with 1,775 points. St. Ben's defeated St. Thomas, ending coach Riverso's sparkling career, 76–68, and then DePauw, 78–67, as Wendorff scored 20 points. Pacific Lutheran and Salem (Massachusetts) State were the next victims, 61–55 and 74–54. But Washington University (St. Louis) was too much for the Bennies in the title game, 74–65, winning their second of three consecutive national championships.

Riverso completed his fifteen years at the Tommies' helm with 337 wins and just 80 defeats for an .808 winning percentage. His record during the '90s was

even better, at 200–37 (.844). His final season of 1999 marked the thirteenth consecutive year that the Tommies qualified for the NCAA Division III tournament. Meanwhile, Coach Durbin at St. Benedict had built a program capable of challenging the Tommies, and 1999 marked the Bennies' eleventh straight year of NCAA tournament play.

In 2000, under first-year coach Trisch Dornisch, the Tommies made it all the way back to the Final Four with a 27–1 record. St. Thomas beat Pacific Lutheran, George Fox, and Hardin-Simmons, as MIAC Player of the Year Molly Hayden from Hopkins High School led the way with 57 points in the three games. Southern Maine shocked the Tommies, 49–42, in the semifinal, however, as St. Thomas shot just 25 percent and Hayden was held to 10 points.

Since 2000, Coach Durbin has surpassed Riverso to become the winningest coach in MIAC history with, as of 2006, a 448–100 (.818) overall record and a 355–65 (.845) conference record.

Meanwhile, St. Cloud State won five conference titles—four in the Northern Sun (NSIC) and one in the North Central (NCC)—in the 1980s, and the University of Minnesota Duluth (UMD) dominated the NSIC with nine championships in twelve seasons beginning in 1989.

St. Cloud went 31–4 in 1983 and hammered UMD for the Minnesota AIAW Division II title, 86–65. The Huskies then moved on to the NCAA Division II tournament, where they lost to Central Missouri State, 65–63. Senior Diane Scherer, from St. Cloud Apollo, won All-America honors and finished her career with 2,349 points. The following year, St. Cloud ran off twenty-six consecutive victories but lost to Dayton in the Great Lakes Regional finals.

The Huskies women joined the NCC in 1985 and finished second in conference play but then shocked regular season champion South Dakota, 56–55, to advance to the NCAA quarterfinals. This time it was Cal Poly-Pomona who ended their season. Three-time All-American Sarah Howard from Stillwater graduated in 1988, yet it was the 1989 team that won its only NCC title. Toni Jameson and Jan Niehaus, from St. Paul Highland Park and Melrose, respectively, earned All-America honors, but Central Missouri State again bounced the Huskies from postseason play in the quarterfinal round, 87–71.

Despite their nine conference championships, the UMD Bulldogs never won more than one NAIA national tournament game. Their best teams were probably those of 1988 through 1991. Led by coach Karen Stromme, who had herself been a star player at St. Olaf, and center Dina Kangas, from Pine River, these three editions of the Bulldogs won seventy-six games while losing nineteen. Each year they won three games and the NAIA Bi-District 13-14 title and then won one game at Kansas City. Kangas finished her career as the top all-time Minnesota college scorer—of either gender and at any level—with 2,810 points. Their best win-loss percentage came in 1996, however, at 23–5. After having moved up to NCAA Division II, the Bulldogs lost to

North Dakota State in a regional semifinal game that year and four times in five years.

Mankato State University (now Minnesota State University Mankato) should also be mentioned as the true pioneers of women's basketball in Minnesota. The Mavericks played an intercollegiate schedule as early as 1966, featuring the traditional girls and women's six-on-six format. They switched to five-on-five in 1969 and won the Minnesota AIAW championship three times in the early 1970s. They defeated the Gopher women four straight times from 1973 through 1975. But Mankato has only one conference championship to show for all its years of hoops play, that being an NCC title in 1986. The 1986 Mavs went 25–4 behind four stars of the early high school tournaments— All-American Lisa Walters, who had led Henderson to the state Class A high school title in 1983; Pat Burns from Heron Lake–Okabena's 1981 Class A champs; point guard Ann Christopherson from Austin Pacelli; and Rhonda House from Spring Valley.

There's a reason that Minnesota State Mankato and St. Cloud State have won only two NCC titles between them—or, rather, there are two reasons: North Da-

Minnesota Women's Small College Champions, 1980–1997

Year	MIAC	NIC
1980	N/A	Bemidji State, St. Cloud State, Southwest State
1981	N/A	Southwest State
1982	Concordia	Minnesota Morris, Moorhead State, St. Cloud State
1983	Concordia, St. Olaf, St. Thomas[a]	St. Cloud State[b]
1984	St. Thomas	St. Cloud State
1985	St. Mary's	Minnesota Duluth, Moorhead State
1986	Concordia, St. Mary's	Bemidji State
1987	Concordia[c]	Bemidji State
1988	Concordia[d]	Northern State
1989	St. Benedict	Minnesota Duluth
1990	Concordia	Minnesota Duluth
1991	St. Thomas[d]	Minnesota Duluth
1992	St. Thomas	Northern State
1993	St. Benedict[c]	Minnesota Duluth
1994	Bethel	Northern State
1995	St. Benedict, St. Thomas[c]	Minnesota Duluth, Northern State
1996	St. Thomas[c]	Minnesota Duluth
1997	St. Thomas	Northern State

Note: These are regular season champions only; there were no postseason conference tournaments through 1997.
[a] MAIAW Division III champion. MAIAW is the Minnesota Division of the Association of Intercollegiate Athletics for Women.
[b] MAIAW Division II champion.
[c] NCAA Division III Final Four participant.
[d] NCAA Division III national champion.

Big Changes for Small College Men

For the better part of forty years, most Minnesota small colleges belonged to the Minnesota Intercollegiate Athletic Conference (MIAC) or Northern Conference—which began as the Northern Teachers Conference, became the Northern Intercollegiate Conference (NIC), and is now known as the Northern Sun Intercollegiate Conference (NSIC). The two conference champions would then meet for the championship of the National Association for Intercollegiate Athletics (NAIA) District 13 and the right to play in the national tournament. The winner of that game would be the best small college team in Minnesota.

The clarity and simplicity of that arrangement went out the window in 1985, and this grand tradition ended with only five NSIC champs ever winning the D-13 title—St. Cloud in 1962 and 1968, Winona State in 1973, and Moorhead State in 1980 and 1982. Otherwise, it was all MIAC all the time.

In 1985, the NCAA split its Small College Division into Division II and Division III, and the MIAC elected to move to the NCAA Division III. Meanwhile, Mankato State (now Minnesota State Mankato) in 1982 and St. Cloud State in 1985 moved to the North Central Conference (NCC), which elected to compete in NCAA Division II. Only the NSIC stayed in the NAIA, at least for the time being; they too moved to the NCAA in the

year 2001. Minnesota's small colleges for fifteen years split into three different postseason tournaments, and who was best among them was purely in the eye of the beholder.

Meanwhile, the men from Minnesota struggled more often than not at the national level. After Hamline in 1953, it was not until 1994 that another Minnesota team made it to a national semifinal game. And it was a not-too-dominant St. Thomas team that won the MIAC at 18–2 and finished 24–6 overall. A dozen times since 1953, MIAC champions had posted better records without getting so far in the postseason—and half of those were earlier editions of the Tommies themselves. These were not the Tommies of stars Steve Fritz and Bob Rosier, but rather the Tommies of the relatively unsung Brent Longval, Jesse Radabaugh, and Johnny Tauer. Yet they beat Central College, 73–62; Hampden-Sydney (Virginia), 80–66; and Greensboro (North Carolina) College, 84–74, before being ousted by NYU, 75–68.

Overall, St. Thomas won six MIAC titles in just seven years (from 1989 to 1995), while Augsburg and Gustavus Adolphus also won five titles each during the 1980s and 1990s. Minnesota Duluth won or tied for eleven straight NSIC titles in 1982 through 1992, while St. Cloud State won three NCC titles in 1986 through 1988.

The first three UMD titles came under coach George Fisher. Dale Race took over in 1984, and from 1985 through 1992 the Bulldogs never won fewer than twenty-three

Minnesota Men's Small College Champions, 1984–1997

Year	MIAC Regular Season	MIAC Conference Playoff	NIC/NSIC Champion
1984	Augsburg	N/A	Minnesota Duluth, Northern State[a]
1985	Augsburg	St. John's	Minnesota Duluth
1986	St. John's	St. John's	Minnesota Duluth
1987	St. John's	Gustavus	Minnesota Duluth
1988	Gustavus	St. John's	Minnesota Duluth
1989	St. Olaf, St. Thomas	Gustavus	Minnesota Duluth
1990	St. Thomas	St. Thomas	Minnesota Duluth
1991	Gustavus	Bethel	Minnesota Duluth
1992	Gustavus, St. Thomas	St. Thomas	Minnesota Duluth
1993	St. John's	St. John's	Northern State[b]
1994	St. Thomas	St. Thomas	Minnesota Morris
1995	St. Thomas	St. Thomas	Northern State[b]
1996	Gustavus	Concordia	Northern State[c]
1997	Gustavus	Gustavus	Minnesota Duluth, Northern State[d]

Note: MIAC initiated a postseason conference tournament in 1985. After the MIAC moved to NCAA Division III in 1985, the NAIA District 13 tournament consisted entirely of NIC teams through 1995, so the NIC did not hold a conference postseason tournament.
[a] The NAIA District 13 four-team playoff final was St. John's 53, Minnesota Duluth 51.
[c] Northern State was ineligible for the NAIA District 13 championship, so Minnesota Morris went instead in 1993 and 1995.
[d] The NSIC moved up to NCAA Division II in 1996, and its postseason play was in a multistate regional, so the teams listed in 1996 and 1997 are the regular season champions only.

games. The best of these teams were its 1988–1991 teams, which won forty-one consecutive home games; center Jay Guidinger earned All-America honors all three times. Race won 293 games, most ever by a UMD coach, while losing 120, for a winning percentage of .709, over fourteen years. But never over this period was UMD able to win more than one game at the NAIA.

St. Cloud won its only three NCC titles before the end of the twentieth century under coach Butch Raymond and All-Americans Kevin Catron in 1986 and Reggie Perkins in 1988. It was the 1987 edition of the Huskies who went the furthest in the postseason, to the NCAA Division II Elite Eight, before losing to Delta State, 78–73, in overtime. Raymond stayed

for thirteen years and compiled a 231–142 (.619) record.

Why did the men from Minnesota's small colleges struggle at the same time that the women were enjoying such great success? Perhaps this reflected the greater sophistication of NCAA Division I "mid-majors" in men's recruiting versus women's. For years, Minnesota boys who were not good enough to play at the U, elsewhere in the Big Ten, or at places like Boston College or Duke played ball in the MIAC and NSIC. Now they were going to Division I schools like Cal Poly, Miami (Ohio), Montana State, Northern Iowa, and Valparaiso. Meanwhile, the second-tier players among the girls were still going to St. Ben's, St. Thomas, St. Cloud State, and UMD. That, at least, is one theory.

kota State (NDSU) and the University of North Dakota (UND). One or the other or both won or shared the regular season or postseason title every year from 1986–1987 to 2004–2005. And in the 1990s, the NDSU Bison or UND Fighting Sioux won the NCAA Division II national title eight times in nine years. The success of both the Bison and the Sioux had more than a little to do with the performance of girls from Minnesota high schools. The Bison's first two all-conference players in 1983 were Kim Brekke from Warren and Shelley Oistad from Fertile-Beltrami. Then came Kristi Kremer of Wheaton in 1987, 1988, and 1989, and Dana Patsie of New York Mills in 1988. Darci Steere from Storden-Jeffers won All-America honors for NDSU's national champions of 1993 and 1994. Kasey Morlock of Stewartville was a four-time All-NCC player and three-time national champion from 1994 to 1996, and in 2006, she was one of only five women named to the NCAA Division II Twenty-fifth Anniversary Team. Amada Gehrke of Cass Lake played for the national runners-up of 2000.

Meanwhile, in Fargo, the Sioux got better when the three Pudenz sisters—Tracey, Tiffany, and Jaime—came over from Storden-Jeffers (later Red Rock Central). Tiffany and Jaime each played on two UND national champions. Then the 2001 NCAA runners-up featured Mandy Arntson of Austin, Jenny Boll from Crookston, Jenny Hoffner from Brooklyn Park, conference MVP and All-American Theresa LeCuyer from Anoka, Becky Moen from Morris, and Janelle Palbicki from Bloomington Jefferson.

NDSU, along with South Dakota State, has now left the NCC after more than eighty years to move up to the NCAA Division I. Minnesota Duluth has also joined the

NCC and renewed its long-time rivalry with Minnesota State Mankato and St. Cloud State. But that is probably little consolation for fans in Fargo and Grand Forks, where it is probably difficult to imagine the NDSU-UND rivalry coming to an end.

Kasey Morlock was named Minnesota's Ms. Basketball in 1993 and then led NDSU to NCAA Division II national titles in 1994, 1995, and 1996. She earned All-America honors three times and was Division II Player of the Year in 1997. In 2006, she was one of only five women named to the Division II twenty-fifth anniversary all-star team.

30 *Hard Times for Gopher Women*

THE GOPHER WOMEN had enjoyed considerable success and appeared to have built a solid foundation by 1983. And with the return of All-American Laura Coenen for her junior year, the prospects for 1983–1984 were good. Unfortunately, a hyperactive thyroid sapped Coenen's strength throughout much of the season. Eventually, medication helped the situation, but Coenen then missed the final four games of the season with bronchitis.

Six-foot-three freshman Molly Tadich of Bloomington, who had played at both Lincoln and Jefferson high schools, had a strong year, often filling in for Coenen. Tadich had her first start on January 22 in place of Coenen and set a team record with 23 rebounds in a loss to Northwestern. Her strong play even compelled Mosher to move Coenen to guard to open another spot in the front court for Tadich to play alongside forwards Carol Peterka and Barb Meredith.

The Gophers slid to seventh place in the Big Ten in 1984, but the team rebounded as did a healthy Coenen in 1984–1985. Coenen had 42 points in the Gophers' first home game of the year against Nebraska, which broke her own women's record and tied the overall Gophers record held by Eric Magdanz and Ollie Shannon. For the season, Coenen averaged more than 25 points per game and had her best year rebounding. She also was the first Gopher women's player to score more than 2,000 points in her career and was recognized nationally, as well, as a Women's Basketball News Service first-team All-American. Coenen was the Gophers' first true first-team All-American—Elsie Ohm in 1978 and Laura Gardner in 1979 are often listed as All-Americans, but their recognition was for their performance in the postseason National Women's Invitation Tournament (NWIT) only.

Then, with Coenen's graduation, the Gophers found that the cupboard was almost bare. Tadich put in two more years of yeoman work, scoring 18 and then 19.5 points per game to finish her career with 1,706 points. She also finished as the (then) number two rebounder in school history with 1,135; her record for double-doubles still stands. Peterka graduated in 1986 as the (then) number four scorer in Gophers history. Still, the Gophers dropped to overall records of 8–20 in 1985–1986 and 9–19 in 1986–1987. For both years, they were 4–14 in conference play, finishing ninth in the Big Ten in 1986 and tying for eighth in 1987.

The 1986–1987 season was also marred by a locker-room incident between Tadich and coach Ellen Mosher Hanson (who had married Scott Hanson in 1984). Following a loss at Kansas State in early December 1986, Hanson got in Tadich's face and berated her. There was physical contact between the coach and player, including pulling of Tadich's hair by Hanson. The confrontation prompted an investigation by women's athletic director Merrily Baker. Later in the month, Hanson suspended Tadich for violations of team rules. Eventually Tadich was reinstated, and Baker cleared Hanson of any serious wrongdoing, although she also made it clear that the department would not condone abuse of players.

Hanson left after the 1986–1987 season, resigning in August; she and her husband were in the process of purchasing a resort in Hayward, Wisconsin. Assistant Chris Howell also moved to Hayward to take a teaching position, although she later returned to the university athletic department.

The remaining assistant, LaRue Fields, was named interim head coach. The university conducted a national search for a new coach but eventually settled on Fields, who signed a three-year contract during the 1987–1988 season. Fields became the first black coach of the Gopher women and only the second black women's basketball coach in the Big Ten, after Vivian

Stringer at Iowa. Fields was popular and respected by her players, but the team continued to struggle on the court. In three years under Fields, the Gophers had an overall record of twenty-four wins and sixty losses and finished no higher than eighth in the Big Ten.

Fields left the Gophers after the 1989–1990 season, citing the stress of the job and a desire to pursue other career opportunities. Although she had been plagued by the same problems Hanson had in her final years— a lack of good players—Fields was leaving just before Carol Ann Shudlick was about to begin a phenomenal career at Minnesota.

The Shudlick Era

Playing for Apple Valley High School, where she averaged 23 points and 13 rebounds per game her senior season, Shudlick was named Miss Basketball Minnesota in 1990. Though recruited by Fields, Shudlick would spend her career playing for coach Linda Hill-MacDonald. Hill-MacDonald came to Minnesota after spending her earlier playing and coaching career in the Philadelphia area. Most recently, she had spent ten seasons as head coach at Temple University, compiling a 166–130 record with the Owls.

It took a couple of years to get going under Hill-MacDonald: the team finished last and then tied for last in the Big Ten during her first two seasons as coach. The Gophers improved to 14–12 in 1992–1993 for their first winning season since 1985, and with the improved performance came larger crowds to Williams Arena. On January 17, 1993, in its first home conference game of the season, Minnesota beat Illinois before 3,657, the largest crowd to ever watch the women. The record lasted only a week as the attendance was 6,746 the following week, when Minnesota defeated twenty-third ranked Indiana behind Shudlick's 26 points.

The women had a new home for the 1993–1994 season. During the summer of 1993, Williams Arena underwent an extensive renovation. The hockey arena on the west end of the building was converted into the Sports Pavilion, with a capacity of 5,700, that would be home to many of the women's and some of the men's sports.

While the arena was being converted, Shudlick played with a Big Ten all-star team in Hungary and was named to *Street and Smith's* preseason first-team

All-America squad. The Gophers returned three other starters, Crystal Flint, Nikki Coates, and Cara Pearson, while Shannon Loeblein, a five-foot-nine junior guard, was the only newcomer in the starting lineup. The team had high aspirations for the season.

After winning seven of nine nonconference games, the Gophers opened their Big Ten schedule by losing three of four. They came back, however, to finish in a fourth-place tie with a 10–8 conference record. Their chances for one of the thirty-two at-large bids to the NCAA tournament improved on the final day of the Big Ten season, when Indiana and Northwestern both lost, and the Gophers were able to tie Indiana for fourth place in the conference. The next day the Gophers got together to wait for the news, and the gathering turned into a celebration with the announcement that Minnesota had received a berth in the NCAA tournament for the first time in the team's history.

The Gophers were the tenth-seeded team in the East Regional, and they drew a game against seventh-seeded Notre Dame, on Notre Dame's home court in South Bend, Indiana. Surprisingly, it was the visiting Gophers who came away with the win, beating the Fighting Irish, 81–76. Minnesota's reserves came through in the second half, building their lead as Shudlick got into foul trouble and took a seat on the bench with nine and a half minutes left. By the time Shudlick returned, the Gophers were up by 10 points and held on for the win.

The next opponent was Vanderbilt, and this time the Gophers fell, 98–72, ending a season that appeared to signal a resurgence of the program. Shudlick received the Margaret Wade Trophy, one of two awards given to the top female college basketball player in the country. (Lisa Leslie of the University of Southern California received the other, the James Naismith Award.) Shudlick was also named 1994 Big Ten Player of the Year and a first-team All-American by the Women's Basketball Coaches Association (WBCA) and Kodak.

Shudlick, Flint, and Coates were gone after the season. But the Gophers got off to a good start in 1994–1995, led by seniors Loeblien and Pearson and freshman Angie Iverson. On February 10, Minnesota destroyed Illinois, 92–46, to up its conference record to 7–5. No one could have guessed that it would be nearly two years before the Gophers would win another Big Ten game.

The conference losing streak reached thirty regu-

Gopher Women's Annual Record, 1983–1997

Year	Overall Record	Big Ten Record
Coach Ellen Mosher Hanson		
1983–1984	12–15	9–9
1984–1985	18–10	13–5
1985–1986	8–20	4–14
1986–1987	9–19	4–14
Hanson Totals	47–64	30–42
1983–1987	.423	.417
Hanson Grand Totals	172–125	43–47
1977–1987	.579	.478
Coach LaRue Fields		
1987–1988	9–18	5–13
1988–1989	7–21	4–14
1989–1990	8–21	3–15
Fields Totals	24–60	12–42
1987–1990	.286	.222
Coach Linda Hill-McDonald		
1990–1991	6–22	2–16
1991–1992	8–19	3–15
1992–1993	14–12	9–9
1993–1994	18–11	10–8
1994–1995	12–15	7–9
1995–1996	4–23	0–16
1996–1997	4–24	1–15
Hill-McDonald Totals	66–126	32–88
1990–1997	.344	.267
Gopher Totals	137–250	74–172
1983–1997	.354	.301

Carol Ann Shudlick, who received the Margaret Wade Trophy in 1993–1994, broke Laura Coenen's single-game scoring record with 44 points in a game during her sophomore season. Two years later, she matched that total and finished with a then school record of 2,097 points.

lar-season games (thirty-two, counting games in the Big Ten tournament) before Minnesota pulled out a 2-point win over Ohio State on February 2, 1997. The victory was the Gophers' only regular-season Big Ten win through the entire 1995–1996 and 1996–1997 seasons, and they of course finished last in the conference both years. Minnesota pulled off a surprise in the Big Ten tournament by beating Wisconsin in the first game behind 19 points by Mindy Hansen and 15 rebounds from Iverson.

A week later, Hill-MacDonald resigned under pressure from the athletic administration.

Not Enough Minnesota Talent

The sorry truth about this mostly disappointing era is that the Gophers' roster consistently was stacked with the greatest schoolgirl ballplayers that the state had to offer. Before Shudlick there were Diane Kinney from Burnsville (1982); Lea Blackwell from Edina, Peterka from St. Cloud Apollo, and Susie Piram from Derham Hall (all 1984); and Jennifer Hall from Burnsville (1990). After Shudlick came St. Paul Harding teammates Loeblein and Pearson, Lori Lawler of Rochester Lourdes (1991), and Iverson of Owatonna (1992). After losing out on Janet Karvonen in 1980, the Gophers recruited pretty much every Minnesota girl they wanted. And yet, with the exception of the Shudlick years, the losses mostly piled up.

Peterka, Ellen Kramer, Iverson, and Loeblein completed their careers with more than 1,000 points scored, and the first three are all among the program's top ten all-time rebounders. Debbie Hilmerson from Little Falls, Peterka, Holly Thompson, Nikki Coates, and Loeblein are among the Gophers' all-time leaders in both assists and steals. All of the women mentioned racked up impressive individual statistics, but the talent pool was never deep enough. The only winning seasons the Gophers enjoyed between 1985 and 2002 came when they had a truly extraordinary player such as Shudlick to pick up the slack.

That, and the fact that few if any Minnesota girls of note were playing major college ball elsewhere, was a pretty powerful indication that the caliber of girls basketball in the state had fallen behind.

31

A School for Scandal

IN JANUARY 1985, Minnesota Gophers freshman forward Mitchell Lee was charged with third-degree criminal sexual conduct. He was charged with raping a female student at Centennial Hall, the dormitory where Lee and the woman were residents. Lee's legal situation took nearly a year to resolve, but on January 14, 1986, he was acquitted of the charges against him. Lee rejoined the team but did not play in the Gophers' next game two days later, a win over number two ranked Michigan. Then Minnesota pulled off another upset, beating Michigan State despite a 45-point performance by the Spartans' Scott Skiles. Lee played thirteen minutes in the Michigan State game and scored 5 points.

The winning streak continued the following week, and the Gophers evened their conference record at 3–3 with a 67–65 win at Wisconsin on January 23, as Todd Alexander sank a tie-breaking basket with one second left.

The players celebrated their win over the Badgers at the Concourse Hotel. The next morning as the team boarded a plane for their flight home, Madison police ordered them off the plane. After they were back in the terminal, each player was led out to a car in which sat an eighteen-year-old woman who claimed she had been raped by three of the Gophers at the hotel early that morning. Based on her identifications, Lee and Kevin Smith were taken into custody. The rest of the players were questioned for several more hours at the airport, and some of them were finally allowed to leave. Others were taken to police headquarters, where a third player, George Williams, also was charged. The arrests came exactly one year to the day after Lee had been arrested for sexual assault in Minnesota. Lee, Smith, and

Bobby Jackson, the Big Ten's MVP in 1997, drives to the basket against Kentucky in the 1997 Final Four. The Gophers' appearance in the Final Four was later erased from the record books because of an academic scandal that was uncovered two years later.

Williams were eventually acquitted, but the repercussions of the incident were dramatic. On January 25, University president Ken Keller announced an investigation and declared that the team would have to forfeit its next game, scheduled for the following day at Northwestern. A few hours later, Jim Dutcher resigned as the Gophers' coach.

Assistant Jimmy Williams, who had been with the team since the arrival of Bill Musselman in 1971, took over as interim head coach. Like his first team at Minnesota, in 1971–1972, this one would be shorthanded for the rest of the season. So the Gophers again completed their season with a lineup that became known as the "Iron Five." In the next game, Ray Gaffney, Tim Hanson, John Shasky, Kelvin Smith (not the Kevin Smith who had been arrested in Madison), and Marc Wilson played nearly the entire game, as the Gophers beat Ohio State, 70–65. The second Iron Five won only one more game, however, and finished in eighth place. For the second time in little more than a decade, the Gophers would be looking for a new coach to bring them success on the court and respectability off of it.

The Clem Haskins Era Begins

A new chapter in Minnesota basketball began when the university hired Clem Haskins as head basketball coach. Haskins had played nine years in the NBA and then returned to his alma mater of Western Kentucky University to coach the Hilltoppers.

The Gophers started well under Haskins in 1986–1987, winning seven of ten nonconference games and their first two games in the Big Ten. But Minnesota then lost its final sixteen conference games to finish in a tie for last place. Despite the poor finish, the Gophers had several players—including guard Ray Gaffney, forwards Willie Burton and Richard Coffey, and center

Jim Shikenjanski—who would lead a resurgence of the basketball program.

Haskins's rebuilding job was complicated by serious problems that he inherited from his predecessor. Following an eighteen-month investigation, in March 1988, the NCAA placed the basketball team on probation for two years. The Gophers were cited for forty rule violations; thirty-five of them concerned the basketball team, and thirty-three of those occurred when Dutcher was coach. The report said that Dutcher and Jimmy Williams had demonstrated "a knowing and willful effort on their part to operate the university men's intercollegiate basketball program contrary to the requirements and provisions of NCAA legislation." Dutcher said he had violated rules "out of compassion," including responding to a request of a booster group to help pay the tuition for Darryl Mitchell after Mitchell had completed his athletic eligibility but was still in school. Dutcher had also had Mitch Lee's mother to his home for dinner during Lee's first trial for sexual assault.

In addition to the violations under Dutcher, the program was guilty of two violations involving the structuring of the salaries of assistant coaches under Haskins. The university paid a consultant more than $300,000 for an internal investigation as well as the design of a compliance program to ensure adherence to NCAA rules in the future. Because of the university's cooperation in the investigation, the NCAA kept the sanctions relatively light. They prohibited the Gophers from postseason play in 1988, which was not a problem as the team finished with a 10–18 record, and imposed a limit on the number of coaches who could be engaged in off-campus recruiting over the next year.

Minnesota may have dodged what could have been more serious penalties, but another situation was developing that would threaten the entire athletic department. In April 1988, university administrator Luther Darville was fired after an audit revealed nearly $200,000 missing from his department, the Office of Minority and Special Student Affairs. Darville was later tried and convicted of three felony counts of theft. In his testimony, Darville said he had given much of the money to athletes. He also stated that several members of the football coaching staff and basketball coach Clem Haskins had knowledge of the situation—a charge that Haskins denied. By this time, the university was con-

ducting another internal investigation, this one with a price tag of nearly $600,000. Ultimately, the NCAA found Minnesota guilty of seventeen rule violations related to the football, basketball, and wrestling teams. The result was another two years' probation for the men's athletic program, but the only penalty against the basketball team was the loss of one scholarship.

Despite the distractions of the investigations, the Gophers were improving. They doubled their Big Ten victory total from two to four in 1987–1988. Then, in 1988–1989, they won seventeen regular season games while losing eleven, breaking even in the Big Ten at 9–9. Minnesota was nearly unbeatable at Williams Arena, where fourteen of the seventeen wins occurred. The biggest of the wins was an upset of Illinois, the top-ranked team in the country at the time. Although they struggled on the road, Minnesota finished their conference season with a win at Ohio State, a game they needed to have any hope of making it to the NCAA tournament.

By this time the tournament field encompassed sixty-four teams, and there was no limit on the number of teams that could come from any one conference. As such, the Gophers' fifth-place finish in the Big Ten was enough to earn them a tournament berth as the number eleven seed in the East Regional. In the first round, Minnesota beat the sixth-seeded Kansas State Wildcats, 86–75. Despite a broken nose that required a protective mask, Willie Burton had a great game, scoring 29 points and grabbing 13 rebounds.

The Gophers' next opponent was Siena, the fourteenth-seeded team, which had knocked off Stanford, the number three seed in the tournament. Minnesota beat Siena, 80–67, to advance to the Sweet Sixteen and a meeting against Duke, the number two seed in the East. Led by Danny Ferry and Christian Laettner, Duke ended the Gophers' season with an 87–70 win. The tournament appearance was a great boost for the basketball program, however, and the team had even higher expectations for the following season.

The starting lineup in 1989–1990 consisted of four seniors—Coffey, Burton, Shikenjanski, and guard Melvin Newbern—along with junior guard Kevin Lynch. After an opening loss at Cincinnati, Minnesota won their next ten games. From there, the Gophers went on to a regular-season record of 20–8, including 11–7 in the Big Ten. One of the wins was a shocking 108–89 rout of Bobby Knight's Indiana Hoosiers. Minnesota entered the NCAA tournament with a much higher seeding—sixth in the Southeast Region—than the previous year, but struggled to win its first two games, against Texas-El Paso and Northern Iowa.

The team would have to play better to compete in the regional tournament, and it did. Minnesota's next opponent was the Syracuse Orangemen, whose Derrick Coleman, Billy Owens, LeRon Ellis, and David Johnson all became first-round draft picks in the NBA over the next three years. Syracuse led by 4 points at halftime, but the Gophers caught fire in the second half, sinking 79.2 percent of their shots from the field. Employing a variety of defenses, Minnesota held the Orangemen to a 43.5 percent shooting percentage for the game. The backcourt of Newbern and Lynch led the defense, and the pair also scored 38 points between them. Outscoring Syracuse by 11 points in the second half, Minnesota won the game, 82–75, to advance to the regional final against Georgia Tech. A win against the Yellow Jackets would send the Gophers to the NCAA Final Four for the first time in their history.

Yellow Jackets' forward Dennis Scott sank 7 shots from three-point range and scored 40 points against the Gophers. Freshman point guard Kenny Anderson added 30 points, and senior guard Brian Oliver added

19. Yet the Gophers built a 12-point lead before a late first-half rally by Georgia Tech cut the Minnesota lead to 2 at halftime. The game remained close through the second half. Trailing by 2 points with under a minute to play, the Gophers had a shot at tying the game as Lynch went to the free throw line. He made just one of the two attempts, however, leaving Minnesota a point behind. Georgia Tech increased its lead to 93–88, but Burton sank a three-pointer to bring the Gophers back to within 2 points. The Gophers immediately fouled Anderson, who went to the line for a one-and-one. He missed his first shot, and Coffey rebounded. Out of timeouts, the Gophers had to race downcourt and try for a shot that could tie or win the game. The ball found its way to Lynch, who was on the run as he fired a jumper from the right corner as six-foot-nine defender Johnny McNeil flew through his line of vision. It was a desperation shot that would have won the game for Minnesota had it found its mark. But the ball sailed wide of the basket as the buzzer sounded to end the game.

As Georgia Tech celebrated on the court, the Gophers had trouble absorbing the fact that they had lost. "It didn't seem like they had won the game," said Willie Burton afterward. "They were out there jumping up and down, celebrating, and I couldn't get it through my

The Minnesota Gophers' Melvin Newbern (left) passes to Willie Burton (right), who is being guarded by Duke's Danny Ferry in the 1989 NCAA tournament. Minnesota made it to the tournament's third round before being beaten by Duke. Burton, Newbern, and company made it to the Elite Eight, however, in 1990.

head that they had won. I didn't believe it was over." Radio announcer Ray Christensen recalled, "We broke for a commercial immediately after the game. As I sat there, I felt so good—not disappointed—because I knew the Gophers had played as well as they could have played, and they had gotten this far with talent that really wasn't as good as most of the teams they had beaten. Even though they had lost [to Georgia Tech], that Syracuse game was the best I had ever seen a Gopher team play, and it really was one of the great thrills of my life."

For the Gophers, four players scored more than 10 points, led by Burton with 35. Coffey was the only starter who did not hit double figures in scoring, but he was the game's leading rebounder. Although the Gophers fell short of the Final Four, the team's performance in its final two games was a fitting ending for the seniors—Coffey, Burton, Newbern, and Shikenjanski— who had endured twenty-one straight Big Ten losses in their freshmen and sophomore seasons.

Minnesota finished with a 12–16 record in 1990–1991 and did not make a postseason tournament. The following year, the Gophers went to the National Invitation Tournament (NIT) but lost their opening game. Haskins had another solid backcourt with Voshon Leonard and Arriel McDonald, and after the 1992–1993 season, the Gophers had another shot in the NIT. They got to play their opening games at home—though not at Williams Arena, where work on a massive renovation had begun immediately after their final regular season home game. The fate of Williams had been in doubt at various times over the previous two decades. Issues with fire and safety codes came up in January 1980, and it appeared that the Gophers might have to abandon the Barn at the end of the season. Emergency concessions were made, however, and the Board of Regents approved more than $250,000 to give the arena a reprieve. Through the 1980s, the university considered moving basketball and hockey, which also used the building at that time, to another Twin Cities arena. Finally, university administrators came up with a multiphased plan to upgrade a number of athletic facilities, including the Barn.

With the work on Williams Arena underway, the Gophers instead played at the Target Center, the home of the Minnesota Timberwolves. A good crowd turned out to see the Gophers beat Florida in their first NIT game. An even larger crowd turned out for the second game,

Voshon Leonard was the Minnesota Gophers' leading scorer in 1992–1993 when the team won the National Invitation Tournament. He remains the Gopher men's all-time leading scorer with 2,103 career points.

a win over Oklahoma. Because of the large crowds and enthusiasm in Minnesota, the NIT decided to allow the Gophers to remain at home for a third game. This time "home" was the Met Center in Bloomington, where the Minnesota North Stars played in their final season before moving to Dallas. A standing-room-only crowd packed the arena and watched the Gophers beat Southern California, 76–58, to earn a trip to New York for the NIT Final Four.

"Many of the fans stayed to join the band and cheerleaders in singing 'Hail Minnesota,'" said Christensen. "They were savoring the moment, not wanting to leave. It was beautiful. The Gophers' performance in the NIT had brought out the most resounding basketball fan phenomenon I can remember." Many of the fans followed the team to New York for the games at Madison Square Garden. In the semifinal game, the Gophers fell behind by 11 points to Providence. But Minnesota came back and won the game, 76–70, behind Lenard's heroics. For the second time ever, the Gophers were in the NIT championship game.

Their opponent was the Georgetown Hoyas, and the game was a defensive battle. With four and a half minutes left the Gophers opened up a 62–51 lead, as McDonald corralled a loose ball, dribbled past a horde of players who had fallen to the floor, and laid the ball in the basket. The points were the last ones that Minnesota would score, and Georgetown roared back. The Hoyas had a chance to tie the game in the final minute, but six-foot-ten freshman center Othella Harrington made only 1 of 2 free throws. Still down by a point, Georgetown got the ball back and had several chances in the final seconds. But Minnesota's Randy Carter blocked a shot by Kevin Millen. Millen got the ball back and missed another shot, but the ball went out of bounds off a Minnesota player, giving the Hoyas one last chance with four-tenths of a second left. Lenard intercepted the inbounds pass to preserve the Gophers' 62–61 victory and its first NIT championship.

On-Court Success as Another Scandal Brews

With all five starters from the NIT champions returning in 1993–1994, the Gophers had high hopes that for the most part were not achieved: Minnesota finished in a fourth-place tie in the Big Ten with a record of 10–8. One of the wins came on a strange Saturday evening, February 5, at Williams Arena against Northwestern. The Wildcats had won all nine of their nonconference games but then lost their first seven conference games going into their game against the Gophers.

Minnesota snapped a three-game losing streak with a 79–65 win. For no apparent reason, Northwestern head coach Ricky Byrdsong turned over the coaching duties to an assistant and spent much of the game seated in a folding chair at the end of the court. He did get involved in the game, drawing a technical foul from the officials in the second half, at a time when the Wildcats were leading by a point. The technical allowed the Gophers to take the lead, as Lenard sank 2 free throws in addition to taking possession of the ball. The Go-

phers quickly opened up their lead and maintained it for the rest of the game. Byrdsong then began roaming the aisle behind the Northwestern bench, bantering with fans, and taking an open seat in the stands. After the game, Byrdsong sent one of his players to the scorer's table with a request to change the scoreboard to read Northwestern 35, Minnesota 34.

Whether Byrdsong's erratic behavior was an attempt to motivate his team, as he claimed, or indicative of some type of mental breakdown was never clear. He took a brief leave of absence from his coaching duties but returned to the Wildcats, who played better over the remainder of the season and nearly secured a postseason tournament berth. Several years later, Byrdsong was fired by Northwestern, the result of the team's perennially poor record rather than issues related to his behavior in Minnesota.

In July 1999, a white supremacist targeted racial and ethnic minorities in a series of drive-by shootings over two days. Eight people were injured, and two were killed, one a Korean student outside a church in Bloomington, Indiana, and the other a black man taking a stroll with two of his children near his home in Skokie, Illinois. The latter was Ricky Byrdsong.

The Gophers made it to the NCAA tournament in 1994, reaching the second round before losing to Louisville. Another 10–8 conference record in 1995 earned the team another NCAA berth, but the Gophers lost to St. Louis in the first round.

The 1995–1996 team produced a 10–8 record in the Big Ten for the third year in a row, although the Gophers missed the NCAA tournament and had to settle for an NIT bid. The entire starting lineup, however, would return in 1996–1997. The Gophers had six-foot-nine John Thomas, from Minneapolis Roosevelt, at center. Courtney James, from Indianapolis, was the power forward, and he shared the frontcourt with Sam Jacobson, who had been a star at Park High School in Cottage Grove, Minnesota. The guards were Eric Harris, from New York, and Bobby Jackson, who had come to Minnesota after two years at Western Nebraska Community College. Jackson did not play organized basketball until his sophomore year of high school in Salisbury, North Carolina. He had wanted to play at nearby Wake Forest but did not qualify academically. He was to be the leader of the team that went further than any other Minnesota basketball team.

After winning eleven of its twelve nonconference games as well as its first two Big Ten games, Minnesota traveled to Indiana for a game against the Hoosiers on January 8. Indiana led 79–72 with 58.2 seconds left in the second half when the Gophers rallied. Harris sank a three-point basket, and, after a pair of free throws by Indiana's Neil Reed, Jacobson hit a three-pointer to cut the lead to 3 points. James then stole the inbounds pass and got the ball to Jackson, who sank a game-tying three-pointer from the top of the key. Minnesota had erased a 7-point deficit in just twenty-five seconds. The Gophers got the ball back but were not able to score again during regulation play.

All five Minnesota starters had 4 fouls entering the overtime period. It had been thought that Jacobson had fouled out with four and a half minutes remaining in the second half. Jacobson went to the bench but returned to the game when it was determined that the foul he thought had been called on him had actually been called on Jackson. Jacobson's presence was significant: he scored the first 6 points in overtime before eventually fouling out. By that time, the Gophers were on their way to a 96–91 victory.

The Gophers then beat Michigan to up their Big Ten mark to 4–0 before dropping a game at Illinois. Minnesota won their next twelve games before losing again, and the Gophers finished with a 16–2 record in the Big Ten to capture their first conference title since 1982.

Despite the loss in their final game, the Gophers finished the regular season as the third-ranked team in the nation. Haskins received Big Ten Coach of the Year honors, and Bobby Jackson was named the conference's Player of the Year in addition to being named a second-team All-American by the Associated Press. The Gophers' leading scorer, averaging 14.5 points per game, Jackson also led the team in assists. Jacobson was second in scoring with 13.4 points per game.

Minnesota got a number one seed in the Midwest Region for the NCAA tournament and had little trouble in winning its first two games. The Gophers' regional semifinal game was against Clemson, a team they had beaten more than three months before in the championship game of the San Juan Shootout in Puerto Rico. Minnesota opened up a 15-point lead, but the Tigers closed to within 6 at halftime and went ahead briefly in the second half. The Gophers got the lead back and were up by 4 points with twenty seconds left. But Clem-

son scored a pair of field goals, sandwiched around 2 missed free throws by Minnesota's Quincy Lewis, to tie the game. Eric Harris was on the bench with an injured shoulder, suffered with seven minutes left in the second half, and three Gophers starters—Jacobson, Jackson, and Thomas—had 4 fouls as the game went into overtime. Clemson built a 6- point lead, but the Gophers came back to force another overtime period. This time, they scored 8 of the first 9 points. Led by Jackson's career-high 36 points, Minnesota won the game 90–84.

The Gophers then met UCLA for the regional championship. After trailing by 10 points early in the second half, Minnesota came back to defeat the Bruins, 80–72. A pair of reserves, Lewis and Charles Thomas, ignited a 16–4 run that put Minnesota ahead. Lewis scored 10 points during that stretch and finished the game with 15 points.

For the first time in its history, the Minnesota basketball team was headed for the Final Four, in Indianapolis. The Gophers' opponent in the semifinal game was the defending national champion, the Kentucky Wildcats. The Wildcats scored the first 6 points of the game and later built a 10-point, 35–25 lead. The Gophers closed the gap to 5 at halftime, as Jacobson scored Minnesota's final 4 points on a pair of jump shots. Jacobson then hit a three-pointer to start the second half, and Minnesota was within 2.

The score was 47–43 for Kentucky with fourteen and a half minutes left when Courtney James had a dunk; however, the basket was nullified when he was called for a player-control foul. The decision enraged Haskins, who whipped off his jacket—his trademark move for protesting an official's call—and was charged with a technical foul. Kentucky coach Rick Pitino inserted Derek Anderson into the game to shoot the free throws. Anderson, who had not played since tearing knee ligaments two months before, made both his shots, and Ron Mercer followed with a field goal to give Kentucky a 51–43 lead. Still, Minnesota came back. Jacobson hit a jumper. Jackson did the same and then followed with a layup. Jackson then completed the comeback by burying a three-pointer from the left wing

Former paratrooper Richard Coffey (33) was called the "heart and soul" of the Gophers' great class of 1990 that played in the Sweet Sixteen in 1989 and the Elite Eight in 1990. He was also one of the greatest rebounders in Gophers history.

Television 4
MINNESOTA
33
MINNESOTA
34
Badgers
44
MINNESOTA
40

to put the Gophers ahead by a point. This was Minnesota's only lead of the game, however. Kentucky steadily built its lead back and went on to a 78–69 win.

Although they had fallen short of the championship, it was a memorable year for the Gophers. Unfortunately, soon after began a series of negative incidents, followed by revelations of wrongdoing that would eventually negate their season of glory.

On April 12, 1997, two weeks after the Gophers' loss to Kentucky, Courtney James was arrested on a domestic assault charge after allegedly hitting his girlfriend, Melanie Olsen. James was convicted in August and suspended from the University of Minnesota. Rather than serve the suspension, he left school and pursued a career in professional basketball. That same month, a woman reported to the University of Minnesota police that a Gophers basketball player had forced her to have sexual contact with him, although she declined to press charges. The player was one of two basketball players accused of similar behavior the previous November; in that case, the woman also had declined to press charges. The disturbing allegations continued. In May 1997, a woman told the university police that a player had raped her. No charges were filed, although it was later charged that university officials may have intervened with the university police department in the situation.

In 1998, the Big Ten began holding a conference tournament at the end of the regular season. The Gophers were seeded eighth out of the eleven teams (Penn State had joined the conference in 1992) after a 6–10 record in the Big Ten. Minnesota won its first game, against Northwestern, and then played top-seeded Michigan State. Despite being outrebounded, the Gophers had a 37–34 lead at halftime, as Eric Harris scored 23 points. Harris finished the game with 29, and Minnesota upset the Spartans, 76–73. The Gophers lost their next game, but the win against Michigan State allowed them to finish their regular season with a .500 record, which was necessary for a berth in the NIT.

The Gophers won their first three NIT games to advance to the semifinals in New York, where the combination of Lewis and Clark helped them defeat Fresno State. Quincy Lewis was the game's leading rebounder and also hit a three-pointer with 4.8 seconds left in regulation to tie the game. Minnesota won in overtime, 91–89, as guard Kevin Clark topped all scorers in the game with 24 points. Two nights later, the Gophers beat Penn State for the championship, their second NIT title. Clark had another big game, scoring 28 points, and was named tournament MVP. Sam Jacobson, in his final game for the Gophers, added 23.

The Gophers finished with an 8–8 record in the Big Ten during the 1998–1999 season and, despite a loss to last-place Illinois in the conference tournament, received a berth in the NCAA tournament as the number seven seed in the West Regional. On March 9 the Gophers flew to Seattle to prepare for their opening-round game against Gonzaga two days later. But on Wednesday, the *St. Paul Pioneer Press* broke a series of stories regarding academic fraud within the university's men's basketball program.

The Haskins Era Comes to an End

Jan Gangelhoff, the academic counseling unit's office manager, had told reporter George Dohrmann that from 1993 to 1998 she had completed research papers and done other course work for at least twenty team members. Four of the twenty were members of the 1998–1999 team—Antoine Broxsie, Kevin Clark, Jason Stanford, and Miles Tarver. Gangelhoff also said she had received $3,000 from Clem Haskins to continue tutoring Broxsie after she had been ordered by Elayne Donahue, the counseling unit's director, to stop. Gangelhoff later clarified that she had received the money from Haskins through an intermediary. Haskins denied any connection with the money paid to Gangelhoff.

The story went back to the fall of 1992, when Alonzo Newby was hired as an academic adviser for the basketball team. He initially worked out of the academic counseling unit and reported to Donahue. Two years later, Newby was moved to the men's athletic department. The transfer had been sought by Haskins and approved by McKinley Boston, then the men's athletic director. (Boston later became the university's vice president in charge of athletics and student development and was in this position at the time that Dohrmann's stories came out.) Removing Newby from the control of Donahue and having him report directly to the athletic department was called an experiment to help academically at-risk student-athletes. It was similar to a system that Haskins had had in place in his final six years at Western Kentucky.

The impact of this arrangement at Minnesota was to remove the checks and balances that turned out to be a necessary part of the academic oversight process. In fact, Gangelhoff said that having Newby independent of the academic counseling unit was what allowed them to avoid getting caught. "We put up roadblocks, and Alonzo going into men's athletics was the biggest one," Gangelhoff told Dohrmann.

The university suspended Broxsie, Clark, Stanford, and Tarver. Clark and Tarver had been starters for the Gophers—and Tarver the team's leading rebounder—leaving Minnesota shorthanded in its game against Gonzaga.

Minnesota fell behind by 21 points in the second half but came back to close the gap to 2 with under two minutes left. Freshman Dusty Rychart, who started in place of Tarver, led the charge and finished the game with 23 points and 17 rebounds. But Gonzaga held on to win.

With Minnesota's season over, attention turned to the scandal. University president Mark Yudof ordered an internal investigation of the alleged cheating. The investigation was expanded two months later when the *Star Tribune* came out with a blockbuster of its own. In May 1999, the *Star Tribune* reported, university officials had intervened, sometimes with the cooperation of the university police department, in sexual misconduct and assault investigations of football and basketball players, "helping negotiate agreements in cases that were never submitted to prosecutors." The story also alleged that several of the athletes were later accused of assaulting other women.

Yudof immediately announced that he was broadening the probe of the men's athletic department, asking investigators to answer the question, "Is there a pattern or system in men's athletics that systematically tries to discourage, dissuade, coerce, or cajole women from filing grievances?" The report on this aspect of the investigation came back in July. The conclusion was that

Clem Haskins coached the Minnesota Gophers from 1986 to 1999 and led the Gophers to the Big Ten title and the NCAA Final Four in 1997. The Gophers had to forfeit those achievements, however, and Haskins resigned amid a major academic scandal two years later.

there did not appear to be "systematic interference" on the part of athletics officials in investigations of sexual misconduct. However, the investigators documented one instance of interference and added that they found a "pattern of favoritism" on the part of officials toward athletes accused of sexual misconduct. In response to the report, Yudof issued a series of policy changes, including prohibiting the athletic department from participating in criminal investigations of athletes.

The report on the academic scandal was still to come, but heads were already rolling. In June Newby was fired for refusing to cooperate with investigators. By the end of the month, Haskins was gone, too. Yudof acknowledged that early findings in the investigation had revealed numerous incidents of academic fraud, although there was no evidence linking Haskins to the misconduct. Nevertheless, Yudof made it clear that a coaching change was necessary to "restore public confidence in the school's academic integrity." Without the ability to fire Haskins with cause, the university instead negotiated a buyout package worth more than $1.5 million to Haskins.

The university released its report in November 1999. With it came the announcement that several people—including Boston and men's athletic director Mark Dienhart—would not have their contracts renewed. In addition, the university determined that Haskins had been aware of the fraud. It also learned later that Haskins admitted to the NCAA that he had paid Gangelhoff $3,000 for continuing her tutoring of Broxsie, a charge he had repeatedly denied to university officials. The university filed a lawsuit against Haskins, claiming that he had misled them during the negotiations to buy out his contract, and eventually received a ruling in Hennepin County District Court that ordered Haskins to repay, over time, $815,000.

The report and sanctions from the NCAA infractions committee were finally issued in the fall of 2000.

The committee determined that Haskins had been aware of the course work being done by Gangelhoff for the players, in addition to then providing false information and directing four former players to lie after the story of the cheating scandal came out. The committee was also critical of Newby for violating "the principles of ethical conduct" and, in essence, prohibited Haskins and Newby from working in college athletics for seven years while administering a similar prohibition on Gangelhoff for five years.

Beyond public reprimand and censure, the NCAA placed the men's basketball program on probation for four years and cut its scholarships, as well as visits by recruits, over the next three years. The ban on postseason play was not extended beyond the one-year ban that the university had already implemented. But the NCAA also ordered that team records from 1993–1994 through 1998–1999 be vacated. The Gophers' 1998 NIT championship and 1997 Big Ten title and Final Four appearance would now join the 1972 NCAA tournament appearance in the dustbin of history. As far as the NCAA is concerned, they never happened.

Gopher Men's Annual Record, 1985–1999

Year	Overall Record	Big Ten Record
Coach Jimmy Williams (interim)		
1985–1986	2–9	2–9 (8th)
Coach Clem Haskins		
1986–1987	9–19	2–16 (9th)
1987–1988	10–18	4–14 (9th)
1988–1989	19–12	9–9 (5th)
1989–1990	23–9	11–7 (4th)
1990–1991	12–16	5–13 (9th)
1991–1992	16–16	8–10 (6th)
1992–1993	22–10	9–9 (5th)
1993–1994	21–12	10–8 (4th)
1994–1995	19–12	10–8 (4th)
1995–1996	19–11	10–8
1996–1997	31–4	16–2
1997–1998	20–15	6–10
1998–1999	17–11	6–10
Haskins Totals	238–165	106–124
	.591	.461
Gopher Totals	240–174	108–133
1975–1999	.580	.448

Authors' Choice:
Minnesota All-Stars, 1983–1997

Center Carol Ann Shudlick, Apple Valley High School and University of Minnesota. In 1994, Shudlick led the Gopher women to their best season between 1983 and 2002, scoring 23.4 points per game and winning national Player of the Year honors. When she graduated, she was the top Gophers scorer, man or woman, with 2,097 career points.

Forward Laura Coenen, University of Minnesota. Coenen was the first Gopher to earn first-team All-America honors in 1985, when she also set a record for scoring average (25.3 points per game) that still stands. She earned first-team All–Big Ten honors both in 1983 and 1985.

Forward Willie Burton, University of Minnesota. Burton was the athletic star of a Gophers team that improved in the first four years of the Haskins era from 2–16 in the Big Ten to 23–9 overall. In the penultimate game of his career, Burton scored 35 points in the Gophers' biggest win in years, an 82–75 upset over Syracuse in an NCAA Regional semifinal game.

Guard Voshon Leonard, University of Minnesota. From 1991 through 1995, Leonard led the Gophers to seventy-eight wins and an NIT championship in 1993. He completed his career with 2,103 points and remains to this day the all-time leading scorer among Gopher men. His NBA career has extended more than a decade, during which time he has scored almost a dozen points per game over more than five hundred games.

Guard Kevin Lynch, Bloomington Jefferson High School and University of Minnesota. Lynch led the Jaguars to state Class AA titles in 1986 and 1987 and then was a starting guard and major contributor to the Gophers' great NCAA tournament runs in 1989 and 1990.

SECOND TEAM *Center* Laurie Trow, Rochester John Marshall High School and St. Thomas University; *forwards* Richard Coffey, University of Minnesota, and Tony Campbell, Minnesota Timberwolves; *guards* Joel McDonald, Chisholm High School and St. Cloud State University, and Mary Jo Miller, Milroy and Tracy-Milroy High Schools.

32 *The NBA Returns*

THE DEPARTURE OF the Minneapolis Lakers in 1960 was offset in part by the arrival of major league baseball and football the following year. Meanwhile, the Minnesota Gophers football team was winning and making two consecutive Rose Bowl appearances, so there was still plenty of sports entertainment for area fans.

Professional men's basketball maintained some presence over the next decade. The Lakers came back to Minneapolis to play a regular-season game each season from 1961 through 1965, and two other neutral-site games were played in the Twin Cities during the 1966–1967 season. The Boston Celtics–Detroit Pistons game in December 1966 even sold out Convention Hall, a newly built annex to the Minneapolis Auditorium, and the average attendance at all seven of these games was more than 7,400.

Those types of crowds were conspicuously lacking for the American Basketball Association (ABA) Minnesota Muskies and Minnesota Pipers from 1967 to 1969. Each team lasted only a year before moving elsewhere, as it played in front of mostly empty seats at the Metropolitan Sports Center in Bloomington.

In the ensuing years, an occasional NBA exhibition game was played at Williams Arena or the Met Sports Center, and Minnesota remained without an NBA team of its own. This situation gnawed at some. In 1984, Minnesota governor Rudy Perpich appointed a twenty-member task force headed by former Lakers great George Mikan to research the possibility of acquiring an NBA franchise for Minnesota, whether through expansion or relocation. The formation of the task force signaled the state's strong desire for an NBA team and focused attention on the efforts. Soon after the group began its work, a pair of lifelong friends entered the scene.

Harvey Ratner and Marv Wolfenson were chums from childhood and later business partners in a variety of ventures. They started off selling real estate and then branched off into the construction of single-family homes and apartment complexes. In the late 1960s, the duo parlayed their interest in tennis into an empire of racquet-fitness clubs throughout the Twin Cities. They had owned some shares of the Minneapolis Lakers in the 1950s, and in the 1980s, they made an unsuccessful bid to purchase the Minnesota Twins. After that foray, Wolfenson said they had no plans to enter into the sports business again. But soon it became known that a few financially troubled NBA franchises might be available. In rapid order, Ratner and Wolfenson made overtures to the Milwaukee Bucks, San Antonio Spurs, and Utah Jazz. "The trouble is," Wolfenson said, "that the minute you start looking at a team, the city forces unite to protect the franchise."

In early 1986, however, the NBA made it known that it was finally ready to address the issue of expansion. On March 4, Wolfenson and Ratner, accompanied by Governor Perpich, task force chair Mikan, and their attorney, Bob Stein, traveled to the league offices in New York to deliver $100,000 in earnest money and to formally apply for an expansion franchise. Miami and Anaheim had already applied, and before long there would be more cities—Charlotte, Orlando, and Toronto—joining the hunt. The expansion applicants looked toward the league's annual meetings, set for that October in Phoenix, and hoped that final answers on their applications would be received at that time.

Ratner and Wolfenson then turned their attention to the question of where their team would play. Having looked at the Cities' existing—and not particularly appealing—options, they decided to build an arena of their own. They reached an agreement with the Minneapolis Community Development Agency to build an 18,000-seat multiuse arena in downtown Minneapolis. While many of the other expansion applicants were having municipal facilities built for them, this was not the case in Minneapolis. "We're building our own arena with our own resources. The city helped us only to the extent of letting us use their good credit to get bonds to buy the land," said Wolfenson. He added that this aspect of acquiring a team was "the hardest part of the whole thing, at least from a financial standpoint."

A new arena could be ready for the 1990–1991 season. In the meantime, the Metrodome could be used. All that was left was to get a team. Following a presentation by the Minnesota contingent and other hopeful cities at October 1986 league meetings, the NBA Board of Governors voted to add from one to three expansion teams to the league over the next four years.

And They Shall Be Called "Timberwolves"

Ratner and Wolfenson had hoped to have been granted a franchise to begin in 1987, but they were still happy with the results. And so confident were they now that Minnesota would be returning to the NBA that they announced a contest to name the team. Over six thousand applicants featuring nearly 1,300 different names were received. The Abominable Snowmen, Snoose, Fighting Walleyes, Brrs, and Jumpstarts were among the monikers that did not make the final cut. Two names were selected and passed on to the 842 City Councils in Minnesota for the final decision. By a two-to-one margin, the local municipalities preferred the nickname "Timberwolves" over "Polars." The team, if there was to be one, had a name.

On April 3, 1987, came the news that the NBA expansion committee would recommend to league owners that Minnesota be awarded a franchise for the 1989–1990 season. The committee also recommended that Charlotte receive a franchise for the 1988–1989 season and that either Miami or Orlando be awarded a team to begin in either 1988 or 1989. Nineteen days later, it became official. But the Board of Governors went one better than the expansion committee—they voted to award franchises to both Orlando and Miami in addition to Minnesota and Charlotte.

The first step Ratner and Wolfenson took toward staffing the organization was to hire Bob Stein as president and chief executive officer. Stein was hardly a stranger to the pair. In addition to being Wolfenson's son-in-law, Stein, as attorney for Wolfenson and Ratner, had been their principal representative during the long process to acquire a franchise. An All-America defensive end for the University of Minnesota in the 1960s, Stein then played eight years in the National Football League. He also received his law degree and began a legal practice while still playing football. After retiring as a player, Stein stayed active in the sports world, as much of his legal practice was devoted to serving as an agent for professional athletes.

Stein hired Billy McKinney, a former college star at Northwestern who went on to a seven-year career in the NBA, as the director of player personnel. A month later, the team selected a coach. The choice was Bill Musselman, who had resigned from the University of Minnesota and left the state amid more than one hundred NCAA violations thirteen years earlier. From there, Musselman embarked on a professional coaching career that encompassed four different leagues—the ABA, Western Basketball Association, NBA, and Continental Basketball Association.

His one stint in the NBA was with the Cleveland Cavaliers. Musselman took over the team in the 1980–1981 season and produced a 25–46 record before being moved up to the front office, where he served as a vice president and director of player personnel. He came back as coach briefly the next season and posted a 2–21 record. Five seasons in the Continental Basketball Association followed, during which time he became the league's all-time leader in regular-season winning percentage and in postseason victories. He built and coached the expansion Tampa Bay/Rapid City Thrillers to three consecutive titles beginning in 1984. He then moved to the Albany Patroons, where he produced an incredible 48–6 regular-season record en route to another league championship.

It was clear that Musselman knew how to win, but many wondered if he could learn how to lose, something that would be inevitable for an expansion team. During his time with the Cavaliers, he had traded away four first-round draft picks as he tried to bring in players who could help the team immediately. As a result, the Cavs were not getting top players out of college that could help their chances in the future.

With the Timberwolves, Musselman was a coach without any players for nearly a year, until the expansion draft in June 1989. Minnesota' first selection was Rick Mahorn, a power forward from the Detroit Pistons, who two days before had won their second consecutive NBA title. The next two picks were forward Tyrone Corbin from Phoenix and center Steve Johnson from Portland. All three players indicated that they wanted their contracts renegotiated, however. Stein took a hard line in refusing to do so, and the players held out. Mahorn never played for the Wolves, and Johnson held out until after the season had started and played in only four games before being traded. Corbin missed the entire exhibition season and signed right before the opening of the regular season. Corbin quickly moved into the starting lineup and became one of the team's top contributors.

In the college draft Minnesota added point guard Jerome "Pooh" Richardson from UCLA, who was the Pacific Ten conference's all-time leader with 833 career assists. Over the next few months, the Timberwolves also signed a number of free agents, including forwards Sam Mitchell and Tod Murphy and guard Sidney Lowe and forward/guard Tony Campbell. All became key members of the team.

Minnesota's first game was an exhibition contest against Magic Johnson and the Los Angeles Lakers at the Metrodome in mid-October. Then on November 3, 1989, the Timberwolves played their first regular-season game against the SuperSonics in Seattle. Minnesota opened up a 10-point lead in the second quarter, but Seattle went on to win the game, 106–94. Corbin led Minnesota with 20 points and 8 rebounds.

The Timberwolves had another game on the West Coast, losing to Portland before coming back to Minnesota for its home opener against Michael Jordan and the Chicago Bulls on November 8. A crowd of more than 35,000 saw a great battle in which the Wolves held a lead with five minutes left. But Jordan hit a three-pointer from the top of the key with 4:18 to play to put the Bulls ahead for good. The basket gave Jordan 35 points in the game, and in the final minutes he added 10 more to finish with 45 points as Chicago beat the Wolves, 96–84.

Minnesota's first regular-season win came two nights later against the Philadelphia 76ers. Corbin sank 2 free throws to tie the game with three seconds

Guard Jerome "Pooh" Richardson was the first player taken by the Minnesota Timberwolves in the college draft for the team's inaugural season. He remained the Wolves' point guard for three years, averaging 15 points and 8 assists per game.

left in the fourth quarter, and the Wolves went on to win in overtime, 125–118. Corbin, who played all fifty-three minutes in the game, finished with 36 points, and Tony Campbell led all scorers with 38.

In January 1990, the Timberwolves made a trade with the Milwaukee Bucks that brought center Randy Breuer, a star at Lake City High School and with the Gophers, back to Minnesota. Breuer averaged 10.2 points per game after joining the Timberwolves.

One of the biggest wins for Minnesota in their first season came on February 2 against the Boston Celtics. The Timberwolves had played one of their worst games against the Celtics in Boston in November, and they hoped to do better before a national cable-television audience. Minnesota led throughout much of the game and had a 10-point lead in the fourth quarter. Larry Bird and Kevin McHale of the Celtics led a comeback that put Boston ahead 102–101 with 1:50 left to play. Tony Campbell then took over. His basket put Minnesota back in front, and he solidified the lead by making 10 free throws in the final minute and a half. In addition to setting a team record with 44 points, Campbell also had 14 rebounds.

Despite a slump at the end of the year, the Timberwolves won twenty-two games in their initial season, more than any of the other three recent expansion teams. Large crowds were turning out at the Metrodome, and with four home games left the Wolves needed another 158,000 in attendance to set an NBA record. The Timberwolves sold tens of thousands of tickets for $1 to corporations, who were then to give the tickets to youth groups. Whether the deeply discounted tickets turned into actual fans in the seats or not, the effort did achieve its desired result: Minnesota finished with an official attendance total of 1,072,572, topping Detroit's mark by more than 6,000.

In every way, the Timberwolves' first season was seen as a success. Now the team prepared to move into its permanent home, the Target Center, for the 1990–1991 season. For the second year in a row, Campbell and Corbin finished one-two on the team in scoring. After having led Minnesota in rebounding its first year, Corbin finished second in that category to center Felton Spencer, who had been the Timberwolves' first draft choice in the 1990 college draft. The team improved by seven games over the previous season, finishing the year with a record of 29–53. However, not all was well in the Timberwolves' front office.

The Decline and Near Fall of the Wolves

McKinney left the team early in the season, his contract bought out through a mutual agreement with the team

Tony Campbell was the Timberwolves' leading scorer in their first three seasons. He scored a career-best 23.2 points per game in 1989–1990, including 44 points against the Boston Celtics in a February game.

amid reports of a souring relationship among Musselman, McKinney, and Stein. Then, the day after the season ended, the Timberwolves fired Musselman.

One of the reasons cited was Musselman's lack of communication with and general treatment of the players. More significantly, Stein and Wolfenson had become disenchanted over Musselman's refusal to develop younger players, characterized as a "win-every-game mentality" rather than a "build-for-the-future approach." While the management philosophy of focusing on long-run success rather than short-term results was reasonable, it left the question of why the Timberwolves had hired Musselman in the first place.

Under new coach Jimmy Rodgers the Timberwolves posted a 15–67 record, worst in the NBA, in 1991–1992. Once again, the Timberwolves would be in the lottery to receive the top selection in the college draft, and having the poorest record meant the team would have the best chance of getting the number one pick. This was significant, since center Shaquille O'Neal had decided to leave Louisiana State University following his junior season and enter the draft.

The Timberwolves did not win the lottery and instead ended up with the number three selection. O'Neal went to the Orlando Magic, and the Charlotte Hornets drafted Alonzo Mourning of Georgetown with the second selection. The Timberwolves then selected Christian Laettner of Duke, which had won its second straight NCAA tournament at the Metrodome in April. Laettner had been a center at Duke, but he moved to forward with the Timberwolves and gave the team its first big name. As a rookie in 1992–1993, Laettner was Minnesota's leading rebounder and averaged 18.2 points per game, second on the team to Doug West's 19.3 points.

West, a second-round draft choice in 1989, was the last of the original Timberwolves. Two original players, Pooh Richardson and Sam Mitchell, had been traded before the season to Indiana for forward Chuck Person and guard Micheal Williams. Person and Williams were third and fourth on the team, respectively, in scoring, and Williams distinguished himself toward the end of the season with his free throw shooting.

He began a streak of successful free throws on March 24. More than a month later, he still had not missed and was closing in on Calvin Murphy's NBA record of 78 consecutive free throws. Williams was four short of that on April 25, as the Timberwolves played their final game of the season. He got to the line ten times and made all 10 free throws to pass Murphy and extend his streak to 84. He extended his streak the following season to 97 straight free throws, which remains an NBA record.

In the record-breaking game, Minnesota beat Utah to snap a twelve-game losing streak and end its season with a record of 19–63. The poor performance during the year had cost Jimmy Rodgers his job: he was fired on January 11 and succeeded by Sidney Lowe, the team's first point guard. The Timberwolves' first draft choice in 1993 (and the fifth overall selection) was Isaiah "J. R." Rider from the University of Nevada, Las Vegas. A talented guard, Rider was eventually determined to be more trouble than he was worth.

Minnesota hosted the NBA All-Star Game in 1994. No Timberwolves player participated in the game itself, but Rider participated in the slam-dunk contest the day before the game. With a dunk in which he transferred the ball from one hand to the other between his legs before slamming it through the basket—a move he had developed on the playgrounds of his hometown of Oakland and dubbed "East Bay Funk"—Rider won the contest. He finished his rookie season with a scoring average of 16.6 points, second to Laettner's 16.8 points per game. The Timberwolves won their twentieth game of the year, surpassing their previous year's total, on April 6, with more than two and a half weeks to play. They did not win again, however, losing their final ten games to finish the 1993–1994 season with a record of 20–62.

There were greater worries for the team than its win-loss record, however. As the season was winding up, the future of the Timberwolves in Minnesota was in doubt. Even before the Target Center had opened

Bill Musselman came back to Minnesota to become the first coach of the Timberwolves. The team did well under him, but he was terminated after two years in favor of a coach who would "build for the future."

in 1989, the arena had become a financial burden to Wolfenson and Ratner. With their initial financing having fallen through with the demise of their lender, Midwest Federal Savings and Loan, the pair had been forced to borrow at high interest rates to complete construction. The financial situation was taking a toll on the owners, who eventually determined that they would have to sell the team as well as the arena, seeking to have the state take ownership of the latter. In 1994, fueled by fears that Minnesota could lose its NBA team only a year after having lost its National Hockey League team, the North Stars, the Minnesota Legislature considered a public buyout of the Target Center. The buyout bill made its way through ten different committees in the state Senate and House of Representatives, and on May 7, the final day of the 1994 legislative session, a deal was reached for the public purchase of the Target Center. It appeared that the Timberwolves had been saved, although barely two weeks later, the outlook was vastly different. On May 23, Wolfenson and Ratner sold the Timberwolves to a New Orleans group that intended to move the team to that city.

At this point, the NBA stepped in. Citing concerns regarding the finances of the new ownership group as well as its gambling connections, the NBA did not allow the sale.

A Turnaround Begins

In the summer of 1994, Glen Taylor, a Mankato entrepreneur and former state senator, came forward to buy the Timberwolves.

As the ownership situation was playing out, Minnesota again had a high pick in the draft. Selecting fourth overall in June 1994, the Timberwolves took Donyell Marshall, a forward from the University of Connecticut. Two months later, the Timberwolves hired a new head coach, Bill Blair, who had been an assistant coach for a number of NBA teams.

In Minnesota's first regular-season game of the 1994–1995 season, Marshall was the team's top scorer, with 26 points in a loss to Denver. The Timberwolves ended up losing their first six games as well as thirteen of their first fourteen.

Rider emerged as the team's top scorer, and Laettner had another solid year, finishing second on the team in scoring while leading in rebounds, assists, and minutes played. In February 1995, the Timberwolves traded Marshall to the Golden State Warriors for Tom Gugliotta, a forward who was able to help Laettner with the rebounding chores while also averaging in double figures in scoring.

Despite the poor start, the Timberwolves improved their record for the third year in a row. It was only by a game, however, as they finished with a record of 21–61, becoming the first NBA team to lose at least sixty games for four straight seasons. If this was progress, it was barely perceptible. But over the summer of 1995, the team made a number of moves that would provide stability over the next decade while finally putting the franchise on a winning track.

The Second Golden Age of Minnesota Basketball, 1997–2006

Forty years ago, before the advent of girls and women's basketball, Minnesota high schools used to produce one or two Division I college prospects in a year. Maybe there were a dozen bona fide prospects in the entire decade of the 1960s.

Now, in the twenty-first century, more Minnesota boys than that win Division I college basketball scholarships every single year. In 2005–2006 more than sixty Minnesota men were on the rosters of major college teams. And there were an even greater number of women—about eighty of them—on major college basketball rosters.

The most obvious evidence of this great explosion of basketball talent was the high school class of 1997. Khalid El-Amin of Minneapolis North and Coco and Kelly Miller of Rochester Mayo were among the most highly recruited Minnesotans ever, and all went on to great success at the college level. Then there is the success of the Minnesota Gopher women under coach Pam Borton. The Gophers had won a miserable fifty-nine Big Ten games in the sixteen seasons from 1985 to 2001. Then they won about as many in one season under Brenda Oldfield and four years under Borton.

But the real news was bubbling along beneath the radar of the major media—and therefore outside of the view of casual basketball fans. Some suggested that the increased popularity of basketball among Minnesota youth was due to the influence of the Minnesota Timberwolves after their founding in 1989.

No. The real news was the creation of the private basketball clubs that enabled Minnesota's elite youth to play almost twelve months of the year under the supervision of qualified coaches and under game conditions. Now, for the first time in almost one hundred years, kids were playing more basketball outside the schools than in. The creation of this private market for youth basketball in the late 1980s and into the 1990s—this is the reason why we are now enjoying a second golden age of Minnesota basketball.

Khalid El-Amin of Minneapolis North perfectly represented the change from the low post to the transition game as the predominant fact of life in the game of basketball. He led the Polars to a state championship three-peat and then led the University of Connecticut to an NCAA title.

33 *The Transition Game*

IT ALL STARTED WITH THE THREE-POINT SHOT. But it was only at the 1997 state high school tournaments, both boys and girls, that it suddenly became clear to Minnesotans, at least, how much the game of basketball had really changed. It was one of those moments—like the sudden appearance of Jim McIntyre in the low post in 1944 and that of the Lynd Panthers with their fast break in 1946—when the changes could no longer be ignored. But now it was Khalid El-Amin, Coco and Kelly Miller, the boys from Wabasso High School, and "the transition game."

The men who make the rules had simply wanted to open up the lane for more of that good old low post offense that had dominated the game for forty years. They thought that "bonus" points on long jump shots would bring jump shots back into favor, thereby achieving the real goal of spreading the defense and opening up the lane. It worked beyond their wildest dreams. But faced with the threat of the three-point shot, the defense did not simply fall into the trap and overextend itself. It compensated. It went on the attack.

Once upon a time, the defense guarded the basket. Old-timers would be lying if they said the zone defense of the 1930s through the 1950s wasn't a bit passive. Today, the defense attacks the ball and denies the passing lanes, while still defending the basket. It double-teams opportunistically, it rotates rapidly to cover the open man, it helps out relentlessly, and it challenges every shot.

If fouls come, they come. Eight to ten players are rotating in and out of the lineup anyway, at least among the elite teams, because most players cannot sustain

thirty-two or forty, much less forty-eight, minutes of pressure defense. You need fresh troops to do the job, which had been understood as far back as the late 1930s and early 1940s, when "racehorse basketball" had enjoyed a brief vogue.

The defense plays this style because it must but also because it can. It takes quick, well-conditioned athletes to play it, even in hockey-like shifts. And, sure enough, today's athletes are quicker, stronger, more athletic, and in better physical condition than at any time in history. It is the perfect and timely convergence of strategy and ability, and it is here to stay—at least until the next innovation comes along.

Then it was the offense's turn to react and adapt. Faced with the pressure defense, the offense is more active than it has ever been. Movement away from the ball and constant screening and bumping of the defensive players all over the court are the foundations of the new offensive style—that and outstanding ball-handling skills, meaning that the point guard has replaced the big player in the low post as the key member of the contemporary roundball squad.

Then there's the actual "transition." Throughout the history of the game, the goal has been to get a high-percentage shot—that is, a shot close to the basket. Today, the high percentage shot means getting a good look at the hoop, not having a defender in your face. And that does not necessarily happen close to the hoop and rarely in a classic low post set. Often, the open shot comes before the defense can get into its half-court set—in transition.

The transition is different from the classic fast break. Both look for a numerical advantage. But the fast break was designed to get a layup—if not, the ball came back out into the half-court set. The transition simply looks for an open shot. With the three-point shot providing compensation for the lower shooting percent-

Lindsay Whalen put what had been a struggling Minnesota Gopher women's program on the map with her great ball-handling skills and mastery of the full-court game. She had the unique ability to find open shots, for herself and for her teammates, all over the court and at any time. For that, she won All-America honors twice and was a first round draft pick of the Connecticut Suns.

age, an open shot from the outside is as good as any.

One of the outcomes of all of this would have been considered a paradox in earlier years. When elite teams match up, you often get a faster paced game, but with lower scoring. The 1999 boys Class A championship was such a game—a highly entertaining, fast-paced, competitive game in which the loser ended up scoring just 50 points (Southwest Minnesota Christian defeated Fergus Falls Hillcrest Academy). The 2000 boys Class AA title game went even further, providing an even faster-paced, scrambling, full-tilt, full-court style of play and a 42–28 score (Litchfield over Waterville-Elysian-Morristown).

Of course, everyone knows that after shooting percentages had climbed right from the game's founding through about 1990, now they're falling—in the NBA, in the NCAA, and in the high schools. And the conventional wisdom holds that it is because kids do not practice the jump shot anymore—much less, their free throws—instead whiling away the hours in the gym and on the playground practicing the dunk or the behind-the-back dribble. Well, try telling Ben Johnson of DeLaSalle, Shane Schilling of Minnetonka, or Shannon Schonrock of Winnebago and Blue Earth Area High School that the jump shot is extinct. Or try telling Jake Sullivan of Tartan, who set a national high school career free throw record of more than 90 percent, that kids cannot shoot free throws anymore. All won Division I scholarships based on their shooting skills.

Another explanation centers on the defense—and the officiating. Once upon a time, basketball was a non-contact sport. Now the rule is "no harm, no foul." In reality, it more often looks like "no blood, no foul," and that applies equally to boys and girls and men and women.

The sum total of all these changes is that no longer can the offense take the air out of the ball, kill the clock, and bore the defense into inattention. Those days are gone, at least when elite athletes with top-notch coaching get together. The great teams and great players today are the ones who've mastered the new offensive and defensive game.

And it all started with the three-point shot.

El-Amin and the Rabbits

No, this is not a fairy tale. But if Minnesota basketball fans had not seen it with their own eyes, they might not have believed it. Khalid El-Amin, Minneapolis North's five-foot-nine waterbug, and the Wabasso Rabbits came along with just the right skills and the right strategies at just the right time to symbolize the arrival of "the transition game." The new game called for quickness, ball-handling skills, and court sense, and El-Amin brought exactly those attributes to the court in abundance. He could penetrate and finish in the paint, he could penetrate and dish or kick the ball back out for the three, or he could stop and take the open three himself. He did it all on offense, and nobody ever made his teammates look as good as he did.

Not known as a great defender, his rambling, gambling, overplaying, risk-taking style—never more than a half-step away from transition—was better suited to the 1990s than any other time in history. By the time his high school eligibility was completed in 1997, El-Amin had joined Jim McIntyre as the two most dominant players in boys tournament history. Consider El-Amin's achievements:

- He and teammate Jabbar Washington were the first boys to both start and win three state title games;
- He was one of only eight boys to that time to earn all-tournament recognition three times;
- Despite a pass-first, shoot-second mentality, he finished as the all-time leading career scorer in the boys tournament with 238 points;
- He produced one of only a dozen 40-point games to that time in boys tournament history.

He did not dominate the way McIntyre did, of course. He did it his own way, the '90s way. McIntyre led his team in scoring with at least 21 points in every state tournament game he played—at a time when 24 points was the previous *single-game* record. El-Amin led the Polars in scoring in seven of his eleven games and scored as few as 10, 12, and 13 points. But when necessary, or when the defense rested, he could explode, as he did against St. Thomas (41 points) as a junior and Rochester Mayo (35 points) as a senior. When really pushed to the wall, he produced one of the most electrifying moments in tournament history. That happened in 1996 in that 41-point effort. El-Amin swished two three-point buckets in the final eleven seconds of play, the second at the buzzer, to bring North from the brink of defeat to a 67–65 quarterfinal win over St. Thomas Academy.

Nobody who saw that game was at all surprised when he scored 22 points in his first college game at the University of Connecticut and then two seasons later led the Huskies to the NCAA title. His NBA career ended unsatisfactorily, however, as El-Amin averaged about 6 points and 3 assists per game in one season with the Chicago Bulls.

The transition offense is just a part of the new game of basketball, but a few teams adopted it without embracing the other parts. This theory seems to have been invented by coach Paul Westhead and Loyola Marymount in the late 1980s. At least, they popularized it in a shocking 149–115 embarrassment of defending national champion Michigan in the second round of the 1990 NCAA tournament. Basically, this weird, unprecedented style of play was the transition without the pressure defense. It meant shooting nothing but layups and threes, and always within about ten seconds.

Here in Minnesota, this all-transition-all-the-time style was adopted by the aptly named Wabasso High School Rabbits and coach Larry Larson. Laboring in the relative obscurity of the southwestern Minnesota prairie and lacking in any particular basketball tradition, they rode the transition game to their first boys state tournament ever in 1997 with a lusty 87-point scoring average. "Our goal is to score at least three points per minute," Larson said.

They did better than that against Bloomington Trinity in the first round, hitting 99 with three minutes left and then, miraculously, staying there for a 99–74 win. In the semifinal against Red Lake, all hell broke loose. The Rabbits took the early lead 29–23 after one quarter, 53–47 at the half. Then in the third quarter they got hot, extending their lead to 81–62.

Forced to play at the Rabbits' tempo, the Warriors of Red Lake responded with the most astounding comeback in tournament history. Wabasso still led by 14 with four minutes left and by 10, 102–92, with 1:15 left. Then Red Lake guard Gerald Kingbird scored an incredible 13 points in fifty-seven seconds. His last three-pointer swished through with 17.7 seconds on the clock, tying the score at 105.

In overtime Red Lake took their first lead since 10–8 at 111–109, but that was to be their last lead, as the Rabbits pulled away once again to a 117–113 final. Kingbird finished with 37 points, while Delwyn Holthusen added 30 for the Warriors. Wabasso was led by Derrick Jenniges and Bob Moore with 31 and 29. No tourna-

ment game before or since has ever seen the following numbers:

- Most points by a winning team, most points by a losing team, and, of course, most points by both teams—all three records had been set previously in 1968, when Moorhead beat St. Paul Highland Park, 107–89, in the first round;
- Most field goals and most field goal attempts—surprisingly, it was the losing Warriors who set these records, making 48 of 87 field goals (the Rabbits were right behind, with 46 of 75; the old records were 41 and 81);
- Most points in one quarter—Red Lake's 43 topped Moorhead's top quarter in that 1968 game by 6;
- Most three-point field goals—Wabasso tied this record with eleven.

The running game also seemed to make it tough for both sides to settle down and shoot free throws. The Rabbits were so-so at fourteen-of-twenty-five, but the Warriors could easily have won their amazing comeback had they made more than just eight-of-twenty-two from the line. Kingbird was a respectable five-of-seven, but the rest of the Warriors made just three-of-fifteen (20 percent) compared to thirty-five-of-fifty-seven (61 percent) from the field.

By tournament's end, Wabasso had demolished LeSueur's record of 255 points in a three-game tournament with a total of 274. But Hancock did not let the Rabbits run in the final, edging them, 60–58, to deny them a title and coach Larson's three-points-per-minute goal for the tournament. In 1997, Hancock was the only school in tournament history to win both the boys and the girls titles in the same season, despite an enrollment of just sixty-seven students. (Minneapolis North and Hopkins joined this exclusive club in 2003 and 2006, respectively.)

Miller Time

The girls equivalent of El-Amin and the Rabbits was the Miller twins, Coco and Kelly, from Rochester Mayo.

It has often been said that the difference between girls and boys hoops is that boys play is more vertical and more physical. The truth is, however, that at the high school level only the most elite boys consistently are able to play "above the rim." And there is just as much contact in the girls game; it is just as much of a "test of strength." The real difference between the girls and boys games is neither of these things. The girls, with their smaller hands, have a harder time controlling the ball—even with the smaller girls and women's ball—especially in traffic. That is why the girls (and women) routinely have 10 or 12 more turnovers in a game than do the boys (or men). Superior ball handling, therefore, is a real game breaker in girls play, and a transition game that keeps the ball out of traffic is an even more potent weapon for the girls than it is for the boys. And that is why, from 1993 to 1997, it was Miller Time.

Anyone who saw Coco and Kelly Miller of Rochester Mayo as eighth graders in 1993 knew they were something special. The Miller twins led Mayo that year in a gallant but losing effort, 73–67, against a great Bloomington Jefferson squad that finished 26–1 and won their other tournament games by 19 and 8 points.

In 1994, Mayo was upset by Apple Valley in the regional tournament. Then Mayo came back in 1995 with a devastating three-guard offense featuring Laura Paukert and the Miller twins. The result was a 68–40 rout of nemesis Apple Valley, followed by equally decisive wins over Tartan and another old nemesis, St.

Cloud Apollo, in a replay of the 1982 title game, 73–44 and 74–49. Coco and Kelly scored 75 and 74 points, respectively, in the three games.

In 1996, Mayo took third place after losing to Osseo in the semis. Kelly led all scorers with 63 points, but Mayo missed Paukert and lacked an inside presence against a physical Osseo team.

Then, in 1997, Mayo faced what must have been the toughest girls bracket ever, including Jefferson, Osseo, and Mayo. For Mayo, it was a replay of 1995: a three-guard offense featuring Kiersten Kramer and the Millers compensated for a lack of inside power. Jefferson edged Osseo, 65–60, in the first round and then lost to Mayo, 78–70, in the highest scoring, best played, and probably the most exciting game in the history of the girls tournament. Mayo then easily defeated Woodbury in the final. Coco and Kelly led all scorers again with 72 and 71 points, respectively.

No one who saw the Millers play were surprised when they led Georgia to the NCAA Final Four in 2000. They were also honored with the Hickok Award as the top amateur women athletes in the United States. Both went on, as of 2005, to average more than 7 points per game in more than 150 WNBA games.

The twin sisters Coco Miller (35, left) and Kelly Miller (background, right), from Rochester Mayo, were to the girls' game what Khalid El-Amin was to the boys'. They thrived in the new full-court style of play, leading Mayo to state titles in 1995 and 1997. In 2000, they shared the Hickok Award as America's top amateur female athletes.

34 *Youth Basketball Booms*

THE HIGH SCHOOL CLASS of 1997 amazed and delighted Minnesota basketball fans and Division I college recruiters alike. At the top of the pyramid were, arguably, three of the top half-dozen high school stars in history—Mr. Basketball, Khalid El-Amin from Minneapolis North, and co–Ms. Basketball award winners, Coco and Kelly Miller from Rochester Mayo. Right behind them were three women who became honorable mention All-Americans—Jesse Stomski of Tartan High School and the University of Wisconsin, Megan Taylor of Roseau and Iowa State, and Maren Walseth of Bloomington Jefferson and Penn State. Erica Haugen of Osseo joined Taylor as a starting player for an Iowa State team that achieved a top ten rating, while Theresa LeCuyer of Anoka started her career at the University of Minnesota and then transferred to North Dakota, where she won a national title and Division II Player of the Year honors.

Among the boys, Brian Giesen of New Prague and Indiana State; Jared Nuness of Hopkins and Valparaiso; Martin Rancik, a Slovakian native who played at St. Louis Park and Iowa State; and Dusty Rychert of Grand Rapids and Minnesota all went on to start in NCAA tournament play. Chris Bjorklund of Brainerd and Cal Poly, San Luis Obispo, scored more than 2,000 career points and earned all-conference honors. Greg Buth of Edina scored more than 1,000 points at Dartmouth. And Kyle Behrens of Hayfield and North Dakota, Chad Koenen of Clara City and Southwest State, and Kyle Schlaak of New Richland and Winona State all earned NCAA Division II All-America recognition.

The class of 1999 was almost as good. The top-rated recruit was Nick Horvath of state champion Mounds View, who went to national powerhouse Duke. Michael Bauer of Hastings, Ben Johnson of DeLaSalle, and Shane Schilling of 1998 state champion Minnetonka

all went on to start for the Minnesota Gophers, though Johnson started his college career at Northwestern. Troy Bell of Holy Angels went to Boston College, where he scored more than 2,000 career points. Mauri Horton of Minneapolis North went to Rutgers, where she became captain of an NCAA tournament entry.

By 2001, there were a remarkable ten Minnesota women playing in the NCAA tournament. Not already mentioned are Tara Bjorklund of Sibley East and Colorado, Janelle Johnson of Park Rapids and Wisconsin-Milwaukee, Tamara Moore of Minneapolis North and Wisconsin, and Kelly Siemon of Edina and Notre Dame. The following year, there were five men—Bell, Horvath, Nuness, Alan Anderson of DeLaSalle and Michigan State, and Nick Jacobson of Roseville and Utah—and five women—Bjorklund, Moore, Stomski, Tia Battle of Maple Grove and Vanderbilt, and Jana Peljto of Osseo and Harvard.

By the fall of 2005, the *Star Tribune* was able to list eighty Minnesota women and sixty men on NCAA Division I rosters, with Division I scholarships. Eleven of the women played for the Minnesota Gophers, who fifteen years earlier were able to recruit virtually any Minnesota girl they wanted and lost games by the batch. Now the Gophers were a top twenty team nationally for the fifth straight year.

The Gopher men featured ten Minnesotans, though the results were substantially less satisfactory than for the Gopher women. The reason was simple: unlike Minnesota girls, many of the very best boys were choosing to play college ball elsewhere. Most prominent among them was Minneapolis North grad Kammron Taylor, starting at guard and scoring 16 points per game for the top twenty–rated Wisconsin Badgers. Also, Patrick O'Bryant of Blaine and Bradley led the nation in rebounding throughout much of the 2005-2006 season. Meanwhile, the Bison of North

Dakota State (NDSU) were playing .500 ball in just their second season in Division I with a roster that was almost equally loaded with Minnesotans—and the same goes for the NDSU women.

In short, Minnesota was now producing more Division I talent in a year than it had done in entire decades past. How did this happen? Most basketball fans understand that it has something to do with increasing opportunities for kids to play youth basketball outside the schools. But youth basketball is rarely covered in the newspapers, so the details are almost as murky as events in Minnesota basketball that occurred fifty or seventy-five years ago.

The Clubs Are the Heart of the System

The story of "youth basketball," which means basketball for school-age kids but played outside the schools and outside the school season, is in fact pretty simple. In the 1950s and 1960s, the Minnesota State High School League (MSHSL) ruthlessly restricted the opportunities of Minnesota kids to play both in and outside the schools. The regulations gradually were relaxed, and by the 1980s, a variety of youth basketball clubs had been founded, mostly in the Twin Cities area.

The purpose of the clubs, initially, was to enable kids to receive coaching and to play in game conditions virtually all year long. But the clubs had limited capacity, so there were tryouts to get in. They functioned essentially as elite, metro all-star camps. By the mid-1980s, the crème de la crème at six or eight of the leading clubs made up traveling teams that played against the other clubs in the so-called Metro League. (It was about this time that the metro area girls began to dominate the state high tournament, whereas the Greater Minnesota teams had done just fine previously.)

Having achieved their initial goals, the clubs now wanted the opportunity to play at a national level in order to give the kids exposure to recruiters and college scholarship opportunities. So in 1988, a group of volunteers—including Jerry Geisler of Osseo; Fred Harris of Fridley; John Sherman, founder of the Minnesota Magic club; and many others—created the necessary structure to gain sanction by the Amateur Athletic Union (AAU). State AAU tournaments were held for both boys and girls, with the winners advancing to the AAU nationals.

Success came rapidly. In 1989, a boys team from the Magic club won a national AAU title. Jon Bryant, later of Armstrong High School and the University of Wisconsin, and Robert Mestas, later of Minneapolis Roosevelt and Miami (Ohio), were the star players, while John Barth of Elk River High School was the head coach.

By this same year, there were about eighty to ninety girls teams in the Metro League; two years later there were about 250. By the mid-1990s there were more than four hundred boys teams. A strictly volunteer organization could not administer a program of such scope. In 1992, the volunteers elected Minnesota Youth Athletic Services (MYAS)—which had been founded the previous year by Dan Klinkhammer and Reggie Powell—as administrator for Minnesota's AAU-sanctioned basketball play. From this beach head, MYAS gradually expanded its services to include several hundred events—AAU events, events sanctioned by other youth basketball authorities, and nonsanctioned events for teams that did not want to play at a national level.

MYAS also expanded its programs to include Division II and Division III opportunities as well as Division I. "The Minnesota program was built from the top down and from the bottom up," Klinkhammer, MYAS executive director from its inception to the present day, said. "The elite clubs call for tryouts for all-star caliber traveling teams. But MYAS also has Division II and Division III programs so that kids who aren't elite can also play."

"This happened," Klinkhammer continued, "because small town teams would come down here and play all-star teams representing three or four school districts, and they would be getting beat by 60 or 70 points. The coach would ask, 'Why should I play in your tournament?'" Now clubs can select the level of play that is appropriate for their kids, though the national AAU considered this to be "blasphemy," according the Klinkhammer. "They are pretty much into the more elite caliber of ball."

As a result, however, Minnesota has 14,000 boys playing youth basketball, while Wisconsin has 4,000 from a slightly larger population. Illinois, with two and a half times the population, has just one-quarter as many clubs. "The clubs are the heart of the system," Klinkhammer said. "They play when and where they want to play."

The Shannons—Shannon Schonrock (11, left) from Winnebago and Blue Earth Area High School and Shannon Bolden (20, right) from Marshall High School—had already been teammates before coming to the University of Minnesota in 2002. They played together at the North Tartan club, with Bolden winning All-America honors in 2001 and Schonrock, in 2002.

The Ace of Clubs

The most prominent of the clubs among basketball fans is the North Tartan girls, founded by Bob Meyers. Tartan first gained prominence in 1991, when its thirteen-and-under team finished second at the national AAU tournament. Kinesha Davis (later of Blake, Western Illinois, and Nevada, Las Vegas), Jenny Hoffner (Brooklyn Park and North Dakota), and Megan Taylor earned All-America honors.

The following year a new group of thirteen-and-under girls, including All-Americans the Miller twins and Walseth, won the Tartan's first national title. The same girls finished third in the fourteen-and-under class and ninth in the fifteen-and-unders and then won another national title as sixteen-and-unders. The Millers and Walseth earned All-America honors again. They finished fourth as seventeen-year-olds in the eighteen-and-under class and won their third national

title as eighteen-year-olds. The Millers repeated as All-Americans—Kelly for the fifth time, Coco for the fourth. More often than not it was Del Schiffler, who coached Mark Olberding at Melrose and also coached Woodbury to the 1983 boys Class AA state title, on the sidelines with this fabulous cohort.

There were other national championships as well, including a 1999 Junior Olympics title in which Susan King (Holy Angels and Stanford) won All-America and MVP honors. And in 2003, the eighteen-and-under team won; Jamie Broback (Eastview and Minnesota), Lindsay Dietz (Elk River and Minnesota Duluth), and Liz Podominick (Lakeville and Minnesota) were named All-Americans. Dietz was the tournament MVP.

In 2005, Tartan's fifteen- and sixteen-year-olds participated in the Nike End of the Trail Tournament. Amy Beggin (Roseville), Tara Steinbauer (Bloomington Kennedy), Jackie Voigt (Park of Cottage Grove), Macie Michaelson (Marshall), and Heather Cook (Eden

Prairie) earned all-tournament honors, and Bri Zabel (Northfield) was named tournament MVP. Seven Tartan teams qualified to play in national tournaments in 2006, the most of any club in Minnesota. By 2006, Tartan boasted almost one thousand alumnae, fourteen AAU All-Americans, eight high school All-Americans, and one college All-American—Kelly Miller of Georgia in 1999, 2000, and 2001.

Minnesota girls also won two national championships in 2001, and neither was won by the Tartan club. Rather, the Minnesota Express won the sixteen-and-under title at the National Invitational West, and Minnesota Power Play under coach Willie Taylor won the same age class at the AAU Shootout. That same year, the Minnesota Summit took fifth in the seventeen-and-under national championships behind Katie Alsdurf (Forest Lake, Marquette, and Minnesota), and their eighteen-and-unders took a ninth place. Tartan took a seventh place in the sixteen-and-under class, as Shannon Bolden (Marshall and Minnesota) won All-America honors. Janel McCarville's (University of Minnesota) Velocity Red from Wisconsin took seventh place in the eighteen-and-unders, and McCarville also earned All-America recognition. Other leading girls clubs have included the Minnesota Ice, the Minnesota (or Lake Conference) Lakers, and North Winds from Rochester.

Among the boys the Minnesota Magic has continued as one of the elite programs with seventeen national champions, not only at the AAUs but also in national tournaments sponsored by the Basketball Congress International (BCI), Mid-America Youth Basketball (MAYB), National Youth Basketball Championships (NYBC), and Youth Basketball of America (YBOA). More than one hundred Magic alumni have won Division I scholarships, four have played in the NBA, and two—Bell and Kris Humphries (Hopkins and Minnesota)—have been first-round NBA draft picks. In 2004, the Magic fielded forty-eight teams with almost five hundred players.

The Minnesota Glory, founded and led by Charlie Paxson, former coach at Meadow Creek Christian, provides "a Christian Perspective on Athletics." Glory alumni include forty Division I scholarship athletes and two BCI All-Americans—Ryan Brinkman (Mayer Lutheran and Winona State) in 1998 and Ben Paxson (Meadow Creek Christian) in 1999.

Minnesota basketball fans know that Kris Humphries has played for Hopkins High School, the University of Minnesota, and the Utah Jazz. It is possible, however, that Humphries played more youth games with the Minnesota Magic and the Howard Pulley Club than he did for the Royals, Gophers, or Jazz.

Klinkhammer describes the Howard Pulley and Minnesota Select clubs, however, as "the elite of the elite." The Pulley program was founded by Rene Pulley in 1985. Alumni include Bauer, Bell, Adam Boone (Minnetonka, North Carolina and Minnesota), El-Amin, Devean George (Benilde-St. Margaret's, Augsburg, and the Los Angeles Lakers), Johnnie Gilbert (Minneapolis Henry and Oklahoma), Jeff Halbert (White Bear Lake and Ohio University), Moe Hargrow (St. Paul Highland Park and Minnesota), Horvath, Humphries, Nick Jacobson, Ben Johnson, Darius Lane (Totino Grace and Seton Hall), Joe Mauer (Cretin and the Minnesota Twins), Bruce Price (Minneapolis South and Tennessee State), Rick Rickert (Duluth East and Minnesota), and Jake Sullivan (Tartan and Iowa State)—plus about one hundred more recipients of Division I men's scholarships.

Tournaments, and Exposure Tournaments

One of the misconceptions about youth basketball is that it is synonymous with the AAU. The BCI and YBOA have already been mentioned as holding national tournaments of some prominence. The fastest growing sponsor, however, is the U.S. Sport Specialties Association (USSSA), whose national tournament was by 2005 almost as large as the AAU. The MYAS administers USSSA as well as AAU events in Minnesota, and in 2005, it held four state and regional tournaments in Minneapolis to select qualifiers for the national championships. In addition, USSSA national invitational tournaments for boys and girls in grades three through eleven were held in Minneapolis.

But the most prestigious tournaments are now those sponsored by the shoe companies Adidas, Nike, and Reebok. This is where "the elite of the elite" compete, because this is where exposure to the Division I recruiters is most likely to be found. At the Nike camps, for example, college recruiters can watch thirty or forty games and see most of the nation's top Division I prospects. At the AAU tournament, they would have to watch several hundred games to see the same number of serious Division I candidates.

In 2005, the Pulley Club played in the Boo Williams, Kingwood, Memorial Day, Rumble 'n' Bronx, and Peach Jam tournaments—all sponsored by Nike—in Georgia, Louisiana, New York, Texas, and Virginia. The club also participated in the Wisconsin Shootout, whose promotional materials state, "College coaches at the Division II, Division III, NAIA, [and] Junior College level[s] in the midwest are sent a letter in May to come and recruit at this tournament. This will be an exposure tournament for all players who have the ability to play college basketball at the Division II, Division III, NAIA, and Junior College level[s]." The season concluded in July with the AAU Super Showcase in Orlando, Florida, and Jerry Mullen's/Kansas City Premiere Last Chance Summer Showcase in Kansas City, Missouri.

Meanwhile, MYAS administers "a couple hundred tournaments a year," according to Klinkhammer. One is the Gopher State Prep Showcase, also held in the summer after the club teams have been together, playing regularly and presumably at their best for several months. "Upholding the belief that the upper Midwest is home to many truly talented high school basketball players who are not receiving the exposure necessary for college recruitment, the Minnesota Youth Athletic Services created the Gopher State Prep Showcase," says the event Web page. "As Minnesota's premier showcase of high school talent . . . this tournament will give eligible boys and girls teams an opportunity to play competitively in the off season with an audience that will include hundreds of Division II and III college coaches. . . . Don't miss this opportunity to 'showcase' your players to hundreds of college coaches and recruiters."

So What's the Problem?

According to Klinkhammer, youth basketball—unlike school sports—functions as a market. Kids play for the club of their choice, and the clubs play "when and where they want to play" and under the jurisdiction (AAU, USSSA, etc.) they choose. So what's the problem?

Some say that kids' lives today lack balance—that playing one sport all year long is bad for young people. The amount of basketball youth could play was constrained for a long time by the regulatory authority of the schools. Now the youth sports market enables kids and their parents to decide for themselves how much basketball is enough or too much.

Then there is a presumption that coaches and administrators in the schools have the best interests of the young players at heart but that those working within a "market system" do not. This is surely unfair. MYAS, for instance, operates out of dingy and cramped quarters in Columbia Heights—quarters that are not nearly as pleasant as those at the MSHSL offices or in many modern schools. There's a serious limit to what the market— the kids and their parents—can bear in the way of fees and expenses, and youth basketball is not subsidized from outside of the market. So nobody is getting rich administering youth sports programs.

Klinkhammer acknowledges that there are a few "street agent" coaches who try to steer a kid to a particular college or toward a professional contract and to get a "piece of the action." This, he says, is "very rare" in Minnesota. More frequently we hear complaints about high school basketball players taking advantage of "open enrollment" to change schools for athletic purposes. What has this to do with youth basketball? Often kids play together in the summer leagues, and they transfer in order to continue to play with their summer league "all-star" teammates.

There are, in short, legitimate concerns about the operation of a free market in youth sports. But no one believes that returning to the days when kids were limited to sixteen games in a year is a solution. The truth is that one hundred years ago, no one knew whether athletics would—or should—become entrenched in the schools. Now that an alternative structure for youth sports has grown up outside the schools, some are wondering again whether youth basketball belongs in the private clubs operating in a market economy. The writer of a 2002 letter to the editor in the *Star Tribune* asked if "there may be a better way to run sports that wouldn't involve teachers, and . . . a better way to teach that wouldn't involve sports."

Authors' Choice:
Minnesota All-Stars, 1997–2006

Forward Kevin Garnett, Minnesota Timberwolves. KG is surely the most skilled basketball player ever to wear a Minnesota uniform of any kind. His signature season came in 2003–2004, when, with 24.2 points and a league-leading 13.9 rebounds per game, he was named the NBA's Most Valuable Player.

Wings Coco and Kelly Miller, Rochester Mayo High School. How many eighth graders have led their team to a Minnesota state championship semifinal? Just two. Four years later, they had shared two state championships, scored more than 200 tournament points apiece, and owned seven all-tournament trophies between them. Another three years later, they were honored with the Hickok Award as the greatest amateur women athletes in the country.

Guard Khalid El-Amin, Minneapolis North High School. No other male athlete had in eighty-five years accomplished what El-Amin did in the Minnesota state high school tournament—that is, winning three titles and earning three-time all-tournament recognition. (Since then only Isaiah Dahlman has duplicated this feat.) He also graduated as the top boys career scorer in tournament history with 238 points (Dahlman finished his career with 236), and later he led the University of Connecticut to an NCAA championship.

Guard Lindsay Whalen, Hutchinson High School and University of Minnesota. The Gopher women went from their worst teams ever to their very best, and that was almost entirely because of Lindsay. She is perhaps the most creative player, both scoring and passing (male or female), in Minnesota history and completed her Gopher career with 2,285 points, best ever for any Gopher regardless of gender.

SECOND TEAM *Center* Janel McCarville, University of Minnesota; *forwards* Isaiah Dahlman, Braham High School, Devean George, Benilde-St. Margaret's High School and Augsburg College, and Sam Jacobsen, Park High School, Cottage Grove, and University of Minnesota; *guard* Kelly Roysland, Fosston High School and University of Minnesota.

35 *The Return of David and Goliath*

THE BIG NEWS in high school basketball circles is the continuing decline of interest in the state tournament, coupled with a vast increase in the numbers of Minnesota youth—both boys and girls—earning Division I athletic scholarships. It is not clear that fans are losing interest in youth basketball (through age eighteen) overall, but the focus of attention more and more is on key regular season games as well as the players' exploits outside of the high school season.

The Four-Class System

After what was regarded as an unsuccessful experiment with the boys Sweet Sixteen format, the Minnesota State High School League threw tradition completely out the window in 1997 and leaped from two classes to four. The four-class format quickly met its putative objective of giving more teams the opportunity to compete at the state tournament level. In 1999, for example, St. Paul Highland Park became the first St. Paul public school to win a boys championship in fifty long years. Also, five of the first eight boys Class A finalists made their first tournament appearance. (That is, if you count Win-E-Mac's 2000 appearance as their first—McIntosh had participated in 1924 and McIntosh-Winger in 1978.) Another, 1997 champion, Hancock, made their first tournament appearance in seventy-five years, and 1998 runner-up Carlton made their first appearance in thirty-nine years. Clearly, the four-class format is giving many boys teams an opportunity to succeed that they had not had under previous formats.

The impact among the girls was much less significant, as only two of the first thirty-two finalists were making their first tournament appearance. During the two-class era, girls from the relatively smaller schools within each class (today's Class A and AAA) had already had a lot more success competing against the relatively larger schools (now Class AA and AAAA) than the boys from smaller schools had had. School size, in other words, has been less a determinant of success among the girls than the boys.

The problem, as always, is attendance. After peaking at 59,000 in 1990, by 1995 attendance at the girls tournament had plummeted to barely 30,000. Only once has attendance at the new four-class tourney topped 40,000. Boys attendance peaked at almost 88,000 (17,600 per session) in the early 1960s and topped 100,000 (in almost twice as many sessions) throughout most of the 1970s. Attendance bottomed out at 55,000 for the two Sweet Sixteen tournaments and then increased to almost 80,000 with the extra sessions that four classes provide. Still, attendance was back down to 61,395 in 2004.

The complaints about the four-class tournament have continued. *Tribune* reporter Roman Augustoviz had written way back on March 16, 1996: "If they were given the choice between the present two-class state tournament and going to four classes, the coaches in the girl's basketball state field would stay with the status quo." Augustoviz cited second-year coach Kris Bennett of Red Lake Falls, who said, "I just hate [four classes]. You've got such good rivalries right now." Erin Herman of Hill-Murray was quoted as saying, "I like two classes. I could live with three, but four is too many." In all, eight coaches favored two classes, three liked three, and just one opted for four. Yet the four class format was adopted in 1996 for implementation beginning in 1997 for both the boys and the girls tournaments. First-round games were played at sites scattered throughout the state.

Four years later, the MSHSL surveyed coaches and athletic directors whose teams had played in the boys or girls tournaments of 1999 or 2000. An overwhelming majority wanted a three-class tournament with all games in the metro area. Half of this preference was ac-

Rick Rickert (44) tries to get off a shot against Osseo in the 2001 boys Class AAAA state tournament final. Rickert scored 26 points to finish with 90 points as the tournament's top scorer, but Osseo clobbered Rickert's Greyhounds 73–48 to take the title.

commodated in 2004, when all games were played in the Twin Cities for the first time.

Then, on March 23, 2001, Sid Hartman wrote that the tournament had been "ruined" because small-town teams no longer had the opportunity of "coming in and knocking off the big-city teams." Forget that they had so infrequently actually done so; they had had the opportunity.

David and Goliath

It is a myth, however, that Minnesota's small and large school powers do not play one another anymore. It just does not happen in the postseason. But fans who wonder which of the four champions each year (for each gender) is really the best have seen good indicators from some celebrated regular season matchups among the leading boys teams.

Isaiah Dahlman launches a shot against Martin County West in the 2004 Class AA final. Dahlman and Braham won, 73–47, and then repeated their performance in 2005 and 2006.

The most celebrated came in 2000, when eventual Class AAAA champion Tartan (26–1) was thrashed, 74–49, by eventual AA champ Litchfield (29–0) in a holiday tournament. Most observers thought that Minneapolis Henry's AAA champs were the best team of the year, however. The Patriots' only loss was an 88–67 loss to national power Oak Hill, Virginia, in a tournament in Virginia.

In 2005, the Braham Bombers' Class AA champs (33–0) staked their claim as the best team in Minnesota by defeating Richfield, AAA runner-up, 72–63, and perennial power Minneapolis North, 71–56. North later lost to Mounds View (23–9), which finished third in Class AAAA, in the Section 6AAAA final, 53–47. By tournament time Braham was slowed by point guard Josh Vaughan's injury, however, and most thought that

Kelly Roysland of Fosston (35) drives around Kaley Sorenson (5) of Hawley in the 2003 Class A final. Fosston won, 48–36, its third state championship in four years, a feat that would not have been easily accomplished by a small school in either the single- or the two-class era.

Hopkins's AAAA champs (31–1) were the state's best team, despite the Royals' need to go to two overtimes in their final.

In the metro area the relative strength of the best AAAA and AAA teams has been measured in such conferences as the Minneapolis City and Classic Suburban, which mixed teams from both classes. In 2005, Class AAA runner-up Richfield (26–5) lost two regular-season games to Class AAAA fourth-place Tartan (25–7), but both by just 1 point. And 2005 Class A champ Russell-Tyler-Ruthton (28–3) lost to Class AA third-place Luverne (21–9), 61–60. That the best AAA teams can compete with the best AAAA teams—and the best A teams with the best in AA—seems clear enough. And

Litchfield and Braham have shown that an occasional AA team can compete even at the highest levels.

The success of the Minneapolis North boys, with five state titles since 1980, also provides powerful ammunition for those who believe that smaller schools can compete against larger ones. North's enrollment, generally in the eight hundred to nine hundred range from year to year, would place it in Class AAA, but the Polar boys choose to compete in Class AAAA. Its most recent titles came with victories over Stillwater (enrollment about 1,800) in 1997 and Osseo (enrollment about 1,600) in 2003.

Among the girls the small schools historically have had plenty of success competing with larger schools, though in the four-class era there has been less play than the boys across class lines. But in girls volleyball, many of whose superstars are also great basketball players, competition between the classes is customary, and the small schools have enjoyed great success. In 2005, Faribault Bethlehem Academy, to cite just one example, played in its fourth straight Class A final. The Cardinals had defeated three Class AA and AAA tournament entries, including AA finalist Stewartville, plus perennial AAA powers Apple Valley and Eagan. They also gave AAA finalist Marshall a tough match before losing, 25–22, 25–20, and 25–16. So there is reason to believe the girls from the small schools could compete against the larger schools if given the chance.

Polars' Success Goes over the Top

With four classes and thirty-two tournament teams—both among the boys and the girls—there are plenty of opportunities to win state championships, and the state's better programs do not need to face one another to win one. So great teams no longer distinguish themselves by winning a state title but rather by returning to the tournament year after year and winning multiple championships.

Two programs dwarf all others as the greatest dynasties of the era just before and after the new millennium—the Minneapolis North and Rochester Lourdes girls. At North, of course, the boys also completed their three-peat in the first year of four-class play and then added another Class AAAA title—their fifth overall—82–73 over Osseo in a double overtime thriller in 2003. The Polars now lead all Minnesota high schools with their combined total of ten boys and girls championships.

The Lady Polars, under coach Faith Patterson—who as Faith Johnson played for Minneapolis Marshall-U in the earliest girls tournaments—did not win their first title until 1998 but quickly matched the boys' five titles, and in their case in the remarkably short space of just eight years. North played in every one of the first nine Class AAA tournaments, made it to the championship game in eight out of nine tries, and took third place in that ninth tournament.

First, there were the Tamara Moore-Felicia Bell-Mauri Horton years. North lost to Alexandria in the 1997 title game, but the next year clobbered three opponents by an average score of 68–37. Moore led all AAA scorers both years with a total of 123 points (20.5 per game) and then went on to earn All-America honorable mentions at Wisconsin and to play in the Women's National Basketball Association (WNBA). In her senior season of 2002, Bell led her Florida Tech team to the NCAA Division II Elite Eight.

With Moore and Bell gone, Horton returned in 1999, and Tiara Medlock did her best Tamara Moore impression. North romped again by an average score of 65–36. The 1998 and 1999 teams combined for fifty-six wins against just two losses. Horton played college ball at Rutgers, where she was team captain her final two seasons, and then played professionally in Israel. Medlock played hoops at Minneapolis Community and Technical College and then emerged as a track and cross-country star at Texas A&M-Commerce.

Then came the Mia Johnson years. The slight five-foot-nine point guard became the first player (boy or girl) ever to earn all-tournament honors four times—and that was in her junior year in 2003. In 2004, she earned them for a fifth time, though North won only two state championships during her five years at the point.

The Polars slumped to second place in Johnson's freshman season of 2000, losing to New Prague and center Randi Wirt in the final, 64–62. Marshall and Shannon Bolden blocked North in 2001 and 2002, winning two straight titles and defeating North, 55–37 in a 2001 semi and 61–46 in the 2002 final. Krystal Taylor, along with Johnson, won all-tournament honors a third time in 2002, however.

Johnson finally won her first state title in 2003, as

Mia Johnson of Minneapolis North was the first player (boy or girl) to earn all-state tournament honors four times, and that was by her junior year. She repeated as a senior in 2004, when North played in its seventh Class AAA final in eight years. In 2005, without Johnson, the Lady Polars won their fifth state title in eight years.

North dominated again by an average margin of 51–28 to finish with a 28–3 record. Johnson, Faith Buchanan, and Laraea Starr won all-tournament honors. They repeated in 2004, despite a mediocre 22–8 record, but Johnson had missed a good portion of the regular season with a knee injury. In the tournament she led the Polars with 46 points, and North won two of the three games easily. In between they survived a 63–61 thriller against Worthington. Johnson played one year of college ball at Saint Louis University, ranking fifth in Conference USA scoring with 17.1 points per game. Her 441 points was also the fifth best in school history, but then she transferred to Michigan State, where she has three years of eligibility remaining as of this writing.

Lawrence McKenzie (1) sets up the Minneapolis Patrick Henry offense against Red Wing in the 2002 Class AAA championship game. Henry won, 61–44, to become the first boys program to win five state titles. The following year, the Patriots became the first boys program to win six championships.

Despite Johnson's departure, North had two starters back in 2005, and that was enough: North hammered Holy Angels, 71–45, in the final to finish 24–4.

Eagles Prey on Tournament Opposition

Rochester Lourdes entered the four-class era with five state titles, then added three more in 2000, 2003, and 2005 to continue to lead all programs with eight championships, all of them under coach Myron Glass. The

Eagles do it with solid defense and a healthy spirit of revenge. Never in its eight championship seasons has it allowed more than 38 points per game over the three games, and only once in twenty-four games did an opponent score 50 points. That was an unbeaten Albany team in 2003, featuring two daughters of coach Jon Noreen in future small college stars Darby (St. Ben's) and Joanne (Minnesota State Mankato).

As for the revenge angle, in 1999 Lourdes lost in the semifinals to eventual champion Blake. On the way to its 2000 title, the Eagles clobbered Blake, 58–35. In 2002, it was Breck beating Lourdes's defending champions in the first round, 59–39. In 2003, the Eagles returned the favor, 35–22, in the final.

Coach Glass is famous for his meticulous preparation. After the 2003 semifinals, he and his staff worked until 2:30 A.M. preparing a game plan for the title game against the Breck Mustangs. At 10:30 A.M., his girls all received an eight-page scouting report. "In 1986, we came here for the first time and lost twice," Glass said. "We learned our lesson on what to do and how to prepare."

"We've learned that defense comes first," all-tournament forward Ellen Hake said. "We are a very organized team."

And since the 1990–1991 teams led by Lori Lawler and Stacy Sievers, Lourdes has won without great talent like the Noreens; Blake's Kristin Ambrose and Kate Baumann (1999–2001); or Kelly Finley and Melissa Miller of Breck (2002–2003)—all of whom have tasted defeat at the hands of Glass's teams. Over the course of the past five championships, only guard Anne Breland won all-tournament honors more than once, in 2003 and 2005. It didn't hurt that Lourdes had the services of sisters Laurie and Missy Decker, Lori and Kate Lawler, and Monica and Ellen Hake, however. The Hakes led the Eagles in scoring in 2000 and 2003 with 56 and 50 points, respectively.

The only real constant through it all is Glass himself. In twenty-two years, his girls have won 571 games while losing just 69 (.892). And not only has he won eight state basketball titles, he and his Eagles have won four boys cross-country, two girls cross-country, and two girls track and field titles as well.

More Four-Class Dynasties

Until 1997, Minnesota had seen exactly two three-peat high school champions—the Edina boys in 1966–1968 and the girls from New York Mills in 1978–1980. Now that the North boys and girls have both joined that exclusive club, it is no longer so exclusive. More exclusive yet is the four-peaters' club, which includes only the boys from Southwest Minnesota Christian in Edgerton (1999–2002) and Minneapolis Henry (2000–2003).

Southwest Christian rang up a 106–8 record over four years and had to win only three of twelve state

tournament victories by less than double-digit margins. They did it with defense, as only one opponent ever scored as many as 60 points—that being Win-E-Mac in the 2000 final, a 72–61 win for Southwest. Forwards Robbie Holleman and Cody Kuipers each won all-tournament recognition the first two years, while it was center Jeff Schaap who did so during the second pair of championships.

Henry, meanwhile, became the leading boys program with six state titles overall. Its first champions of the four-class era (and third overall) in 2000 was perhaps the best boys team of the era, going 28–1 and outscoring state tournament opponents an average of 74–46. Guards Greg Patton and Tony Travis dominated games with their pressure defense and quick transitions to the offense in the open court. But whenever a little muscle was needed, Johnnie Gilbert was there in the paint. All three won all-tournament honors.

Henry remained a perimeter and pressure-oriented team throughout its run. In 2003 and 2004, Lawrence McKenzie and Terry Pettis made the Patriots go to 28–2 and 29–4 records. Forward Zerek Knight also made all-tournament both years. Never was there a margin below double figures—in fact, the average score over three years was 71–50. The 2003 edition appeared merely mortal by comparison. McKenzie was back, but Henry had to scrap to a 59–54 win over Red Wing in a semifinal and finished up at 26–6. McKenzie, son of coach Larry McKenzie, first joined Gilbert at the University of Oklahoma and then transferred to the University of Minnesota for his final two years of college play.

Meanwhile, the Lake Conference has been creeping back to the prominence it had in the 1960s. Bloomington Jefferson was the only Lake school to win a boys state title between 1968 and 1998, and the Lake girls won only two of the first eleven Class AA titles. But the Lake boys won five of the first ten Class AAAA championships and four of five from 2002 to 2006. Moreover, the Lake supplied both finalists in three of those championship seasons. Hopkins, under coach Kenny Novak Jr., won in 2002 and 2005 over Jefferson and Eastview, respectively, and Chaska defeated Burnsville for the 2003 title. The Jefferson girls matched the Jaguar boys with a fourth state title in 1998. And all six of the Class AAAA girls finalists in 2004, 2005, and 2006 came from the Lake, Lakeville, Hopkins, and Bloomington

Kennedy each having won a state title—Lakeville and Hopkins twice—in the twenty-first century.

The Lake has also produced such star players as Liz Podominick (Lakeville and University of Minnesota), Kris Humphries (Hopkins, Minnesota, and NBA), Ryan Amoroso (Burnsville and Marquette), Leslie Knight (Hopkins and Minnesota), Spencer Tollackson (Chaska and Minnesota), Jenna Smith

(Bloomington Kennedy and committed to Illinois), and Jillian Schurle (Hopkins and Princeton).

The Hopkins boys in 2005 produced perhaps the most electrifying moment of the four-class tournament era (along with the Red Lake-Wabasso game of 1997) in a thrilling double-overtime marathon with conference rival Eastview. Eastview was "sitting" on a 60–58 lead with 2.5 seconds left in overtime. The Royals

Girls High School Champions, 1997–2006

Year	Championship Game Score	W–L	Authors' Choice: Postseason MVPs
1997	A Hancock 56 Red Lake Falls 50	24–3	Kelly Miller, Rochester Mayo, F-G
	AA N. London–Spicer 55 Minnewaska Area 51	29–1	Coco Miller, Rochester Mayo, G-F
	AAA Alexandria 52 Mpls. North 43	25–3	
	AAAA Rochester Mayo 78 Woodbury 57	27–0	
1998	A Christ's Hshld of Faith 45 Red Lake Falls 36	19–10	Tamara Moore, Mpls. North, F
	AA Blake 73 Caledonia 57	19–7	
	AAA Mpls. North 66 Chaska 33	29–0	
	AAAA Jefferson 70 Cretin-Derham Hall 41	24–2	
1999	A Brandon-Evansville 61 Red Rock Central 46	24–5	Kate Townley, Cretin-Derham Hall, G
	AA Blake 53 Minnewaska Area 44	25–4	
	AAA Mpls. North 72 Owatonna 44	27–2	
	AAAA Cretin-Derham Hall 62 Moorhead 45	26–2	
2000	A Fosston 64 Minnesota Valley Lutheran 50	28–1	Hana Peljto, Osseo, C
	AA Rochester Lourdes 57 Sibley East 25	28–2	
	AAA New Prague 64 Mpls. North 62	27–1	
	AAAA Osseo 80 Eastview 53	24–3	
2001	A Fosston 50 Eden Valley–Watkins 45	29–0	Liz Podominick, Lakeville, C
	AA St. Michael–Albert. 63 N. London–Sp. 59 (OT)	27–3	
	AAA Marshall 56 North Branch 39	28–1	
	AAAA Lakeville 42 Elk River 31	27–2	
2002	A Kittson Central 63 Elgin-Millville 41	30–1	Shannon Bolden, Marshall, F
	AA N. London–Spicer 43 Yellow Medicine E. 31	29–2	
	AAA Marshall 61 Mpls. North 46	29–0	
	AAAA Lakeville 55 Blaine 46	29–0	
2003	A Fosston 48 Hawley 36	30–2	Kelly Roysland, Fosston, G
	AA Rochester Lourdes 35 Breck 22	30–2	
	AAA Mpls. North 57 Duluth East 32	28–2	
	AAAA Woodbury 61 Eastview 42	29–0	
2004	A Wabasso 59 Underwood 48	29–4	Leslie Knight, Hopkins, F
	AA Breck 39 Hawley 23	29–3	
	AAA Mpls. North 56 Willmar 39	22–8	
	AAAA Hopkins 63 Lakeville 45	31–1	
2005	A Elgin-Millville 43 Fosston 34	31–2	Jenna Smith, Kennedy, C
	AA Rochester Lourdes 50 Pequot Lakes 33	30–1	
	AAA Mpls. North 71 Holy Angels 45	24–4	
	AAAA Bloomington Kennedy 44 Hopkins 38 (OT)	28–2	
2006	A Fulda 57 Granada–Huntley–East Chain 49	26–4	Cory Montgomery, Cannon Falls, C
	AA Cannon Falls 66 Crookston 50	28–6	
	AAA Benilde-St. Margaret's 54 Marshall 39	27–4	
	AAAA Hopkins 65 Bloomington Kennedy 48	30–2	

Minnetonka's Shane Schilling (34) scores in a 55–53 win over Minneapolis North in a 1998 Class AAAA semifinal. 'Tonka went on to win the championship the following night, and Schilling went on to play for the Minnesota Gophers.

had the ball, but they were ninety-six feet away from the basket on their own baseline. Hopkins threw a pass three-quarters of the length of the court that was batted around for a second and then landed in the hands of sophomore guard Blake Hoffarber. Unfortunately, Hoffarber had fallen to the court in the scramble and was literally sitting on the three-point line. Still, he managed to throw up a two-handed shot that swished through the hoop as the buzzer sounded. With luck like that, Hopkins could hardly lose in the second overtime, and it did not. Andrew Henke scored 7 points in the second OT as the Royals pulled away to a 71–60 win.

Finally, DeLaSalle won its third, fourth, and fifth state titles in just thirty years of tournament eligibility in 1998, 1999, and 2006, respectively, moving up to AAA for the 2005–2006 season. The Islanders lost to

Boys High School Champions, 1997–2006

Year	Championship Game Score	W–L	Authors' Choice: Postseason MVPs
1997	A Hancock 60 Wabasso 58	26–2	Khalid El-Amin, Mpls. North, G
	AA Caledonia 69 DeLaSalle 47	29–0	
	AAA Simley 61 New Prague 47	25–3	
	AAAA Mpls. North 61 Stillwater 53	25–3	
1998	A Norman County East 75 Carlton 48	27–2	Shane Schilling, Minnetonka, F
	AA DeLaSalle 53 Long Prairie–Grey Eagle 52	24–3	
	AAA St. Thomas 60 Mpls. Henry 49	22–6	
	AAAA Minnetonka 65 Eagan 57	25–2	
1999	A SW Christian 63 Fergus Falls Hillcrest 50	27–1	Nick Horvath, Mounds View, C
	AA DeLaSalle 50 Watertown-Mayer 44	24–3	
	AAA St. Paul Highland Park 56 Rocori 48	27–2	
	AAAA Mounds View 69 Minnetonka 64	24–3	
2000	A SW Christian 72 Win-E-Mac 61	27–1	Jake Sullivan, Tartan, G
	AA Litchfield 42 Waterville-Elysian-Morristown 28	29–0	
	AAA Mpls. Henry 59 St. Thomas 45	28–1	
	AAAA Tartan 62 Maple Grove 51	26–1	
2001	A SW Christian 65 Christ's Household 55	25–4	Rick Rickert, Duluth East, C
	AA Kenyon-Wanamingo 53 Hayfield 30	28–3	
	AAA Mpls. Henry 74 St. Thomas Academy 61	28–2	
	AAAA Osseo 73 Duluth East 48	30–1	
2002	A SW Christian 66 Ortonville 56	27–2	Kris Humphries, Hopkins, F
	AA Litchfield 62 Lewiston-Altura 51	30–2	
	AAA Mpls. Henry 61 Red Wing 44	29–4	
	AAAA Hopkins 54 Bloomington Jefferson 40	28–2	
2003	A Mankato Loyola 65 Ellsworth 55	32–0	Humphries
	AA Litchfield 51 DeLaSalle 33	30–2	
	AAA Mpls. Henry 69 Sauk Rapids-Rice 55	26–6	
	AAAA Mpls. North 82 Osseo 73 (2 OT)	28–3	
2004	A Russell-Tyler-Ruthton 59 Nashwauk-Keewatin 29	23–6	Ryan Amoroso, Burnsville, F
	AA Braham 73 Martin County West 47	31–2	
	AAA Mankato West 50 Red Wing 42	24–4	
	AAAA Chaska 71 Burnsville 57	30–2	
2005	A Russell-Tyler-Ruthton 58 Rushford-Peterson 55	28–3	Isaiah Dahlman, Braham, G
	AA Braham 63 Crookston 39	33–0	
	AAA Shakopee 57 Richfield 46	31–1	
	AAAA Hopkins 71 Eastview 60 (2 OT)	31–1	
2006	A Rushford-Peterson 55 Ellsworth 52	23–9	Cory Johnson, Duluth East, F
	AA Braham 72 Breck 53	31–2	
	AAA DeLaSalle 65 Duluth East 47	27–5	
	AAAA Hopkins 69 Robbinsdale Cooper 53	30–2	

Liz Podominick of Lakeville wheels in the lane against Blaine in the 2002 girls Class AAAA final. Podominick scored 25 points to lead Lakeville to a 55–46 win and their first of two straight state titles. Podominick went on to play for the Gopher women for three years before concentrating on track and field in her fourth year of eligibility.

Caledonia, 69–47, in the 1997 Class AA final, as Aaron Middendorf scored 45 points for the Warriors. Then, DeLaSalle edged Long Prairie–Grey Eagle, 52–51, and beat Watertown-Mayer, 50–44, in 1998 and 1999, respectively. Ben Johnson played in all three finals, earned all-tournament honors three times, and scored 227 points in nine games, the third-best all-time performance among the boys, behind Khalid El-Amin and Mark Olberding. He went on to play basketball at Northwestern and the University of Minnesota. Then in 2006, the Islanders clobbered Duluth East, which had just moved down from Class AAAA, 65–47.

36 *The Gopher Women Come Out of Nowhere*

BY THE END OF THE 1996–1997 season, it had been twelve years since the Minnesota Gopher women had fashioned a winning record without the supernatural efforts of Carol Ann Shudlick. So women's athletic director Chris Voelz hired Cheryl Littlejohn, an assistant for the women's basketball team at Alabama, as the new coach and made note in the announcement of the new coach's recruiting skills.

It is difficult to assess Littlejohn's recruiting skills because she struggled so mightily when it came to actual coaching. The Gophers finished last or tied for last in the Big Ten in Littlejohn's first three seasons. In her fourth and final year, Minnesota finished out of the cellar with a 1–15 record only because Northwestern posted a winless season. And beyond the lack of on-court success was turmoil with her players and, eventually, NCAA rule violations that led to Littlejohn's dismissal.

Her first season, in 1997–1998, ended with Littlejohn suspending seven players from the opening (and, for Minnesota, the last) game in the Big Ten tournament for violation of a team rule by going to a bar after the team's final regular-season game. The suspensions left the Gophers with only seven players as they lost to Wisconsin.

One of the suspended players was senior Angie Iverson, who watched the final game of her college career from the bench, dressed in street clothes. Iverson had achieved personal success with the Gophers, even leading the nation in rebounding her junior year. But like others, she had experienced only frustration in terms of team success.

Within a few months of the end of the 1997–1998 season, Littlejohn found herself shorthanded for another reason: five players left the team. The group included three of the players who had been suspended—Kiauna Burns, Lynda Hass, and Sarah Klun—as well as

Andrea Seago and Rachel Young. Burns moved on to North Dakota State, where she enjoyed greater success before completing her college career.

Young cited financial problems as her reason for leaving, but the others cited abuses and mistreatment on the part of Littlejohn. The charges included claims that Littlejohn had refused to let the players eat after a loss and that the coach forced Seago, when she returned to practice following knee surgery, to run baseline-to-baseline sprints known as "suicides" until she repeatedly vomited.

Burns cited comments from Littlejohn that she perceived as racist. (Burns and Littlejohn are both black; the comments involved Burns' guardians, who are white.) Klun and other players questioned Littlejohn's commitment to academics. Hass was disturbed by Littlejohn's admonition that other players should avoid Hass and Iverson because "when you hang around dogs, you get fleas."

The university investigated the situation and acknowledged incidents that would not be repeated, such as not allowing players to eat after a game, but Littlejohn coached the Gophers for another three seasons.

The end came when Littlejohn was fired in May 2001, following revelations of NCAA violations. The university issued a report that detailed twelve violations committed by Littlejohn during her four years with the Gophers. The charges included payments made to a player, interference with the university's investigation into the violations, and practices outside of NCAA-approved times.

The Gophers won twenty-nine games and lost eighty-one during Littlejohn's tenure, fashioning a

Janel McCarville (4) from Stevens Point, Wisconsin, was a dominating center for the Gophers who won 98 games during her four years on the team. In the Final Four season of 2003, she set a record for most rebounds in an NCAA tournament.

7-57 record in regular-season Big Ten play. Including the Gophers' final two years under Hill-MacDonald, the team was 8–88 over its previous six seasons in the Big Ten. Yet, as had been hoped, Littlejohn had recruited some players who, under the leadership of a new coach, would bring about a stunning turnaround in team performance.

Lindsay Whalen, a guard from Hutchinson, was a freshman in Littlejohn's last season. Other players who would return for the 2001–2002 season included sharpshooting guard Lindsay Lieser from New London, Minnesota, and forwards Kadidja Andersson from Stockholm, Sweden, and Corrin Von Wald from Hudson, Wisconsin. Just before she was fired, Littlejohn also had recruited six-foot-two center Janel McCarville from Stevens Point, Wisconsin, who had been the co-High School Player of the Year in Wisconsin in 2001.

A New Beginning

Minnesota had some talented players, then, and they would get an able leader when the university hired Brenda Oldfield as its new coach in June 2001. Some of the Gophers already knew Oldfield from her time as recruiting coordinator at Iowa State. From there, Oldfield went to Ball State as head coach, taking over a team that had a 66–169 record over the past nine seasons. Under Oldfield, the school posted records of 16–13 and 19–9.

It was not expected that Oldfield could perform a similar feat at Minnesota, at least not that quickly, but the turnaround that the Gophers experienced in 2001–2002 was even more amazing. The Gophers' only loss in nonconference play was by 33 points to Stanford, a team ranked in the top ten nationally. Their next loss, in their Big Ten opener, was to twenty-fourth-ranked Penn State by a score of 88–83.

Pam Borton took over as the head coach of the University of Minnesota women in 2002. During her first four years at the helm, the Gophers won 95 games while losing 34 for a winning percentage of .736. The program received a setback in 2006, however, when five women with eligibility remaining left the team.

Three weeks later, the Gophers went to Madison and beat fifth-ranked Wisconsin, 92–85, behind 32 points by Whalen. The win not only put the Gophers into the national rankings at number twenty-three in the Associated Press poll but generated excitement back home.

"Pack the Pav" was the theme of an effort already underway to generate a large crowd when the Gophers were scheduled to return to the Sports Pavilion for a game against Indiana on January 27. The day before the Gophers won in Wisconsin, however, a sprinkler had burst at the Pavilion, spraying approximately 40,000 gallons across the arena. The pipe break necessitated a move of the game to Williams Arena, in the other half of the building, and the theme became "Ride the Wave to Williams." A record crowd of 11,389 came out to see Minnesota defeat Indiana, 75–60.

It was doubtful that the Pavilion would be available to the Gophers for the rest of the season, but they were more than happy with the larger capacity of Williams Arena and have never moved back to the smaller arena. Later, more than 12,000 fans turned out to see them play Michigan State, and Minnesota's average attendance of more than 7,300 in its six games at Williams Arena was much greater than the total capacity at the Sports Pavilion.

The Gophers finished the conference season with an 11–5 record, tied with Penn State for second place, two games behind Purdue. The Gophers made the NCAA tournament for only the second time and beat Nevada, Las Vegas, 71–54, in their first-round game, as Whalen scored 29 points and McCarville had 12 rebounds. Despite getting into foul trouble, McCarville matched her rebounding total in the second game, and Whalen topped her scoring total with 31 points. The Gophers still fell to the host team, North Caro-

The Big Game
Minnesota 82, Duke 75
March 30, 2004

The Gopher women had had an up-and-down year in 2003–2004. After finishing in second place in the Big Ten the previous two years, they lost four of their final six games and dropped to fourth place. And, while there was never any doubt that they would play in the NCAA tournament for a third straight year, they were disappointed with a seventh seed in the Mideast Regional.

Lindsay Whalen's broken hand had not helped matters, but now she was back in the lineup, though wearing a soft cast on her right (shooting) hand. Moreover, their first- and second-round games would be played in the friendly confines of Williams Arena. The Gophers could not help capitalizing on all of that good fortune, and they stormed to the regional final in Norfolk, Virginia. Unfortunately, their opponent would be the number one ranked team in the nation, Duke—though the Blue Devils somehow managed only to be the number two seed in the region. Nevertheless, Duke, led by All-America guard Alana Beard, entered the game with a 30–3 record (to the Gophers' 24–8) and heavily favored.

The Gophers took their first lead, 10–7, on a Whalen three-pointer at the 13:53 mark of the first half and then extended the lead to 26–16 late in the half. Defensive stopper Shannon Bolden made Beard's life miserable, and after Bolden went out with 2 fouls at 9:33, Kadidja Andersson did the same. Beard finished the half shooting two-for-seven with 5 points. After McCarville sat down with 2 fouls at 2:42, Andersson made 2 free throws and then defended a Beard miss, and the Gophers were ahead 33–26 at halftime.

Duke stormed back, hitting 6 of their first 7 shots after the break and trimming the Gophers' lead to 42–40. A McCar-ville steal keyed a Gophers run, but again Duke came back to within 50–49. Then, with 11:46 left, McCarville was called for a controversial foul on what looked like a charge by Duke's Monique Curry. But Bolden swished a three-pointer, and Andersson scored 4 quick points. Still, Duke came back, finally tying the game at 59 for the first time since 7–7. Incredibly, Bolden hit the third of her 3 (for 3) three-pointers. McCarville then checked back into the game with about 5:30 left and scored 10 points the rest of the way. But with just under a minute remaining, Duke was still within 70–68 when Whalen took the ball coast-to-coast for a layup. It became a free throw shooting contest after that, and the Gophers hit 10 of 12 in the final forty-nine seconds.

Whalen and McCarville led the way, as usual, with 27 and 20 points respectively, while McCarville added 18 rebounds. By the end of the Final Four semifinal loss to Connecticut four nights later, McCarville owned the NCAA record for rebounds in the postseason tournament. Andersson scored 17 and joined McCarville and Whalen on the all-region team. Whalen was chosen the Most Outstanding Player.

The Gophers' stars, in other words, did what they always did. Andersson, on the other hand, chose the right moment to play the game of her life, and likewise Bolden, whose three-for-three from three-point land was the statistical difference in the game. She held Duke's All-American, Beard, to a draw at 10 points apiece, but took just those 3 field goal attempts to Beard's 14.

McCarville also won sweet revenge over Duke center Mistie Bass. McCarville and Bass had opposed one another in the 2001 Wisconsin Division I high school title game. McCarville won the individual battle, but her Stevens Point team lost the war to Bass and Janesville Parker, 51–44. Bass scored 7 of Duke's first 9 points but added only 4 more points the rest of the night.

lina, 72–69, as Whalen's three-point attempt missed at the end of the game.

The Gophers finished the season ranked in the top twenty-five in the country after having risen as high as fourteenth, and the honors came in for a number of individuals. Whalen was named the Big Ten Player of the Year and McCarville the conference's Freshman of the Year. Oldfield was named the national Coach of the Year by Associated Press.

The success the Gophers had achieved created demand from other schools for Oldfield's services. Less than a month after the end of the season, Oldfield announced she was leaving Minnesota to become head coach at the University of Maryland. The news was a shock to Gophers fans, and the university began a search for a successor. In May 2002, the Gophers hired Pam Borton, an associate head coach at Boston College who had also been the head coach at Vermont.

Borton would have a team with all five starters returning to go with a number of incoming Minnesota freshmen—defensive specialist Shannon Bolden from Marshall, point guard Shannon Schonrock from Winnebago, and forward/center Christina Collison from Eden Prairie. Schonrock eventually moved into the starting lineup ahead of Lieser, and the rest of the returning starters—Andersson, McCarville, Von Wald, and Whalen—all had another year under their belts.

Minnesota had another strong season in 2002–2003, finishing in a second-place tie in the Big Ten for the second year in a row and getting another bid in the NCAA tournament. With wins over Tulane and Stanford in the opening rounds, the Gophers advanced to the Sweet Sixteen before falling to Texas, 73–60. Minnesota finished the season ranked in the top twenty by both Associated Press and USA Today/ESPN, and Whalen, who averaged more than 20 points and 6 assists per game, was named to the WBCA All-America team.

Despite the loss of Lieser and Von Wald, expectations were sky-high for Whalen's senior year. In February, the Gophers beat fifth-ranked Penn State at home before a record crowd of 14,363. But in the next game the Gophers lost at Ohio State, and, worse yet, Whalen collided with two Buckeyes and broke her right hand.

Freshman Kelly Roysland, from Fosston, took Whalen's spot in the lineup and performed well, but Minnesota lost four of its last six Big Ten games. McCarville also stepped up in Whalen's absence and had a number of outstanding games, including a triple-double in the Big Ten tournament with 23 points, 11 rebounds, and 10 steals to go with 6 assists.

Minnesota got a number seven seed in the Mideast Regional of the NCAA tournament and played host for the first two rounds of play at Williams Arena. Whalen was back and scored 31 points and added 9 assists despite wearing a soft cast on her lead hand. The Gophers beat UCLA, 92–81. In the second round, the Gophers faced Kansas State, the region's number two seed. McCarville, who had had 17 rebounds against UCLA, topped that against Kansas State and their highly regarded center Nicole Ohlde (later a member of the Minnesota Lynx). McCarville pulled down a career-high 18 rebounds as Minnesota won, 80–61.

The win put the Gophers in the Sweet Sixteen for the second year in a row. The next opponent was Boston College, where Borton had been an associate head coach only two years before. The Gophers won, 76–63, as McCarville had 25 points and 15 rebounds with Whalen getting 10 assists. In the regional final, the

Gophers faced and defeated Duke, the nation's top-ranked team.

The following week a large contingent of Gophers fans followed the team to the Final Four in New Orleans, where Minnesota faced the new number one ranked team, the Connecticut Huskies, in the semifinal game. Led by Diana Taurasi, the Huskies opened up an 8-point lead at the half. The Gophers cut the margin to two with under eight minutes to play, but the Huskies held on for a 67–58 win.

The Gophers' top players again received postseason honors. Both McCarville and Whalen made the WBCA All-America first team, and Whalen was also named a second-team All-American by the Associated Press. Despite missing seven games with the hand injury, Whalen finished her college career with 2,285 points, first on the list of Minnesota scorers of either gender. She was then a first-round draft choice of the Connecticut Sun of the Women's National Basketball Association (WNBA), becoming the first Gophers player ever to be drafted by the WNBA.

The Post-Whalen Era

Whalen was gone, though not forgotten, but the Gophers were determined to show that they could win without her. Her spot in the backcourt was taken by April Calhoun, the state's Ms. Basketball in 2001 at Armstrong High School in Plymouth. Calhoun started at the University of Iowa, playing there for two seasons before transferring to Minnesota. In the Gophers lineup, Calhoun was called upon to do a variety of things; in addition to her tenacious defense, Calhoun eventually took over the playmaking, allowing Schonrock to roam the perimeter in search of open three-point shots.

Jamie Broback was the other newcomer to the starting lineup, taking over Andersson's power forward spot. A six-foot-three sophomore from Eastview, Broback became the team's second-leading scorer—leading the team in scoring in seven straight games late in the year—and also provided rebounding help to McCarville. McCarville, the lone senior on the squad, led the team in points, rebounds, steals, blocked shots, and assists per game. She was named to the WBCA All-America team for the second year in a row and was also named a second-team All-American by Associ-

Gopher Men Rebuild . . . Again

As the investigation into the academic situation under coach Clem Haskins unfolded, the Gophers hired as their new coach Dan Monson, head coach of the Gonzaga Bulldogs and the one who had given Haskins the final defeat of his Minnesota career. For the third time in a quarter century, the university brought in a coach to rebuild a program decimated by scandal.

In addition to the sanctions he knew the program would be facing, Monson had additional problems in his first year of 1999–2000. Joel Przybilla, the Gophers' star seven-foot-one center from Monticello, had developed an antipathy toward attending classes. In the aftermath of the Haskins's academic fraud scandal, the U had demanded and Monson had promised to run the cleanest program in the country, and Przybilla's antics were not what anyone had in mind. He was averaging 17.2 points in Big Ten play and leading the conference in rebounding, but he was suspended by Monson. Przybilla then quit the team and announced his intention to enter the NBA draft. The Gophers finished the season with a 12–16 overall record, 4–12 in the Big Ten. The university had already issued its own sanctions that prohibited the Gophers from participating in postseason tournaments, other than the Big Ten conference tournament, but with their record Minnesota would not have qualified for tournament play anyway.

Early in the 2000–2001 season, the NCAA placed the basketball program on probation for four years and cut its scholarships, as well as visits by recruits, over the next three years. The ban on postseason play was not extended beyond the one-year ban that the university had already implemented. With these issues finally settled, the Gophers were able to focus on basketball again and win twelve of thirteen nonconference games. Although not as successful in the Big Ten, the Gophers made the National Invitation Tournament

(NIT) and beat Villanova in the first round before losing to Tulsa. The season's finish also marked the end of Ray Christensen's career as the radio voice of the Gophers, a post he had held since 1956. A few months earlier, Christensen also had concluded a fifty-year run of play-by-play announcing of Minnesota football.

In the coming years, the Gophers had a pair of home-grown stars who performed well although only briefly. Rick Rickert from Duluth East High School played two seasons before deciding to turn pro. His spot in the front court was taken in 2003–2004 by Kris Humphries from Hopkins High School. Humphries stuck around even less time, playing one season before entering the NBA draft. Humphries led the Big Ten in scoring and rebounding and was named the conference's Freshman of the Year. Minnesota as a team did not do as well. With a 3–13 record, the Gophers tied for last place in the Big Ten and, with an overall record of 12–18, could not even qualify for the NIT.

Even with Humphries gone, the Gophers improved greatly in 2004–2005. Senior starters Brent Lawson, Jeff Hagen, and Aaron Robinson had solid seasons, and junior-college transfer Vincent Grier was third in the Big Ten with 18 points per game during conference play. Minnesota finished with a surprising 21–11 record—10–6 in the Big Ten, good for fourth place—and made their first appearance of the Monson era in the NCAA tournament. Iowa State beat the Gophers in the opening round of the tournament, although the season was seen as a step forward for Monson and his program.

The continuing challenge of recruiting elite talent to the U was again illustrated during the following off-season, however. The state's top rising senior, Isaiah Dahlman of Braham, announced that he would be playing basketball for Big Ten rival Michigan State, and a month later the state's top rising junior, Cole Aldrich of Bloomington Jefferson, announced that he would be attending Kansas University.

Gopher Men's Annual Record, 1999–2006

Year	Overall Record	Big Ten Record
Coach Dan Monson		
1999–2000	12–16	4–12
2000–2001	18–14	5–11
2001–2002	18–13	9–7
2002–2003	19–14	8–8
2003–2004	12–18	3–13
2004–2005	21–11	10–6
2005–2006	16–15	5–11
Gopher Totals	116–101	44–68
1999–2006	.535	.393

ated Press. In addition, McCarville was a finalist for the Wooden Award, one of the awards for the player of the year, and she was the first player selected in the WNBA draft in April 2005.

The Gophers had a strong nonconference season, losing only two games. One was in overtime to Washington, the second of two regular-season games that McCarville missed with a broken hand. The other loss was to Louisiana State, the nation's top-ranked team. Even though she was double-teamed and dogged much of the game by LSU's six-foot-five freshman, Sylvia Fowles, McCarville scored 31 points and had 13 rebounds, 5 steals, 4 assists, and 3 blocked shots.

Despite some of the explosive scoring performances from Broback and McCarville, as well as the long-range shooting of Schonrock, the team's trademark was defense in 2004–2005. On December 2, 2004, the Gophers set a team record for the fewest points allowed in an 86–34 win over Detroit. Minnesota performed well against several ranked teams, including a 75–35 win over New Mexico, which was rated number twenty-three in the country.

In the Big Ten the Gophers beat the teams they were expected to beat and lost to the ones they were not expected to beat: Ohio State, Michigan State (twice), and Penn State. Minnesota finished fourth in the Big Ten with a 12–4 record during the regular season. In the conference tournament, the Gophers beat Purdue as expected and then finally pulled off the big upset over top-seeded Ohio State to advance to the title game. In the final the Michigan State Spartans beat the Gophers for the third time, but the Gophers qualified for the NCAA tournament as the number three seed in the West region.

In the first round at Williams Arena, the Gophers easily defeated St. Francis (Pennsylvania), 64–33, once again setting a team record for fewest points allowed. They then beat Virginia, 73–58, to advance to the Sweet Sixteen for the third consecutive year. This is where the road ended for Minnesota, however, as the region's second-seeded team, Baylor, defeated the Gophers, 64–57. Gopher fans took solace in the fact that the Bears then steamrolled their way to the NCAA title and that none of their other opponents came as close as Minnesota had in its 7-point loss.

For the 2005–2006 season, the Gophers' roster boasted the Ms. Minnesota Basketball from each of the

Jamie Broback (33) led Eastview High School to the Class AAAA state tournament final in 2003 and then starred for the Minnesota Gophers for two seasons.

five previous years—Calhoun; Bolden; Liz Podominick from Lakeville; Leslie Knight from Hopkins; and Ashley Ellis-Milan from St. Paul Central. In addition, Coach Borton did what none of her predecessors could do: she signed highly regarded and heavily recruited players from outside the Gophers' "natural" recruiting area—players like Brittney Davis from Portland, Oregon; Emily Fox from Colorado; and Lauren Lacey and Natasha Williams from the Chicago area. Korinne Campbell of Lawrenceville, New Jersey, the number-two-rated small forward in the nation, was also set to come to the U in the fall of 2006.

This season saw Schonrock surpass Lieser as Minnesota's all-time three-point shooter, and the Gophers again contended for the Big Ten title, until a four-game losing streak in February dropped them into third place behind Ohio State and Purdue. Then came a pair of even more disheartening upset losses in the first round of the Big Ten and NCAA tournaments.

Two weeks later, Gopher fans were shocked when Broback, Davis, Lacey, Podominick, and Williams announced that they were leaving the program, largely due to what Borton called "roster management"—i.e., playing time—issues. Borton acknowledged that "we have challenges in our program" but also pointed out that the Gophers' recruiting class had been rated as the fourteenth best in the country. Still, going into the 2006–2007 season, there were more questions about the program than at any time since the firing of Cheryl Littlefield.

Gopher Women's Annual Record, 1997–2006

Year	Overall Record	Big Ten Record
Coach Cheryl Littlejohn		
1997–1998	4–23	1–15
1998–1999	7–20	2–14
1999–2000	10–18	3–13
2000–2001	8–20	1–15
Littlejohn Totals	33–81	7–55
1997–2001	.289	.113
Coach Brenda Oldfield		
2001–2002	22–8	11–5
Coach Pam Borton		
2002–2003	25–6	13–4
2003–2004	25–9	9–7
2004–2005	26–9	12–4
2005–2006	19–10	11–5
Borton Totals	114–40	56–25
2002–2006	.740	.691
Gopher Totals	167–129	74–85
1997–2006	.564	.465

37 *New Small College Powers Emerge*

S̄T. THOMAS HAD A PRETTY GOOD DECADE in the 1990s. The men won five regular season and three postseason Minnesota Intercollegiate Athletic Conference (MIAC) basketball championships. The women won six regular season titles, went to the NCAA Division II Final Four four times, and won the national championship in 1991. But since the turn of the new millennium, the Tommies have been supplanted as *the* MIAC powers, at least for the moment, by the Carleton women and the men from Gustavus Adolphus.

Carleton Women Come Out of Nowhere

The MIAC held its first women's postseason playoff in 2001, and Carleton, who had never before won a women's conference hoops title of any kind, won each of the first four playoff titles. In 2001, the Knights shocked the Tommies on their home turf, at Schoenecker Arena, 61–58. St. Thomas was the regular season champ and won two NCAA tournament games to Carleton's none. Still, Carleton coach Tammy Metcalf-Filzen, who had played for Northfield High School's Class AA runners-

up in the 1979 state tournament, won Coach of the Year honors.

Third-place (tied) Carleton won at first-place (tied) St. Thomas again in 2002, 71–62, and then won at first-place (tied) St. Ben's, 79–63. Renee Willette, from Minneapolis South, led the Knights in scoring for the second consecutive year, and this time Carleton won its first NCAA tournament game ever before bowing to Chapman College, 87–74.

The Knights tied for the regular season title in 2003 and easily won the postseason tournament. They did it with balance, as leading scorer Megan Vig, a freshman from Northfield and the league's Sixth Player of the Year, scored just 10.8 points per game. Linnea Engel, a junior from Mounds View, excelled on defense but also increased her scoring to 10 points per game. It was Engel, too, who hit a career-high 24 points in the playoff final against Gustavus. In the NCAA, however, the Knights went cold and lost to St. Norbert, 60–47, on their home court.

Carleton tied for the conference title again in 2004 and then clobbered Concordia, 62–40, for postseason honors. They defeated Lakeland (Wisconsin), 58–42, before losing to Buena Vista (Iowa), 69–61, in the NCAAs. Vig blossomed into a star, averaging 16 points and 7 rebounds per game and earning all-conference honors.

In 2005, Carleton won its first outright regular season title but lost to St. Ben's, 77–74, in the playoff final and failed to get an NCAA tournament bid. The following year, the Knights gained a measure of revenge, upsetting the regular season champion Bennies, 74–73, in the playoff semifinals. They lost at Concordia (Moorhead) in the final, however, 65–56.

Minnesota Women's Small College Champions, 1998–2006

Year	MIAC Regular/Playoff	NSIC Regular/Playoff
1998	St. Benedict, St. Thomas	Minnesota Duluth, Northern State
1999	St. Benedict[a]	Minnesota Duluth
2000	St. Thomas[a]	Minnesota Duluth/Minnesota Duluth
2001	St. Thomas/Carleton	Southwest State/Minnesota Duluth
2002	St. Benedict, St. Thomas/Carleton	Southwest State/Southwest State
2003	Carleton, Gustavus, St. Benedict/Carleton	Minnesota Duluth/Minnesota Duluth
2004	Carleton, St. Benedict/Carleton	St. Paul Concordia/Minnesota Duluth
2005	Carleton/St. Benedict	Moorhead State/St. Paul Concordia
2006	St. Benedict/Concordia	Wayne State/Wayne State

Note: The first MIAC women's playoff was in 2001, and the first NSIC postseason tournaments were in 2000.
[a] Played in NCAA Division III Final Four

Overall, from 1999 to 2006, St. Ben's won 155 games to Carleton's 148, but the Carls claimed three regular-season and four postseason titles in five different championship seasons. St. Ben's won four regular-season titles (including ties) but just one playoff title, also in five different seasons. Meanwhile, the Tommies slumped to the first nonwinning and then losing seasons in almost twenty years, at 13–13 in 2004, 11–14 in 2005, and 10–15 in 2006.

Gustavus Men Keep on Coming

A quick glance at MIAC records show the St. Thomas men with nine conference titles in the nineteen years from 1988 to 2006 and Gustavus Adolphus with six, while the Tommies went 208–76 (.732) in the 1990s (from 1989–1990 to 1999–2000) to the Gusties' 198–87 (.695). But that's all a bit misleading. A strong case can be made for Gustavus as the MIAC power of the past twenty years.

Even during the Tommies' glory years from 1988 to 2003, Gustavus won more postseason titles, by a margin of six to four. Then there is the fact that the Gusties won the 1987 playoff and 1988 regular season titles and won both in 2004 and 2005. Add it all together, and in the twenty-one years through 2006, Gustavus has fourteen MIAC titles (both regular and postseason) in twelve different seasons to

the Tommies' thirteen titles in nine different years.

In 2003, Gustavus Adolphus became the first Minnesota men's team since Hamline in 1951 to play for a national championship. This was despite the fact that St. Thomas won the regular season MIAC title at 16–4 to the Gusties' 15–5. But Gustavus snapped the Tommies' twenty-three-game home winning streak at Schoenecker Arena, 62–36, in the playoff final. Guard Tim Brown, from Bloomington Jefferson, and forward Eric Nelson, from Mendota Heights and Sibley High School, each scored 15 points for the Gusties.

Gustavus then beat Whitworth (California) at home on Gus Young Court, 65–55. Brown was the only Gustie in double figures with 22 points. From then on Gustavus, with its unimposing 22–6 record, was the underdog in every game but continued to defy the odds by putting on a shooting clinic. They won at Wisconsin-Stevens Point, 75–62, by shooting 56 percent from the field, including 50 percent on three-point attempts. Brown again led the way with 20 points and three-of-four shooting from three-point land.

The next two rounds were held at Buena Vista (Iowa), where the Gusties knocked off 25–1 and heavily favored Hanover (Indiana), 79–66, and then 25–2 Occidental, 74–56, with shooting percentages of 53 and 60 percent. Against Hanover they also shot 85 percent from the charity stripe, and against Occidental they hit 67 percent (10 of 15) of their three-point

Carleton star Megan Vig snares a rebound against archrival St. Benedict's. The Knights won three MIAC regular season titles and two postseason championships during Vig's career. She was All-MIAC four times and finished as the Carleton women's second-leading all-time scorer.

Minnesota Mysteries and Myths
Community College Women Are Best-Kept Secret

Compared to its peers, the women's Minnesota Community College Conference (MCCC) is the toughest college basketball conference in America. The vaunted Atlantic Coast Conference (ACC) or the Big Ten can only wish to do this well: since 1994, a Minnesota junior college has appeared in all but two women's NJCAA Division III Final Fours. Five different schools have won a total of nine national titles, including six straight from 1994 to 1999.

Anoka-Ramsey Community College has led the way, winning Minnesota's first NJCAA title in 1994 and continuing from there to win five national championships in seven tournament appearances. Meanwhile, Central Lakes (Brainerd), Fergus Falls, Minneapolis, and Rainy River (International Falls) Community Colleges have made just one national tournament appearance apiece, but all came home with the heaviest hardware.

The Anoka-Ramsey Golden Rams got the ball rolling in 1994, knocking off Triton, 69–62, for the first of six straight NJCAA titles by Minnesota junior colleges. Dan Mielke of Anoka-Ramsey took Coach of the Year honors.

Rainy River and Central Lakes took the next two national titles. Rainy River clobbered Montgomery County (Maryland), 83–60, in the 1995 final as Autumn Racker scored 33 points and a record 81 for the tournament. Then Central Lakes of Brainerd beat Monroe (New York), 71–57, in 1996 to finish 27–2 for coach Dennis Eastman. Central's seven postseason wins were by an average of 19 points. Jill Casper of Isle led the scoring at 15.9 points per game, while Angie Klockman from McLeod West added 15.2 points and 9.9 rebounds.

Anoka-Ramsey came back with three straight titles and 25–4, 27–2, and 23–6 season records. The 1997 championship was won with almost ridiculous ease, by scores of 97–59, 98–39, and 80–47. Liza Kunzmann, from Mounds View, was named tournament MVP with 17 points per game and a record 7 three-pointers in a single game. Katie Regnier, from Cold Spring Rocori, led the way in the final with 13 points and 11 rebounds, and Julie Anacker, from Shakopee, had 11 points and 11 rebounds in the semi.

The 1998 title was almost as easily won, 111–80 over W. R. Harper in the semi and 73–48 over DuPage (Illinois) in the final. Anacker had 12 points, 5 assists, and 5 steals in the final. Jefferson (New York) made the Golden Rams work for the 1999 title before succumbing, 68–62, in the final. Jessica Arbogast, from Osseo, scored 79 points in the last three play-off victories and snared 29 rebounds in the final two games alone. Amber Benson tied Kunzmann's tournament record by making 7 three-point shots in one game. Paul Fessler coached the Rams to the 1998 and 1999 titles.

The Rams finished second in 2000, losing to DuPage (Illinois), 72–61, in the final, but Fergus Falls brought the MCCC back into the winner's circle in 2001. The women from Fergus—now the Fergus Falls campus of Minnesota Community and Technical College—defeated Montgomery-Tacoma Park (Maryland), 92–66; Northern Essex (Massachusetts), 77–50; and Manhattan (New York), 61–58.

Anoka-Ramsey fell short again in 2003, but Angel Leon set a tournament record with 29 rebounds in one game.

Then, in 2004, Minneapolis Community and Technical College (MCTC) brought the title back to Minnesota, beating DuPage, 79–77, in overtime. Tory McClenton, from St. Paul Johnson, hit 2 free throws and blocked DuPage's last-gasp attempt to secure the win. Tiara Medlock and Nakia Carlisle, both from Minneapolis North, scored 23 and 22 points apiece. Carlisle was named the tournament MVP.

In 2005, Anoka-Ramsey won its fifth title, now under coach Keith Lindahl. The Rams defeated Bunker Hill (Massachusetts), 84–63; Mohawk Valley (New York), 70–67; and Monroe (New York), 64–60. Their imposing front line of six-foot-three Selina Thiesen from Centennial High School, six-foot-two Stephanie Westman from Blaine, and six-foot Bonnie Johnson from Osseo all averaged double-doubles for the three games and earned all-tournament honors. Johnson was named the tournament MVP, though Westman scored 70 points (including 33 with 27 rebounds against Bunker Hill) and Thiesen 60. Thiesen went on to set both rebounding and free throw shooting records for Augsburg of the MIAC.

The Rams' 2005–2006 season was cancelled for lack of players. After its run to the 2005 title, Lindahl left to take over at four-year Missouri Valley College. New coach Dave DeWitt was only hired in late July, and only one player from the 2005 roster was returning. It was just too late in the recruiting season to assemble a roster, though DeWitt even held several practice sessions with four players before pulling the plug. Ironically, at the time the season was cancelled, Anoka-Ramsey was ranked fourth in the nation in the preseason poll of NJCAA coaches.

attempts. Only senior center Dave Newell, from Fergus Falls, scored in double figures in both games for a total of 30, and he also gathered 13 rebounds against Hanover. Seven different players scored in double figures in one or the other of these games, including Doug Espenson, who came off the bench against Occidental to contribute 11 points.

Hampden-Sydney College was the next victim, 79–68 in the national semifinal at Salem, Virginia. Espenson, from Mankato East, exploded for 24 points and 8 rebounds, again coming off the bench. Brown added 20 points, and Gustavus once more shot better than 50 percent, including 59 percent in the first half. Now the Gusties would face Williams (30–1) for the title.

Gustavus led through the entire game and still led 63–55 with 3:16 left. But the Ephs stormed back and took their first lead at 64–63 on a Tim Folan three with forty-eight seconds left. Derek (not Eric) Nelson, from Lyle, put the Gusties back ahead with a layup at the thirty-two-second mark. Williams held the ball for a final shot, but Ben Coffin was fouled with 4.6 seconds remaining. He made his first shot to tie the score but

missed the second. Folan grabbed the rebound, however, and drew what game reports called a "touch foul." Gusties coach Mark Hanson later said that "deciding a national championship game on a loose ball with four seconds left is difficult to feel good about."

Folan made both free throws for the final 67–65 margin and then intercepted the Gusties' desperation, last-second, full-court pass. Brown led all scorers with 19, while Espenson again came off the bench to add 13 points and 10 rebounds. Folan scored 15 for Williams, while point guard Michael Crotty dished out 12 assists and had just 2 turnovers. The Ephs committed just 4 turnovers total, while Gustavus had 17. Coffin and Crotty made the all-tournament team, while only Espenson won all-tournament honors for Gustavus.

As of 2006, Gusties' coach Hanson has a record of 325–118 (.734) in sixteen years at the St. Peter school, while St. Thomas coach Steve Fritz has a 464–228 record (.671) in twenty-five seasons. Both Fritz and Hanson were All-MIAC players at the same schools where they coached.

Minnesota Men's Small College Champions, 1998–2006

Year	MIAC Regular/Playoff	NSIC Regular/Playoff
1998	Augsburg/Gustavus	Northern State/N/A
1999	Augsburg/Gustavus	Northern State/Winona State
2000	St. Thomas/St. John's	Wayne State/Wayne State
2001	St. John's/St. John's	Southwest State/Winona State
2002	St. Thomas/St. Thomas	Northern State/Minnesota Duluth
2003	St. Thomas/Gustavus[a]	Northern State/Minnesota Duluth
2004	Gustavus/Gustavus	Northern State/Northern State
2005	Gustavus/Gustavus	Winona State/Northern State
2006	Carleton, St. Thomas/St. Thomas	Winona State/Winona State[b]

Note: The first NSIC postseason tournaments were in 2000.
[a] Williams 67, Gustavus 65 in the NCAA Division III national title game.
[b] Winona State 73, Virginia Union 61 in NCAA Division II national title game.

David Zellmann earned All-America honors and led the Winona State Warriors to the NCAA Division II national championship in 2006. Here, he scores the winning basket after making a steal against Minnesota State University–Mankato in North Central Region play. The Warriors, coached by Mike Leaf, were down by 16 points with just over eight minutes to play and came back to win, 74-71.

Community College Men Keep on Running

Minnesota's community college men have enjoyed nowhere near the success of the women, though there is a 1998 NJCAA Division III men's championship trophy on display at what is now the Minnesota Community and Technical College–Fergus Falls campus. In 1998, Fergus Falls defeated Cobleskill (New York), 73–61, for the NJCAA championship; Tom Schlieman was named tournament MVP, and Tom Chatman also earned all-tournament honors.

Vermilion Community College in Ely almost duplicated this achievement in 1999, making it to the national championship game before losing to Richland College (Texas), 80–76. Ronald Hearns, son of world champion boxer Thomas "The Hit Man" Hearns, was the leading scorer for the Ironmen at 26.3 points per game, and Hearns and Duane Williams made the all-tournament team.

The Ironmen under coach Paul McDonald returned to the NJCAA in 2001 and 2002, winning one game and losing two each year. Edward Smith was the team's leading scorer each year, though he failed both years to earn all-tournament recognition. As his father, coach Bob McDonald, of Chisholm High School, said, "[Paul] loves to press and run the floor." So his Ironmen scored more than 85 points per game at the NJCAA and ranked in the top five in the nation in scoring for seven years in a row.

Minnesota Mysteries and Myths

Who is Minnesota's Winningest Small College?

According to the MIAC's official records, St. Thomas surpassed Hamline as the conference's winningest program when it won its twentieth regular season title in 2003. Hamline had won its nineteenth title way back in 1960 but none since then. The truth is that the Tommies also tied for the championship of the Minnesota Collegiate Conference (MCC), forerunner to the MIAC, in 1918. And they won an MIAC title in 1944, but for reasons having something to do with World War II, the MIAC no longer recognizes that title. In other words, the Tommies' 2006 MIAC title was in fact their twenty-third conference championship. Hamline, meanwhile, won three MCC titles in 1913, 1914, and 1915, so, in fact, St. Thomas only surpassed Hamline's total of twenty-two conference championships in 2006.

Here's the rub. Carleton won five MCC titles from 1915 through 1920 and then won the first three MIAC titles in 1921, 1922, and 1923. After that, Carleton left the MIAC in search of tougher competition, which it found in the Midwest Conference. Still, the Carls won fourteen conference titles in the Midwest before rejoining the MIAC in 1990. Add them up, and their 2006 cochampionship, like the Tommies', is their twenty-third conference championship. (Neither has won a postseason tournament in a year in which they had not already won the regular season title, so each has enjoyed twenty-three championship seasons.)

Meanwhile, Minnesota Duluth (formerly Duluth Teachers College, formerly the Duluth Branch) won sixteen regular season championships in the Northern Teachers/Northern/ Northern Sun Conference between 1934 and 1997, and four championships of the MIAC, of which it was a member from 1949 through 1976. More recently it won two NSIC postseason titles in 2002 and 2003, after Northern State had won the regular season championships. So the Minnesota Duluth men have enjoyed twenty-two championship seasons and were tied with Carleton and St. Thomas at the head of the pack until 2006.

Still, none may be the state's winningest small college program, depending upon your taste. St. Cloud State won sixteen championships in the Northern Teachers/Northern/ Northern Sun Conference between 1943 and 1976. The Huskies (formerly Indians) moved to the North Central Conference (NCC) in 1983 and won four regular season and two postseason titles there for a total of twenty-one championship seasons.

St. Cloud also claims six championships of the old Minnesota State College Conference (MSCC) in 1909, 1910, 1913, 1920, 1928, and 1930. But the then-Indians competed in the MSCC with Minnesota's junior colleges as well as the old teachers colleges, so there's a legitimate question whether these should count as "collegiate" championships or not.

For the record, UMD easily is the winningest women's program with eleven regular season and two additional postseason titles for a total of thirteen championship seasons. Put the Bulldog men and women together, and their combined thirty-five championship seasons puts them two ahead of St. Thomas.

38 Two Kevins, a Flip, and, Finally, Respectability

IN MAY 1995, the Timberwolves made Kevin McHale vice president of basketball operations. After finishing a thirteen-year career in 1993 with the Boston Celtics—one that eventually got him elected to the Basketball Hall of Fame—McHale returned to his home state to become an analyst on the Timberwolves' television broadcasts. He would also serve as a special assistant coach. A year later, McHale was named assistant general manager and vice president. At the same time the Timberwolves hired McHale's old Gophers teammate, Phil "Flip" Saunders, as general manager and coach-in-waiting, as it turned out.

Following his college playing career, Saunders immediately began coaching. He spent four seasons at Golden Valley Lutheran College before returning to Minnesota, where he served as an assistant under Jim Dutcher. Saunders later moved to the Continental Basketball Association, where he had been coaching for seven seasons before joining the Timberwolves.

The Timberwolves had the fifth pick in the 1995 draft and selected Kevin Garnett, who became the first player in twenty years to go directly from high school into the NBA. A six-foot-eleven forward, Garnett had spent his final year of high school in Chicago and was named National High School Player of the Year by *USA Today*. Although they were taking a chance drafting a player out of high school, the Timberwolves thought that, had he attended college, Garnett would have been the top pick in the draft two years later.

Minnesota got off to another poor start in 1995–

Flip Saunders came to the Minnesota Timberwolves to join his former college teammate, Kevin McHale, in 1996. Saunders originally was the team's general manager, but he became their coach a few months later and led the Timberwolves to their most successful seasons.

1996, however, and on December 18, Bill Blair was fired as coach. Not surprisingly, Saunders took his place. Garnett got his first start of the season three weeks later against the Lakers in Los Angeles. He jumped for the opening tip-off and then had 9 points and 8 rebounds before leaving the game in the second half after cutting his hand while dunking.

Garnett went back to coming off the bench for the next few weeks, but he started the Timberwolves' final forty-two games and averaged 14 points and 8.4 rebounds in those games. His presence was needed, particularly after the Timberwolves traded Christian Laettner to Atlanta in February. Garnett helped Minnesota improve its record to 26–56, finally ending the team's streak of sixty-loss seasons.

J. R. Rider led Minnesota in scoring, but his behavior was a problem. Since joining the Timberwolves, he was frequently fined for missing practices and team flights as well as more serious problems. Rider was convicted of first-degree assault for kicking a woman who was manager of a sports bar in Bloomington in 1994, and he eventually served four days in jail for his failure to stay in contact with his probation officer and to complete an anger-counseling program. He got into more problems in Oakland when he was arrested for possession of illegal cellular phones and on another occasion for public gambling in addition to being questioned in a sexual-assault investigation.

On the court, Rider could be just as much trouble. In a game in March 1996, Rider was ejected from a game and refused to leave until his mother came onto the floor from her courtside seat and pointed him toward the locker room. So in July, the Timberwolves traded Rider to Portland. What they received in return was not nearly so significant as the fact that the Wolves finally were rid of him.

In the draft, which took place a month before the trade, the Timberwolves had the number five pick, just behind the Milwaukee Bucks. The Bucks picked point guard Stephon Marbury, from Georgia Tech, and the Wolves picked Ray Allen, a shooting guard from Connecticut. But within the hour, the Wolves had traded Allen and a future first-round draft pick to the Bucks for Marbury. Not only did the Wolves get the point guard they wanted, they also obtained a player who had been friends since high school with Garnett, the two having met at summer all-star games.

Marbury was a valuable addition to the Timberwolves. He averaged 15.8 points and 7.8 assists his rookie season. He complemented a strong front court that included Garnett, who was second on the team in scoring and rebounding, and Tom Gugliotta, who led the team with 20.6 points and 8.7 rebounds per game. Minnesota finished with a record of 40–42, the sixth-best record in the Western Conference, and made the playoffs for the first time. There they were swept in three games by the Houston Rockets, but the improvement on the team was evident and would continue in the ensuing years.

That fall, before the 1997–1998 season began, the Wolves signed Garnett to a seven-year contract extension for $126 million that would begin with the 1998–1999 season. Combined with the fact that Garnett had initially turned down an offer of $102 million, the contract produced shock waves through the NBA. It was widely rumored that the league would reopen the collective bargaining agreement with the players and perhaps institute a lockout in 1998.

Minnesota posted its first winning record, 45–37, in 1997–1998 and faced the Seattle SuperSonics in the opening playoff round. The Timberwolves won two of the first three and had a chance to wrap up the series at home. Instead, the SuperSonics won at the Target Center and then again in Seattle to end the Wolves season. Garnett emerged as the team's leading rebounder, while Gugliotta played in only forty-one games because of injuries.

Gugliotta was a free agent at the end of the season and signed with the Phoenix Suns in the summer of 1998. The Timberwolves did not need to worry about filling Gugliotta's spot immediately, since the 1998–1999 season was delayed and nearly wiped out. The owners had decided to go ahead with a lockout over the issue of the players' rapidly escalating salaries. Garnett was Exhibit A.

The labor dispute was settled in early January 1999, and the season finally got underway a month later. Meanwhile, the Timberwolves had signed free-agent forward Joe Smith. Smith had been the first player taken in the 1995 draft, by the Golden State Warriors, and had averaged more than 16 points and nearly 8 rebounds per game in his first three years in the league. The manner in which he had been signed, however, would come back to haunt the Timberwolves.

Smith was the leading scorer, with 23 points, in Minnesota's first game of the year, an 18-point win at Denver on February 5. Minnesota won seven of its next nine and was off to a good start in a regular-season that would extend into May but last only fifty games because of the lockout.

Marbury was in his third season with Minnesota and would be a free agent at the end of the season. He made it known that he was likely going to be leaving Minnesota, giving the reason as a desire to return to his native East Coast. It was widely reported, however, that Marbury was jealous of Garnett—of both his huge contract and his status as the Wolves go-to guy—a charge that both players denied. (What made matters worse was the fact that Gugliotta's earlier defection was attributed to his dislike of Marbury and his shoot-first mentality at the point guard spot.) In any event, rather than lose Marbury to free agency, the Timberwolves traded him to the New Jersey Nets in a three-team deal. The Wolves got Terrell Brandon, another point guard, from Milwaukee.

Brandon did well in his twenty-one games with Minnesota over the remainder of the season, averaging nearly 15 points and 10 assists per game, but the

Wally Szczerbiak (10) was drafted out of Miami University of Ohio and quickly became the Timberwolves' second option on offense. He scored about 15 points per game over six and a half seasons before being traded to the Boston Celtics during the 2005–2006 season.

Timberwolves slipped to a final record of 25–25. In the playoffs they were eliminated in four games by the San Antonio Spurs, who went on to win the NBA title.

The addition of Wally Szczerbiak, a forward from Miami (Ohio) University, in the 1999 draft helped the Timberwolves reach fifty wins for the first time in 1999–2000. Garnett had now become one of the most dominating players in the league, averaging 22.9 points and 11.8 rebounds. Brandon again played well, both scoring and distributing the ball. In addition to Garnett and Brandon, Szczerbiak and Malik Sealy averaged more than 10 points per game. Reserves Smith and Anthony Peeler averaged nearly that many points.

One of the biggest wins of the season came on January 17, 2000, when the Timberwolves beat the Indiana Pacers, 101–100, as Sealy banked in a three-point basket at the buzzer. Less than three weeks after the team's season ended, however, Sealy was dead. He had been at Garnett's birthday party at a downtown Minneapolis night club and was returning home at approximately 4 A.M. the next morning when a car going the wrong way on the highway hit Sealy's vehicle head on. In his memory, the Timberwolves retired Sealy's uniform number 2.

Hopes for the postseason were higher than ever, yet the Wolves again were knocked out of the playoffs in the first round, this time by Portland.

Just before the 2000–2001 season opened, the Timberwolves found themselves in hot water with the NBA. It turns out that they had attempted to circumvent the league's salary-cap rules when they had signed Smith. Free-agent salaries are tightly constrained, but teams are not bound by the salary limits when re-signing a player who had been with them for at least three years. The Timberwolves and Smith reached a secret deal that would take effect after Smith had played for them for three seasons. Such subterfuge was suspected as being relatively common, but the Timberwolves had put their agreement with Smith in writing. After discovering the illicit document, the league voided Smith's contract, fined the Timberwolves $3.5 million, and took away their first-round draft choices for the next five years. One of those draft picks was later restored when owner Glen Taylor agreed to accept a suspension and vice president of operations Kevin McHale agreed to a leave of absence until the summer of 2001. The penalties were mitigated somewhat by

the winning records that the Timberwolves continued to produce, meaning that their lost draft picks would not have been worth as much as they would have, had the team been losing and putting themselves in a position for higher selections.

A forty-seven-win season in 2000–2001 was followed by a 50–32 record in 2001–2002 and a 51–31 record in 2002–2003. Garnett continued averaging more than 20 points and more than 10 rebounds per game. Yet Minnesota still could not advance beyond the first round in the playoffs each year.

The trend continued even in 2003, when the Timberwolves had the home-court advantage in the playoffs for the first time. The Wolves and the Los Angeles Lakers split the first two games at Target Center, and the series then shifted to Los Angeles. In Game 3, Garnett had 33 points and 14 rebounds, although he fouled out twelve seconds into overtime. Even without him, the Timberwolves won, 114–110, to take a two-games-to-one lead and the home-court advantage. Enthusiasm briefly was sky-high. But the Lakers won the next three games to take the series and continue Minnesota's postseason frustration.

Veterans Sam Cassell and Latrell Sprewell came to Minnesota in a pair of trades in the summer of 2003 and averaged 19.8 and 16.8 points per game, respectively, during the 2003–2004 season. Garnett had his best season, averaging 24.2 points and leading the league with 13.9 rebounds, to win the NBA's Most Valuable Player award.

The Timberwolves were only 9–8 at the end of November, but they raised their record to 20–10 by the end of the year and kept on winning. Minnesota finished the regular season with a 58–24 record, best in the Western Conference, which meant they would have home-court advantage throughout the conference playoffs.

They opened the postseason by beating the Denver Nuggets, three games to one. Next they faced the Sacramento Kings in a best-of-seven series. The Kings won the first game despite 40 points from Cassell and 18 rebounds by Garnett. Minnesota evened the series with a win in the second game and had a 13-point lead with just over two minutes left in Game 3 in Sacramento. The Kings roared back to tie the game and send it into overtime, but the Wolves held on to beat the Kings, 114–113, to take a two-game-to-one lead.

The series finally came down to a seventh game at

Minor Professional Leagues Struggle in Skeeter State

During the 1980s and 1990s, several teams representing Minnesota cities played in the minor professional leagues, the Continental Basketball Association (CBA) and the International Basketball Association (IBA). The first was the Rochester Flyers, who enjoyed precious little success in the CBA from 1987 through 1989. After a last place finish in 1988–1989, the franchise was moved to Omaha.

A new Rochester team, the Renegade, joined the CBA for the 1992–1993 season, along with the Fargo-Moorhead Fever. The Fever was a Minnesota team in name only, however, as it played its home games in the Fargodome in Fargo, North Dakota. The teams finished with the two worst records in the CBA—Fargo-Moorhead at 18–38, and Rochester at 6–50.

Rochester was back in 1993–1994 as the Renegades (plural), and with a new coach in Bill Musselman. Under Musselman, the Renegades improved their record to 31–25. Although they finished last in the four-team Mideast Division, they had the fifth-best record in the eight-team CBA American Conference.

The league playoffs encompassed four teams from each conference, but to determine the number four team, a special playoff-entry tournament was held in Bismarck, North Dakota. The fourth-, fifth-, and sixth-place teams from each conference played one another to determine who would get the final playoff spots. Rochester beat Fort Wayne before losing to the Quad City Thunder in overtime to finish its season.

This marked the end for Minnesota in the CBA, as the Fever moved to Mexico City and the Renegades to Harrisburg, Pennsylvania, where the team folded during the 1994–1995 season.

In 1995–1996, the IBA was launched as a regional league with five teams: the Black Hills Posse, based in Rapid City, South Dakota; Dakota Wizards, in Bismarck,

North Dakota; Fargo-Moorhead Beez; Minnesota Rockin' Rollers, in St. Cloud; and Winnipeg Cyclone. A pair of former Minnesota Gophers played for the two IBA teams with Minnesota connections, Townsend Orr for Fargo-Moorhead and Nate Tubbs for Minnesota. Black Hills had the league's best regular-season record at 20–4, but the Beez won the IBA title by defeating second-place Winnipeg and then Black Hills in the playoffs.

The following year, the Minnesota Rockin' Rollers, were out and the St. Paul Slam was in. Some now say that the Rockin' Rollers moved from St. Cloud to St. Paul, while others report that the Slam was an expansion team. Either way, the Slam played in the mostly empty Roy Wilkins Auditorium, a remnant of the old St. Paul Auditorium. The Slam added former Gopher Melvin Newbern to their roster at midseason and found themselves in a battle for one of the four playoff spots. St. Paul and Winnipeg were tied for fourth place as the teams completed their regular seasons with two games against one another in St. Paul. The Cyclone, coached by former Rochester Flyers coach Bill Klucas, won the first game, meaning the Slam would have to win the finale to regain a tie. The league then decided that if this happened, the teams would immediately play a "fifth quarter" to break the fourth-place tie and determine the playoff representative.

In the game, St. Paul beat the Cyclone, 108–92, to force the additional period. The Slam then outscored Winnipeg, 28–25, in the fifth quarter to make the playoffs. St. Paul's postseason ended quickly, however, as the Black Hills Posse, the eventual league champion, beat the Slam in two games.

The Slam played one more season in St. Paul but produced the league's worst record. The Beez had the best record and went on to win its second IBA title in three years. In 1998, the Beez became the Rochester (Minnesota) Skeeters, and Klucas returned to Rochester to coach them. The Skeeters lasted only two seasons, however, and the IBA only another three before the entire league folded after the 2000–2001 season.

Target Center on May 19. Garnett came up huge, scoring 32 points and grabbing 21 rebounds, and the Timberwolves held on for an 83–80 win. Sacramento's Chris Webber had a three-point attempt rattle in and out at the buzzer.

The emotional series put Minnesota into the conference finals against Minnesota's former team, the Lakers. The Timberwolves had the home-court ad-

vantage against the Lakers for the second year in a row, but the Lakers prevailed again. Los Angeles and its dueling superstars, Kobe Bryant and Shaquille O'Neal, won three of the first four games and took the series, four games to two. The Timberwolves' most successful season to date left them one step short of the NBA finals.

The strong playoff run created the Wolves' highest

Kevin Garnett was drafted out of high school by the Timberwolves in 1995, and he became one of the best players in the NBA. He was the league's MVP in 2003–2004, when he averaged 24.2 points and 13.9 rebounds per game.

expectations yet, but instead it was followed by a disappointing season in 2004–2005. With the team struggling in February, Flip Saunders was fired as head coach. Kevin McHale took over, and the Timberwolves went 19–12 under his leadership. It was not enough to make the playoffs, however. Minnesota's 44–38 record was one game behind the Memphis Grizzlies for the final playoff spot. Garnett led the league in rebounding while averaging 22.2 points per game, and he was also named to the NBA All-Defensive Team.

The Wolves added guards Marko Jaric (via trade) and Rashad McCants (via the draft) but continued to struggle in 2005–2006. So, on January 26, 2006, McHale traded swing man Szcerbiak to the Boston Cel-

tics as part of a seven-player deal. Ricky Davis replaced Szcerbiak as the Wolves' second option on offense, while young Marcus Banks eventually took over for Jaric at point guard. But Minnesota won only one-third of its games in the month following the trade, so additional rebuilding was anticipated before the 2006–2007 season (and before the final three years of Garnett's current contract run out).

The epitaph of the Timberwolves' first decade with the two Kevins is this: The Wolves have struggled to surround their superstar, Kevin Garnett, with an adequate supporting cast. The loss of four first-round draft picks due to the Joe Smith contract fiasco was just too much for the Wolves to overcome.

39 *The Lynx Find Fans Elusive Prey*

THE WOMEN's National Basketball Association (WNBA) typically selects nicknames for its teams by playing off the nickname of the local NBA team. There's the Utah Starzz of the WNBA riffing off of the NBA Jazz, for example, and the Charlotte Sting of the WNBA getting their buzz from the then Charlotte Hornets.

So the nickname Lynx was a natural for the Minnesota WNBA team, what with their NBA counterpart having the name of another endangered predator, the Timberwolves. A different spelling of their chosen name also might have been appropriate, however, as the Lynx, in their first year of play in 1999, had many links to a former team in the American Basketball League (ABL). The Lynx's links included a coach and a high-scoring forward who had been members of the Columbus Quest, which won the championship in both of the full seasons of the ABL. Although there was no formal connection between the Lynx and the Quest, nearly half of the original Lynx's roster, in addition to head coach Brian Agler, had been with Columbus.

The ABL had begun in 1996–1997, playing a traditional winter schedule. The WNBA started in 1997, playing over the summer. The ABL, having had a head start, was seen as the more accomplished league in terms of player talent, but the clout of the WNBA, backed by the NBA, made it a strong adversary.

In 1998, the WNBA announced the expansion of its organization with the addition of teams in Minnesota and Orlando. And even before the new Minnesota team had a nickname, it had the beginnings of a roster.

In the early years of the WNBA, the league owned all of the franchises and contracts and often allocated players for the overall good of the league. For example, in 1997, the league signed Lisa Leslie, who had been a high school and college star in Southern California, and then assigned her to the Los Angeles Sparks. The allocation of players became even more common with expansion teams.

In September 1998, the WNBA allocated six-foot-two forward Kristin Folkl to Minnesota. Folkl, who had signed with the league in April but had sat out the season to rehabilitate a torn knee ligament, had been a volleyball and basketball star at Stanford University. Two months later, the newly named Lynx signed Agler as head coach. Agler had led the Quest to regular-season win-loss records of 31–9 and 36–8, along with the two league titles. The ABL was struggling, however, and his duties and pay had been cut. The Quest allowed him to accept the position of head coach and general manager with the Lynx as long as he stayed in Columbus for the remainder of their 1998–1999 season.

Agler did not have to wait that long to leave Columbus, however, as the entire league folded in mid-December. Free of duties in the ABL, Agler's new quest would be building the Lynx. He did not forget his former team, though. At the WNBA draft in May 1999, he selected four of his former Columbus players—guards Tonya Edwards and Sonja Tate and forwards Angie Potthoff and Andrea Lloyd (who became Andrea Lloyd Curry upon her marriage the following weekend).

This group was reunited with guard Katie Smith, who had been allocated to the Lynx by the WNBA the day before the draft. Smith had been a star at Ohio State and held the Big Ten record for points in a career, since broken by Kelly Mazzante of Penn State, before joining the Quest. In the third game of the 1998–1999 ABL season, Smith tore the anterior cruciate ligament in her knee, and her status was doubtful for the start of the 1999 WNBA season. She proved to be a player worth waiting for, as she became the top scorer not just for the Lynx but for the entire league.

Soon after, the Lynx looked at adding another former Quest player—Carol Ann Shudlick, whom they in-

In July of 2005, Katie Smith (30) of the Minnesota Lynx became the first U.S. woman to score 5,000 points in her professional career. A few weeks later, she was traded to the Detroit Shock.

vited to their training camp. Shudlick had been a star with the Minnesota Gophers and then played with Columbus in 1996–1997 before playing the next season in Sweden. Shudlick did not make the team, however, and the number of former Quest players, including the injured Smith, stayed at five when the Lynx played their first regular-season game on June 12, 1999.

Their opponents were the Detroit Shock, which had produced a record of 17–13, nearly good enough for a playoff berth, as an expansion team in 1998. While the Lynx were also an expansion team, they faced high expectations, as they had a roster stocked with proven veterans from the ABL rather than the usual band of castoffs and rookies. Joining the former Questers in the starting lineup for Minnesota was Brandy Reed, the Lynx's top pick in the expansion draft.

Edwards, Reed, and Tate combined for 48 points as the Lynx beat Detroit, 68–51, before an announced crowd of 12,122 at the Target Center. Two nights later, the Lynx picked up their second win by beating the Starzz by 24 points, leading to a matchup with the league's other undefeated team, the Houston Comets. Led by Sheryl Swoopes, Tina Thompson, and Cynthia Cooper, the Comets were the two-time defending WNBA champions. Much was made of the fact that they would be facing a team predominantly comprised of ABL champions from Columbus.

Smith returned from rehabilitation of her injured knee to play against Houston, and the Lynx and Comets were evenly matched in the first half, which ended with the score tied. Houston got off to a quick start in the second half, however, scoring 10 of the first 12 points and going on to a 69–55 win over the Lynx.

Minnesota stayed at or above .500 for most of the season, finally falling below for the first time on August 7. The Lynx finished their season two weeks later with a 15–17 record, which put them in a three-way tie for fourth place in the six-team Western Conference. Reed, the one starter that season who had not come from the Quest, led the Lynx in scoring and rebounding.

Reed had come from the Phoenix Mercury, who had left her unprotected in the expansion draft earlier in the year. Reed's performance in Minnesota, however, caused Phoenix to want her back badly enough to give up a first-round draft choice to the Lynx. With this trade, Minnesota had the fifth and sixth picks in the WNBA draft, which they used to draft two guards, Grace Daley and Betty Lennox.

The higher of the two picks, Daley, played sporadically in 2000, but Lennox moved right into the starting lineup and averaged 16.9 points while also leading the team with 5.6 rebounds per game. Lennox was voted the league's Rookie of the Year. Smith was the Lynx's leading scorer at 20.2 points per game and set a WNBA record with 88 three-point field goals. Smith led the league in minutes played for the first of three consecutive years, with 37.3 per game in 2000.

Led by Smith and Lennox, the Lynx were 9–5 at the end of June 2000. Minnesota won its first game in July to go five games over .500 for the first time but then lost its next eight games. For the second year in a row, the Lynx finished with a record of 15–17 and missed the playoffs.

The Lynx dropped to 12–20 in 2001 despite some outstanding individual performances. Smith led the WNBA with 23.1 points per game and scored 40 points in a win at Detroit on June 17. Lennox, who was scoring more than 10 points per game and leading the Lynx in rebounding, suffered a hip injury in the same game, however, and missed the next twenty games.

The Lynx activated six-foot-two rookie Svetlana Abrosimova from St. Petersburg, Russia. Abrosimova attended the University of Connecticut and was the Lynx's top draft pick in 2001, but a torn ligament in her left foot had kept her out of the first six games of the season. Abrosimova and Smith handled most of the scoring load the rest of the season, and one or the other was the team's high scorer in each game, except for an 18-point performance by Lennox after she returned in August. Abrosimova ended up leading the Lynx in rebounding and was second in scoring. Smith recorded another big game in July by scoring 46 points, a league record, in an overtime loss in Los Angeles.

In 2002, for the second year in a row, the Lynx used their first-round draft choice to select a six-foot-two forward from Connecticut. This time it was Tamika Williams, who started all but one game during the season and averaged 10.1 points, third on the team behind Smith and Abrosimova, and led the Lynx in rebounding.

The Lynx made a couple more significant moves before the end of the season. One was the trade of Lennox, who had started only one of five games, to Miami for guard Tamara Moore in June. The following month, Agler was relieved of his duties as head coach, although he remained as the team's general manager. The Lynx had a win-loss record of 6–13 at the time, and they did not do any better under Heidi VanDerveer, an assistant coach who was promoted to succeed Agler on the bench. Minnesota finished the season with a record of 10–22, in last place in the Western Conference.

Early in 2003, the Lynx hired a new head coach, Suzie McConnell Serio. As a point guard at Penn State, she set an NCAA record for career assists and also played on the U.S. Olympic basketball team in 1988 and 1992. From 1998 to 2000, McConnell Serio played for the Cleveland Rockers in the WNBA while also coaching Oakland Catholic High School in Pittsburgh.

That spring, the Lynx drafted point guard Teresa Edwards, an Olympic teammate of McConnell Serio's. Considering the number of Olympics in which she participated—five, or every one from 1984 to 2000—Edwards was a former Olympic teammate of many, including Katie Smith in 2000. Edwards had played in the ABL, but, at the age of thirty-eight, she would be making her WNBA debut with the Lynx in 2003. Another significant newcomer was forward Sheri Sam, selected in a dispersal draft of players from the Miami Sol team that had folded. Sam averaged 11 points per game, second on the team to Katie Smith's average of 18.2 points. Edwards started every game and set a new team single-season record with 148 assists.

With a win-loss mark of 18–16, the Lynx finished with a winning record for the first time in 2003 and also made it to the playoffs for the first time. They faced the Los Angeles Sparks in a best-of-three series with the opener at the Target Center in Minneapolis on August 28. The Sparks had a 49–32 lead at halftime and increased their margin to 21 points less than a minute into the second half. But the Lynx turned up their defense, holding Los Angeles to 32 percent field goal shooting in the second half, after the Sparks had hit 67 percent of their shots in the first half. Helped by Lisa Leslie going to the bench in foul trouble, the Lynx closed the gap and eventually took a 62–61 lead with a little more than five minutes to play. The teams battled back and forth, exchanging the lead into the final minute. The Sparks

were ahead 72–69 when Katie Smith sank a three-pointer to tie the game with 24.4 seconds left.

Los Angeles had the ball, when Edwards kicked it away from Tamecka Dixon, resulting in a whistle and an inbounds pass for the Sparks. Williams stole the inbounds pass, raced downcourt, and laid in the game-winning basket with 7.4 seconds left.

It was the most exciting victory in the history of the franchise, although it was witnessed by a crowd of only 3,622. It was also the last victory for the 2003–2004 Lynx. The Sparks won the two games in Los Angeles to take the series and end Minnesota's season.

By trading Sheri Sam to Seattle in April 2004, Minnesota ended up with an additional first-round draft choice, giving them the sixth and seventh picks in the 2004 draft. Neither was high enough to get the player most fans were hoping for. The Connecticut Sun, with the fourth selection in the draft, selected Gopher superstar Lindsay Whalen. The Lynx were criticized by some for not working out a trade to get the popular Whalen, while others protested that they would have to give up too much to move up in the draft.

Whalen's lasting popularity in Minnesota was evident when the Lynx set a new attendance record—16,227—when they hosted the Sun in a weekday game in mid-July. It was Connecticut's only appearance at the Target Center during the season. How many more fans Whalen would have helped the Lynx lure on a regular basis is unclear, but it seems likely that Minnesota would have drawn better than the 7,163 per game that they averaged in 2004 had they had Whalen on their team.

With their first-round choices, Minnesota took six-foot-five forward Nicole Ohlde from Kansas State and six-foot-four forward Vanessa Hayden from Flor-

ida. Ohlde had a strong rookie season, finishing second on the team with 11.7 points per game, behind—you guessed it—Smith, who averaged 18.8. Ohlde was also second on the team with 5.7 rebounds per game behind Tamika Williams, who averaged 6 a game. Despite turning forty during the season, Teresa Edwards again started every game, although it was Helen Darling who led the Lynx in assists during the season.

Matching their record of 18–16 from the previous season, the Lynx made the playoffs again, and McConnell Serio was named WNBA Coach of the Year. The Lynx's season ended abruptly, however, as they were swept in the first round by the Seattle Storm, who went on to win the WNBA title.

After making the playoffs for two years in a row, the Lynx had a setback in 2005, losing eleven of their final fourteen games to sink to a 14–20 record for the year. Abrosimova led the team in scoring and rebounding average. In a game against the Detroit Shock in July, Katie Smith scored her five-thousandth career point—which included her years in the ABL—to become the first professional woman to reach that level in the United States. A few weeks later, the Lynx traded her to Detroit.

The Lynx's troubles were not confined to the court. Their attendance dropped by 10 percent over 2004 to an all-time low of 6,670 per game, twelfth in the league. Meanwhile, Whalen led Connecticut to the WNBA finals,

In 2004, the Lynx drafted too low to get Lindsay Whalen, and in 2005, they were not able to get Gophers star Janel McCarville, who was the first overall pick in the draft. But in 2006, the Lynx won the top pick in the WNBA draft, which they used to select Seimone Augustus of Louisiana State, giving them hope for more wins on the floor and more fans in the seats.

Guard Teresa Edwards (4) played for every U.S. Olympic team from 1984 to 2000. She made her WNBA debut with the Lynx at age thirty-eight in 2003 and played two seasons with Minnesota.

Essay on Sources

THE AUTHORS WISH TO ACKNOWLEDGE the many sources of information that were consulted in developing this history of basketball in Minnesota. We wish in particular to thank those who made themselves available for interviews or responded to questions via e-mail. All such sources are detailed below, by chapter, with one exception.

The *Star Tribune* has billed itself as the Newspaper of the Twin Cities, and in the world of sports and over the 115 years covered in this book, it and its predecessor in the morning news cycle, the *Minneapolis Tribune*, were more than that. They were the newspapers of record for sporting news throughout the state, and the authors reviewed most issues published during basketball seasons from 1892 to 2006. Articles from these issues are the primary source for information on team matchups, game dates, winners and losers, key players and coaches, game strategies, and key plays and for the opinions and observations of coaches, fans, players, and sportswriters.

Columnists and reporters cited include but are not limited to Roman Augustoviz, George Barton, Dennis Brackin, Bill Carlson, Ben Cohen, Jackie Crosby, Dick Cullum, Randy Furst, Dick Gordon, Sid Hartman, Joe Hendrickson, Chris Ison, Charley Johnson, J. Lawler, Gary Libman, Paul McEnroe, Bill McGrane, John Millea, Gregor W. Pinney, Joel Rippel, Patrick Reusse, Jon Roe, Pam Schmid, Mary Jane Smetanka, James Walsh, Jason Wolf, Jerry Zgoda, and Todd Zolecki. Many of the early news reports, prior to about 1940, are not bylined.

A bibliography with full publication information for selected newspaper articles and books cited follows this essay.

---

1. The Four Pioneers

The career of Dr. Louis J. Cooke, both at the Minneapolis Y and the University of Minnesota, is described in *Gopher Glory*. His activities as physical director at the Minneapolis YMCA were clarified by reference to the archives of the Minneapolis Y (and specifically the minutes of the meetings of the Board of Directors from 1895 through 1897), which are held at the Elmer L. Andersen Library at the University of Minnesota Twin Cities.

The appearance of basketball in 1892 at the Minneapolis Y under physical education director Dr. James C. Elsom is mentioned in *Gopher Glory* and also in the Wiley and Lehmann history of the Minneapolis YMCA, *Builders of Men*. Information about Elsom's later career is from the *Big Ten Records Book*.

The primary sources on Max Exner and Ray Kaighn are the histories of Carleton and Hamline by Leal A. Headley and Merrill E. Jarchow (Carleton) and David W. Johnson (Hamline), respectively. Information about Exner's later life and career came from his file in the Carleton College archives. The program for the re-enactment of the first intercollegiate basketball game (originally 1895, reenacted at Hamline on April 2, 1992) also provides additional information about Kaighn and his early activities at Hamline.

Background concerning Dr. James A. Naismith's invention of basketball is found in Naismith's own monograph, *Basketball*, and also in three histories of the American YMCA movement by Doggett, Hopkins, and Morse. The early spread of basketball through the turn of the twentieth century is discussed in all of the standard histories of the game—including those by Bjarkman, Douchant, Isaacs, McCallum, and Shouler et al. It is also worth noting that the archives of the YMCA in the United States are also held at the Andersen Library and contain a vast collection of contemporaneous publications of the Y that trace the game's growth in detail.

2. The Birth of Golden Gophers Basketball

Sources of the early history of the Minnesota Gophers include contemporaneous reports and *Gopher Glory*.

Information concerning the Premo Poll and Helms Foundation awards are from Douchant's history written under the banner of *Inside Sports* magazine. Information about Gopher opponents comes from the standard histories and the *Big Ten Records Book*.

The Gophers' annual win-loss records are compiled from five different sources—two different versions of the *Big Ten Records Book*, *Gopher Glory*, and the University of Minnesota men's basketball media guides for 2002–2003 and 2005–2006. The many discrepancies found were resolved against actual lists of opponents and game scores for each year.

3. Minnesota's First Hoops Hotbed

The primary source concerning basketball in Red Wing is the *Red Wing Republican-Eagle*. Most issues published during the basketball seasons from 1895 to 1916 were consulted. Additional information is from the histories of Red Wing and Goodhue County by Angell, Irvine, F. Johnson, and Rasmussen.

Finally, a script of a speech delivered by Edmund P. Neill to the fraternal organization the Red Wing Tribe No. 31 of the Independent Order of Red Men (IORM) in 1933 was provided courtesy of the archives of the Goodhue County Historical Society, Red Wing. Neill was very much engaged in basketball activity in Red Wing from 1896 to 1906, and the speech consists of his reminiscences about that first decade of basketball in the Queen City.

4. The High Schools Take the Court

The early history of high school basketball, prior to 1913, is drawn from contemporaneous reports in such local newspapers as the *Brown County Journal*, *Madison Western Guard*, and *Stillwater Gazette*, in addition to the *Minneapolis Tribune*.

Physical education and basketball won their way into the high school curriculum largely due to the philosophy of muscular Christianity. This philosophy is discussed in detail in Naismith's *Basketball* as well as the Doggett, Hopkins, and Morse histories of the YMCA movement in the United States.

The details of the founding of the tournament at Carleton in 1913 are found in the college weekly, the *Carletonia* (later the *Carletonian*), and also in Headley and Jarchow's history of the college. Rev. Fred B. Hill and Claude J. Hunt files at the Carleton archives were

also consulted. Francis J. "Dobie" Stadsvold's story is from the pages of *The Thirteen Towns* as well as the city of Fosston's *Centennial History*.

Sources concerning the Northfield tournaments of 1913–1922 include the local newspapers of the participating high schools, including the *Mankato Free Press*, *Mesabi Miner*, *Red Wing Republican-Eagle*, *Rock County Herald* (Luverne), *The Thirteen Towns* (Fosston), and the *Virginia Daily Enterprise* as well as the *Carletonia* (later *Carletonian*) and the *St. Paul Pioneer Press*. Programs for the 1920 through 1922 tournaments also were obtained from the Carleton archives.

Information about the later careers of the Nordly brothers comes from a variety of sources, including obituaries from the *Red Wing Republican-Eagle* supplied by the Goodhue County Historical Society. An obituary of Carl Nordly in the *Journal of Physical Education, Recreation and Dance* (August 1990) and an oral history interview with C. Nordly, conducted through the auspices of the American Alliance for Health, Physical Education, Recreation and Dance (AAHPERD) were provided by the Carleton archives.

The list of state public high school basketball champions is from the *Minnesota State High School League Yearbook & Record Book*.

5. Victorian Attitudes Trump Women's Basketball

Information about early girls basketball at Carleton College and the cities of Fosston and Red Wing is from the Headley and Jarchow history of Carleton and *The Thirteen Towns* and *Red Wing Republican-Eagle*, respectively.

Other information about girls high school basketball is drawn, in part, from *Daughters of the Game* by Marian Bemis Johnson and Dorothy E. McIntyre. Additional information is from newspaper articles that appeared in the *St. Paul Pioneer Press*, on July 7, 1998, under the byline of Mary Divine, and the *Star Tribune*, on June 27, 1999, based on interviews with and information provided by Bemis Johnson.

Joel Rippel, *Star Tribune* sports reporter and author of *75 Memorable Moments in Minnesota Sports* (Minnesota Historical Society Press, 2003), generously shared his research concerning the Minnesota Gopher women's basketball program from 1900 to 1908.

A number of scholarly papers by Beran, Cooper, Epstein, Gerber, and Lee were consulted concerning the reasons for the demise of girls and women's competitive athletics in the period from 1908 to 1942.

6. The Best of the Rest
This section draws almost entirely on contemporaneous newspaper reports. In addition to the *Minneapolis Tribune*, as always, the *Brown County Journal*, the *Carletonia* (later *Carletonian*), *Duluth Herald*, and *St. Cloud Journal Press* were consulted. The Headley and Jarchow book and the D. Johnson history were consulted regarding Carleton and Hamline, respectively. The Carleton archives also provided copies of the college yearbook, the *Algol*, for the years from 1913 through 1921.

7. The Ups and Downs of Doc Cooke's Gophers
See sources for chapter 2.

8. The Midwestern Style and
9. March Madness Captures the High Schools
The career of Wisconsin coach "Doc" Meanwell is outlined in most of the standard histories of basketball, while those of his disciples—from Levis and Dean, to Cowles, Hutton, and Nordly, and to Haddorff, Hutton Jr., and Kauls—are constructed from contemporaneous newspaper reports. Information about the later careers of Levis and Dean also was supplemented by the *Big Ten Records Book* and the standard histories.

Likewise, all information about high school play through this era are from newspaper reports of the day. Reports from the *Minneapolis Tribune* were supplemented with a March 24, 1984, article by Charley Walters of the *St. Paul Pioneer Press Dispatch*. The list of public high school champions from 1925 to 1942 was cross-checked against the *Minnesota State High School League Yearbook & Record Book*.

10. Get the Ball, Pass the Ball, and Put It in the Basket
This section is supplemented with information from the University of Minnesota Sports Information Department and the *Minnesota Daily* ("Huge Fieldhouse Will Open Tonight," February 4, 1928). Additional information about the Gophers' 1937 Big Ten champions and 1938 season are from a personal interview with John Kundla conducted by coauthor Stew Thornley on June 10, 1988, and a follow-up telephone interview on September 19, 2004.

The Gophers' win-loss records are compiled from the five different sources listed for chapter 2.

11. The Heyday of Senior Men's Play
All information is from reports of the *Minneapolis Tribune*.

12. The Low Post, the Fast Break, and the Jump Shot
The vast majority of information in this section is from contemporaneous newspaper reports. This was supplemented by information about the careers of Hank Luisetti, Slim Wintermute, Bob Kurland, George Mikan, and Wilt Chamberlain, which are reported in all the standard histories of the game.

The story of the Lynd Panthers has also been told by Steven R. Hoffbeck in "Hayloft Hoopsters" in *Minnesota History*, and the story of Whitey Skoog's experimentation with the jump shot while still in high school is highlighted in John Christgau's *The Origins of the Jump Shot*.

The list of public high school champions from 1943 to 1960 was cross-checked against the *Minnesota State High School League Yearbook & Record Book*.

13. The March of the Pied Pipers
Thanks to Dana Johnson, Director of Development, Hamline University Athletics, for reviewing and correcting details of this chapter. Johnson also shared the manuscript and provided feedback from Hamline alumni Jim Fritsche, Al Frost, Joe Hutton, Jr., Roger Johnson, Dick Klaus, Vern Mikkelsen, Rollie Seltz, and Bill Williams. Supplemental information about the career records of coach Joe Hutton is from the Web site of the NAIA (http://www.naia.org). Information about various professional careers (Clint Wager, Arnie Johnson) is from Shouler et al., *Total Basketball*.

14. Ozzie Cowles Brings Back the Control Game
Contemporaneous reports are supplemented by information from Perlstein, ed., *Gopher Glory*, and "Jim McIntyre" (*Sport* magazine).

Information about the Gophers' efforts to hire John Wooden in 1948 was developed with the assistance of Joel Rippel, *Star Tribune* sports reporter. A number of other sources were also consulted, including Wooden's book, *They Call Me Coach*; articles from the *Los Angeles Times* and *Terre Haute Tribune*; and Dave MacMillan's letter of resignation provided by the University of Minnesota archives.

The Gophers' win-loss records are compiled from the five different sources listed for chapter 2.

15. The Greatest Show On Earth

Contemporaneous reports are supplemented by interviews conducted by Stew Thornley with the following Lakers: John Kundla, George Mikan, Vern Mikkelsen, Don "Swede" Carlson, Bud Grant, Sid Hartman, Tony Jaros, and Dick Schnittker. Since there has been some dispute over Hartman's age, the authors consulted his birth certificate, on file at the Minnesota Historical Society archives, to determine his age, which places his birth date on March 15, 1920.

16. Shooting Stars of the Golden Age

District champions are as listed in Edward Simpkins, *The History of Minnesota State High School Basketball Tournaments, Supplemental Issue*. The career point totals are from "Minnesota High School 1,000 Point Club" in *Minnesota Basketball Yearbook & Preview 1983–1984*.

George Borgerding and Jonas Holte's single-game scoring records are listed on Minnesota High School Basketball Records at http://www.infolink.morris .mn.us/~mattnet/. Borgerding's record was confirmed by reference to the *Belgrade Herald* for December 22, 1945, and his performance in the 1944, 1945, and 1946 seasons was reviewed in the local paper. Meanwhile, the *Glenwood Herald* for December 25, 1919, reports that Starbuck defeated Barrett 92–2 on the date that Holte is credited with his 58-point effort, but Holte's individual effort could not be confirmed.

Neil Fedson's performance in 1948–1949 was reviewed via the *Austin Daily Herald*. Jon Hagen's 1957 season was tracked in the *Redwood Gazette*.

17. The Lakers after Mikan

See sources listed for chapter 15. In addition, concerning the Lakers' nearly disastrous air flight of January 18, 1960, Thornley interviewed copilot Harold Gifford and Eva Olofson, widow of pilot Vern Ullman.

18. Good, Natural Basketball Talent?

Information about early black basketball in Minnesota (before 1960) is from the African American Registry (http://www.aaregistry.com/african_american_

history). Black population data is from the U.S. Census Bureau (http://www.census.gov/population/www/ documentation/twps0056.html).

Sources regarding Terry Kunze's academic suspension in 1964 include a column by Dick Cullum and an article by Bill McGrane in the December 17, 1964, *Minneapolis Tribune*.

Paul Presthus shared his anecdote about Bill Fitch with Stew Thornley in a telephone interview on January 1, 2005.

Concerning the 1972 "basket-brawl," the usual sources were supplemented by reference to articles by Mike Augustin, Max Nichols, William F. Reed, Patrick Reusse, and Dan Stoneking in the *Minneapolis Star*, *St. Paul Pioneer Press*, and *Sports Illustrated*. *Sid!* by Hartman with Reusse is also referenced.

Concerning the NCAA rule violations under coach Bill Musselman, articles by Augustin, Terry Brown, Marshall Fine, Dick Gordon, Chan Keith, Joe Marcin, and Nichols, appearing in the *Star*, *Minnesota Daily*, *Pioneer Press*, and *The Sporting News* contributed to our version of those events. The NCAA's voiding of the Gophers' 1972 appearance in the NCAA tournament is noted in the *Big Ten Men's Basketball Media Guide*, pp. 68 and 71. An additional source was a 1976 radio interview of Mark Olberding conducted by Stew Thornley when Thornley was the sports director at KMSR Radio in Sauk Centre, Minnesota.

The forfeiture of Mychal Thompson and Osborne Lockhart's Florida high school state championship was reported by Bob Fowler in the *Minneapolis Star*. The incident was clarified by Stew Thornley by reference to the Florida High School Athletic Association Boys Basketball Championship Records and through correspondence with Jack Watford, Florida High School Athletic Association, December 2004.

Concerning NCAA violations under coach Jim Dutcher, the customary sources were supplemented with an article by Stephen Lorinser in the *Minnesota Daily* and a report in the "Notebook" section of *The Sporting News*.

The Gophers' win-loss records are compiled from the five different sources listed for chapter 2.

19. The Decline and Fall of the Single Class

The career point totals are from "Minnesota High School 1,000 Point Club" in *Minnesota Basketball*

Yearbook & Preview 1983-1984. The list of public high school champions from 1961 to 1983 was cross-checked against the *Minnesota State High School League Yearbook & Record Book.*

20. From John Kundla to Bill Musselman
See sources listed for chapter 18.

21. Small Colleges Achieve Parity
Information from contemporaneous reports was supplemented by information from the Minnesota Intercollegiate Athletic Conference (MIAC), http://www .miac-online.org/mbbrec.html and http://home.cord .edu/dept/sports/mbbmiac.html.

22. The Red, White, and Blue Ball
Information was drawn from contemporaneous reports.

23. The Triumphs and Trials of Jim Dutcher
See sources listed for chapter 18.

24. The MSHSL and Fans Embrace Girls Hoops
The early impetus for girls high school sports in Minnesota is discussed by Dorothy E. McIntyre, "Reflections from the Front of the Bus," in *Leveling the Playing Field,* edited by Ridder. Additional information about McIntyre's career is from "Two Illustrious Alumnae" in the *Link* magazine (Spring 2004) of the University of Minnesota College of Education and Human Development.

A variety of sources was consulted concerning the impact of Title IX, including monographs by Karen Blumenthal and Welch Suggs and a report by Richard W. Riley of the U.S. Department of Education.

Other information in this chapter is from the *MSHSL Yearbook & Record Book.*

25. A Good Start for Gopher Women
Published sources were supplemented by interviews conducted by Stew Thornley with Ellen Mosher Hanson and Diane Scovill, and with information from the Minnesota women's basketball media guide for 2002–2003.

The sidebar concerning the evolution of women's intercollegiate athletics from the old WAA is from an article by Eloise M. Jaeger, "Breaking Barriers," in *Leveling the Playing Field,* edited by Ridder.

26. "They Were Concerned about Being Basketball Players"
Primary sources include telephone interviews conducted by Stew Thornley with Scooter (DeLorme) Barnette, Doris Draving, Lusia Harris-Stewart, Dick Higgins, Dee Hopfenspirger, Marie Kocurek, Terry Kunze, Gordy Nevers, and Lynnette Sjoquist; correspondence with Julia Yeater dated January 2005; and a conversation between Thornley and Mary Manderfeld.

In addition to the usual printed sources, newspaper and magazine articles by Fitzgerald, Grow, Levy, Herman, Lieber, Maly, Moss, Nightingale, and Pileggi, appearing in the *Chicago Tribune, Des Moines Register, Milwaukee Sentinel, Minneapolis Star, New York Times, Omaha World-Herald, San Francisco Chronicle,* and *Sports Illustrated* were consulted.

Other secondary sources include Lannin's *A History of Basketball for Girls and Women,* the Minnesota Fillies media guide for 1979–1980, and the Web site WBL Memories (http://www.wblmemories.com).

27. New Patterns in Girls Hoops
This chapter was developed primarily from contemporaneous newspaper reports and the *MSHSL Yearbook & Record Book.* The later careers of Minnesota high school basketball players are documented in the Minnesota State University Mankato Mavericks 2004–2005 women's basketball media guide.

28. Living in the Past
This chapter also was developed primarily from contemporaneous newspaper reports and the *MSHSL Yearbook & Record Book.* The later careers of Minnesota high school basketball players are documented in *North Central Conference Men's Basketball Record Book.*

Bob McDonald's state record for coaching wins was documented in "Top 10 in Victories" on the *Star Tribune* Web site in 2003, which in turn cited *Minnesota Basketball News* and *Star Tribune* staff research. Tom and Joel McDonald's scoring records are cited at the Minnesota High School Basketball Records Web site.

29. Small College Women Overachieve
Information from contemporaneous newspaper reports was supplemented by information from the Minnesota State University Mankato Mavericks 2004–2005 women's basketball media guide and a number of Web sites, including those of the College of St. Bene-

dict, the University of St. Thomas, the Minnesota Intercollegiate Athletic Conference (MIAC), and the North Central Conference (NCC).

This information was supplemented by e-mail correspondence from coach Mike Durbin, St. Benedict's; sports information director Eugene McGivern, St. Thomas; and coach Lori K. Ulferts, St. Cloud State.

30. Hard Times for Gopher Women
The usual sources were supplemented by information from the University of Minnesota women's basketball media guides for 2002–2003 and 2005–2006.

31. A School for Scandal
The usual sources were supplemented by information from newspaper articles by Borger, Dohrmann, McKenzie, and Oseid appearing in the *Minnesota Daily* and *St. Paul Pioneer Press*. The Gophers' win-loss records are from the men's basketball media guide.

32. The NBA Returns
Contemporaneous reports are supplemented by information from the Minnesota Timberwolves media guides.

33. The Transition Game
The transition game is described in the Murrey book as well as videos by coaches Bonnie Henrickson and Bob Huggins, among many others. Transition defense is described in a video by Steve Barnes.

34. Youth Basketball Booms
Our understanding of the administrative origins and organization of youth basketball is thanks to an interview by Marc Hugunin with Dan Klinkhammer, Executive Director, Minnesota Youth Athletic Services.

Records of girls and boys national AAU tournament participation is from the AAU Web site.

Thanks to Alan R. Holst, who has tabulated Minnesota high school graduates who have played Division I college basketball for many years and who graciously shared his research with the authors. Charley Walters also mentioned in 2000 that there were thirty-seven Minnesota men on Division I rosters at that time.

35. The Return of David and Goliath
This chapter is based primarily on contemporaneous reports and the *MSHSL Yearbook & Record Book*. Information about the future careers of Minnesota high school products come primarily from their college Web sites—including those of Emporia (Kansas) State, Florida Tech, Michigan State, Rutgers, and Saint Louis University—as well as the Web site of the WNBA (http://www.wnba.com).

Blake Hoffarber's "sitting shot" in 2005 was described as "the greatest shot" in tournament history by Bob Olson, Aurora, Minnesota, in correspondence with Marc Hugunin. Olson is the brother of former Edgerton and Virginia High School coach Richie Olson and has seen approximately fifty state tournaments.

36. The Gopher Women Come Out of Nowhere
Contemporaneous reports are supplemented by reference to the University of Minnesota women's basketball 2002–2003 and 2005–2006 media guides. Additional comments concerning the Gopher men are by Christenson.

37. New Small College Powers Emerge
Contemporaneous reports are supplemented by reference to numerous Web sites including the MIAC, Anoka-Ramsey Community College, Carleton, St. Benedict's, and St. Thomas women's basketball pages and the MIAC, Gustavus Adolphus, St. Thomas, and Vermilion Community College men's pages.

Additional information was provided via e-mail correspondence between Marc Hugunin and Mark Hanson, Gustavus Adolphus men's basketball coach; Karen Kraft, Anoka-Ramsey Community College athletic director; and Paul McDonald, Vermilion Community College men's basketball coach.

Additional accounts of the Gusties' 2003 NCAA Division III title game are from D3hoops.com.

38. Two Kevins, a Flip, and, Finally, Respectability and
39. The Lynx Find Fans Elusive Prey
Concerning the Timberwolves, contemporaneous reports are supplemented by information from the Minnesota Timberwolves media guides. Concerning the Lynx, contemporaneous information is supplemented by information from the Minnesota Lynx media guides and Web site.

Bibliography

Asterisked entries denote the standard histories of basketball mentioned in the essay on sources.

Angell, Madeline. *Red Wing, Minnesota: Saga of a River Town.* Minneapolis: Dillon, 1977.

Augustin, Mike. "'U' Cagers Lose; Game Ends in Riot." *St. Paul Pioneer Press,* January 26, 1972, 17.

——. "U Player Ruled Ineligible in Ticket Scalping." *St. Paul Pioneer Press,* Saturday, January 17, 1976, 1.

Beran, Janice A. "Lou Henry Hoover: Crusader for Causes Benefiting Children and Women." Proceedings of the North American Society for Sport History, 1988.

Big Ten Records Book. 58th edition. Park Ridge, IL: Big Ten Conference, 2006. http://bigten.collegesports.com/trads/big10-recordbook.html.

Bjarkman, Peter C. *The Biographical History of Basketball.* Chicago: Masters, 2000.*

Blumenthal, Karen. *Let Me Play: The Story of Title IX: The Law That Changed the Future of Girls in America.* New York: Atheneum Books for Young Readers, 2005.

"Body Is Found; Believed to Be Connie Kunzmann." *Minneapolis Tribune,* Sunday, March 29, 1981, 12C.

Borger, Judith Yates. "Lack of Contact with Instructors Creates Chances for Cheating." *St. Paul Pioneer Press,* March 10, 1999, 9A.

Brackin, Dennis. "'U' Basketball Team Placed on Probation for 2 Years by NCAA." *Star Tribune,* Tuesday, March 8, 1988, 1A.

Brown, Terry. "ACIA Slaps Basketball Program, Expects More from NCAA." *Minnesota Daily,* Friday, January 9, 1976, 1.

——. "Officials Lament NCAA Penalties, but Say They Are Deserved." *Minnesota Daily,* Thursday, March 11, 1976, 1.

Carlson, Bill. "Grant to Lakers; Fort Wayne Here." *Minneapolis Sunday Tribune,* December 25, 1949, S1.

Christensen, Ray, with Stew Thornley. *Golden Memories.* Minneapolis: Nodin Press, 1993.

Christgau, John. *The Origins of the Jump Shot.* Lincoln: University of Nebraska Press, 1999.

Cooper, Carol. "Lou Henry Hoover: Vanguard for the Girl Scout Movement." Proceedings of the North American Society for Sport History, 1988.

Cullum, Dick. "Gophers Can Rally from Loss of Kunze." *Minneapolis Tribune,* Thursday, December 17, 1964, 33.

Divine, Mary. "Early in the Game." *St. Paul Pioneer Press,* July 7, 1998.

Doggett, Lawrence Locke. *History of the Y.M.C.A., 1844–1861.* New York: Association Press, 1922.

Dohrmann, George. "U Basketball Program Accused of Academic Fraud." *St. Paul Pioneer Press,* Wednesday, March 10, 1999, 1A.

Dohrmann, George, and Judith Yates Borger. "U Considers Whether to Bench Four Players." *St. Paul Pioneer Press,* Thursday, March 11, 1999, 1A.

Douchant, Mike. *Inside Sports College Basketball.* Detroit: Visible Ink, 1995.*

Epstein, Karen V. "Sameness or Difference? Class, Gender, Sport, the WDNAAF and the NCAA/NAAF." Proceedings of the North American Society for Sport History, 1988.

"Fillies Leave Floor Before Game against Chicago, Are Suspended." *Minneapolis Tribune,* Sunday, March 22, 1981.

Fine, Marshall. "Cagers May Face NCAA Probe." *Minnesota Daily,* Friday, May 11, 1973, 1.

——. "Quitting Cagers Cite Neglect, Insults by Coach Musselman." *Minnesota Daily,* May 11, 1973, 40.

Fowler, Bob. "Forfeit Prep Title, Too? More Woes for Thompson, Lockhart." *Minneapolis Star,* Thursday, March 11, 1976, 1E.

Gelfand, M. Howard. "Former 'U' Player Says Musselman Gave Him Money." *Minneapolis Tribune,* Friday, August 22, 1975, 4A.

Gerber, Ellen. "The Controlled Development of Collegiate Sport for Women, 1923-1936." *Journal of Sport History* 2, no. 1 (1975).

Gordon, Dick. "Will 'U' Appeal Saunders? Ineligibility Predicted." *Minneapolis Star*, March 10, 1976, 1D.

Grow, Doug. "Fillies Ritual: Sweating Out Payday." *Minneapolis Star*, Wednesday, February 18, 1981.

———. "She Spoke Up, Got Shipped Out." *Minneapolis Star*, Friday, February 20, 1981, 9C.

———. "Last Nail Driven in Fillies' Coffin." *Minneapolis Star*, n.d.

Hartman, Sid. "Grant Ineligible; Out for Season: Superior Cager Plays Last Game." *Minneapolis Tribune*, Friday, December 16, 1949, 18.

Hartman, Sid, with Patrick Reusse. *Sid! The Sports Legends, the Inside Scoops, and the Close Personal Friends*. Stillwater, MN: Voyageur, 1997.

Headley, Leal A., and Merrill E. Jarchow. *Carleton: The First Century*. Northfield, MN: Carleton College, 1966.

Heller, Bill. *Timberwolves Stalk the NBA: Obsession: Bill Musselman's Relentless Quest to Beat the Best*. Chicago: Bonus Books, 1989.

Herman, Robin. "For Female Basketball, a Big Bounce Forward." *New York Times*, Wednesday, July 19, 1978, A14.

Hoffbeck, Steven R. "Hayloft Hoopsters." *Minnesota History* (winter 1997–1998).

Hopkins, Charles Howard. *History of the Y.M.C.A. in North America*. New York: Association, 1951.

"Huge Fieldhouse Will Open Tonight." *Minnesota Daily*, February 4, 1928.

Irvine, S. T. *History of Red Wing to 1942*. Unpublished manuscript. Collection of Minnesota Historical Society.

Isaacs, Neil D. *All the Moves: A History of College Basketball*. New York: Harper Colophon Books, 1984.*

Ison, Chris. "Trouble Has Followed the Gopher Basketball Program." *Star Tribune*, March 11, 1999, A9.

Ison, Chris, and Paul McEnroe. "'U' Officials Intervened for Athletes." *Star Tribune*, Friday, May 21, 1999, 1A.

"Jim McIntyre." *Sport* magazine, February 1949.

Johnson, David W. *Hamline University: A History*. St. Paul: Hamline University Press, 1994.

Johnson, Frederick. *Goodhue County, Minnesota: A Narrative History*. Red Wing, MN: Goodhue County Historical Society, 2000.

Johnson, Marian Bemis, and Dorothy E. McIntyre. *Daughters of the Game: The First Era of Minnesota Girls High School Basketball 1891-1942*. Edina,

MN: McJohn, 2005.

"John Wooden Signed as Bruin Cage Mentor." *Los Angeles Times*, April 21, 1948, 8.

Keith, Chan. "McCutcheon: Couldn't Take Any More." *Minneapolis Star*, Friday, September 8, 1974, 6B.

———. "NCAA Notes 100 Violations by 'U.'" *Minneapolis Star*, Wednesday, July 23, 1975, 1A.

———. "Four Ex-University Athletes Talk of Extra Money." *Minneapolis Star*, Friday, July 25, 1975, 1A.

———. "Ex-Aide Blames Musselman." *Minneapolis Star*, Wednesday, October 27, 1976, 1D.

"Killer of Pro Basketball Player Paroled after 9 Years in Prison." *Omaha World-Herald*, Saturday, June 20, 1990, 35.

Lannin, Joanne. *A History of Basketball for Girls and Women: From Bloomers to Big Leagues*. Minneapolis: Lerner Sports, 2000.

Lee, Mabel. "The Case For and Against Intercollege Athletics for Women and the Situation since 1923." *Research Quarterly* (May 1931).

Levy, Paul. "No Bed of Roses for Suspended Fillies." *Minneapolis Star*, Tuesday, March 24, 1981, 12B.

———. "Fillies May Be Headed for Detroit." *Minneapolis Star*, Wednesday, April 22, 1981, 13B.

———. "Bizarre's Word for Fillies Deal." *Minneapolis Star*, Friday, July 17, 1981, 7B.

Libman, Gary. "'U' to Ask Supreme Court to Lift Probation." *Minneapolis Tribune*, Wednesday, August 10, 1977, 1A.

———. "Fillies Bow to Iowa in Debut." *Minneapolis Tribune*, Saturday, December 16, 1978, 1C.

Lieber, Jill. "Does Players Blast Boss." *Milwaukee Sentinel*, Thursday, February 1, 1979, part 2, 1.

Lorinser, Stephen R. "Can the U Administer Itself?" *Minnesota Daily*, September 21, 1989, 1.

Lyons, Andrew M. "Red Wing Basketball." In C. A. Rasmussen, editor, *A History of the City of Red Wing, Minnesota*. Red Wing, MN: C. A. Rasmussen, 1933.

Maly, Ron. "Sour Note by Cornets: Coach Fired." *Des Moines Register*, Tuesday, December 12, 1978, 1S.

———. "Oh, Sister! Cornets Sail in Debut: Uhl Hits 22, Green 12 in 103-81 Breeze." *Des Moines Register*, December 16, 1978, 1S.

Marcin, Joe. "Minnesota-NCAA Skirmish Goes to the Supreme Court." *The Sporting News*, October 22, 1977, 65.

McCallum, John D. *College Basketball U.S.A. Since*

1892. New York: Scarborough Books, 1980.*

McGrane, Bill. "No 'Feeling Sorry,' 'U' Girds for Future." *Minneapolis Tribune,* Thursday, December 17, 1964, 33.

McKenzie, Sarah. "Report Shows Officials' Roles in Investigations." *Minnesota Daily,* Monday, July 12, 1999, 1.

McKenzie, Sarah, and Tammy J. Oseld. "Inquiry Examines Assault Claims." *Minnesota Daily,* Monday, May 24, 1999, 1.

"Minnesota Loses to Ohio in Overtime, 42-40: 11,000 See New Plant Dedicated: Regulation Periods End with Teams Deadlocked at 32 to 32." *Minneapolis Tribune,* Sunday, February 5, 1928, Sports, 1.

Morse, Richard C. *History of the North American Y.M.C.A.* New York: Association Press, 1913.

Moss, Al. "Pioneers Rout Fillies, 122-61, in WBL Finale." *San Francisco Chronicle,* Wednesday, April 1, 1981, 64.

Murrey, Bob. *Coaching the Fast Break: By the Experts.* Coaching Cards for Basketball, 2002.

Naismith, James. *Basketball.* Reprint. Lincoln: University of Nebraska Press, 1996.

"New Candidate Enters Bruin Cage Picture." *Los Angeles Times,* April 13, 1948, A9.

Nichols, Max.. "Two Cage Suspensions Are Just." *Minneapolis Star,* Saturday, January 29, 1972, 7A.

———. "Musselman Admits He Violated NCAA Rules." *Minneapolis Star,* Thursday, July 31, 1975, 1A.

———. "NCAA Probation Likely for 'U' Men." *Minneapolis Star,* Friday, September 17, 1976, 1A.

———. "Judge Blocks Probation by NCAA." *Minneapolis Star,* Thursday, December 2, 1976, 1D.

"Nicodemus New Coach at Milwaukee: Ex-Cornet Boss 3rd Does Mentor." *Des Moines Register,* Thursday, December 14, 1978, S1.

Nightengale, Dave. "Hustle Suspends 2, Plans Trade." *Chicago Tribune,* Saturday, January 27, 1979, Section 2, 1.

"Notebook." *The Sporting News,* March 21, 1988, 17.

"Ohio Governor Demands Action." *Minneapolis Star,* Thursday, January 27, 1972, 1B.

Perlstein, Steve, editor. *Gopher Glory: One Hundred Years of University of Minnesota Basketball.* Minneapolis: Layers, 1995.

Pileggi, Sarah. "Full of Heart in an Empty House." *Sports Illustrated,* March 10, 1980, 32.

Pinney, Gregor W. "Specific Violations in University

Report on Basketball Scandal." *Minneapolis Tribune,* Thursday, March 11, 1976, 3D.

Reed, William F. "An Ugly Affair in Minneapolis." *Sports Illustrated,* February 7, 1972, 18.

Rekela, George R. *State Champions: The Story of the Buhl Bulldogs' Rise to Glory in 1941 and 1942.* Minneapolis: Milkees, 1991.

Reusse, Patrick. "Opposing Coaches, Taylor, Musselman, Accuse Other." *St. Paul Pioneer Press,* January 26, 1972, 18.

Richardson, Ray. "Players Cite Problems with Borton," *St. Paul Pioneer Press,* April 7, 2006, D1.

Ridder, Kathleen C., editor. *Leveling the Playing Field: Stories by Minnesota Women in Sports.* St. Cloud: North Star, 2005.

Roe, Jon. "NCAA Places All Gopher Men's Teams on Probation." *Minneapolis Tribune,* Friday, October 22, 1976, 1A.

———. "'U' to Fight NCAA Ruling in Court." *Minneapolis Tribune,* Saturday, October 23, 1976, 1A.

———. "2 Players Declared Ineligible by 'U.'" *Minneapolis Tribune,* Tuesday, October 25, 1977, 1A.

———. "Thompson Ruled Out of 7 Games, Winey to Miss 3." *Minneapolis Tribune,* Tuesday, November 15, 1977, 1A.

———. "'U' Cager Would Change 2 Things." *Minneapolis Tribune,* Tuesday, November 15, 1977, 1C.

———. "Nevers Promises Game Despite Fillies Walkout." *Minneapolis Tribune,* Monday, March 23, 1981, 1C.

———. "Report Links Death of Ex-Gopher Hall to Cocaine Use." *Star Tribune,* Wednesday, November 16, 1988, 1C.

Shouler, Ken, Bob Ryan, Sam Smith, Leonard Koppett, and Bob Bellotti. *Total Basketball: The Ultimate Basketball Encyclopedia.* Toronto: Sport Classic Books, 2003.*

Simpkins, Ed. *The History of Minnesota State High School Basketball Tournaments.* Prior Lake, MN: Ed Simpkins, 1964.

———. *The History of Minnesota State High School Basketball Tournaments, Supplemental Issue.* Prior Lake, MN: Ed Simpkins, 1965.

Sinker, Howard. "Ex-Fillies Watch New Group Go for Broke." *Minneapolis Tribune,* Tuesday, March 24, 1981, 1C.

Stoneking, Dan. "Father of Witte Blasts Musselman." *Minneapolis Star,* January 27, 1972, 1D

Suggs, Welch. *A Place on the Team: The Triumph and Tragedy of Title IX*. Princeton, NJ: Princeton University Press, 2005.

"Two Illustrious Alumnae Recognized with University's Outstanding Achievement Award." *Link* 20, no. 2 (spring 2004); http://education.umn.edu/alum/link/2004Spring/OAA.html.

Walters, Charley. "'31 Tourney Vet Appreciates Today's Skills." *St. Paul Pioneer Press/Dispatch*, March 24, 1984, 2C.

Wiley, S. Wirt, and Florence Lehmann. *Builders of Men: A History of the Minneapolis Young Men's Christian Association, 1866-1936*. Minneapolis, 1938.

Wolf, Jason. "Littlejohn Fired as 'U' Coach: Investigation Uncovers NCAA Rules Violations." *Star Tribune*, Tuesday, May 15, 2001, 1A.

"Women's Pro Cager Reportedly Murdered." *Minneapolis Tribune*, Wednesday, February 11, 1981, 1C.

"Wooden Goes to California: Leader of Indiana State Basketball Team Takes New Field." *Terre Haute Tribune*, April 20, 1948, 1.

Wooden, John R., and Jack Tobin. *They Call Me Coach*. New York: McGraw-Hill, 1988.

Zolecki, Todd. "Will Iverson's Career End on Sideline? She and Six Other Gophers Will Sit Out Tournament Opener." *Star Tribune*, Friday, February 27, 1998, 5C.

———. "Littlejohn Endures Tumultuous Rookie Season: Complaints of Mistreatment and Defections among Women's Baseball Players Prompt a University Investigation of the Coach." *Star Tribune*, Sunday, May 3, 1998, 1C.

Index

Photo Credits

Pages iv, 2, 8, 10, 11, 24, 31, 33, 46, 51 (both), 52, 54, 60, 76, 77, 82, 96, 97, 104, 106, 110, 111, 112, 125, 129, 139, 140, 143, 145, 147 (all), 158, 159, 160, 161, 162, 163, 180, 192, 194, 197, 198, 201, 203, 214, 221 (Schonrock), 222, 237, 238, 242, 249—Courtesy of the University of Minnesota

Pages ii, 25, 43, 44, 53, 59, 62, 83, 85, 86, 90, 91, 92, 93, 101, 109, 127, 136, 153, 154, 164, 168—Minnesota Historical Society Collections, St. Paul

Pages 121, 174, 176, 178, 183 (both), 212, 221 (Bolden), 226, 229, 232—Courtesy of the MSHSL

Pages 19, 27, 47, 66, 67, 98, 114, 116, 118, 179—Courtesy of the *Star Tribune*/Minneapolis–St. Paul 2006

Pages 207, 208, 210, 251, 254, 256, 258—Courtesy of NBAE/Getty Images

Pages xii, 7, 34, 71, 72, 73—Courtesy of the Hamline University Archives

Pages 4, 20, 36, 37, 38, 40—Courtesy of the Carleton College Archives

Pages 227, 228, 230, 235—Courtesy of www.20-20photo.com

Pages 13, 14, 18—Courtesy of the Goodhue County Historical Society

Pages 119, 122, 218—Courtesy of the *St. Paul Pioneer Press*

Pages 132, 185, 186—Courtesy of the University of St. Thomas

Pages 48, 95—Courtesy of George Rekela

Pages 64, 172—Courtesy of the Concordia College Archives

Pages 148, 156—Courtesy of the *New York Mills Herald*

Page 17—Courtesy of the Lac qui Parle County Historical Society

Page 80—Courtesy of Ray LeBov

Page 133—Courtesy of St. John's University

Page 150—Photo by Buzz Magnuson, courtesy of the *St. Paul Pioneer Press*

Page 177—Photo by the *Marshall Independent*, courtesy of Chris and Mary Jo (Miller) Hmielewski

Page 189—Courtesy of North Dakota State University

Page 245—Photo by Tom Dahlin, courtesy of Tom Dahlin

Page 247—Photo by Doug Sundin, courtesy of Winona State University Athletics